# Somerset Maugham
# and the Maugham Dynasty

# Somerset Maugham
# and the
# Maugham Dynasty

BRYAN CONNON

SINCLAIR-STEVENSON

First published 1997

1 3 5 7 9 10 8 6 4 2

Copyright © Bryan Connon 1997

Bryan Connon has asserted his right under the Copyright,
Designs and Patents Act 1988
to be identified as the author of this work

First published in the United Kingdom in 1997 by
Sinclair-Stevenson
Random House, 20 Vauxhall Bridge Road, London SW1V 2SA

Random House Australia (Pty) Limited
20 Alfred Street, Milsons Point, Sydney,
New South Wales 2061, Australia

Random House New Zealand Limited
18 Poland Road, Glenfield,
Auckland 10, New Zealand

Random House South Africa (Pty) Limited
Endulini, 5A Jubilee Road, Parktown 2193, South Africa

Random House UK Limited Reg. No. 954009

ISBN 1–85619–274–1

Typeset in 12 on 14 point Ehrhardt
by Deltatype Limited, Birkenhead, Merseyside
Printed and bound in Great Britain
by Mackays of Chatham PLC

For
Patrick Brock
Andrew Harvey
John Wiles
and the rest of the family

# Contents

# *Illustrations*

## Section 1

Robert Maugham *(Private Collection)*
Edith Maugham *(Private Collection)*
Willie, aged eleven *(Private Collection)*
Willie, aged seventeen *(Private Collection)*
Freddie Maugham on the cover of *Granta (Peter Burton Collection)*
Harry Maugham *(Private Collection)*
The Tivoli Theatre, Strand *(Author's Collection)*
Charles Frohman
*Punch* cartoon of Shakespeare and WSM's posters
Billie Burke
Ethel Irving
Gladys Cooper
Constance Collier
Syrie Maugham in *The American Sketch (Author's Collection)*
Syrie, Liza and Willie *(Private Collection)*
Alan Helm *(Private Collection)*
Gerald Haxton *(Private Collection)*
Beverley Nichols *(Author's Collection)*
Cyril Butcher *(Author's Collection)*
The Villa Mauresque *(Peter Burton Collection)*

ix

Freddie Maugham, Robert Bruce, Kate Mary Bruce, unknown and Noël Coward *(Private Collection)*

## Section 2

Freddie Maugham *(Private Collection)*
Nellie and Robin *(Private Collection)*
Robin at Highfield *(Private Collection)*
Robin at Eton *(Private Collection)*
Helen 'Nellie' Romer Maugham *(Private Collection)*
The Maugham sisters: Diana, Kate and Honor *(Private Collection)*
A scene from *He Must Return (by permission of Peter Noble*)
Robin as a subaltern, 1940 *(Private Collection)*
Programme for *He Must Return (by permission of Peter Noble)*
Rebecca West, 1951 *(Author's Collection)*
Derek Peel, *c.* 1956 *(Author's Collection)*
Robin with Michael Davidson, 1953 *(Private Collection)*
Colin Spencer, 1952 *(by permission of Colin Spencer)*
Keith Monk *(Peter Burton Collection)*
Alan Helm *(Private Collection*)
Robin with Peter Burton, Casa Calapada *(Peter Burton Collection)*
Casa Calapada *(Peter Burton Collection)*
Peter Burton, Ibiza, 1971 *(Peter Burton Collection)*
William Lawrence *(photograph by Mike Gill, Peter Burton Collection)*
Robin with Honor *(Private Collection)*
'Robin Maugham, England 1977' by Ian McGee *(Peter Burton Collection)*
Robin Maugham by Michael ffoulkes for *Punch*, 1975 *(Peter Burton Collection)*

# Acknowledgements

I am most grateful to the sisters of the late Lord Maugham for their kindness and co-operation in the preparation of this book, but I must emphasise that co-operation is not to be taken as being synonymous with approval.

I am greatly indebted to Mr Peter Burton to whom obfuscation is anathema. He was a close friend and colleague of Robin Maugham for twelve years and worked with him on a series of novels, memoirs and biographies. Mr Burton has permitted me to adapt and/or quote from: *Talking To*, *Parallel Lives*, *Conversations with Willie* and *Enemy*, as well as articles written by him for the British and American gay press. In addition he has allowed me access to his Maugham files.

I am indebted also to the many authors who have analysed W. Somerset Maugham as a writer and as a man; in particular the work of the Canadian scholar Professor R. L. Calder and the distinguished American journalist Mr Ted Morgan. Following Maugham's death, freed from legal restraint, they were able to encompass the complex subject of his sexuality. However, as both wrote from a heterosexual perspective only, much that was germane to his character eluded them, along with those subtleties of the English gay scene and class structure with which they were unfamiliar.

I would like to thank the following individuals and institutions who have contributed in a lesser or greater degree and I trust that none has been omitted due to oversight: Mr Gordon Anderson; Mr Timothy d'Arch Smith; Mr Robin Baird-Smith; Mr John Bedding; Mr Andrew Boxer; Mr John Brennan; Mr Rex Bunnett; Mr Cyril Butcher;

Professor Robert L. Calder; Mr Walter Cerroece; Mr William E. Colby; Mr John Constable; Mr Tom Corbett; Lady Daubeny; Mr Hugh Dean; Mr Marshall Dill Jnr; Mr John Durnford; Hon. Mrs Honor Earl; Mr Vivian Ellis; Mr Melvin Fell; Sir Charles Fletcher-Cooke; Mr Bryan Forbes; Mrs Jeanne Francis; Sir John Gielgud; Mr Eric Glass; Lord Glendevon; Mr Derek Harmer-Morris; Mr Alan Helm; Mr Frank Henley; Mr Myles Hildyard; Mr Ken Hoare; Mr Philip Hoare; Mr Francis King; Mr Roy King; Mr William Lawrence; Mrs Peggy Lloyd; Mr James Blair Lovell; Mr Michael Lowrie; Mr Peter Madok; Hon. Mrs Diana Marr-Johnson; Mr John Middleton; Mr Stanley Millar; Mrs V. Milne-Connon; Mr Billy Milton; Mr Keith Monk; Mr Sheridan Morley; Mr Patrick Newley; Mr Beverley Nichols; Mr Peter Noble; Mr Michael Pitt-Rivers; Sir Peter Quennell; Mr Carl Rollyson; Mr Anthony Rudd; Mr Kenneth D. Schlessinger; Miss Elizabeth Sellars; Mr Donald Sinden; Mr Colin Spencer; Miss Gloria Swanson; Mr Martin Taylor; Mr Donald Thomas; Mr Michael Thornton; Mr Martin Tickner; Mr William Uncles; Mr Hugo Vickers; Mr Dick Vosburgh; Mrs Gillian Warr; Mr Tony Warren; Mr Godfrey Winn; Mr John H. Wright and Mr Peter Yan.

I would also like to thank the British Home Office; the Imperial War Museum; the Swiss Embassy; Central Library, Eastbourne; Dixon Ward, Solicitors; Samuel French Ltd; *Punch* magazine; Lambeth Local History Forum and the Central Intelligence Agency, Washington.

The following have permitted me to quote from the named texts: Lady Daubeny: *My World of Stage* and *Stage by Stage* by Sir Peter Daubeny; the Hon. Mrs Honor Earl: *Better Than I Dared Hope*; Mr Colin Spencer: *The Two of Us* and *The World, the Flesh and Myself* by Michael Davidson, as well as letters written by him; Mr Francis King: *Yesterday Came Suddenly*; and the literary executors of the late Sir Cecil Beaton for the Beaton diaries and his other works.

I am indebted to Mr Andrew Harvey for his assistance and to Mr Derek Harmer-Morris for his invaluable help in preparing the manuscript. Finally I acknowledge with gratitude the encouragement of Mr Christopher Sinclair-Stevenson, Miss Penny Hoare and my editor at Reed Books, Ms Eugenie Boyd.

# A Note on Sources

A number of informants agreed to assist in the preparation of this book on condition that they were not to be named, nor their contributions used in a manner which might identify the source. A similar condition was applied to certain documents and private papers. I have therefore been obliged to protect my sources in these instances or lose the use of privileged information. In consequence it has not been possible to supply detailed reference notes. Where it has been possible, information is given in the text or may be deduced from the selected bibliography.

# Introduction

I originally called this book 'The Maughams' and I planned that Willie Maugham would take his place in a cavalcade of characters without receiving undue prominence. I quickly realised that this was impossible, and that, unbidden, he would dominate and shape the book's structure.

I have been an admirer of his work for over fifty years: over sixty if I count my visit to the Queen's Cinema, Bayswater when I was seven to see *Of Human Bondage*. I remember little of it except that I disapproved of Miss Bette Davis as Mildred because her peculiar Hollywood-Cockney was not in the least bit like the friendly voices of the waitresses who served in the tea-rooms of Whiteleys or Derry & Toms.

By the age of seventeen I had read almost everything the seventy-year-old author had written and, with the dogmatic certainty of youth, had decided he was one of the best story-tellers of all time; a view that remains unchanged now that I am seventy myself.

When I read *The Razor's Edge* in 1944 it never occurred to me that the author was an old man. He spoke from the page, face to face, as an equal; there were no barriers of obscurity, verbosity or pretention. It is this plainness that has often annoyed critics but pleased the public. The style, based on colloquial speech, did not always come easily to him. He could spend an entire working day writing and re-writing a single page in meticulous longhand, until he felt he had done as much as he could, even if the result did not please him. He then copied the 'finished' page into a notebook or pad. In later years this step in the process was omitted. Before he passed his work on to be typed he would go through it yet again and make revisions. This painstaking routine may seem unnecessarily arduous, but Willie derived intense pleasure from the physical act of writing, and even created a cell-like room at his home where, like a mediaeval monk, he could work in uninterrupted solitude.

Away from his cell, Willie was a joyful libertine, indulging all his senses and often flirting with danger to satisfy his sexual needs. As with so many homosexual men of his generation, he was a casualty of Victorian hypocrisy and the victim of his own fears. This does not explain, or excuse, his unpredictable and frequently irrational behaviour. One moment he could be Dr Jekyll, the next Mr Hyde. In 1941 when he was on the film-set watching Spencer Tracy playing the dual role in Stevenson's tale, he was heard to remark: 'Which one is he now?' A similar question might apply to Willie, for it was not always evident which of his dual, or even multiple, personalities was in control.

Sadly the publication of *The Razor's Edge* marked the decline of Willie's abilities as a story-teller. It seemed for a while that his nephew Robin Maugham would replace him, given the evidence of his writing debut with *Come To Dust*, followed by *The Servant*. But it remained to be seen if he had the creative resources, stamina and self-discipline of his uncle. Of all the male Maughams Robin was probably the most likeable, but in the long term his boyish charm and the need to be popular worked against him.

After I had completed the final draft of this book I suffered the disappointment of most biographers at the loss of material discarded during progressive re-writes. One of my favourite sections was a polemic on Frederic Maugham and the Munich Crisis, but it did not suit the overall concept. Other sections were entertaining but too frivolous, and one or two sexually shocking, even in this apparently unshockable age. It was also easy to be tempted into attractive by-ways, such as a description of the theatre in London and New York when Willie was a favoured dramatist, or to analyse in greater depth the impact Syrie Maugham had on interior design.

With the book finished, I will miss the company of the Maughams and their friends. They have been part of my life for the past five years; I trust that you will find them as lively to be with as I have done.

Bryan Connon
1997

# Prologue:
# Looking Back

The life-support system was disconnected on 13 March 1981 and Robert, Second Viscount Maugham of Hartfield was pronounced legally dead. It was the end of a dynasty that had lasted for over one hundred and fifty years and left its mark on the law, politics and the arts.

In his memoirs, Robert, or Robin as he was always called, described himself as 'queer and alcoholic', a startlingly honest confession for a public figure to make in 1972. This was very different from his uncle Willie Somerset Maugham's autobiography, *Looking Back*, of ten years earlier in which Willie eliminated any clue that suggested he was actively homosexual. If he had resided in England this might have been seen as a wise precaution as the law that had trapped Oscar Wilde was still in force, but Willie had chosen exile in France in the 1920s precisely to escape from the law and to be with his lover.

Irrational as it may seem, the consequences of the Wilde trials increasingly haunted Willie as he grew older; he feared that he too might suffer vilification and see his work banned if the general public knew the truth about his sexual orientation. So paranoid did he become that he concocted an elaborate fiction, in *Looking Back*, to present himself as a red-blooded womaniser, the very antithesis of a homosexual.

His friends might have colluded with the deception, treating it as the caprice of a senile old man, had he not attacked his deceased ex-wife Syrie in terms so vituperative that he could not be forgiven by those who loved and admired her. The maliciousness of his simultaneous litigious activities against his daughter Liza provided additional scope for his critics and he was condemned and ridiculed. *Looking Back*, therefore, not only failed in its intention but became, ipso facto, a licence to expose Willie's life, warts and all. Robin led the way when Willie died in 1965, with *Somerset and All the Maughams*, but he was constrained by libel laws and family sensitivities from expressing himself as bluntly as he might have wished.

# I

# Maugham & Sons, London & Paris

When Victoria was crowned in 1838, Robert Maugham, lawyer
and writer, had already made a name for himself, the first of the
Maughams to do so. His entry in the *Dictionary of National
Biography* mystifies by beginning when he was an adult, as if he
had arrived fully-formed from another planet, but the register of
the old church of St Dunstan's in the West shows that he was
baptized on 6 April 1788: 'Robert, son of William and Catherine
Maugham, born March 9th in Chancery Lane'.

His father, William, was one of several Maughams who had left
Westmorland during the slump following the Napoleonic wars
hoping to find work in London. At first they settled in the Covent
Garden area, but how they made a living is unknown. William
may have been a cabinet-maker like one of his uncles or a
bookbinder like another, or a glazier like his father. After he
married he was continuously in debt, and then in 1802 he, his
wife and their four children vanished from the official records.
They may have returned to Westmorland to escape financial
problems or even have been removed to Marshalsea Prison for
debt. If the family did go to the Marshalsea it might explain
Robert's silence about his early years, unless he was too ashamed
of his humble antecedents to acknowledge them.

Reticence about the past persisted among the Victorian
Maughams. Instead of accepting their origins, they preferred
generalities and myths – for example, a story of their descent from
Mahon, son of Murtagh Mor O'Brien, King of Ireland – but
there was no Irish connection at all; it was wishful thinking based

on phonetic confusion. Two of Robert's grandsons, Frederick and William (always known to family and friends as Freddie and Willie), had their own theories. Freddie, who became the first Viscount Maugham, believed that they were descended from John of Gaunt, Duke of Lancaster, and he was delighted when the *Genealogists' Magazine* of June 1952 published an article tracing the female line back to Edward I of England. This, and the family coat of arms and crest, were proof enough for him. After his death, however, his son Robin checked these with the College of Heralds which dismissed them as bogus.

Willie thought that a Scottish Maugham had crossed the border and started his own clan in Westmorland, but there is no proof of this. He was fascinated by the story of his mother's ancestors, the Breretons, and the possibility of a trace of royal blood in his own veins but he thought a connection with the unfortunate Edward II should be played down: 'I wouldn't like my blameless reputation to be sullied.' Ironically, if the Victorian Maughams had looked into the matter, they would have discovered enough to satisfy any snobbish longings for noble ancestry. In the early 1960s Dr P. H. Reaney, the eminent etymologist, researched all the possibilities and concluded that the likeliest link was with the ancient de Malgham family, wealthy landowners in Norfolk and Yorkshire.

Robert Maugham's early years remain a mystery but he reappeared in London at the age of seventeen as a clerk to George Barrow, an attorney in the City of London with an office near the Royal Exchange. In 1817 he qualified as a lawyer and rapidly showed that he had the instincts and ambitions of a modern marketing executive. At the time, apart from a collection of statutes and decisions, there was a complete lack of legal text-books, so he wrote a series which became standard works of reference. The cumbersome titles constitute the list of contents, and typical was his second book, *A Treatise on the Law of Attornies, Solicitors and Agents: with Notes and Disquisitions, A Treatise on the Laws of Literary Property, comprising the Statutes and Cases relating to Books, Manuscripts, Lectures and A Complete*

*Collection of the Statutes and Rules and Orders relating to Attornies.*
This is generally seen as his most important work and he used the
preface to prepare the ground for a further development:

> It is indeed most remarkable, that the Attornies of the Metropolis,
> two thousand four hundred of them in regular practice (beside many
> uncertified), are destitute of all facilities to cultivate the higher
> branches of their profession . . . We possess neither college nor hall,
> library nor society, yet the necessity of every possible assistance in
> legal studies is surely equal to that of any other science, and none can
> be more important than the LAW.

He led the campaign to win the recognition and status that
other professions enjoyed and, in 1825, became one of the
founders of the Law Institution, now known as the Law Society.
As a reward for his success, he was elected secretary, with a salary
of £400 a year and an apartment for himself and his family in the
Institution's newly-built premises in Chancery Lane which he had
helped to plan. His role as secretary was a sinecure and he carried
on in private practice with a young attorney, Thomas Kennedy, at
100 Chancery Lane, a short step from his own front door.

Robert found time to fill another gap in the market in 1830 by
launching the *Legal Observer* which carried topical items, reports
of cases and articles of practical interest to lawyers. It succeeded
where earlier attempts had failed because he used the nation-wide
network of coaches to distribute his newspaper, so it was possible
to have the latest copy in most centres within twenty-four hours.
He remained its sole owner, editor and frequent contributor until
1856 when he sold out to the rival *Solicitors' Journal* which had
successfully copied and modernised his concept.

He was also actively engaged in the development of legal
education, the Solicitors' Acts of 1843 and 1860, and, in 1844, was
a founder member of the Law Assurance Company. An article
describing his manifold achievements in *The Law Society's
Gazette* of December 1959 dubbed him 'the father of legal
journalism'. He died a wealthy man in 1862.

His son, also named Robert, became a solicitor and formed a
prosperous partnership with a William Dixon. In 1848, they

3

opened a branch in Paris and William's brother Albert joined them. Once the Paris office was established, Robert took sole charge and moved it to 54 Faubourg St Honoré. This was almost opposite the British Embassy, and he became its unofficial legal adviser. The London practice was run by the Dixon brothers (whose name survives in the Surrey firm, Dixon, Ward & Co.).

During these years Robert enjoyed travelling and at various times explored Greece, Turkey, Asia Minor and North Africa, collecting artefacts which he displayed in his home, a large, elegant apartment at 25 Avenue d'Antin, now renamed Avenue Franklin D. Roosevelt.


# Beauty and the Beast

Robert, an ugly little man, did not marry until he was nearly forty. It is not known how he met the formidable Mrs Anne Alicia Snell and her two pretty daughters. As a young woman, Anne had married an army officer and gone to India where she was left with her two little girls when he died. Instead of returning to her family in England, she decided to settle in Paris and add to her army pension of £265 a year by writing stories. She became a great success and is reputed to have written some seventy romantic novels as well as books for children. Her younger daughter, Rose, also became a writer and had six short novels to her credit before she died of tuberculosis in 1869 aged twenty-seven. Unfortunately, except for some of the children's books which are uplifting moral tales typical of the period, no trace of their work remains.

Edith, the elder daughter, was the one who attracted Robert. She was nearly half his age, a small, frail girl with delicate features, large brown eyes and a mass of russet-coloured hair, her beauty emphasised by a tubercular condition. They were married by Robert's clergyman brother, Henry, at the British Embassy church on 1 October 1863. On her part there may have been affection, but no love, because years later, when she was asked why she was faithful to such an ugly man, she merely replied that he had never hurt her feelings. It seems she was glad to escape from the shadow of her dominating mother, for, after her marriage, she saw as little of her as possible.

From the outset, Edith was ruthlessly determined to become a figure in Paris society, an objective which needed considerable expenditure to compete with the aristocracy and the nouveaux riches. Dressed by Worth or one of his imitators, she was constantly out and about accompanied by Robert. Paris society dubbed them 'Beauty and the Beast'. They went to balls, dinners, concerts and theatres: the Opéra, the Comédie-Française and the Eldorado, a chic palace of varieties. They entertained at the latest fashionable restaurants and for dinner parties at home the catering was left to one of the firms used by smart Parisians. Edith soon became one of the few foreigners to be listed in the annual directory, *La Société et la High Life*, and, as her obituary in *La Gaulois* was to say on 1 February 1882, 'She graced the most elegant salons.' It is a pity that her journals have been lost because they would have given us the story of her social climb and an insight into the flamboyance of Parisian society during the Second Empire.

Their first son, Charles, was born in November 1865, Freddie in October 1866 and Harry in June 1868. In addition to other servants, Edith had staff to cope in the nursery and may have employed a wet-nurse to breastfeed the children. As soon as she was able, she carried on with her social life and, in the manner of her class, saw very little of her children except on holidays in Deauville. Freddie remembered her 'speaking pleasant words to her sons' and 'watching over their happiness' but Willie's comments were too off-hand to give any indication of her personality. This does not support Robin Maugham's highly romantic account of her as a doting mother in *Somerset and All the Maughams*.

Life continued serenely until the outbreak of the Franco-

5

Prussian war in 1870. In his autobiography, *At the End of the Day*, Freddie described a large map pinned up in the billiard room with little red and blue flags representing the opposing forces. With the German flags moving closer to Paris, the family joined other English residents and left France. The children stayed with Grandma Mary Maugham in London at her house at 20 Westbourne Street, Lancaster Gate, while Robert and Edith went off to Italy for a holiday. Edith's intrepid mother refused to leave France: it is said that she organised a hospital for the wounded and was rewarded with a civic reception when peace came. It seems in character, but any evidence has disappeared. Neglected by her grandsons, enduring a lonely life in Le Mans, she eventually died on 24 October 1904, having outlived her daughter Rose by thirty-five years.

In 1871 the Maughams returned to a Paris ravaged by five months of siege and then by fighting between rival political factions. The family's servants had convinced first the Germans and then the mob that the apartment was British and it had been left alone, but around it were the wrecks of burned-out buildings. In time life returned to normal, but Maugham et Dixon did not recover its prosperity and Robert had to work long hours to maintain the standard of living his family expected.

Edith's whirl of social activities, accompanied or not by Robert, continued much as before, but her tubercular condition began to limit her. As childbirth and an active sex life were then believed to alleviate the illness, she was urged by her doctors to have more children. Following several miscarriages, she became pregnant again in 1873 and, with rest, managed to go the full term. Because of a new decree that all children born on French soil must automatically take French nationality, her confinement took place in the British Embassy. On 25 January 1874 a son was born, and baptized William Somerset Maugham. The unusual middle name came from great-uncle Henry Somerset Todd who in turn had been given it to honour a godfather, General Sir Henry Somerset.

Willie spent his early years with his brothers, but when he was nearly four, they were sent to boarding school at Dover College in England. It was intended that they should go from there to Winchester but, instead, they stayed on. Freddie bemoaned this in his autobiography, suggesting that Winchester might have given him advantages on the old-boy network that a minor public school could never do. Before this, the boys had attended the local French lycée, a fee-paying school with a classically-based curriculum. At Dover they were treated contemptuously as 'Froggies' until they lost their French accents. Freddie said that it took him years to pronounce words with a French derivation in the English manner, and even in old age he still had to pause before using them, which, in common with Willie, gave him a speech hesitancy.

Age had always separated Willie from his brothers but without their high spirits the apartment seemed empty and he became, in effect, an only child, his main companions the series of female servants employed to look after him. He rarely saw his father and was allowed only a few minutes each day with his mother and, apart from holidays, when he shared her with his brothers, he saw little of her.

During the next few years, Edith's health grew worse and she was forced to give up most of her social life. She still entertained friends to tea, though, among them Isabella Williams-Freeman whose husband was a second secretary at the British Embassy. Isabella's daughter Violet, later Mrs Arthur Hammersley, spoke to Robin Maugham of going with her mother to visit Edith:

> Her great brown eyes were always sad. She must have suffered a lot of pain from her terrible consumption and she was sometimes terribly ill. My mother always took me to visit her in the afternoon. Your grandmother would give me a doll to play with. I would take it under the tea table. I could hear them above me talking in low and earnest tones. It seemed the whole trend was one of sadness.

By the time she said this, Mrs Hammersley, an alert old lady of eighty-seven, relished gloom and doom. Nancy Mitford teased her unmercifully about her pessimism and, because she was also a hypochondriac, Osbert Sitwell wrote a short story about her,

'That Flesh is Heir To', in which he pictured her as a carrier of disease with a bag crammed full of germs. Given her reputation, Robin was surprised by a description that she gave of Willie as a child which was the reverse of the gloom he expected. According to her, Willie was mischievous and loquacious, had a lively imagination, and was good at inventing games and telling 'wonderful stories'. But this proved to be the prelude to her despondent opinion of him as an adult. Just before she died in 1964 she wrote to Robin about the praise showered on Willie in the press on his ninetieth birthday, saying that the dissertations on his dignity, benignity and deep loving kindness made her feel she hardly knew him at all.

As Edith's illness became more serious, various expensive cures were tried but had little effect. For several winters she went to Pau, a health resort near the Spanish frontier, taking Willie and her maid with her. On these visits she needed to conserve her strength and there is no evidence that she ever played with him or had much contact. He was there as a precautionary measure because his state of health suggested that he might develop tuberculosis when he was older. This prognosis proved correct and he not only suffered himself, but later infected the only person he ever cared for.

Horrifyingly cruel as it now seems, and despite her rapid physical deterioration, Edith's doctors still demanded that she have children. When a boy was still-born she was left weaker than ever but still they insisted and, in 1881, she was pregnant again, spending months in bed exhausted by pain. She knew instinctively that she had not long to live and persuaded her devoted maid to dress her in her best evening gown so that she could have a photograph taken as a memento for her sons. Perhaps she wanted to remind them that her reputation as a society personality was justified by her beauty. She died on 31 January 1882, seven days after the birth of a son, Alan Edward, who lived for only twenty-four hours. His death on 25 January cannot have made Willie's eighth birthday much of a festive occasion, but by then he had become used to the hushed gloom of the apartment which, for several years, had become steadily more like a hospital, with its pervading smell of scent combined with disinfectant.

It was probably misguided kindness which stopped Robert dismissing Edith's personal maid; instead, he asked her to become Willie's nurse. For the next two and a half years she dominated the little boy's life and influenced the development of his character, yet past biographers have ignored her crucial role. In *The Summing Up*, Willie said that he knew little of his parents apart from hearsay. Did his nurse cocoon the child with her own grief, filling his mind with stories that made Edith seem like a figure from an enchanting fairy tale? When he was an old man, he often became emotional about Edith's early death and would burst into tears. Alan Searle and Beverley Nichols, among others, sentimentalised these scenes and Willie's devotion to her photographs, which he revered as if they were holy icons. But perhaps he wept for a conceptual figure based on hearsay, and for the conventional idea of a loving mother, just as he wept in churches for the concept of salvation and the idea of a loving God – with regret, bitterness and anger – because to him it was all a cruel deception.

In 1883, Robert's deteriorating health gave his partners such cause for concern that they recruited a young solicitor, John Sewell, to help run the Paris office. We do not know if Robert realised how ill he was; perhaps not, because he designed a summer residence which was built at Suresnes, then a country area on the outskirts of Paris, and often took Willie to see how the work was progressing. If he did know his illness was fatal, however, he may well have been carrying out a scheme agreed with Edith, intending the house as a memorial to her and as a gift to his sons. Robert had had the glass in the windows engraved with a sign he had found on his travels in Morocco which was supposed to ward off the evil eye and it impressed Willie so much that he later adopted it as his logo.

Robert died on 24 June 1884 'after long suffering from cancer of the stomach' as *The Times* put it. Once his sons had recovered from the shock of his death so soon after that of their mother, they were faced with the fact that, contrary to appearances, Robert was not a wealthy man. After a three-day sale of the contents of the Paris apartment, enough was raised to provide each of the sons with an annual income of £150, then adequate for their foreseeable needs, provided these were modest. The house at Suresnes, completely furnished and ready for occupation, was not sold but kept by his executors for the boys.

# Youth Has a Kingdom Waiting for It

Robert's executors, his brother the Reverend Henry Maugham and Albert Dixon, became the boys' joint guardians. Charles, aged eighteen, was at Cambridge, while Freddie, seventeen, and Harry, sixteen, were still at Dover College. For several years, Willie had attended the local lycée but, with his long absences at Pau, Robert had realised that this was insufficient preparation for Dover College so had engaged a clergyman attached to the British Embassy church to coach Willie and improve his English. The cleric chose an odd way of doing this, making him read from the crime reports in the *Standard*, a British newspaper. It may have seemed an imaginative method: firstly, it underlined the Bible teaching that the wages of sin, if not always death, was a prison sentence and, secondly, it prepared the young mind for the legal career he was expected to follow. In *The Summing Up*, Willie recalled his horror at one particularly gruesome report of a murder and this may have put the impressionable young boy off a legal career for good. At the same time, it probably implanted a vicarious interest in crime, for detective fiction became his favourite bedtime reading in later years.

Willie's future might have been different if he had gone to live with the Dixons where he would have had surrogate brothers and sisters and enjoyed the advantages of a household used to children. But Henry and his German-born wife Barbara, both in their fifties and childless, agreed to take him; probably it was Christian duty on his part and sentimentality on hers. Willie's nurse was ordered to bring him to England. As he told his nephew Robin: 'My nurse was the only person in the world I loved.' For over two years she had devoted herself solely to him, providing far more love than his own mother had ever done. As soon as they arrived at All Saints Vicarage, Whitstable, Henry told Willie that she was to be dismissed and sent back to France as there was no money to pay her wages. This was a lie, but Henry must have thought that a complete break with the past was advisable. For her it may have been heartbreaking, but the feelings of servants counted for little in Victorian England. For Willie it was a parting as dramatic as death, the prelude to years of loneliness.

The Vicarage was run entirely for the comfort of Henry. No concessions were made to the child and he had to fit into the established routine; the contrast with his recent life in Paris could not have been greater. Both Maughams did their best to show affection but seem to have been baffled by him. They soon indoctrinated him into their narrow-minded brand of Christianity and into their equally powerful code of British middle-class behaviour with its attendant intolerance and snobbery. In 'Society', those who attended the local Baptist chapel or were 'in trade' (which grouped such skills as cobbling and carpentry with banking) did not exist, while the working classes were tolerated provided they accepted with meek gratitude the situation to which God had called them. By sharp contrast, fawning deference had to be paid to social betters irrespective of their stupidity or loutish behaviour.

In due course, Willie was sent as a boarder to King's School, Canterbury where he suffered the unthinking cruelty and crass bullying of boys and masters who mocked the ease with which he spoke French and the stammer which developed over his pronunciation of English. While in the senior school his health, never good, suddenly deteriorated and, when tuberculosis was suspected, he was sent to spend several months at Hyères in the South of France. By the time he returned, his work had slipped behind and his few friends had lost interest in him. After another enforced period in Hyères, it was easy to persuade his uncle and aunt to let him go to Heidelberg to study, probably because they assumed he did not have long to live, an idea he may have encouraged but did not share. He was only sixteen but at last making a bid for independence and freedom from the claustrophobic atmosphere of the Vicarage and the parochialism of Canterbury and Whitstable.

It is difficult to accept Willie's assertion in *Looking Back* that he was sexually innocent when he arrived in Germany: English public schools were notorious for their homosexuality but, in his case, erotic dreams and masturbation may have been sufficient to satisfy his urgent physical needs. Perhaps, like many boys, he fantasised about a handsome older lover and, in the freedom he found away from England, was ready to seduce or be seduced.

At school he had had some scholastic success, but in Heidelberg he was in control of his own education and the two years he spent there were years of learning and self-revelation. Staying at the same *pension* was a young American professor who taught Greek at Harvard and had come to Europe to pursue his studies. He became great friends with Willie, even taking him on a fortnight's holiday to Switzerland and paying all his expenses. When he moved on to Berlin, his room in the *pension* was taken by twenty-six-year-old John Ellingham Brooks, a young man who had studied law at Cambridge but had given it up to live a pleasant life of aestheticism in Germany. As Willie was destined to be another Maugham lawyer, it must have been startling for him to meet someone who had rebelled against this profession. Brooks, poetically handsome, was unashamedly homosexual and, as Maugham admitted to Glenway Wescott years later, they became lovers. More importantly, Brooks took on the role of intellectual mentor and it was under his influence that Willie

abandoned his Christian allegiance, while retaining an appreciation of mysticism and religious theatricality. He was introduced to
Wagner's music, the works of Schopenhauer and Spinoza and saw
the revolutionary drama of Ibsen which became a significant
influence on the structure and characterisation of his own
dramatic writing in later years.

In *Looking Back*, Willie remarks that both Brooks and the
professor were attracted to him physically, but that he was too
innocent to realise it at the time. It is an unnecessary comment,
similar to that of a guilty schoolboy denying a misdemeanour
before it is found out. As we know, contrary to Willie's denial,
that Brooks was indeed his lover, it leaves the impression that the
Harvard man may have been as well. But Walter Adney Payne,
another young man that Willie met in Heidelberg, became more
important to him than Brooks. Payne and Willie were to remain
close friends for nearly sixty years and to live together for over
ten.

When he was eighteen, Willie returned to Whitstable with his
increasing sophistication concealed behind a reserved manner he
could drop at will but use as an armour against inquisitive fools
and potential enemies. This characteristic remained with him for
life and was often assumed to be shyness by people too vain to
realise that Willie was unprepared to expend much time on them.

While he had been away, Willie had written a life of
Meyerbeer. This was not an obvious choice of subject, but as a
small boy he could have heard about the lavish productions of the
composer's work in Paris. (*Le Prophète* of 1849, for example, had a
sensational ice-skating sequence achieved by using roller skates for
the first time on stage.) Though he destroyed the manuscript, it
served its purpose, proving to him that he had ability, a view no
doubt supported by Brooks. He was now determined to be a
professional writer but, wary of mockery, he kept his goal a secret
from his guardians. In a decision he may have later regretted, he
refused to follow his three brothers to Cambridge. He rejected law
and, after a brief spell in an office, accountancy. A Whitstable
doctor then suggested medicine. After a spell at a crammer, Willie

passed the entrance exams to St Thomas's Hospital, Lambeth. As he said in *The Summing Up*, he had no vocation for the medical profession but it meant living in London and this meant freedom.

London was a centre for all those sins that horrified the religious revivalists who banged their drums for Jesus. Sex was easy to come by and nobody thought too much about the wider effects of a laissez-faire attitude, provided behaviour was not too outrageous. Camp young men striking poses were featured in *Punch* and fun was poked at Oscar Wilde, the leading aesthete who had already featured in Gilbert and Sullivan's *Patience* in 1881. By the time Willie began exploring the town, Wilde had started his fated affair with Edward Shelley, the teenager who worked as an office boy at his publisher, Elkin Matthews and John Lane. It is interesting to note that this firm published poems by Willie's aesthetic brother Harry who, apparently, was also attracted to the likes of young Shelley.

St Thomas's Hospital was a grandiose structure on the Thames opposite the Houses of Parliament. Behind it sprawled some of the worst slums in London and only a short walk away was the Waterloo Road, a notorious street offering every kind of sexual pleasure at a price. Only a few weeks after Willie began his medical studies on 27 September 1892, the trial began of Dr Thomas Neill Cream for the murder of four local prostitutes with strychnine. He had a room at 103 Lambeth Palace Road opposite the hospital and even tried to implicate a young doctor at St Thomas's. Cream was found guilty and was hanged on 15 November.

Willie must have followed the case with avid interest in the *Star*, the newspaper he bought on Lambeth Bridge as he walked home in the evenings to his lodging at 11 Vincent Square. The house, built in the previous century, overlooked the large playing fields of Westminster School and from his sitting-room window Willie could watch boys and young men in sporting kit swarming over the grass. He occupied two small rooms on the ground floor for which he paid eighteen shillings a week. Lunch at the hospital cost three or four pence for a bun and butter, and a glass of milk or hot drink. He could live quite comfortably on his income which paid for fees, medical equipment, stationery and clothes, still leaving enough to enjoy his leisure, and for an attractive young man there was much to enjoy.

The training Willie received at the hospital was thorough but frequently unpleasant and not for the squeamish. The first two years were tedious, though enlivened by the anatomy course. He worked just hard enough to scrape through exams, and when he should have been studying he was writing drama in imitation of Ibsen. Boldly, he sent the scripts to theatre managers and was crestfallen when they were returned, rejected, to Vincent Square. He blamed ignorance and the low expectations of the public rather than himself. Perhaps, he decided, it might be wise to build a reputation as a novelist, after which his dramatic masterpieces would receive the serious consideration they deserved.

From 1892 he kept notebooks in which he jotted down ideas, descriptions of characters, scraps of overheard conversation and felicitous phrases or lines of epigrammatic wit that came into his mind at inopportune moments and had to be held in the memory until he reached his pen. The ability to remember was fully stretched in his final three years when he was attached to the out-patients department, or delivering babies in the putrefying slums on the other side of Lambeth Palace Road (where his doctor's bag protected him from 'robbery and violence'). The notebooks rapidly filled with reports and conclusions, the most pertinent being that suffering did not ennoble the spirit and provide contact with the Kingdom of God. Instead it degraded and made men selfish, mean, petty and suspicious.

Willie never provided a reason for studying medicine and may not have had one beyond his explanation that it gave him freedom. A Freudian might argue that subconsciously he was influenced by his mother's illness and the constant parade of doctors attempting to save her. Perhaps someone had suggested, in the irresponsible way that adults sometimes have with children, that when he grew up he should become a doctor and 'make her better', or had cruelly informed him that the only reason he was born was in order to cure her. Such a burden of guilt, deeply implanted, might explain much about Willie.

# Elders and Betters

The elder Maugham brothers accepted without question their dynastic obligation to go into law. After taking his law tripos and obtaining his degree as Bachelor of Law at Cambridge, Charles was admitted to the Roll of Solicitors in 1889, followed by Harry, and together they joined the Paris firm which was now known as Sewell et Maugham.

Freddie might also have become a solicitor and joined them in Paris had he not met Mark Romer at Trinity Hall, Cambridge. Both were studying maths and shared an intense interest in sport; they took an instant liking to each other and remained friends for life. When Freddie left Cambridge in 1889, *The Granta*, in a eulogistic article of 1 March, recorded his prowess as a rowing man: twice in the Head of the River crew and twice in the Varsity races. The piece omitted to mention that he also became captain of the Trinity Hall Rugby team. He was outstanding in debate at the Union and was elected President, though *Granta* suggested his wit had a sarcastic touch. It also noted that he played the piano, 'sings a good song' and proved conclusively that drinking is the only occupation suited to an undergraduate. The eulogy ended: 'He has a supple body but unbending principles and is an emphatic exception to the general rule which has defined a "charmant garçon" as one "qui avait tous les vices".' The cynic might think this compliment slightly double-edged, suggesting a primness in Freddie's make-up. Scholastically, he did not do as well as expected because he spent too much time in rowing practice: as *Granta* quaintly put it: 'He eventually came to anchor in the second class of the Mathematical Tripos.'

Mark Romer introduced Freddie to his parents over Christmas 1885 and they promptly adopted him as a surrogate son. If the Maughams tended to be introspective, the Romers and their five sons and two daughters were gregarious, amusing and boisterous, providing Freddie with the demonstrative family affection which he lacked. As he said in his autobiography in an unusually fulsome sentence, they had 'a great and happy effect on my life'.

The Romer parents – Robert, popularly known as Bob, and his wife Betty – had an exotic family history. Their common ancestor, Wolfgang Rhomer, a military engineer and architect, had arrived in England with William of Orange. Although the name 'Rhomer' was originally given to pious Catholics who made the pilgrimage to Rome, Wolfgang was as Protestant as his monarch. His father, Mathias, who hailed from Düsseldorf, married Anna Duppengiezeer in 1637 and Wolfgang was the third son of a family of eleven. He served in Ireland and in America where he was a member of the council of the province of New York. Several of the maps he made are in the British Museum, including one of the Hudson River and adjoining country. Much of his architectural work was on the harbour defences of Boston and Portsmouth, England. He died in 1713 and was buried in Düsseldorf. His son, John Lambertus Rhomer, who is buried in St Margaret's, Westminster, was equally distinguished as a military architect. He married May Hammond in 1711 and had one son, also named John.

By the 1800s, the surname had been anglicised and in 1837 a portrait of John Romer, surrounded by his large family, was exhibited at the Royal Academy. He had married a gipsy girl, Sarah Cooper, whom he had met at a fair in a boxing booth. What she was doing in such a brutally masculine setting is a puzzle. Honor Earl, Freddie's second daughter, suggested she was an orange-seller like Nell Gwyn. It is believed that John Romer was disinherited following the marriage, but he later built his own fortune as an architect.

Among their nine children were Robert, a popular actor, Frank, who made a name for himself as a composer under the pseudonym Keisar, and Emma, a leading opera singer of the day. Following her marriage to a wealthy army contractor, George Almond, Emma went into management to present operas in English. She died in 1868 and is buried in Brompton Cemetery. Emma's sister Helen, also a singer, married Mark Lemon, a founder and first editor of *Punch*. He was Falstaffian by nature and appearance and, indeed, played the role on tours around England, often appearing with his great friend Charles Dickens. He published reams of his comic verses in *Punch* which may have seemed hilarious at the time, but now lie defunct on the page. He also wrote novels, the best of which was *Mr Nightingale's Diary*, and successful farcical comedies with titles such as *Mind Your Own Business*, all now forgotten.

Many believed Lemon to be of Jewish origin. He maintained that he was not and on one occasion attested to this under oath in court, but the supposition persisted. At the time, Jews were literally second-class citizens and the term 'Jew' was used by the ignorant in denigration. It was not until a law was eventually passed in the 1850s that Jews were given equal rights. Lemon was so incensed when Disraeli, the son of a converted Jew, voted against the bill that he pilloried him in *Punch* with cartoons and satiric verse that he wrote himself. This of course convinced the prejudiced that he was Jewish after all.

The rich combination of Romer and Lemon blood produced Betty, a high-spirited beauty, who caused a stir when she married her first cousin, Bob Romer, in 1864. A brilliant Cambridge man, he became private secretary to Baron Lionel de Rothschild and, for a time, Bob and Betty lived in Paris. While he was mathematics professor at Queen's College, Cork, he 'ate his dinners at Lincoln's Inn' and was called to the Bar in 1867. He was knighted by Queen Victoria at Windsor in 1890 and became a Lord Justice in 1899.

Their son Mark was determined to emulate his father and undoubtedly influenced Freddie's decision to become a barrister. Mark and Freddie left Cambridge together and were called to the Bar together in 1890. It was Betty who found rooms for Freddie in Sydney Street, Chelsea, but he spent much of his leisure time at the Romer home, a large corner house in Harrington Gardens, South Kensington.

In his autobiography Freddie gives a succinct sketch of life in London when he first arrived. Public travel was by small horse-drawn buses with open tops reached by a sort of ladder. They would stop anywhere on request, which was hard, if not cruel, on the horses when they were suddenly jerked to a halt. Most young men used to jump on and off the buses while they were moving and Freddie remembered with some nostalgia the days when he was able to do this easily, running after them and jumping on when they were going at top speed. In wet weather the streets were so filthy that his trousers were covered in mud to the knees and often a passing bus would splash him from head to foot. Dry-cleaning was unknown and he hated the time spent in brushing his clothes every day and looking after the top hat he had to wear. He usually walked the four miles from his lodgings to the Law Courts, arriving about ten o'clock and working through until six o'clock, except on Saturdays when he stopped at about two. There was a lunch break of half an hour and he usually had an egg or sardines on toast, a roll and butter, and coffee. In the evenings he ate at the Holborn where, for ten pence in today's money, he got a mutton chop, bread and cheese, and a pint of beer.

Except for the Romers he hardly knew anyone, and to meet people he took up fencing at the School of Arms where he reached competition standard. He also joined the Harlequin Rugby Club but on one Saturday, when he was playing as a three-quarter back, an opponent fell on his right leg and wrenched his knee so badly that Freddie needed surgical treatment at St George's Hospital. Betty Romer insisted he stay with them until he could walk properly again. He never completely recovered from this knee injury but it did not stop him playing golf or taking up winter sports. In addition to skating, tobogganing and bob-sleighing he grew to love curling. 'There is no better game for those who are no longer young', as he put it.

Soon after his arrival in London, Willie was introduced to the

Romers by Freddie. Willie never acknowledged the debt he owed to the family. Their friendship provided him with his first experience of the way an affluent upper-middle-class English family lived. Until then he had never so much as set foot inside a grand London house. It was the beginning of an education for the eighteen-year-old youth, which eventually allowed him to write his sharply observed drawing-room comedies with the authority of an insider allied with the objectivity of an outsider.

Distance has blurred and made comic the class distinctions that existed in Victoria's reign. As professional people, the Romers were looked down upon by the leisured aristocracy and they, in their turn, looked down upon people in trade, be they stock-brokers, grocers, shipbuilders or theatricals. On one occasion Willie took an actor friend to a dance at the Romer house. The actor was charming and handsome with the demeanour of a gentleman, but Bob Romer was incensed when he heard he was there; to him, it showed a lack of taste and savoir-faire to bring such a person into a private house. The fact that the Romers had theatrical blood in their veins meant nothing to him. The social mores of the time excluded actors from decent company and so the unfortunate young man was spirited away.

It was not until Edward VII ascended the throne in 1901 that the situation altered and, to the chagrin of many of the professional class, the King openly retained his friendships with those in 'trade' and allowed them into court circles. The consequent battle between the rigidity of old class-distinctions and the new liberality was to be reflected in much of Willie's work.

At this stage in his life Willie had met few women whom he could admire and now he had two: Betty, and her younger daughter, Nellie. The mother was gracious, sympathetic, wise and always feminine, while her daughter combined these attributes with spirit and an infectious sense of humour. Willie never spoke of the mother–son relationship he enjoyed with Betty but it became something of a family joke that he preferred to spend time with her in her sitting room than with the men. Nor did he speak of the influence that Nellie had upon him. It was Nellie who became the prototype of the women whom he later singled out for friendship. It is unlikely that he ever thought of her romantically, because at this stage Willie was completely homosexual in behaviour and outlook; also it had become increasingly obvious that Nellie and Freddie were falling in love.

In 1894 the four Maugham brothers were reunited when Charles married Mabel Hardy at St Stephen's Church, Bayswater. The daughter of the artist Heywood Hardy, Mabel, or Beldy as she was known from her student days at the Paris Conservatoire, was nineteen, pretty and vivacious. (It is remarkable that the three Maugham brothers who married chose women who had this latter quality as a conspicuous characteristic.) Charles by contrast to his wife was a grave individual, described by several members of the family as 'a saint'. The couple were to have five children, four daughters and one son, Ormond, born in 1909. The English Maughams saw little of the 'French' Maughams except when Charles occasionally rented a house on the Sussex coast for a few weeks. Most of the family's holidays were spent at his villa near St Brieuc and there is no record of the English cousins visiting them. When Ormond, only twelve years old, was confined to a wheelchair for life after falling from a tree and damaging his spine, Willie was deeply moved by Beldy's devotion and the boy's uncomplaining courage. In his play *The Sacred Flame* Willie examined a similar situation and his treatment provided an example of the important influence Ibsen had on his work for the theatre.

After Charles retired from the Paris business, he and the family moved to London to a flat at 23 Cadogan Gardens and it was here that Ormond died when he was twenty-five. It is said that the tragedy broke Charles' spirit and probably precipitated his death six months later.

Freddie and Nellie were married in 1896 and began their new life in a small rented house in The Boltons only minutes away from Harrington Gardens. By Romer standards they were poor, but the term is relative. A bank clerk of the time on £200 a year considered himself reasonably well-off but, unlike them, he could not afford a cook, parlour maid and nannies, or a home in fashionable Kensington. During the first few years of the marriage, their income rose from £400 to £1,000 per annum which included £100 a year settled on Nellie by her father, but Freddie was forced to raid what was left of his inheritance to pay large bills. He had been fortunate to be taken into the chambers of Charles Macnaghten as a 'devil' and did not have to find the entire sum normally called for. He was required to write drafts of legal documents and soon began to earn small sums for his work. Professionally, he lacked recognition because solicitors preferred to place briefs with men of more experience, but after 1900 things improved dramatically and his annual income soared to over £4,000.

Freddie had to work long hours and then spend most of his evenings at home preparing for the following day; when he began to be professionally successful, he was often shut away in his study working until the early hours. He found time, however, to enjoy his new enthusiasm, photography, for which he installed his own darkroom. He also had a voracious appetite for books on every subject from fiction to mathematical theory. On the way home, he occasionally spent an hour or two playing billiards and dining at the Savile Club, then at 107 Piccadilly. During vacations, he took to travelling abroad on his own, explaining in his autobiography that Nellie preferred to stay with her young family.

He didn't mention that he and Nellie were keen on the theatre and tried to go at least once a week. They usually had dinner at the Carlton Grill or Kettners before a play, though sometimes they preferred to have a late supper at the Savoy. In the early years the Savoy was an occasional extravagance, but Freddie enjoyed Nellie's pleasure at being taken there so much that he did not begrudge the cost. They often went away together for weekends, often to Brighton where they stayed at the Grand or the exclusive Princes Hotel in Hove. Sometimes they went to

France and once, while they were in Paris, he took her to the Folies-Bergère which she thought quite awful; she much preferred Sarah Bernhardt.

In his autobiography, surprising for its almost complete lack of reference to Nellie, he complimented her on her good housekeeping during the difficult years. Their first daughter, Kate, born on 8 November 1897, remembered her mother joking about the lack of money, saying it was just as well she liked rice pudding because it was cheap and filling and satisfied her craving for food when she was pregnant. She also saved money by making all her children's clothes instead of buying from the fashionable shops her friends frequented.

Honor, their second daughter, born in 1901, recalled the discomfort of the clothes children were made to wear in her early childhood. From autumn until late spring they were enveloped in thick wool combinations, covered by a heat-inducing bodice with suspenders to hold up thick woollen black stockings and then a flannel petticoat. The final touch was another petticoat of starched white cotton which rubbed, scratched and tickled the neck and arms. Complaints were not allowed but on hot spring days when the discomfort became unbearable children could not restrain themselves. The reply was always the same as nurses chanted, 'Cast n'er a clout till May be out.' The relief when at last June came and lighter clothes were permitted was reflected in the faces of the children in the parks, playing under the sentinel gaze of nannies. But they were, of course, still swaddled in outdoor clothes, though made of rather less heavyweight materials than winter wear.

Honor thought one of the oddest practices was the use of the formal 'Miss Honor' or 'Miss Kate', which style of address servants were expected to use even when she and her sisters were little more than babies. Nurses were exempt from this but only if they were 'college trained'. She later refused to allow her own sons to be addressed as 'Master Julian' or 'Master Stephen' and she was sure her neighbours thought her behaviour eccentric and 'let the side down'. She also remembered with some incredulity the huge quantities of food eaten in the nursery and dining room. Typically, breakfast might consist of porridge, bacon, eggs, sausages and mushrooms with an alternative for the adults of kippers or kidneys, followed by toast and hot rolls with tea, coffee or, in the nursery, warm milk. Lunch was three large courses and in the afternoon tea was served with plates piled high with carbohydrates in some form or other. When the children were considered old enough they joined their parents for dinner which always consisted of four courses. Yet, Honor admitted, she spent all her holiday pocket-money on sweets; chocolate and toffee were a penny for two ounces and some sweets were only a penny for four ounces.

Nellie was a loving mother but could be a strict disciplinarian. She taught the girls self-control from an early age and forbade childish tantrums. If one of them made a scene and cried, she would say 'You are overwrought' and would send the culprit to bed until she had recovered. She had no patience with minor illness and taught them to be ashamed of it and not to complain. When Honor was eight, she developed an agonising pain during the night but dared not wake the nurse. By morning she was seriously ill and the doctor was called. Her appendix had burst and for several days it was thought that she would die. During the crisis, straw was laid in the street to muffle the sound of horses and a silent gloom pervaded the house. After Honor recovered, Nellie was not quite so insistent on stoicism, especially when Diana, born in 1908, proved to be a delicate child.

Honor, who described herself as the dunce of the family, recalled sobbing bitterly over her first lesson book entitled ironically, *Reading Without Tears*. Its contents were incomprehensible to her and no amount of repetition could fix them in her mind. Once, when she failed to spell a simple word, her nurse angrily slapped her and induced a trauma that made her unwilling to learn: 'So certain was I of being incapable of understanding that I never listened to a word I was taught.' She was not helped when her governess shouted at her: 'You have a clever mother and father, why are you so stupid?'

The family became so anxious about her lack of progress that Nellie took her to see a doctor. He could find nothing wrong with her and the family reluctantly accepted that she was 'a backward child'. In the early 1900s this was a euphemism for mental deficiency. Far from treating her kindly, her governess behaved as if it was Honor's own fault. Locked in her misery she wept in sympathy when she heard unemployed men in the street singing a lament that concluded 'When will this awful time end?'

Many years later Honor realised that her childhood unhappiness was caused by dyslexia, a condition unknown at that time. Her 'salvation', as she described it, came unexpectedly when she was about seven years old. She had just completed a tracing of a swan when her mother came into the nursery. 'Did you do that picture out of your own head?' Nellie asked. Instinctively Honor assured her that she had.

From that moment my life changed. True, nurses and governesses were still beastly to me and my family still teased me for my stupidity, but I felt that at last they had some hope for my future ... all my energies were directed towards proving that, however unintelligent I was in other ways, I could at least paint and draw.

# II

## The Wilde Legacy

Willie created the myth that for most of his time as a medical student it was all work, very little play and that he was 'lonely'. By this, he did not mean the loneliness of authorship but lack of friends. This may have been true while he was on hospital premises, and it is borne out by an article in *St Thomas's Hospital Gazette* of autumn 1966. The writer, Dr James Lurie, then completing his own studies, tried to discover any residual traces that Willie might have left, but found nothing. It seems he was a loner, aloof and retiring, who did not socialise with fellow students. He had, however, one special friend with whom he was constantly seen. If this was not a member of the hospital community, who was he and where were they seen?

In *A Writer's Notebook* Willie gave a clear description of male friendship as it seemed to him in 1894. There were two kinds, he said: the first was the friendship of animal attraction which drew one to a man, but was not due to any particular qualities or gifts. It was akin to love, it arose in the same way and probably declined in the same way. The second kind of friendship was intellectual and he elaborated on this theme, concluding that the perfect friendship would combine both intellectual and animal attraction, but that it was like crying for the moon. At the time his experience was entirely homosexual and this may explain why, when *A Writer's Notebook* was published nearly sixty years later, this section included a disclaimer emphasising that sex had no active role in the animal attraction he described. Initially, as the notes were for his eyes only, a disclaimer was unnecessary and was

26

presumably added during editing. It is significant that he destroyed all his notebooks once he had made extracts from them.

In contrast to the 'Boy's Own' view of male friendship, the evidence indicates a less inhibited side to Willie's nature. Shortly after he left St Thomas's, he was taken to a party given by Gordon Spry at his home in Vincent Square. Remarking that he had lodged at No. 11, he asked to see over the house. When he and his host went into one of the bedrooms, Willie closed the door, took a tube of petroleum jelly out of his pocket and boldly demanded sex. Spry, telling this story to Timothy d'Arch Smith, remarked that he was astonished because at first sight young Maugham seemed so reserved. During these early years, too, Ellingham Brooks, his lover from the period in Heidelberg, was a regular visitor to London and probably introduced Willie to his particular circle of friends, some of whom were likely to be homosexual.

Harry also stayed in London from time to time, having decided to be a writer rather than work as a solicitor in the Paris firm. He was a regular visitor to the Romer house and became part of that set, but he had a separate circle of homosexual friends to which he introduced Willie. One of this circle was a young man, Wentworth Huyshe, who was to be a beneficiary of Harry's will and may have been his lover. Willie and Huyshe became close friends and the two explored London together with the latter acting as a guide to art galleries and museums. Perhaps he also acted as a mentor and discussed and encouraged Willie's ambitions, but the precise nature of their relationship can only be guessed at. As a token of his gratitude Willie sent him a copy of his first novel, *Liza of Lambeth*, when he received his small, precious supply from the publishers and thanked him for his kindness when he was a 'stupid boy'. This has been taken to mean 'ignorant', but between gay men it can have a camp, sexual connotation. Typically it might refer to someone making a fool of himself while infatuated with another man, or becoming involved with someone who then blackmailed him.

Whatever other male friendships he may have had, the man at

the centre of Willie's life was Walter Adney Payne, to whom he dedicated *Liza of Lambeth*. In a preface to a bibliography of his work compiled by Fred T. Bason and published in 1931, he commented that he named a friend who had been close to him in his lonely youth. Presumably the use of 'lonely' was intended to be ironical. The dedication is a rare example of an expression of affection. Payne was an accountant who later also became a lawyer; his father George Payne had extensive theatre interests, particularly in the London music halls, including the Canterbury in Lambeth and the vast South London Palace near the Elephant and Castle, both not far from St Thomas's Hospital, and the Tivoli in the Strand. In those days, the Strand had more theatres than any other thoroughfare in London and the restaurants, cafés, pubs and shops stayed open until the early hours to cater for the crowds that thronged it. At the eastern end it petered out into Holywell Street where bookshops specialised in pornography, while in the whole of the area male and female prostitutes smilingly lingered for custom.

Nearly every Saturday afternoon, Willie went to the Tivoli where he saw many of the great music-hall acts including Marie Lloyd, Dan Leno, Vesta Tilley and Albert Chevalier. In the evenings he went to legitimate theatres to see successes such as Oscar Wilde's *A Woman of No Importance*. For the budding playwright, it was an education in style and technique as well as a training in what to avoid. Payne, the heir apparent to his father's business, no doubt obtained free tickets for himself and Willie.

But there were other attractions at the Tivoli. The whole of the Strand frontage consisted of restaurants and private rooms for tête-à-tête suppers, while on the ground floor there was a bar ideal for casual pick-ups. In the auditorium itself, the darkened areas at the rear of the upper tiers were well known for homosexual encounters and, provided behaviour was not too blatant, the staff ignored it just as they did at the Empire and Alhambra theatres in Leicester Square. Strolling around these public places hoping to make eye contact was known as 'bucking', a term later superseded by 'trolling' or 'cruising'.

While Willie enjoyed himself at the Tivoli, not far along the Strand Oscar Wilde was using the recently built Savoy Hotel for occasional nights with Lord Alfred Douglas and other young men. During his subsequent trial the court collapsed into laughter at this exchange:

'Did any of the men who visited you at the Savoy have whiskeys and sodas and iced champagne?'
'I can't say what they had.'
'Did you drink champagne yourself?'
'Yes, iced champagne is a favourite drink of mine – strictly against my doctor's orders.'
'Never mind your doctor's orders, sir!'
'I never do.'

Wilde made no secret of his sexual tastes or of his infatuation for Douglas and yet he must have realised the dangers. There was a distressing scene at the Savoy when his wife Constance begged him to return home, if only to preserve appearances, but he was beyond rational argument. When Douglas's father, the Marquis of Queensberry, left his card on which he had scrawled 'For Oscar Wilde posing Somdomite [sic]' at Wilde's club, Wilde instituted libel proceedings. The Marquis counterattacked with damning evidence that Wilde had committed homosexual acts with a series of rent boys. When Wilde lost the action his arrest was delayed long enough for him to leave the country but he seemed too stunned to do so. For once, there were no polished epigrams: he had lost his wit along with his wits. He was prosecuted under the Criminal Law Amendment Act of 1885 which now permitted the law to pursue men into the privacy of the bedroom; not surprisingly, it was soon to be dubbed 'the blackmailer's charter'. Wilde was found guilty and sentenced to two years' hard labour in May 1895.

The public, with its propensity for hypocritical guilt over practically anything to do with sex, worked itself into a frenzy of moral indignation, spurred on by hysterical press reports. It was as if all their own vices could be expiated by the disgrace of one public figure in a ritual of medieval sacrifice.

The lasting legacy of the Wilde trials was national homophobia where little had existed before. Vast sums of taxpayers' money and police time were to be wasted over seven subsequent decades in a futile attempt to stamp out homosexuality between consenting males. The resultant misery and horror suffered by thousands might have been avoided if only Wilde had left the country when he had the opportunity to do so. Indeed, it is doubtful if the authorities wished to prosecute and to risk embarrassment to the establishment. It was as recent as 1889 that Lord Arthur Somerset had been advised to go abroad following the discovery by the police of his involvement with teenage telegraph-boys at a house in Cleveland Street. Once Wilde stayed in England to face the consequences, every effort was made to isolate and crush him. But Lord Alfred Douglas and other men of privilege who might have been dragged into the scandal were protected from prosecution by a conspiracy acceptable to the authorities.

Wilde's arrest created panic in the gay community, and many fled the country. Willie went to Capri, a favourite with gay men since Tiberius built twelve villas there for the pursuit of pleasure. Ellingham Brooks had settled permanently on the island to enjoy the Bohemian atmosphere in which expatriates theorised endlessly about the arts without the necessity of doing anything. Willie was enchanted, but too shy to speak of his own ambitions and was mortified when he was treated as a philistine medical student who cared for nothing but dissecting bodies. Describing this in *The Summing Up* he wickedly added that they saw him as someone who would seize an unguarded moment to give his best friend an enema. Today the sexual innuendo could not be clearer but presumably he guessed that most readers would miss its coded ribaldry.

On his return to England, Willie got in touch with members of the Wilde set to express his support for Wilde as playwright and author. Ted Morgan, in his biography, believes this was done in a private and circuitous manner, but a simpler explanation is that Willie already knew Robert Ross, Reggie Turner, Laurence Housman, Robert Hitchens and others. It is a possibility that he also knew some of the men involved in the trials, even Wilde himself. In the gay world where the inhibitions of class did not apply, social circles overlapped just as much then as they do today. Willie may even have visited Wilde's fellow defendant Alfred Taylor at his house at 13 Little College Street, not far from Vincent Square, where notorious sex parties were a regular occurrence. If he did not go personally to such parties, he would have known of someone who did. Cosmopolitan though the gay community appeared, it was like a small village where the inhabitants knew each other's secrets but kept them from outsiders.

Willie was only twenty-one in 1895 but for nearly five years he had lived an independent life, able to follow his sexual inclinations with little restraint. Now the effect of the Wilde trials began its insidious work. Legally, Willie was a criminal. Like his gay contemporaries, he was forced to create a façade of overt masculinity, and be on the alert for police activity. He even grew a moustache because it was well known that Wilde liked his young lovers to be clean-shaven. Sporting facial hair was therefore tantamount to a disguise and a statement to the public that the wearer was not queer. As he grew older he became a chameleon personality whose characteristics depended on the company he was in. But he was always haunted by the fate of Oscar Wilde and fear of public disgrace, although he continued to take risks when sexual need overcame caution.

When he fictionalised his life story in *Looking Back*, Willie scattered it with incidents to show that he had always been completely heterosexual. In a burst of apparent candour he recalled that, hearing fellow medical students boasting of their cocksure prowess with women, he felt so ashamed to be a virgin that he picked up a prostitute who charged him £1 for sex. This resulted in gonorrhoea which was treated by one of the doctors at St Thomas's. Undeterred, he said he continued to pay prostitutes whenever he could afford it. His claim to virginity was laughable but curiosity might have induced him to try straight sex. Alternatively he may have caught venereal disease from a boyfriend and like most homosexual men blamed his condition on a mythical female whore because he feared his name might be passed to the police.

To emphasise his alleged heterosexuality further, Willie carefully explained his close relationship with Walter Adney Payne whose flat-mate he became in 1899. Payne, he said, regularly picked up girls and, when he had finished having sex with them, sent them into Willie's bed. The pick-ups were probably boys and group sex the favoured option, though girls may also have been involved.

An avowed bachelor, Payne eventually married in 1933. When he died in 1949, his widow offered to return all Willie's letters, still in the locked cabinet where Payne had kept them secure. Willie arranged for the cabinet to be collected by Harrods and had the letters destroyed. His action gave rise to much speculative gossip about the nature of their contents.

# *Liza*

*Liza of Lambeth* appeared in September 1897, the year Willie qualified as a doctor. He knew instinctively that the story of a clandestine love affair between Liza, the factory girl, and a married man, set against the background of the slums, was daring enough for the middle-class reader without describing conditions in detail. There was nothing of the overpowering stench of the streets or the stink of vermin-infested houses: instead, by omission, he gave a romanticised version of slum life, and the pregnant girl's death at the end provided the tale with a moral twist to satisfy Victorian piety.

Willie did not preach but made his points with irony, alleviating the grimness of the story with humour in the manner of Dickens. Humour, in all its variations, was to be the key to much of Willie's writing and to the man himself. He analysed this point at length in *The Summing Up*. Humour, he contended, teaches tolerance and leads one to take pleasure in the discrepancies of human nature.

The reaction to *Liza of Lambeth* was mixed. *The Academy* magazine accused Willie of imitating the work of Arthur Morrison who had broken new ground in English fiction by recording working-class slum life in all its stark reality. In a furious response Willie denied the accusation: 'It is, perhaps, a little amazing to be charged with plagiarism, when my book was finished three months before [Morrison's] *The Child of the Jago* appeared.' The reference to Morrison's most recent book could only be treated with contempt, for it was obvious that *The Academy* meant *Tales of Mean Streets*, a collection of short stories published in 1894. It caused such a sensation that it was banned in some quarters. One of the most dramatic stories concerned Liza Hunt of Bow, known colloquially as 'Lizerhunt'. Only the most obtuse reader could fail to note the parallels in *Liza of Lambeth*. Willie made some recompense to Arthur Morrison over forty years later in *The Summing Up* by admitting his importance as a pioneer, but he could not bring himself to say he had ever read *Tales of Mean Streets*. Although it was a storm in a tea-cup at the time, this controversy probably laid the foundations for the refusal by many of the literary establishment to give Willie his proper due as a serious author in the years to come.

Nellie was noted for her openness, and one wonders if she told Willie, as she later told her daughters, that she thought *Liza* was a horrible book. But during the ten years when he was struggling to follow up its success, she encouraged him when others were advising him to give up writing and go into medical practice. Willie was a regular visitor to The Boltons as well as to 27 Harrington Gardens and Kate recalled that he was always kind, never talked down or was facetious to them and usually tipped them generously. From an early age, Kate wanted to be a writer and presented Willie with her first childish effort at a play. It contained a proposal scene which went something like this:

Albert. Would you partake of a lemonade, Miss Windsor?
Cecily. Oh, yes please! No. I think I would prefer an ice.
Albert. (Handing her an ice) Miss Windsor, or may I be so bold as to
call you Cecily? I love you. Will you be my wife?
Cecily. (With a maidenly blush) Are you rich?
Albert. Of course. My father owns lots of land.
Cecily. Yes.

Willie approved of the lack of prevarication.

Just before *Liza* was published, Willie had appeared in a series of *tableaux vivants* presented at the Romer house in aid of charity. Years later, Kate produced the programme when Noël Coward and Willie were dining with her. It announced the first tableau as

> Auld Robin Gray in Four Scenes
> Auld Robin Gray – Mr W. S. Maugham
> Song – Miss Maud Ritchie.

Coward gleefully remarked: 'My dear Willie, you must have been terribly, terribly bad!'

Willie protested that, on the contrary, he was a 'succès fou'.

Coward wagged a finger at him and said: 'Nonsense, my dear boy. They always put the worst number on first – and you're never on again!'

In the aftermath of *Liza*, Willie was taken up by Augustus Hare, a famous author of travel books, the darling of royalty, the aristocracy and the nouveaux riches. An avowed bachelor, he had a penchant for young men whom he 'adopted' until they grew tired of him and left, usually having coerced money out of him. Seemingly undeterred by constant disappointment, he always went in search of a successor. (His biographer, Malcolm Barnes, could find no direct evidence of homosexuality and perhaps his adoration of young men did not extend to physical contact.) His enthusiasm for Willie had its useful side, for he introduced him to influential friends who included him on their house-party guest lists. Willie told Raymond Mortimer that this frequently meant sharing a bed with another young man and this sometimes led to sex which, he said, 'turned out to be very pleasant'.

Willie and Hare remained friends until Hare died in 1903 and, in an essay included in *The Vagrant Mood*, published in 1952, Willie wrote an amusing but characteristically guarded account of a typical weekend at Holmshurst where his host lived in luxury with a large staff to look after him. Hare was a dreadful snob and he would have been beside himself with delight if he could have known that, through his great-great-grandmother, Lady Anne Lyon, he would be linked to the present British royal family.

# Harry Maugham

Queen Victoria died on 19 January 1901 and Edward VII was proclaimed King. A few days earlier Willie had completed *The Hero*, his deeply-felt response to the futility of the Boer War. The novel's examination of the smug sexual and moral codes of a nation convinced that God had selected it to rule the world did not appeal to the public. Readers, slowly adjusting to the possibility that the British Empire was not infallible, wanted cheerful diversion, not predictions of gloom. His next novel, *Mrs Craddock*, published in 1902, caused a minor stir. It portrayed an independent-minded woman who nevertheless needed to be sexually dominated, and there was a strong hint of homosexual fantasy in Willie's description of arousal. It failed and was remaindered to a book club run by *The Times* to be sold off cheaply.

In the decade following *Liza of Lambeth*, Willie made little money but he was more successful than his intellectual brother Harry. Some of Harry's poems appeared in collections of verse and there was a series of sixteen articles in *Black and White Magazine* under the heading 'The Amiable Egoist', and there may have been more written under pseudonyms. It is believed that he contributed to *Punch* but it has proved impossible to verify this. There were five books, including *Sir Paul Pinder and Other Plays*, published by Grant Richards in 1899. Apart from *Sir Paul Pinder*, the collection comprised *The Mastery of Men*, *The Landslip*, *The Husband of Poverty* and *The Old and the New*. The titles were scintillating compared to the plays themselves which made no concession to changes in dramatic form and, so far, no record has been found of any of them being staged. The dialogue was stolid and unwittingly bathetic:

> Cedric must die (Stabs him, he dies). Now at last have I relieved my breast of the burden which too long was pressing upon it. (Drops to one knee hands clasped in prayer) Forgive him his sins and forgive me mine too, oh Lord. (Plunges dagger into his own breast and falls dead across the body of Cedric).

In 1903, Grant Richards published Harry's *The Book of Italian Travel* which also appeared in America under the imprint of E. P. Dutton & Co., New York. It was a work of scholarly distinction, the result of years of research, and comprised a collection of writings by travellers to Italy from 1580 to 1900 with his own pertinent comments. It must have proved invaluable as a reference book for subsequent writers but sadly it does not appear to have been reprinted and is now exceedingly rare.

It would be easy to dismiss Harry because he was uncommercial, but E. V. Lucas, the eminent essayist and critic, maintained that he was the only real writer in the family. Willie thought highly enough of him to ask for his opinion of the manuscript of *Liza of Lambeth*. Alarmed and horrified by the frankness of the theme, Harry advised him not to publish. He may have influenced Willie's next choice of subject, *The Making of a Saint*, an historical tale set in medieval Italy, which was written in Capri during the summer vacation of 1897. In 1896, Harry's play *The Husband of Poverty*, *A Drama of the Life of Francis of Assisi* had appeared in print and perhaps Willie, inspired by this and assisted by Harry's extensive knowledge, believed that an historical novel would prove he was a 'serious' author. He later claimed that he was swayed by the assertion of the critic Andrew Lang that the only worthwhile novel young writers could produce was one with an historical theme, because they did not yet know enough about life to 'do much else'. Whatever Willie's intentions, the result was poor and he did not include it in his later collected works.

According to Willie's first literary agent, Maurice Colles, the typescript of a play, *The Fortune Hunters*, was delivered to him in January 1903, the result of a collaboration between the two brothers. Although Colles thought little of it, Willie was convinced it had merit. After Harry's death, he rewrote it as *Worthley's Entire*, but it finally appeared as *Mrs Dot* in 1908 at the Comedy Theatre with Marie Tempest in the lead. By this time, there was probably little of Harry's contribution left; in any event, he received no credit for it.

In February 1903 the Stage Society, which promoted 'non-commercial' drama, staged Willie's *A Man of Honour* for two performances. The venue was the Imperial Theatre, Westminster, which had been lavishly refurbished by Lillie Langtry, notorious as the ex-mistress of King Edward VII. Willie must have been aware of the irony of this: as a small boy walking with his mother and brothers along the promenade at Deauville, they had seen the striking figure of the Jersey Lily coming towards them. After she had passed, one of the boys asked who she was. The reply from Edith had been a contemptuous 'Nobody. A Mrs Langtry.'

The family turned out in force to see the play and Nellie said that Willie was pale with terror until the audience showed its enthusiastic approval. Afterwards, a party was held at the nearby Westminster Hotel, probably paid for by the Romers. The guests were, of course, in full evening-dress but Harry arrived in a 'shabby' suit, slightly drunk, and declared jovially: 'I'm glad my little brother has had some success at last.' This has been interpreted as the patronising comment of a jealous man but the family maintain that jealousy was out of keeping with Harry's disposition. After all, the pair's joint effort, *The Fortune Hunters*, had been given to Colles only a few weeks before.

Although *A Man of Honour* failed when it received a commercial production at the Playhouse Theatre in February 1904, Willie was slowly gaining prestige. Harry, however, was already well-regarded in literary circles for the diversity of his work. He was also a competent painter, a talent said to have been inherited from his father. The basic difference between the brothers was that Willie was a man to watch, capable of surprises, while Harry's writing, however worthy, lacked excitement.

In July 1904, Harry killed himself. The reason remains a mystery. Robin was to give two versions of Harry's suicide, both allegedly based on information provided by Willie. In the account from *Conversations with Willie* it is late at night on 27 July. Willie arrives home from a party to find a message awaiting him. Harry has been found by his landlady in agony, a bottle of nitric acid on the bedside table. She and her husband had heard a crash and, finding his door locked, had broken in. They did not send for a local doctor because attempted suicide was then a criminal offence and the doctor would have been obliged to inform the police. Willie goes immediately by cab and takes Harry to St Thomas's but it is too late to save him. The other version, from Robin's *Somerset and All the Maughams*, is different in some essentials and similar in others.

Both versions are untrue. Freddie, not Willie, was involved, but why Robin changed this in his book is unclear. According to Freddie's diary for 1904 he received a message on 20 July that Harry had been taken seriously ill. He arrived at 9 Cadogan Street to find Harry in agony after drinking nitric acid and immediately took him to St Thomas's Hospital. Harry lingered on until 27 July when he died at seven forty-five in the evening.

The inquest on 29 July recorded that Harry had killed himself 'while of unsound mind'. The funeral was held at Lambeth Cemetery later that day. In accordance with his will drawn up in Assisi in 1895, his executors, Freddie and Charles, arranged for a novel, *Richard Hawkswood*, to be published by William Blackwood and Sons in 1906. There were bequests to the son of Charles' partner, J. T. B. Sewell, to Charles' wife Beldy, and to George Barlow and Wentworth Huyshe, with the residue to go to Harry's brothers. Harry's private papers and manuscripts which might have provided clues to his life no longer exist and if he left a suicide note it was probably destroyed by Freddie to spare family feelings. In 1992 Honor spoke of a male friend of Harry who made it clear that he was one of her uncle's lovers. She would not name him but from her description it may have been E. V. Lucas.

Robin implied in *Conversations with Willie* that Harry was a lover of boys. It may be more than coincidence that Harry's publisher Grant Richards had a list of poets that included Lord Alfred Douglas, A. E. Housman and Horatio R. F. Brown, each of whom wrote about love between men and young boys. There were, of course, many more poets writing similar verse for other publishers, often under pseudonyms. Harry might have been one of them. Although a distinction must be made between men who believed their love for a boy would be violated by sex acts and those whose basic motivation was sexual satisfaction (Lord Alfred Douglas, for example, was a self-confessed paedophile), on this score Harry remains an enigma. When he killed himself he may have been suffering from unrequited passion, threats of blackmail, sexual guilt or irrational despair, but the truth may never be known.

# Le Chat Blanc

At the end of 1904, Willie left Walter Payne and went to Paris with his new lover, Harry Philips, whom he referred to as his secretary. Before Philips returned to England the couple visited Capri in the summer of 1905. Here Willie learned that the unlikely marriage between his ex-lover Ellingham Brooks and Romaine Goddard, a wealthy American lesbian, had ended after two years. (Romaine Brooks later achieved distinction as an artist and became one of Willie's closest friends when she lived in the South of France with her lover Natalie Barney.)

Willie had also developed a close friendship with the young

artist Gerald Kelly whom he had met through Beldy and Charles when he stayed with them after Harry's suicide. In the preface to a catalogue of Kelly's work in 1950, he described him as his oldest friend and pin-pointed his nervous vitality and exuberant loquacity as that which had initially attracted him. While Willie was in Paris, Kelly introduced him to the café Le Chat Blanc. The first-floor room was a regular meeting place for artists and their friends, and it was here that Willie found material for several characters that appear in his novels. Roderick O'Conor, for example, talked of his friend Gauguin and of the time they shared a studio. From this, Willie evolved the basic theme for *The Moon and Sixpence* and obtained technical data to add veracity to the story. Willie bought several of O'Conor's own paintings which were described by Clive Bell, another member of the Le Chat Blanc circle, as full of 'austere intentions unrealised'.

Bell, who became an eminent art critic, was an early link between Willie and those whom the English, with their passion for categories, have dubbed the Bloomsbury Group. Bell had met Leonard Woolf, Lytton Strachey and Saxon Sydney-Turner at Cambridge in 1899. Later, E. M. Forster, Virginia Woolf, Duncan Grant, David Garnett and others formed this 'volatile, irregular entity' as Quentin Bell had described it.

Dominating the regulars at Le Chat Blanc was Aleister Crowley, then in his late twenties. He practised an intellectual form of occultism which sometimes involved homosexual acts. He once attempted to entice spirits from the sea by performing an elaborate ritual on the beach at Eastbourne but, it seems, he was more successful at raising laughter. He became the butt of the press which called him 'The Great Beast' or 'The Wickedest Man in the World'. Willie, at first impressed, later decided he was a fake, though it was rumoured that Willie went through a ritual to sell his soul to the devil in the form of Crowley. This would certainly have been consistent with Willie's academic interest in spiritual cults of every description. In 1908 Willie was to caricature Crowley in his novel *The Magician* as the character Oliver Haddo. Crowley responded in the December issue of

*Vanity Fair* using 'Oliver Haddo' as his pseudonym. With good humour he accused Willie of plagiarism and gave examples to prove it. Instead of losing his temper as he had when a similar accusation was made about *Liza of Lambeth*, Willie kept silent.

Gerald Kelly and Ivor Back, another habitué of Le Chat Blanc, had practised black magic when they were at Cambridge and subsequently became followers of Crowley. Back even edited the master's writings, running to six volumes, which included verse in praise of every conceivable sexual perversion. Willie took a great liking to Back and they remained close friends. Later, Back's wife Barbara acted as Willie's hostess when he entertained during his visits to London after his move to France. Back became a fashionable and wealthy surgeon, but there was a macabre joke about him to the effect that patients never needed to go to him for a second operation because they rarely survived the first.

Following his stay in Paris, Willie travelled to Greece and then Egypt where he remained for three months. Back in England in May 1906, he was reunited with the increasingly prosperous Walter Payne who had taken rooms in Pall Mall. So far Willie had made little or no impression on the public and he began to wonder if he ever would.

# III

## The Wonder of Our Stage!

All these years, Willie had been writing assiduously and had an accumulation of manuscripts including several plays, all of which had been rejected by London managers. Among these was *Lady Frederick* which had a startling final scene in which the middle-aged Lady Frederick deliberately disillusions a young would-be lover by letting him and the audience see her without make-up and with her hair in disarray. This was the last thing the glamorous leading ladies of the day wanted and a succession of famous actresses had shuddered 'no' when they read the script.

There have been several versions of the story of its final acceptance, but there is one which has been overlooked. Among Willie's acquaintances was a young actor, A. E. Matthews, who was to become popular on both sides of the Atlantic, mostly in comedy roles. He introduced Willie to Otho Stuart, the manager of the Royal Court, the most prestigious of the many theatres that fringed the West End. Stuart was always looking for new plays and agreed to read anything that Willie's agent sent him. When his current production failed, he put on *Lady Frederick* as a stop-gap, after persuading the distinguished thirty-eight-year-old Ethel Irving to risk playing the lead.

It opened on 26 October 1907 and Nellie and Freddie noted that Willie, sitting at the back of their box, was very pale and silent. It was a relief to all three of them when the audience warmed to the humour almost at once and the evening became an enormous success. Afterwards they went with Willie to the supper he gave for twenty-two guests at the Bath Club, Dover Street. It cannot be claimed that, like Osborne's 1956 Royal Court success *Look Back in Anger*, Willie revolutionised British Theatre, but it gave him fame and financial security and placed him among the leading creators of well-made, popular plays. Ironically, when he introduced his own brand of revolutionary drama at the end of his playwrighting career he was misunderstood and his work underrated by the critics and public.

*Lady Frederick* was immediately bought by Charles Frohman for Broadway. Frohman was one of the most important figures in British and American theatre at the time. With his partners, he was responsible for hundreds of productions representing the cream of contemporary English-speaking drama. The production starred Ethel Barrymore, who also later appeared in a silent screen version. By 1908 it had transferred to the West End and three more of Willie's plays were produced: *Jack Straw* with Charles Hawtrey, *Mrs Dot* with Marie Tempest and, less successfully, *The Explorer*. With four plays running in the West End at once, Willie had finally gained the success he had craved. *Punch* celebrated his achievement with a cartoon showing a dismayed Shakespeare in front of posters for the four plays.

Willie did not forget A. E. Matthews who was given the role of the gigolo in his next play, *Smith*, but Matthews, to his consternation, found that he was expected to play it in an exaggeratedly camp manner which, he suspected, might prove fatal to his career. He did what he was told at rehearsals but, on the opening night, played the role in a casual and natural manner. 'I got away with the part – even satisfying Somerset Maugham and all concerned.' His manner became famous, and prompted Noël Coward to remark of a performance: 'He ambled through the play like a charming retriever who has buried a bone and cannot remember where.'

Fame had its hazards as Willie discovered when friends, acquaintances and total strangers pressed him to read their amateur attempts at play-writing or offered him ideas for his next comedy. At a weekend house party he was cornered by Winston Churchill who swore he had a 'wonderful idea' but, as he was too busy to develop it into a sparkling comedy himself, he suggested a form of collaboration. Willie, alarmed at the thought of this, tried to put him off, but Churchill was so insistent that he agreed to discuss the matter over dinner at the Athenaeum. The 'wonderful idea' came in the form of an anecdote: travelling on the night train to Edinburgh, Churchill was trapped in a lavatory when he found the door had stuck and nobody responded to his shouting and banging. As the train suddenly lurched, he had an attack of panic and imagined what might happen if it crashed and he was killed, taking with him the answer only he knew to a particularly difficult political problem of the moment. Sitting down, he scrawled out the solution on a sheet of his pocket memo pad and released it through the window. When Churchill stopped speaking Willie waited for him to continue, but then realised that he had heard the wonderful idea in its entirety. Nonplussed, he mumbled that it was not for him.

For some time Nellie had felt that Willie needed a wife and she took to matchmaking with some enthusiasm; he accepted this without any apparent reaction. Undeterred by her lack of success, she now decided that Marie Lohr, who was playing in *Smith*, would make an ideal wife and she held a dinner party with this in mind. She allowed the children to stay up to see the guests arrive; Kate remembered the actress, very slim and blonde, dressed in pink tulle with a rose in her hair. Among the other guests was Walter Payne, and Marie Lohr later remarked pointedly that the two men were 'inseparable'. Nellie's stratagem had failed.

For over a decade, Willie had been popular with hostesses. Mrs George W. Steevens who collected celebrities, among them Max Beerbohm, Henry Arthur Jones and Reggie Turner, was one of the first to take him up. Willie was good-looking, with sexual magnetism, and he was single, an important asset for a hostess making up numbers. His success in the theatre made him even more collectable and he was taken up by a number of ladies of the London literary set. Whatever Nellie may have hoped, however, there was never any question of marriage or romance.

It is fascinating to note that, in Willie's busy social life, his various circles of friends not only overlapped, but individuals within these circles were often linked by their association with Oscar Wilde, as Willie may have been himself. One of these ladies was Julia Frankau, a friend and admirer of Oscar Wilde, who was to express her sympathy by subscribing to the Epstein funerary monument placed over Wilde's remains in Paris. She wrote novels under the pseudonym 'Frank Danby' and her first, *Dr Phillips, A Maida Vale Idyll*, published in 1887, won her notoriety with its exposé of surgical malpractice. Dinner parties at her home at 64 Grosvenor Street were noted for their lavishness. Contrary to normal practice, the ladies did not withdraw but stayed to converse with the men over coffee and liqueurs. Her friends included George Moore, author of *Esther Waters*, Arnold Bennett and Ada Leverson whom Oscar Wilde christened the 'Sphinx'.

On one occasion Julia took Willie to the supper club held on Saturday nights at the Grafton Picture Galleries. Her son, Gilbert Frankau, later to become a popular author, was there with his first wife, Dolly. In his autobiography *Self-Portrait*, Frankau described Willie as shy, awkward, quiet and dull. Unlike his mother, Gilbert was violently opposed to homosexuality and expressed his horror at the revival of Oscar Wilde's plays, suggesting that it needed a battalion of Lord Queensberrys running the risk of a thousand prosecutions for criminal libel to destroy this 'filthy thing' not only in the theatre but everywhere.

Previously it has been thought that Willie did not meet Ada Leverson until 1908, but it now seems likely that he encountered her at Julia Frankau's home several years before this, possibly even earlier still through Robbie Ross. Ada and her husband had risked public ignominy by sheltering Wilde in the time between his two trials and it was through her that Willie met Lord Alfred Douglas in 1909, allegedly for the first time. She proved to be a loyal friend to Willie, one from whom he took advice about his writing; in return, he admired her novels. She marked her affection by giving him a first edition of Wilde's *The Sphinx*.

In Ada's novel *The Limit* (1911), there is a character based on

Willie. He is a playwright, Gilbert Hereford Vaughan, known to everyone as 'Gillie', who has eleven of his plays being performed simultaneously in London, New York, Paris and Berlin. He is a pale, dark, handsome young man and, unless his conversation is listened to attentively, he does not appear too alarmingly clever. Gillie's vivid dark eyes are so full of expression that women often mistake his intense scrutiny for admiration, when it is simply observation. This leads to misunderstandings and invitations to dinner at the homes of women who misread his stare. This accurate portrait, with its oblique reference to Willie's lack of interest in women, led A. E. Housman, whose passion for Moses John Jackson at Oxford was well known, to describe it as 'indiscreet'. Leverson also wove a sub-plot into her novel that involved Gillie in a flirtation with the uneducated daughter of an innkeeper, a neatly coded way of illustrating Willie's interest in boys of a lower class. Perceptively, she commented that Gillie's exaggerated modesty was his armour against envy, pointing out that it is not talent that is envied but the success that follows its recognition.

Netta Syrett, who dedicated her novel *Rose Cottingham* to Willie in 1915, met him in 1903. He was very taken with her young brother Jerrard, persuading Wilde's friend Robbie Ross to give him a favourable review for his novel *A Household Saint* in the *Bystander*. Details of Willie's relationship with both brother and sister are obscure, but there may have been a brief affair with Jerrard.

Mabel Beardsley and her brother Aubrey were both linked to Oscar Wilde. She enjoyed a fair degree of success as an actress and writer and was a popular figure in literary and theatrical circles. When she became terminally ill in 1913, she moved into a Hampstead nursing home and conducted a salon in her room every afternoon; Willie and Henry Arthur Jones were among her frequent visitors.

Yet another link with Wilde came through the novelist Violet Hunt, daughter of the landscape artist Alfred William Hunt and Margaret Hunt, also a novelist. In 1880, when she was seventeen,

Oscar Wilde, who described her as 'the sweetest violet in England', suggested marriage, but she declined. Among her lovers were George Boughton and Oswald Crawford, a British diplomat from whom she contracted syphilis. This scourge, as alarming as the Aids of today, did not restrain her sexually. She flirted with H. G. Wells and Henry James and, for a while, was pursued by Marguerite Radclyffe Hall, author of the classic lesbian novel *The Well of Loneliness*. Violet became the mistress of Ford Madox Ford who refused to marry her. After the affair was over, she pursued him for years in a deranged manner which may have been symptomatic of her disease.

When Willie met her, she was an established writer, a well-known hostess and part of a wide literary circle. Over seventy years later, Rebecca West, talking to Ted Morgan and Robert Calder, revealed that Violet Hunt had told her of her seduction of Willie. This should be treated with caution, however, as Hunt enjoyed giving the impression that men found her irresistible. All we know for certain is that she became a close friend and confidante. Initially, the attraction for him may have been her intriguing association with Wilde; indeed, he might have met her through Robbie Ross at some literary gathering.

These links with Wilde could be dismissed as coincidence were it not for the strong likelihood that Willie was a peripheral member of the Wilde set of homosexual young men.

# The House that Frohman Built

Willie's success as a playwright continued to be consolidated by Charles Frohman. He was a brilliant businessman who had executive flair and backed his own judgement. Sir James Barrie, for example, had had little confidence in the commercial possibilities of *Peter Pan* until Frohman, convinced it would be a success, produced it at his own theatre, the Duke of York's, in

1903. Frohman liked involving himself in the direction of plays. He once offered a suggestion to Mrs Patrick Campbell who went slightly rigid and replied haughtily: 'You forget, Mr Frohman, that I am an artiste.' He snapped back, smiling: 'Don't worry, dear lady, your secret's safe with me!'

When Willie was lost for a theme, Frohman asked him to write a modern version of *The Taming of the Shrew*. The result, in 1913, was *The Land of Promise* which enjoyed a vast success in New York with Billie Burke and Shelley Hull, and in London with Irene Vanbrugh and Godfrey Tearle. The play, a progenitor of 'kitchen sink' drama, had a scene in which the wife had to work at an ironing board while carrying on important conversations with different people. Irene Vanbrugh got too involved with mechanics at rehearsals, prompting Willie to comment that, while her performance as a laundress was admirable, the dialogue rather went by the ironing board.

It seemed as if Willie could not fail in the theatre, but he was soon accused of selling out his ideas for commercial gain, an accusation which he dismissed as 'high-falutin' chatter'. As if in answer to his critics he wrote two plays with serious themes, which Frohman presented: *The Tenth Man* and *Grace*, both of which had very short runs but broke even. The public wanted amusement and Willie reverted to supplying it. (Coward later, and Wilde before him, were also accused of pandering to demand, as if writing popular, frothy comedy was easy.)

Among several ventures independent of Frohman's management was one that Willie preferred to forget: his translation of a German version of Molière's *Le Bourgeois Gentilhomme* for Beerbohm Tree. The play, originally written in 1670, was now to be staged as the introduction to *Ariadne auf Naxos*, a new opera by Richard Strauss. Tree played Jourdain and directed *The Perfect Gentleman*, as Willie called it, while Thomas Beecham took charge of the opera which was sung in German. What in theory may have seemed a commendable artistic endeavour failed with audiences who did not care for the Molière but enjoyed the Strauss or vice

versa. The costly production played its allotted eight performances at His Majesty's Theatre in May 1913 and was not seen again
in this form. Willie's contribution was eventually published in
*Theatre Arts* in 1955 but it is unfair to judge it because in
performance the text was used by Tree merely as a framework for
comic business and music-hall jokes.

In 1911, to reflect his increasing affluence, Willie had bought
the lease of 6 Chesterfield Street, Mayfair, which he had radically
remodelled at great cost before moving in with Walter Payne.
Appropriately, their first dinner guest was Frohman who was
invited to come and see 'The House that Frohman Built'. This
was more than an ingratiating pleasantry, for, without Frohman's
theatrical empire to back him, Willie might not have broken into
the huge American market so decisively, and it was this initial
success in America that laid the foundations for Willie's future
wealth.

There is no detailed record of the dinner party but the
invitation is likely to have included the male friend with whom
Frohman always travelled. Once, when asked why he had not
married, he replied that he had married his profession. Frohman's
social conversation was almost exclusively about the theatre. He
would have had much in common with Walter Payne who had
become a powerful figure in theatre management when he
succeeded his father. (In *Looking Back* Willie attempted to
diminish Payne's role in his life by explaining his status in
Chesterfield Street as that of a paying guest.)

At Frohman's instigation Willie appointed Elizabeth Marbury
as his representative in America. Bessie, as she was generally
known, was the first woman to become a theatre producer and
literary agent. Among her clients was Oscar Wilde, three of whose
plays were presented for the first time to American audiences
under the Frohman banner. Another client was Clyde Fitch, the
most prolific and financially successful American playwright of his
age. Surviving correspondence between Fitch and Wilde suggests
that they were intermittently sexual partners from 1890 but the
relationship petered out when Wilde became infatuated with Lord

Alfred Douglas in 1892. Fitch, who was assumed by New Yorkers to be gay, was consistently attacked by the critics in coded phrases of homophobic abuse and his plays lambasted for their 'femininity'. Most of his work was written to order and often designed to suit the talents of the actors Frohman built into stars, such as Billie Burke and Ethel Barrymore. When Fitch died suddenly in 1909 his friends were asked to contribute to a book: *The Clyde Fitch I Knew*. Willie was among them and described him as 'the most brilliant conversationalist of his period'. This suggested more than a superficial acquaintanceship, but as Willie did not visit America for the first time until 1910, they must have known each other in London. This is probably another instance of social circles overlapping and it is tempting to speculate that there was more to their friendship than a mutual interest in Wilde.

Bessie Marbury's professional brilliance was matched by that of her lover Elsie de Wolfe. Born in New York of British parents, Elsie completed her education in Edinburgh and was presented at court in 1883 before returning to America. As an amateur actress she appeared in plays staged to raise money for charity and was then recruited by Frohman for his permanent company. By now the women were living together in a house in Irving Place entirely decorated and furnished by Elsie. It was here that the couple entertained, among others, Sarah Bernhardt, Melba, Ellen Terry and Oscar Wilde. Elsie also took charge of renovating their summer home at the Villa Trianon, Versailles. This was so successful that her hobby developed into a profession when, in 1907, she was engaged to design the interiors of the new, women-only Colony Club on Madison Avenue in New York. For this she imported chintz from British manufacturers and invented what was to be known as 'the English country house style'. The result caused a sensation and was frequently imitated. Remarkably quickly, Elsie became internationally famous and has had a lasting influence on the design and decoration of house interiors. Elsie and Bessie played an important role in Willie's progress under the Frohman banner when they launched him into New York society. Willie revelled in the uninhibited admiration Americans showed towards him; soon his address book became filled with famous names, from Cole Porter to J. P. Morgan Jnr.

Tragically, Charles Frohman died in May 1915 when the *Lusitania* was sunk off the Irish coast by a German submarine. He had been on his way to London to deal with future plans, including the production of the new play Willie was working on, *Our Betters*.

Descriptions of Willie by his contemporaries are full of contradictions, but the portrait painted by Gerald Kelly in the summer of 1911 entitled *The Jester* is illuminating. Apparently Willie called at Kelly's studio in William Street off Knightsbridge to show him his new top hat. As Billie Burke (the star of *Mrs Dot* in America) shrewdly noted in her memoirs, Willie was always a fastidious dresser with an elegance that owed more to Paris than it did to Bond Street. She omitted to add that in New York or London this would have appeared a touch effeminate. It may have been his daintiness of dress and his excitement over the new hat that amused Kelly enough to want to paint him immediately. The result, which the artist dismissed as 'valueless', shows a youngish man seated in a camply relaxed pose with a predatory gleam in his eyes and his lips near to a smile. Kelly said it was called *The Jester* because Willie's plays made people laugh but, of the innumerable portraits he painted of him, this alone hints at his homosexuality and the title somehow diverts attention away from this while retaining a certain ambiguity.*

# King's Counsel

Until Willie's brilliant success, Freddie had seen himself as the

---

* Willie's sexuality was also to be evident in Graham Sutherland's portrait of nearly forty years later. Kelly joked that though he had known Willie since 1904 he had only just recognised that, disguised as an old Chinese madam, he kept a brothel in Shanghai. But he may also have recognised that what Sutherland had caught was the predatory expression of an old queen.

most prominent of the Maugham brothers. Previously, he had been able to regard his younger brother with amiable indifference and thought him a fool to give up the medical profession to become a writer. Now all this had changed and he felt affronted by being known in his own set as the brother of a fashionable playwright with a Mayfair address complete with butler. He did not approve of Willie's friends, many of whom he considered worthless, and he deplored his homosexuality.

With his increasing income, Freddie had been able to take a large house at 40 Kensington Park Gardens in Notting Hill; though it was not the most fashionable address, socially it was a step in the right direction. He also leased a Tudor cottage at New Romney, easily reached by the South Eastern and Chatham railway and near the golf course at Littlestone-on-Sea where he played regularly. He tried to persuade Nellie to play but she never took to it, describing it as a 'silly game' and saying she could not distinguish between 'a brassie and a stymie'. She much preferred the more graceful game of croquet which, she considered, showed off the feminine figure to advantage.

The cottage, called somewhat grandly Southlands, was relatively small and nothing much had been done to modernise it since it had been built. It had no electricity or gas so oil lamps and candles were used to provide lighting. The only innovation was a supply of tap water in the kitchen which supplemented the hand-pumped source of water in the back yard. Baths were an ordeal for the servants who had to heat water on the coal-fired range and carry jugs up to the bedrooms to fill hip baths. Outside, down the garden path, there was a little hut which served as a lavatory. The bucket beneath the wooden seat was emptied regularly but when it got too full the lavatory paper on top could tickle bottoms. It was not a place to linger in high summer or the depths of winter.

When Nellie moved in with a servant to get the cottage ready for the family, she took her poodle, Chiefie, to keep her company. The first night, the dog reacted to an unseen presence from which it backed away down the stairs and across the hall, barking and growling all the while. Nellie, who was rather proud of her psychic powers, was convinced that, through the noise from Chiefie, she heard a steady bumping sound. The following day the owners told her that it was difficult to persuade servants to stay because of the ghost. A man had murdered his wife years ago and the sound of her body could be heard as he dragged it bumping down the stairs. To Nellie this gave the cottage additional charm, but Honor said no other member of the family ever heard anything and no servants took fright.

Nellie and the girls treated their visits to the cottage as a great adventure and the primitive conditions only added to the fun. As Honor put it: 'London was so dull. In the country we escaped from routine and those boring afternoon walks through dreary streets. At Southlands everyone was happier and there was so much more for us children to see and to do.' One of Willie's anecdotes concerned a family weekend he spent at New Romney. He remarked that Nellie's idea of bliss was to eat cold mutton in a howling draught. Honor commented: 'We can accept this as literary licence mixed with the precocious dash of that cynicism that was going to make him famous.'

Freddie left Nellie to deal with the children. There is no doubt that he loved his family but he found it difficult to express emotion. The children hardly saw him, except at formal meals when he was usually preoccupied and apparently ignored them. Honor said he was congenitally unsuited to going down on all fours to play bears with them or to listen to them lisping their prayers. Once he asked them, in a rare outbreak of conversation, what they thought was the oldest object in the house. 'You, daddy,' they chorused.

Freddie's reputation for aloofness was not helped by his absence from family gatherings. At Christmas he usually went to St Moritz to skate or to 'curl', while at Easter he went abroad to play golf. In 1909, for example, he joined Willie and Walter Payne at a small hotel near Lake Como for twelve days of golf. In 1923 he stayed for ten days in Le Touquet where he played golf during the day and, after dinner, gambled at the casino. On this occasion there appears to have been a coterie of the legal profession among his fellow-players. It is not altogether surprising, then, that his children regarded him almost as a stranger compared to their easy-going Romer uncles. But when he could, Freddie put in an appearance at their birthday parties and he enjoyed taking them to the theatre in the West End, or to the flourishing Coronet Theatre in Notting Hill. It was here that they first saw *Peter Pan* and the operas of Gilbert and Sullivan.

Nellie spent more time with them each day than was usual in upper-middle-class homes. Instead of a formal 'goodnight' in the drawing room, she went up to the nursery for an hour or so each evening to play with them and they usually ended up with a rumbustious sing-song round the piano. Even when she held one of her dinner parties she did not forget them and pretended to be unaware that the girls slipped down the back stairs to the kitchen where Cook let them sample food prepared for the guests. In many respects Nellie was ahead of her time. Later, when the girls were sent to a smart day-school, Kate overheard another girl describe them derisively as 'rather common', a reference to their exuberant Romer assurance which contrasted vividly with what was considered lady-like behaviour.

Freddie was beginning to show petty signs of jealousy of, and irritation with, the very attitudes which had attracted him to the Romers in the first place. He instructed Nellie that she was not to invite all her brothers to the house while he was there, for while he could cope with them individually, he found them overwhelming as a group. Was this the surfacing of a sense of inferiority suppressed since his early days at Dover College? Increasingly, he made fun of any success, major or minor, which his children had, as if he envied them their Romer characteristics, and he seemed unaware of how hurtful this could be. Later, when Diana had her first novel, which he had not even read, accepted by a publisher, his reaction was glacial: 'I suppose you realise that at the present time it is impossible for anyone to write a novel so bad it will not be published by someone.' As for Willie, who was a sort of graduate of the Romer school, Freddie treated him with increasing condescension, maintaining that anyone could be an author and subsequently writing several books to prove it. Conversely, Willie began to show signs of jealousy of Freddie, though the reason was not clear; perhaps it was envy of his brother's superior education and status, although it had been Willie's choice not to go to university but to opt for a medical career instead. Or perhaps he envied Freddie's home life and the support that his wife gave him.

In 1913, when he was forty-six, Freddie applied for silk which was promptly granted. He made the application with 'considerable reluctance' after his colleagues and several judges had urged him to. As a junior he had had a background role but as a King's Counsel the focus was on him and he discovered that he 'thoroughly enjoyed being in charge of a case, with the duty to examine and cross-examine witnesses myself and to address the Judge in my own way'. Perhaps his reluctance had been due to the Maugham brothers' deep-seated inhibition which they could only conquer if they were absolutely certain that the circumstances favoured them. In Willie, this manifested itself in what has been dubbed as 'shyness' but was more likely a fear of exposure and mockery. Honor believed that, when very young, the boys had suffered some form of abuse. Could the culprits have been their 'nurses', a description that did not imply qualifications but was used for any women employed to look after children? If these women lacked kindness or understanding, their methods of controlling their charges could involve frightening cruelty. The possibility that the Maugham brothers suffered psychologically is a strong one; when Freddie and Willie were old men without goals to achieve, they became introspective and often experienced appalling nightmares. Honor suggested that this was a reversion to childhood and a restimulation of some horror of that time.

# IV

## The White Lady

When Syrie Maugham died in 1955, it could be said that her name was little more than a footnote in the history of interior design as the woman who had invented the all-white drawing room. In *Looking Back* Willie resurrected her to support his claim to be wholly heterosexual, but he could not resist revenge. He accused her of multiple misdemeanours including the use of all the tricks of an experienced courtesan to trap him, just as she had trapped other men. (In a gratuitous anecdote he told of a stranger on a train who asked him if he had met that English tart Syrie . . .) Syrie emerged from Willie's self-pitying diatribe as a character owing as much to fiction as to fact. She could have stepped out of one of his plays, a mixture of Lady Grayston from *Our Betters* and the murderess Leslie Crosbie from *The Letter*. Inadvertently, by turning her into such an interesting villainess, he rescued Syrie from obscurity.

Syrie's father, Dr Barnardo, founder of the homes for destitute children, and her mother, after whom she was named, were both driven by the desire to rescue children in distress and to save souls for Jesus. Their principles did not extend to personal sacrifice, however, and they lived in affluent comfort. Syrie's brothers went to expensive private schools and Syrie (known in the family as Queenie) received the limited education then thought sufficient for a lady. When she was sixteen she became engaged to the son of a prosperous family who lived in Richmond, Surrey. As she was so young, her parents insisted the wedding be delayed, but when it was discovered that he had a mistress from whom he was reluctant to part, Syrie broke off the engagement. Shortly afterwards, he was killed in a riding accident. The effect of this on a love-sick young girl may be imagined; she might even have believed that, in some way, she was responsible for his tragic death.

A few years later, the Barnardos played host to Henry Wellcome, the co-founder of Burroughs, Wellcome and Co., the manufacturers of pharmaceutical products. He was a wealthy middle-aged American who had a liking for celebrities, actors and theatre personalities. Among his friends were Gilbert and Sullivan, Henry Morton Stanley and Lord Kitchener; he had also included Oscar Wilde in his social set before 1895. Anything to do with Africa enthralled him and he once bought 800 copies of *With Kitchener to Khartoum* by G. W. Steevens to give to staff and friends. It was Steevens' wife whose salon included Max Beerbohm, Reggie Turner and the then unsuccessful young Maugham and it seems likely that Willie met Wellcome at her house. Unfortunately, little is known of Wellcome's personal or social life because his executors destroyed the papers which might have provided clues.

By the time Wellcome met Syrie he was ready for the respectability that marriage offered. It also meant escape from the insidious rumours that pursued any prosperous bachelor who was known to prefer male company and had been acquainted with Oscar Wilde. Syrie accepted his proposal and they married in 1901; he was forty-seven and she twenty-one. The marriage lasted for nine years, during which time they lived in England and America and toured extensively in Europe and the Middle East. Syrie acquired poise and sophistication but grew weary of an elderly companion who was said by her to be sexually inadequate. If Rebecca West is to be believed, Syrie told her that Wellcome enjoyed stripping nude, dressing in a raincoat and beating her, which roused him sufficiently to be able to have intercourse. True or not, their coupling resulted in the son Wellcome needed to inherit his business empire. When Monty was diagnosed as 'backward', however, he effectively disowned him. This was some

57

years after he had accused Syrie of being unfaithful with the American financier Archer Harman, an accusation she vehemently denied. After a blazing row he refused to see or speak to her again. (Strangely he apparently remained on amicable terms with Harman.) Several mutual friends attempted to effect a reconciliation but failed. In one of her letters to him, in which she conceded nothing, Syrie pleaded movingly for them to be reunited for the sake of the child. This letter was ignored.

A separation was agreed in 1910 that provided an allowance of £2,400 a year, sufficient to maintain Syrie's social status. Monty was to be in her care until he was eleven but would spend three months a year with his father, who would also be responsible for school fees and other expenses. Wellcome's irrational behaviour suggests that he was determined to get rid of a woman who had become an encumbrance to him, just as he would later 'get rid' of his son. It is clear that he did not understand women, nor had any wish to. Even when his mother was dying he wrote letters and cheques but refused to visit her; instead, he went on a sailing holiday. In reply to his brother's letter speaking of her death he cabled that God would comfort. From the start he and Syrie had been ill-matched: the age difference of twenty-seven years did not help, nor did her vivacity and determination. If he expected a passive wife in the mould of Dora Copperfield he was disappointed. He was too firmly established as a bachelor: selfish, self-satisfied, old-maidish and capable of icy cruelty. His alarming changes of mood may have been due to bad health and the indiscriminate use of drugs such as laudanum and cocaine which were then freely available.

The separation agreement was a private matter known to only a few and for the sake of appearances Syrie behaved as the dutiful wife. She continued living in The Nest, a somewhat incongruously named house that Wellcome had rented on Hayes Common. Syrie's father had died in 1905, so her mother may have joined her to help look after Monty, then seven years old.

Under the terms of the agreement Syrie's responsibility for her son virtually ceased when he became eleven. She took the opportunity provided by her new freedom to move to London where she acquired a house, either within the precincts of Regent's Park or in a street adjacent to it, probably on the west side. Among Willie's lurid accusations in *Looking Back* was the allegation that Gordon Selfridge, the American store-owner, had bought the house for her. This story was based on a misconception, as the houses concerned were owned by the Crown and were not for sale. It is more likely that Syrie took the house on an annual tenancy, either paying the rent herself or having it paid for her by Wellcome's solicitors.

Willie also accused her of being Selfridge's mistress and allowing him to pay for the running of the house. He alleged that she permitted other wealthy men to pay for her clothes, car, servants and day-to-day expenses, just as they did for the kept women who formed her circle of friends. In response, Rebecca West, with the best of intentions, made matters worse by claiming, as a virtue, that Syrie was utterly devoted to only one man at a time. She gave as examples Selfridge and a Lieutenant-Colonel Desmond FitzGerald, both of whom, she said, Syrie had lived with 'for years' before falling in love with Willie. This was patently nonsense but, as Beverley Nichols put it, Rebecca West was 'a touch gaga' when she said it.

What Willie and Rebecca West ignored and, indeed, may not have known, was that while Syrie remained Mrs Wellcome she was under the surveillance of her husband's legal advisers and their agents. Wellcome did not want the scandal of a divorce, but neither was he prepared to put up with behaviour that might be an improper influence on his son or reflect badly on himself. If Syrie committed adultery it would have been with the utmost discretion, for fear of repercussions from her husband.

According to *Looking Back* Willie met Syrie in 1913. Superficially they had much in common: both had escaped from the melancholy atmosphere of strict religious homes and both were widely travelled and enjoyed luxurious living. He did not love her, but being seen with her helped to sustain the façade of heterosexuality he was anxious to protect. He eventually introduced her to Nellie and the family, who found her spirit and wit irresistible. Honor remembered the chic of her clothes in contrast to their own and Kate was thrilled when Syrie offered her couture gowns by famous names such as Lanvin, Ospouat and Chanel which she had worn only once or twice. Honor recalled that a striking feature of Syrie's appearance was her magnolia-like complexion, hence her nickname, 'The White Lady'.

# Bondage

In August 1914, Britain declared war on Germany. People on both sides had no perception of the horrors of modern warfare and, initially, seemed to see it all in terms of patriotic pageantry. Willie wrote to Winston Churchill asking for an appropriate job; in the meantime he joined the American Volunteer Ambulance Corps and crossed to France in October. There, it is said, he met and fell in love with Gerald Haxton, a young Anglo-American volunteer, but gossip has it that their affair began before the war and Willie joined the American unit to be with his lover. Much has been written about Haxton, often to his detriment. He was athletically built, dashingly handsome and exuded a dynamism which Willie found compelling. He was self-indulgent when it came to sex, drink and gambling but he had intellectual abilities which were to make a vital contribution to the success of Willie's career as a short-story writer and novelist.

Before Willie had left for France, Syrie had become pregnant and he accepted responsibility. He claimed that he had urged her to have an abortion which she adamantly refused to do; years afterwards, she insisted that abortion was never even discussed. In *Looking Back* Willie told an odd story about the circumstances of Syrie's pregnancy. According to him, he and Syrie were strolling in Richmond Park when she suddenly suggested that they have a child. What he omitted to point out was that, at the time, the theory of eugenics was much discussed. This proposed the production of gifted children by selective coupling and was the basis of the famous anecdote concerning Mrs Patrick Campbell and Bernard Shaw. (When she suggested they have a child so that it would have her beauty and his brains, he replied, 'What if it works the other way around?')

Willie maintained that he was none too keen to father a child, but Syrie became obsessed with the notion, asserting that her understanding with Wellcome gave her complete freedom to live her own life as she saw fit. Finally, under constant pressure, he agreed, apparently on the understanding that he would have no responsibility beyond impregnating her. After a miscarriage, she became pregnant for a second time, and he now claimed that he was dismayed, although why he felt this if pregnancy was the point of having sex with her is unclear.

This explanation of why and how Syrie became pregnant with Liza is elaborate enough to be true, but as so much of *Looking Back* is suspect, one is tempted to see a covert intention behind it. A clue may be found in an incident which took place in the 1920s and which Rebecca West wrote to Beverley Nichols about in her letter of 4 May 1962. Rebecca West and Beverley Nichols had been invited to dinner with Syrie and Willie Maugham at their Chelsea house, after which they all planned to go to a cinema. When they arrived Willie told them that they had just learned that Liza, who was away in the country, had been taken ill and they intended driving down to see her but as their car was not available till eight-thirty, they could all still have dinner together. While he explained, Syrie was on the telephone to Liza's nurse, furious because the women had delayed calling the doctor, preferring to try out some medication of her own. In exasperation Syrie slammed down the receiver and threw the telephone to the floor. During dinner she was fretting about Liza and the delay caused by the unavailability of the car when Willie suddenly told her off for losing her temper on the telephone. She went pale with fury and said: 'When you asked me to have a child, you said you wanted a child but you lied; you didn't want a child, you only wanted to be a father.' Willie took this accusation without protest and West remarked in her letter that it was obvious that Syrie was alluding to something understood between them. Syrie's remark (confirmed by Beverley Nichols) may indicate that, far from being an ineffectual male manipulated by a powerful woman – a role Willie often adopted in *Looking Back* – it was he who persuaded Syrie to have his child. By this time she was in love with him and may have sensed that her future was as Mrs Maugham, not Mrs Wellcome. Of course, another possibility is that Syrie's pregnancy was an accident which Willie dramatised to his own advantage.

Early in 1915, before her condition became too obvious, Willie took Syrie to Rome where they were joined by Syrie's mother, Mrs Barnardo. During the months of waiting Willie was occupied with writing or playing golf. Syrie, he said, suffered because she was not interested in the sights of Rome, she did not care for reading, nor did she have any womanly hobbies such as needlework. Instead she enjoyed gossiping about her male conquests, men madly in love with her, prepared to give her anything to have her for themselves. She cited, among others, a French duke, a Bourbon prince and Gordon Selfridge who, she said, offered to settle £5,000 a year on her. In the context of *Looking Back* this account serves to emphasise Syrie's alleged empty-headedness. But bearing in mind Henry Wellcome's surveillance of his wife's activities, the stories are more likely to be nonsense, whether they were invented by Syrie or by Willie.

The final stages of Syrie's pregnancy proved difficult and she had to be rushed to hospital where it was necessary to perform a Caesarian operation to save her life. On 5 May 1915 a girl was born and named Elizabeth (Liza) Mary. Soon afterwards, in an action hardly compatible with proud fatherhood, Willie went off for several weeks' holiday on Capri to see his old friend and ex-lover, John Ellingham Brooks. The year before, Willie had rented the Villa Cercola with Brooks and their mutual friend E. F. Benson. Benson was the creator of the Mapp and Lucia stories, with their stylish mockery of English society, as well as several homoerotic novels delicately written so as not to offend. He was a member of the Wilde circle and a close friend of Robert Hitchens and Alfred Douglas with whom he travelled in Greece and Egypt. Like Douglas his sexual taste may have been for young boys but was suppressed. Whatever the truth, he was undoubtedly gay, though painstakingly discreet when in England. Michael David-son wrote of the 'stealthy eternal adolescents of the day purring over *David Blaize*' while others hooted over the latest comic pieces which made Benson the Nancy Mitford of the 1910s. 'In either mood, Society or Homosexual, he was an enchanting novelist.'

On this latest visit, Willie and Brooks dined frequently at the home of Compton Mackenzie and his wife Faith. In her memoir, *As Much as I Dare*, she remarked on his intense interest in the English newspaper that arrived by post and described a drawing she did of him showing nothing but a chair, an open newspaper and a pair of crossed legs which she called 'Somerset Maugham Dines With Friends'. He had with him a manuscript of a nearly-completed play which Faith Mackenzie had typed for him and which he finally called *Our Betters*.

Compton Mackenzie had been entangled with Robbie Ross and Reggie Turner when he was only sixteen but, fascinating as he found the homosexual world, he claimed he remained only a spectator. The encounters, however, gave him a freedom from the corseted attitudes of most fellow heterosexuals and nothing inhibited his friendships with gay men or women. Although the Mackenzies' relationship with Willie was pleasant enough, it does not seem to have been close and they may have detected a wariness in his attitude to them. But it was Mackenzie who was able to write several novels with gay themes, and others which illustrated his lack of inhibition, while Willie, for all his worldly wisdom and sophistication, could not.

Willie rejoined Syrie in Rome in June, and all four returned to England. Instead of going to a location where she could be safe from curiosity, Syrie moved into a Mayfair hotel with her mother and the baby, minutes away from Willie's home. The arrival of

Mrs Wellcome with a baby in her arms could not go unnoticed. This made little sense after all the trouble she had taken to conceal the birth. Did she intend to tell her husband and friends that she had adopted it in Italy and planned to raise the child as her own? According to Willie, the original plan was for Liza to be cared for by her relatives for a few years, after which Syrie would adopt her. If so, staying openly at an hotel in London's most fashionable area was hardly consistent with secrecy.

Plans for the future, whatever they might have been, were dramatically halted when Henry Wellcome sued Syrie for divorce, citing Willie as co-respondent. All along, his agents had reported on Syrie's activities, even to the extent of taking sworn evidence from witnesses in Rome, including the doctor who has attended the birth of the child. Wellcome was now ready to take a dreadful revenge on his wife, exposing her as a blatantly immoral woman, the antithesis of her saintly father. He refused to behave like a gentleman in the convention of the time and allow her to be 'the innocent party'. At first, he wanted the whole story, including Liza's birth, to be told in court but when it was pointed out to him that Syrie's lawyers might claim that she had suffered from his sexual cruelty, he agreed to a compromise which eliminated all mention of the child. As part of the procedure agreed by the lawyers, Willie and Syrie provided less sensational evidence by staying openly at the Castle Hotel, Windsor.

The British press reported the divorce case with relish when it was heard in February 1916 and though Freddie wrote a letter of brotherly support and may have assisted him legally, he was furious at Willie's irresponsibility and what was then considered the terrible disgrace that the divorce had brought on the family name. However, the scandal had an unforeseen benefit for Willie because it projected him to the public as a hot-blooded womaniser who had cuckolded the much-respected Henry Wellcome.

Syrie had now become the mask behind which Willie could conceal his homosexuality.

Before the case came up, Willie had long discussions with his solicitor, Sir George Lewis, about the future. Lewis advised him to pay Syrie off and forget her. He believed that she had cruelly trapped Willie and he would be a fool to marry her to comply with the convention that co-respondents should 'do the right thing'. According to *Looking Back*, Willie replied that if he did not marry Syrie he would regret it for the rest of his life. To record this remark nearly fifty years after the event, when the reader knew the marriage was a failure, suggests that it was either ironic or intended to convey that Willie's motives was honourable. He was certainly vindictive, for he added that he could not bear to think what the baby's future might be if he did not marry its mother, thus implying that Syrie was not fit to have charge of a child.

In the event, Wellcome was granted a decree nisi with costs and given sole custody of his son to whom Syrie was to have no regular access. This was unnecessarily cruel and showed no compassion either for her or for Monty.

Later, when Wellcome failed to lessen Monty's learning difficulties by punishment, the boy was fostered out to a farmer and his wife in England. Tragically, he suffered as a result of the social fear of so-called backward children. Time proved that, mentally, there was nothing wrong with him; like Honor Maugham he was dyslexic. In time, he became a farmer himself and eventually married happily. Wellcome showed some compassion for him but, apart from the mention of an existing trust fund which yielded about £500 per year, he made no provision for him in his will when, in 1936, he died worth over £3,000,000. Syrie was allowed to see Monty on a limited basis but, with the tacit agreement of his relatives, he was effectively expunged from memory. It is ironic that Wellcome, a great benefactor and a brilliant businessman, did not spend money on researching Monty's condition. Instead he wasted a fortune on, for instance, his theory that the white race originated in the Sudan. Monty, who was to die in 1987, maintained a tactful silence about his parents, but something may be gauged from the fact that he attended both their funerals. As Monty's wife put it succinctly to Gerald McKnight, 'You see, he needed them both.'

The divorce finally became absolute at the end of August 1916. Willie had left for New York a few days earlier. He was in no hurry to commit himself to marriage and went on a six-month tour of the Pacific. Syrie, who now expected to become Mrs Maugham, was distressed by the delay, but Willie told her the trip was essential to gather material for future work. He took his lover Haxton with him on what, in effect for them, was a prolonged honeymoon.

On this trip, it was their encounter with a Miss Thompson that became the basis of his most famous short story, 'Rain'. She had been expelled from Honolulu for prostitution and they shared a room next to her in a primitive hotel while they waited to embark on the *Sonoma*. The flimsy partitions stopped short of the ceiling to allow circulation of air and both of them were kept awake by the professional activities of the indefatigable Miss Thompson who, expelled or not, did not waste a minute.

In Papeete, they spent two months researching the last years of Gauguin and, by lucky chance, found a painting he had executed on the glass panel of a door which they were able to buy for a few hundred pounds. The panel was later displayed in Willie's study and fetched £37,400 when it was auctioned in 1962. It was also on this trip that they met Bertram Alanson who was to become one of Willie's inner circle of gay and bisexual associates and friends. Alanson, a brilliant financier, was to take charge of Willie's investments and dramatically increase his fortune over the next fifty years. Willie often joked about Alanson's financial expertise along the lines of: 'Give him fifteen thousand dollars to invest and in no time it's worth a million.'

At the end of 1917 Willie returned to New York where Syrie had settled in an apartment with Liza and a nurse. It has always been a mystery why Willie did not make the final break with Syrie at this point when he had given himself ample time to weigh up the pros and cons, and had already admitted to Sir George Lewis that he did not want to marry her. It has been suggested that, unless he married her, Syrie threatened to make public his affairs with Haxton and other males, but it is difficult to envisage how she proposed to do this without suffering social ostracism for the scandal it would create, at the end of which she would have gained nothing. Besides, it is not certain that Syrie yet understood clearly the nature of Willie's relationship with Haxton.

She may have heard rumours about Haxton's sexuality or known of his arrest in London in 1915, however. It was during a raid by military police to round up deserters that Haxton had been discovered in bed with a John Lindsell in an hotel off the Strand. They were both arrested for alleged homosexual offences. (It was subsequently rumoured that Willie was also arrested, but that, with the collusion of the authorities and the co-operation of Haxton and Lindsell, his name was dropped from the charge details.)

Willie was believed to have paid the legal costs for both men and consulted Freddie on who should be engaged for the defence. The case was heard at the Old Bailey on 7 December. Lindsell was represented by Horace Curtis Bennett and Haxton by Roland Oliver, both eminent lawyers. The defendants were found not guilty.

Even if Syrie had some inkling of the truth she may have convinced herself that, once married, Willie would devote himself to his family. If so, she was to find she was mistaken. Willie may have believed that, in return for married status, Syrie would turn a blind eye to his relationship with Haxton – in other words, behave as a compliant wife. He was to discover, as Wellcome had done, that Syrie was a woman of independent mind.

It was on 26 May 1917 that the marriage ceremony was performed quietly in Jersey City with Willie's friends Edward Sheldon and Lady Colebrook as witnesses. The actress Cathleen Nesbitt recorded in her autobiography that Lady Colebrook telephoned her with the comment: 'There is a doomed entanglement if ever there was one.'

Willie did not stop writing during the war years, or accumulating notes of his experiences for future use. *Ashenden*, for example, published in 1928, was based on his adventures while working for

British Intelligence in Switzerland at the end of 1915. It was unique in that it presented for the first time a realistic explanation of what espionage consisted of and a realistic description of its anti-hero, very different from the colourfully romantic figures the public was used to in spy fiction. Willie was bound by a declaration of secrecy, but he skilfully managed to enthral without revealing too much of his real role.

In 1917, Willie spent several months in Russia on an important mission which he believed might have succeeded in preventing the Revolution had he arrived there six months sooner. He told the story of this in *The Summing Up* and in *Looking Back*, mentioning in passing that one of his contacts, Sasha Kropotkin, had been his mistress in London. True or not, it helped to convince the reader that he was heterosexual.

When the war ended, he was in a Scottish sanatorium recovering from a recurring bout of the tuberculosis he had inherited from his mother. His observations were encapsulated in a short story aptly entitled 'The Sanatorium'. There were also two plays: *Our Betters*, which satirises a thinly disguised Gordon Selfridge, based on Syrie's anecdotes and written in Rome while they awaited the birth of their child, and *Home and Beauty*, written when he was in the Scottish sanatorium.

More important than these was his novel *Of Human Bondage*, published in 1915, a heavily revised version of the unpublished work, *The Artistic Temperament of Stephen Carey*, written in 1898 when he was twenty-four. This had been fictionalised autobiography, poorly executed, but the final version displayed the skills and theatrical cunning he had acquired over the years. He gave the hero, Philip, a club foot which neatly defined him as an object of the reader's sympathy. Commentators have agonised over the foot, seeing it as representing Willie's stammer and giving it symbolic importance. If his famous speech hesitancy had inhibited him in his personal relationships their theory might be valid, but there is no evidence that it did so. There has also been much agonising over Mildred, the central female character, with whom Philip becomes obsessed. According to one of Willie's lovers, Harry Philips, she was based on a young man who spurned him, but Alan Searle maintained the character was a portrait of a waitress Willie knew in his student days. They might both be right: Mildred could be an amalgam of two people. Beverley Nichols once explained to Willie that his own novel, *Crazy Pavements*, was actually a homosexual love-story based on his own experience and the leading female character was really a boy. Willie murmured, 'Just like my Rosie.' This lodged in Nichols' mind and, when he wrote his attack on *Looking Back*, he argued mistakenly that Rosie, the female character in *Cakes and Ale*, was not based on a woman. He did not then know that Mildred was originally named Rosie in the first version of *Of Human Bondage*.

Commentators have contended that the opening sequence of the novel, in which Philip's mother dies when he is only eight years old, must be autobiographical. They frequently quote the paragraph in which Philip opens the dead woman's wardrobe and buries his face in her gowns, catching the lingering fragrance of her scent. They go on to describe the occasion in 1944 when Willie broke down at this point while he was recording the book for the blind, so, they argue, proving how deeply he loved his mother and how traumatic was her loss. They also construe Willie's comment on this paragraph during his speech when he gave the manuscript of the novel to the Library of Congress in 1946 as further proof. He was moved, he said, not by the writing but because it recalled a pain which time had not eradicated. But until he was a very old man he appeared to make a clear distinction between the death of a woman he knew little of and the disadvantageous effects it had on his life. This is usually ignored in favour of sentimentality.

Almost from the start of their marriage, Willie's relations with Syrie deteriorated; he saw her as complicating his life whereas Gerald Haxton simplified it. But Haxton had enlisted when America entered the war. Later, when he was sent to train in South Africa, his ship was captured and he became a prisoner in north-east Germany. When he was released, he travelled to

England but officials in Dover refused him entrance because their records showed him classified as an undesirable alien. It has been surmised that this decision by the Home Office was the consequence of the court case in 1915 aided by some string pulling by Syrie. This seems unlikely, but if there was any behind-the-scenes influence, it might have come from Freddie who saw Haxton as undesirable in every sense. When Haxton applied some years later for permission to enter Britain, he was again refused. By this time Freddie was in an even more powerful position to influence the Home Office if he had wished to.

Willie's infatuation for Haxton did not fade; paradoxically, events might have worked in Syrie's favour if her rival had been allowed to live in London. By ignoring him completely and letting Willie work out his passion against the background of his family life, she might eventually have saved the marriage.

In 1919, however, Willie left on his travels, visiting America, where he collected Haxton, before spending four months of the winter of 1919–20 exploring China. After six months in England, he was off once more with Haxton, this time visiting California before going on to the Far East. He did not return until January 1922 and left again for the Far East in September. The reason he always gave for these long absences away from home was the need to collect material for his writing, but it was also the need to be with Haxton who, for Syrie, would always be an unseen but potent presence in her life.

# V

# The Women

In 1915 Nellie again became pregnant. She tried to carry on as energetically as usual but was dogged by illness and took some while to recover from the difficult birth of a son on 17 May 1916. He was christened Robert Cecil Romer, but from the first was known as Robin. Kate, Honor and Diana doted on him, but Nellie, who believed boys should be brought up to be tough and independent, refused to show him much affection. According to Honor, her mother had not wanted another child so late in life, and it was only when Robin was in his teens that Nellie became devoted to him. Honor also commented that Freddie, never comfortable with young children, seemed to remain cold and aloof towards him. In her opinion, Robin had a 'miserable childhood'.

Freddie, too old for any form of military service, was recruited into a group of special constabulary whose particular task was to patrol the grounds of Buckingham Palace. Women were not conscripted into the services but Kate did voluntary war-work most days. In the evenings she and her friends were in demand for dances got up to entertain men on leave.

When the Zeppelin bombing of London became too intensive in 1918, Freddie stayed in London while Nellie and the family moved temporarily to Henley-on-Thames. While they were there one of Kate's young men, Bob Bruce, an ensign in the Grenadier Guards, came down on leave and proposed to her. She was reluctant to give him a firm answer. Too often she had seen the grief of her friends whose fiancés had been killed at the front and she did not wish to tempt fate by accepting the proposal. This was just before the final German offensive in France; the casualties were horrifying, and many of Bob Bruce's friends died, but he came back superficially unharmed. When he proposed again she accepted him. Like thousands of other young men of his generation he was expected to suppress his emotional suffering, never to involve his loved ones by telling them the truth of months spent in muddy trenches and insanitary dug-outs and, above all, never to admit the horrors of the bloody carnage. It was not until he was in early middle-age that problems began to manifest themselves. As Kate told friends years later, his award of the MC for conspicuous gallantry was not of much help when nightmares and relentless depression took over.

When the Armistice was signed on 11 November 1918, the people became hysterical with joy and relief. Nellie and Kate rushed to join the thousands who gathered spontaneously outside Buckingham Palace shouting 'We want the King'. When he appeared with Queen Mary they cheered and wept. In the evening the family went to see *Bubbly*, a revue at the Comedy Theatre, but the audience made so much noise with bells, rattles, cheering and clapping that they stopped the show several times. Afterwards the crowds in the West End were so great that the family became trapped in their taxi and had to get home on foot. As Honor put it: 'Everyone was too happy to care. Londoners had gone raving mad!' But behind the rejoicing was deep grief for the loss of thousands of men and for the thousands more who were maimed physically and mentally. When the cheering faded away, everyone had to get on with life and hope that Lloyd George's promise of a land fit for heroes could become reality.

The following year, on 15 July, Kate married Bob Bruce. The night before, Nellie insisted she burn all her love letters from other men which she dutifully did, setting the chimney on fire in the process. Her sisters and two friends were bridesmaids and little Robin and Liza held her train. Willie and Syrie lent the couple their car and, after the reception, they motored to Henley-on-Thames which they had sentimentally chosen for the first stage of their honeymoon. To their surprise, the town was holding its official and somewhat belated peace celebrations and there was a deafening cacophony of noise as different brass bands processed through the street playing different tunes, while church bells rang continuously until the early hours of the morning. Back in London after dutiful visits to various Bruce relatives at their grand homes in Scotland, Kate got on with the decoration and furnishing of their house at Rutland Gate. In June 1920, the couple had their first son, David, and when Nellie rushed home to tell Freddie, he commented drily, 'Spare me the gynaecological details.' Robin was taken to see the baby and offered him a penny for his money box. The following year, a second son, John, was born.

Shortly after her house was ready for visitors in late 1919, Kate invited Syrie to see it, expecting praise for the startling treatment of the drawing room with its shiny black walls, pillar-box red doors and gold curtains. Syrie could barely conceal her horror. Tactfully she persuaded Kate to let her devise a new scheme in pale apple-green. It was the first time she had used her flair for decorating other than in her own home and it occurred to her that there was money to be made as an interior designer. She could use her extensive social connections as the basis of a client list and become England's answer to her famous friend Elsie de Wolfe whom she had idolised for some years. Elsie, who was awarded the Légion d'Honneur for her hospital work during the war, was to cause a sensation when in 1926 she left her lover Bessie Marbury and married Sir Charles Mendl, an attaché at the British Embassy in Paris.

At first, when Syrie sought her advice, Elsie, scenting a potential rival, was discouraging; then, seeing how determined Syrie was, she became something of a mentor. Beverley Nichols said she did this to keep an eye on Syrie's activities and that their friendship was fuelled by mutual suspicion. He remembered Elsie telephoning from Paris to confirm his invitation to go to a Maugham first night. 'Dear Syrie' must not know about her trip to London because she wanted a valuable carpet that Syrie also hoped to buy. 'I shall be staying at Claridges incognito – meet me at the theatre at seven o'clock heavily veiled [twenties slang for 'disguised'].' When he arrived, he saw an amazing apparition: her hair was a bright acid-green and her evening gown a mass of glittering green spangles with evening bag and shoes to match. A white mink stole did nothing to diminish the effect. Waiting until the audience was seated, Elsie made a noisy entrance to the stalls just before the lights went down, an old actress's trick, and squeaked astonishment at the number of people who recognised her as she blew kisses and waved wildly before settling down. 'It's such fun to be incognito,' she said contentedly.

Elsie's frivolous nature disguised a shrewd business sense and it is said that she invested in Syrie's first shop at 83 Baker Street. At first the stock at 'Syrie' was rather dull, until another investor, Mrs W. Phillipson, proposed a radical change. In her new, ultra-modern house designed by Basil Ionides, Mrs Phillipson had experimented with white interiors and white ornaments, a startling contrast to the conventional ideas of interior decoration at the time. She persuaded Syrie to follow her lead. As Cecil Beaton put it in *The Glass of Fashion*:

> For the next decade, Syrie Maugham bleached, pickled or scraped every piece of furniture in sight. White sheepskin rugs were strewn on the eggshell-surfaced floors, huge white sofas were flanked with white crackled-paint tables, white peacock feathers were put in white vases against a white wall.

To Syrie's friends, she was a neglected wife who was not prepared to sit and mope while her husband was abroad with his lover, and she had no need to justify herself, but Willie was deeply displeased that she went into trade. It reflected badly on him as the breadwinner and it offended his ingrained Victorian snobbery. It might be tolerable for a lady to dabble in something dainty like a florist shop and then, if it failed, her venture could be dismissed as the silly idea of a foolish woman, but Syrie showed tough business acumen and did so well that she was able to move to much grander premises in Grosvenor Square. Friends who were prepared to pay her high consultancy fees included Noël

Coward, Tallulah Bankhead, Lady Plunket, Lady Milbanke, Mrs I. M. Sieff and 'June', the revue star, later Lady Inverclyde.

In *Looking Back* Willie accused Syrie of unethical business dealings and, for good measure, described how she had defrauded an insurance company by claiming for the loss of a valuable piece of jewellery when she had actually sold it. He also complained of the systematic way she made his life a misery by nagging at him into the early hours of the morning. He added that she lacked cultural resources and was completely dependent on him for friends. This was patently untrue; it is a typical example of the feline jealousy with which he regarded her success among a cross-section of the notable people of the day.

In 1921, *The Circle*, generally regarded as Willie's best comedy, had a stormy opening night on 3 March. The gallery booed, the first time one of his plays had suffered this indignity. The trouble appeared to be the bold approach to the moral problem of whether a young wife should leave a dull husband in favour of a more exciting lover. Maugham, in typical Ibsen style, believed she should. *The Times* summed up the reaction of the press, describing the play as 'brilliant'.

After a delay of eight years, the London production of *Our Betters* finally opened in 1923. It had been savaged by sections of the American press for its immorality and bad language when it was produced in New York in 1917. Unknown to Willie, King George V had been disturbed by a comment made to him about the play and had asked Lord Stamfordham to enquire 'whether it was carefully considered by the censor'. He was assured that it had been read by three members of the Advisory Board who saw no reason for refusing a licence and when they added that it had already been performed in New York, the King's fears were calmed. The Lord Chamberlain's office had been sanguine about it when it was submitted to them. George Street, the official who wrote the report on it, found several of the characters vicious, immoral and sordid, but thought that the effect was one of intense scorn, not sympathy, for vice. He noted that a reference to a statesman 'with musical tastes' might suggest a public figure but he did not specify who – the term 'musical' was then a euphemism for 'homosexual'. When Winston Churchill allegedly said that he had been to bed with the composer Ivor Novello, and was asked what it was like, he replied, 'Very musical', but the wit of the double pun has been lost over the years.

*Our Betters* evoked the usual protests from those who looked for and found offensive sexual content where others did not. By using their fertile imaginations, the protesters saw evil in a situation where a woman and her lover spend fifteen minutes in a tea-house in the garden. Of course, the situation was intended to be ambivalent but not any more so than if they had been alone in the library for a similar time. It was the tea-house which seemed to fire the protesters' indignation, possibly because a hint of sex associated with the decorous, English institution of tea was seen as reprehensible.

There is a little-known story of Willie's kindness to Constance Collier who played the Duchesse de Surennes in the play in London. After a severe illness she was unable to work; most of her savings had gone on medical expenses and she was only saved from poverty by a gift of money from Dame Clara Butt. She was staying with Maxine Elliott at her house, Hartsbourne Manor, when Syrie and Willie arrived ostensibly as weekend guests. He and Maxine had devised a plan to tempt Constance back to the stage with a part in *Our Betters*. She took some persuading and then needed Willie's patient support to get her through early rehearsals when she frequently burst into tears for no apparent reason. 'He is the least exacting and most sympathetic author to actors it is possible to imagine,' she later said. As part of her concept she copied the distinctive voice of a well-known but now forgotten society figure of the day. This caused a minor sensation among the smart first-night audience, some of whom thought it in bad taste.

Willie had written the leading role of Pearl for Gladys Cooper, who had just played Paula in *The Second Mrs Tanqueray*, but she thought the role too similar. Willie, far from being upset by her refusal, seems to have admired her for her common sense. He had been introduced to her in 1909 by Charles Hawtrey who wanted her for *The Noble Spaniard*, Willie's translation of a French farce by Grenet-Dancourt. He was struck by her beauty and was not too surprised when Hawtrey, in reply to his question 'Can she act?', said cheerfully, 'I shouldn't think so.' It transpired that George Edwardes would not release her from her contract as one of the Gaiety Girls and it was not until 1919 that she appeared in a Maugham play, *Home and Beauty* (*Too Many Husbands* in America), under the management of George Curzon and herself at the Playhouse Theatre. *The Times* said: 'One is tempted to call Mr Maugham's farce exquisite.' Alexander Woolcott, reviewing the Broadway production in the *New York Times*, described it as 'an evening of unalloyed amusement'.

*The Letter*, which established Gladys Cooper as a dramatic actress, was not written for her but for Margaret Bannerman (who in turn had taken the lead in *Our Betters* which Cooper had declined). Although the facts are vague, it seems that *The Letter* went into rehearsal but Bannerman found the role was not right for her. Willie used all his influence to have Cooper as her replacement but Bannerman's husband, Anthony Prinsep, who held the option, refused: 'I won't have her.' After legal disentangling, Cooper took over the option and presented the play under her own management in 1927, shrewdly inviting Gerald du Maurier to direct her.

The production was a triumph according to the *Sunday Times*: 'sensationally successful and the audience delighted almost to hysteria'. After a long run, it went on a national tour which became a sort of royal progress for Cooper. She was mobbed by fans wanting to see for themselves this legendary beauty whose picture postcards dated from her days as a Gaiety Girl.

Willie was so impressed by her dedication and hard work that he gave her an option on his next three plays; eventually his agent wrote to her representative reminding him that he had offered her *The Constant Wife* which she refused, *The Sacred Flame* which she accepted, and *The Breadwinner* which she had just declined. 'Of course you can tell Miss Cooper that I am sure Mr Maugham will be very pleased to offer her any plays that may hold out any likelihood of being suitable to her, irrespective of contracts.' Ernest Thesiger, the character actor whose performances were the exemplification of high camp (and who did needlework to calm his nerves in the trenches and was once asked what it was like at the front and replied: 'My dear, *the noise*!! and *the people*!!'), asked Willie why he never wrote him a part. 'I do,' was the answer, 'but Gladys Cooper always plays them.'

In November 1923 Willie's farce, *The Camel's Back*, was a resounding flop at both the Vanderbilt Theatre, New York, and, the following January, at the London Playhouse. The stage manager for the American production was a young man, George Cukor, a homosexual, who met Willie for the first time during the pre-New York try-out. This was the start of a friendship important to both men, who each admired the professionalism of the other. Ten years later, Cukor was established as a film director and was assigned by RKO to direct a screen version of *Our Betters*. The producer, David O. Selznick, engaged Elsa Maxwell, a cabaret entertainer, gossip writer and professional party organiser, to advise on the costumes and general tone of the picture. She claimed to be a dear friend of Willie, but he regarded her as unutterably vulgar, though he thought her a useful bridge player. She loathed homosexual men unless she knew them personally, and in her autobiography, *I Married the World*, she took three pages to explain her ambivalent attitude, saying that there should be one rule for homosexuals who were 'rich in mind' and social ostracism for the rest. If, however, Willie had any qualms about her qualifications for the job, these were overshadowed by his disappointment at the screenplay evolved by Selznick. A comparison between the two texts shows that the carefully structured characterisation and wit of the play were removed, leaving the screenplay ponderous and dreary. George Cukor did his best with the diluted version but the result was a box-office failure.

Of the thirty or so film versions of Willie's work, possibly the most famous is *The Letter*, filmed by Warner Brothers in 1940 with Bette Davis, whose performance remains a tour de force remarkably unaffected by subsequent changes in acting techniques. Just as famous is 'Rain', originally dramatised for the theatre by John Colton and Clemence Randolph. This was a huge success in New York in 1922 with Jeanne Eagles as the whisky-swilling whore Sadie Thompson, the mere sight of whom gives the puritanical missionary Reverend Davidson such lustful thoughts that he kills himself out of shame, a clear case of vice triumphing over virtue.

The piece did not do so well in London, though it sounded exciting when Tallulah Bankhead was announced as Sadie. Willie thought her unsuitable and she was sacked after two days of rehearsal. (Noël Coward at once invited her to play in *Fallen Angels* in which she triumphed.) Willie tried to make amends by praising this performance over a lunch but she never forgave him and made certain he saw the excellent reviews she received when she appeared in a New York revival of *Rain* in 1935.

A film version of 'Rain', cleaned up to satisfy the Hays Office censors, appeared in 1925 as *Sadie Thompson* with Gloria Swanson in the lead. She produced it independently against angry opposition from the Hollywood establishment, which had failed to find a way of doing it without offending the censors. When her film was a success, Willie offered her a sequel about Sadie's new adventures in Australia for $25,000, but Swanson was too exhausted to care. In 1979, though, she said:

> Sadie was a success but it nearly killed me to get it made but I sometimes wonder if I shouldn't have produced Mr Maugham's sequel instead of Mr Joe Kennedy's *Queen Kelly* which I never completed, due to Mr von Stroheim's ruinous direction.

Other film versions of 'Rain' starred Joan Crawford and Rita Hayworth and there was an all-black version made for 'blacks only' cinemas in the 1940s. All copies of it appear to have been lost but in the title there lingers a provocative allure: *Dirty Gertie from Harlem.*

All three Maugham sisters suffered the ordeal of being presented at Court and launched in society. By the time it was Diana's turn in the late 1920s, much of the so-called glamour of earlier times had begun to fade. Debs' luncheons were an obligatory chore, an exercise in mutual reciprocity, with the hope that your guests would include you on their invitation list for their coming-out ball. The problem was that the girls, who were unlikely to meet again after the season, were a callow lot with little to say for themselves and the young men, for the most part, were not much better. Bored by the social round, Diana went to see Professor G. B. Harrison at King's College, University of London, and asked to become a student. He was impressed enough to accept her, without the usual paper qualifications, for a two-year diploma course in journalism, with philosophy as a second subject. While still at King's she began writing short stories which she sold to magazines in Britain and America.

By her teens, Honor was a competent, self-taught artist and, through her own initiative, was accepted at the Chelsea Polytechnic Art School. Her speciality became portrait painting but her first paid work was producing pen-and-ink drawings of jewellery for the catalogue issued by Barkers, the Kensington department store. She was also commissioned by magazines to supply sketches of well-known personalities, among them A. P. Herbert and Jessica Mitford. During his sitting Dr Gilbert Murray read a book in Greek and chuckled all the time. When she sketched Margot Asquith, who at her best looked like a benign horse, the lady produced a photograph by Cecil Beaton which she claimed was the only true likeness ever taken of her. 'So many people draw me with a big nose, even photographers give me a large nose,' she complained. Honor gazed at Beaton's portrait with some embarrassment. There was no sign of the famous nose; instead, a young girl peered out through a bower of roses.

In 1924 Honor married Sebastian Earl. The freedom young couples enjoyed during the war had stopped and there was a return to traditional attitudes, so Honor and Seb had to wait until he was twenty-five and she twenty-three before their wedding. Seb had won scholarships to Eton and Magdalen College, Oxford and was a rowing blue with a sporting record similar to Freddie's. When he had finally settled in a job and felt he had enough income to marry, he explained to his future father-in-law that *The Times* had offered him occasional work as a rowing correspondent for major events which, as they took place mostly at weekends, he could easily manage. Freddie advised him to refuse. 'My dear Sebastian, if you are to do your main job properly, you cannot possibly expect to take on anything else.' Seb ignored him and wrote for *The Times* for eighteen years. In those days, the paper did not name its correspondents so that Freddie never learned about Seb's part-time role. Once, when the two men had a misunderstanding about the Oxford and Cambridge Boat Race, Freddie stalked angrily out of the room. 'All I can say, my dear Sebastian, is that my authority is the rowing correspondent of *The Times*.'

Between having children Kate returned to her childhood ambition of becoming a writer. When her first novel, *The Chequer Board*, was published by Heinemann in 1922, she sent a copy to Willie to acknowledge his encouragement. To her surprise she received a long letter from him containing an analysis of the novel: its plot, characterisation and style. In addition he included a transcript of page by page notes that he had made while reading the book. He praised her for her sense of humour and for the frankness with which she had described her heroine's sensual nature, also for the high spirits and verve which distinguished the novel. Against this he listed her faults arising, he implied, from her lack of experience. He ended by saying how glad and proud he would be if she made a success. But, in his Edwardian pomposity, he added a warning note: she needed to work much harder. It was because women did not take the infinite pains that men did that their work was rarely as well-executed.

Willie may have taken extra care over his response to Kate, said to be his favourite niece, but other young writers also found that

Willie treated their aspirations with respect and often spent his valuable time advising them.

# And a Good Judge Too

Freddie was earning large sums at the Bar but he felt that he was in a rut and that his merits had not been fully appreciated. There had been a brief incident in 1922 when he was offered the position of Solicitor General in the new Conservative government, but there was no vacant parliamentary seat and the matter lapsed. In his autobiography, *At the End of the Day*, he commented that he would have welcomed 'a year or two in the Commons in an official position' but consoled himself that, as things turned out, he had been saved a large loss of income.

His ability was exemplified by his handling of the tangled dispute over the ownership of *The Times* after the death of Lord Northcliffe. Lord Rothermere wanted to buy the shares but John Walter, whose family printed the paper and had once owned it, hoped to regain control. There was an option to enable them to do this but legally it was dubious. Freddie, who appeared for the administrator of the estate, proposed that the shares could go to either party provided a certain sum was paid. 'The figure suggested is £1,350,000, payable according to the terms of the document before me, as to £500,000 within fourteen days of the Order approving this agreement, and the balance at certain other dates.' This was a vast sum in 1922 and there was a gasp of astonishment in court at the figure itself and the short time in which it was to be paid. Rothermere was outflanked when John Walter, helped by the Astor family, found the money. It was believed that Freddie had devised the scheme knowing that Rothermere could not meet its terms and that the Astors would come to the rescue. As Rothermere was seen, perhaps unfairly, as a threat to the integrity of *The Times*, Freddie was applauded for having cunningly saved a great national institution.

In 1928 he received the recognition he craved when Lord Hailsham, the Lord Chancellor, offered him a puisne judgeship in the Chancery Division. He was inclined to refuse at first because, at the age of sixty-one, he thought it too late to build a distinguished judicial career. It also meant a dramatic fall in income and if, through illness, he was unable to complete the necessary fifteen years' service to earn a pension, the loss of that as well. Hailsham pressed him to accept but he asked for time to consider and took a sea voyage to Gibraltar to gather his thoughts. He finally agreed under pressure from Nellie who saw that, if he turned the opportunity down, he might not get another and would later regret it.

The family prosperity was marked towards the end of the 1920s by a move into a large house at 73 Cadogan Square. Nellie refused to employ a butler, preferring instead to have a well-trained head parlourmaid because she believed a senior male servant could be a source of trouble with female staff. Altogether, it needed eight servants to run the house, plus a chauffeur and nursery staff. Looking at the vastness of the drawing room, a thought occurred to her but, guessing Freddie might not approve, she used an indirect approach: 'If I die before you, will you spend money on a really handsome tombstone?'

'Of course.'

'That would be very nice but I'd much rather you spent it on a grand piano. Preferably today!'

Amused by this, he did.

The family had sampled several country houses, including Hamswell House near Bath, but Nellie finally chose Tye House at Hartfield in Sussex as a permanent second home. She was anti-blood sports, refused to wear furs and was overjoyed when she discovered a family of foxes in the wood at the bottom of the garden. When the local hunt arrived on the scene, she stood over the earth, protecting it and defying them. The Master of the Hunt admitted defeat and called off the hounds.

She was equally formidable during the General Strike of May 1926 when she took over the vacant 57 Cadogan Square to use as a hostel. It says something for her character that the estate agents gave her the keys without protest. With the help of Diana and the servants she cleaned the place, put up beds and furnished a sitting room. The first to arrive was a group of Cambridge undergraduates who had been enrolled as special constables. Nellie fed them in her own house and they slept at No. 57. She was getting ready to cope with ten schoolmasters from Bradford when the TUC called off the strike on 10 May, so, in celebration, she held a party for her guests instead before they returned to Cambridge.

In her diary of 9 May, Nellie noted that she had met their next-door neighbour, Arnold Bennett, who told her that his new wife and baby were moving into his house. She already knew that the 'new wife' was his mistress but accepted the pretence while not approving of it. Bennett mentioned in his journal that Willie had worked at Scotland Yard during the General Strike because of his knowledge as an experienced secret agent. How he helped is not clear, unless it was believed that agents of Soviet Russia were involved and that Willie could identify them.

The Strike was condemned by many as unpatriotic but it was soon seen as a watershed because it exposed the gulf between the working classes and the complicated social strata above them. Up until then, the frivolity of 'the bright young things' had been accepted as an antidote to the horrors of war but, as the mood began to change, the wild activities of the young well-to-do became inappropriate for the time. This was illustrated by the hostile reaction to a fancy-dress party at which all the guests had to appear as very young children. It was held at a house in Rutland Gate and Kate and Bob, sitting on their first-floor balcony, could see into the garden, decked out with swings and see-saws and lit by Japanese lanterns, with the guests playing with balloons and toys. Several of their younger friends who were being 'babes' dropped in for a reviving gin as a relief from the fizzy lemonade served by their party hosts. It was innocent and rather silly but it featured in the newspapers for weeks, fuelled by indignant letters from readers who treated it as a wild pagan orgy. Beverley Nichols, one of the babes, later capitalised on the disapproval by satirising the party in his novel *Crazy Pavements*.

# Up at the Villa

In 1925, with her business doing well, Syrie created a new home for herself at Le Touquet on the northern French coast and named it the Villa Eliza after her daughter. Not to be outdone, Willie bought the derelict Villa Mauresque on Cap Ferrat between Nice and Monte Carlo which had been the property of a retired Catholic cleric known locally as 'The Black Bishop'. It was said to be cursed because the cleric had practised satanic rites there but this did not bother Willie. However, the reputation persisted and Beverley Nichols, who claimed to be highly susceptible to 'atmospheres', once remarked that sometimes there was a stifling sense of evil about the place. This might be dismissed as the result of too much gin and an over-active imagination, except that other guests made similar comments, among them Peter Quennell and members of the Maugham family, including Honor.

Willie employed Barry Dierks, a young American architect, and his English friend-cum-business partner, Eric Sawyer, to remodel the house extensively as a home and as a setting for his growing collection of art works bought, some sneered, with the mind of a dealer looking for future profit. Dierks' and Sawyer's success led to a commission from Maxine Elliott to build the Château de l'Horizon. Willie had known Maxine for nearly thirty years and was to feature her as one of 'The Three Fat Women of Antibes', the short story that first appeared in 1933. Her house, a miracle of architectural ingenuity built over a narrow strip of coast near Cannes, became a showplace where she entertained the international set. Willie could not compete on a similar scale, but, for

85

sheer comfort, their mutual friends could find little difference between the two homes.

It was under Haxton's direction that life at the Mauresque rapidly achieved a standard intended to emulate the best traditions of the English country house. A full valet and maid service was provided and the bedrooms had a supply of the latest books, baskets of fruit, bottles of Vichy water and a selection of expensive soaps and scents that included the products of Floris of Jermyn Street. As almost everyone smoked in those days, there were several ashtrays dotted about in strategic positions with boxes of matches decorated with Willie's logo. A feature was the writing table, equipped with a supply of headed stationery, pens, pencils and ink. Godfrey Winn described being lectured by Willie for not making use of this facility. He was told he would never succeed in his authorial ambitions unless he imposed a stern daily regime upon himself and he was ordered to spend his mornings writing and to report with the results to Willie. His efforts would then be rewarded or punished but, as Winn derived as much pleasure from one as the other, the regime was of little benefit.

Outside, in the extensive grounds, hidden from onlookers, Barry Dierks had designed a swimming pool which became a focal point for guests. Nude swimming and sunbathing were encouraged and snippets of gossip often appeared in the newspapers. Collie Knox, an author and press columnist, having swum in it, announced to much amusement that he proposed to start a new fashion and not write a word about the famous Maugham swimming pool.

In the early days, Willie employed secretaries to assist Haxton and one of these was a young man, H. E. L. Priday, apparently known only by his surname. Later, he settled in New Caledonia where he died in 1970. He often boasted of his days at the Mauresque and was very proud of a record-breaking swim across the bay of St Tropez. He was only one of a succession of young men who lived for a while at the house; as Beverley Nichols commented, beautiful but obscure young men were part of the scenery. He remembered a pretty youth with an excess of bangles who was employed to work on Haxton's yacht but who proved singularly inefficient when he and Cyril Butcher took it out to sea. Several years afterwards, Nichols met him in New York happily working as a window-dresser.

Among the first visitors to the Mauresque were three of Willie's young Cambridge friends. Ever since Willie had first met his brother's contemporaries he had developed his links with the university as if, by association, he could acquire the advantages he believed he lacked by not going there. It is said that he was easily embarrassed when it was assumed he was a graduate and he had to explain he was not.

The senior man of the trio was George Rylands, known as 'Dadie', an English scholar who was to direct John Gielgud as Hamlet in 1945 and combine his theatre interests with a brilliant career at Cambridge. Eventually, like Willie, he would be made a Companion of Honour. With him was his friend Arthur Marshall who described Dadie as a 'fascinator'. Marshall was something of a fascinator himself and, while still a master at Oundle School, made a name as a female impersonator on radio and later as a witty writer and television personality. He recalled Willie coercing Dadie into giving tutorials over lunch but claimed no part in the proceedings except as an admiring 'apostle'. The third was Victor Rothschild who, after his death, was to be nominated as the fifth man in the Burgess–Maclean spy saga.

One of the more flamboyant visitors to the Mauresque was the twenty-year-old Sir Francis Rose who was beginning to make a name for himself as an artist under the influence of Christian Bérard and the encouragement of Jean Cocteau. He was wealthy, handsome and sexually uninhibited, with a taste for brawny young men and pretty girls. Willie and Haxton were charmed by him and no doubt intrigued when they learned that Freddie was his guardian. Born in 1909 of a line of Spanish and Scottish aristocrats, Rose was brought up in a Firbankian atmosphere of extreme Catholic religiosity and worldly excess. He succeeded to the baronetcy in 1915 following the death of his sailor father and was fought over by his scatterbrained mother and fashion-loving paternal grandmama who loathed each other. In a rare moment of accord they agreed that Freddie Maugham, who little realised what a nightmare this was to prove, should be appointed his guardian. At a disadvantage because of his lack of affinity with children, Freddie was nonplussed by this precocious, pampered boy who demanded to be allowed to study art to the exclusion of conventional education. After running away from a succession of schools, one of which he set on fire, the climax came when he vanished from Beaumont, the Jesuit public school near Windsor, setting off a nation-wide hue and cry when it was thought he had been kidnapped.

Several weeks later, he was picked up by police in Plymouth with two young sailors who were promptly arrested. There was an emotional parting when Jacky, the younger sailor, hugged and kissed him before being led away. Grandmama insisted that they were not to blame and, to the astonishment of the authorities, gave both sailors a gift of £500. In his often heavily-coded memoir, Rose admitted that his relationship with Jacky was intimate and that an ordinary boy might have been sent to an 'approved school', a description which then included institutions for children 'at risk', but he was saved by his upper-class status.

Freddie was furious with him but admitted defeat and reluctantly agreed to let him study art; from then on, the boy lived with his mother or travelled with grandmama in Europe. Perhaps Freddie hoped this was the last crisis he would have to deal with, but when Rose, at the age of fourteen, fathered a child by a girl of good family, he was left to placate them and make a financial settlement; a similar case followed a few years later. In the artistic colony of Villefranche where Rose settled in his late teens, he fell for a beautiful young American drifter called Ski, who later metamorphosed into the Hollywood star, Wayne Morris. What Freddie thought about his ward he kept to himself, never speaking of him in his immediate family circle, but it is not too fanciful to suppose that he viewed similar characteristics in his own son with some alarm, and his attitude, defined by Robin as aloofness, might be more correctly defined as wariness.

Where Rose first met the occupants of the Mauresque is not known, but as Haxton trawled the louche bars of Villefranche, Nice and elsewhere for young men for Willie's bed, the initial encounter might have been there and the link with Freddie a surprising coincidence. Rose appears to have liked Haxton rather more than Willie, whom he described a touch dismissively as 'having a facile Edwardian wit and style'. He credited both men with teaching him about Wagner when he accompanied them to Bayreuth. They were invited to his twenty-first birthday party, lavishly staged in the grounds of his mother's villa, with the guests waited on by dwarfs and entertained by Eddie Coles, the dancer who had starred in the revue *Blackbirds* on Broadway.

Freddie's legal obligation was now ended and Rose seems to have faded out of Willie's life as well, but he became a devoted friend to Syrie in the late thirties. By this time he was a successful artist, partly due to the influence of Gertrude Stein who collected his works. (It is said it was him she meant when she wrote: 'A rose is a rose is a rose.') Syrie employed him on several of her commissions but friendship did not prevent him commenting that her emotions were given entirely to her daughter 'with great force' and comparing this love with that of a lonely woman obsessed by a pet dog. He was to renew his association with the Maughams some twenty years later when he befriended Robin in Brighton.

Willie bought No. 213 King's Road and a smaller house to the rear of it in Glebe Place as the London base for Syrie and himself. The properties were linked to each other by a wide, covered passageway. Syrie redesigned both houses as a showplace to convince potential clients of her skill as she had in their previous London house at 43 Bryanston Square. Her all-white drawing room on the first floor became famous through the pictures of it that appeared in glossy magazines. Cecil Beaton described it as so immaculate and hygienic that 'Margot Oxford, who had been somewhat taken aback on entering the room, recovered herself to give the advice, "Dear Mrs Maugham, what you need are a few old varnished maps on the wall." '

The business element annoyed Willie, though he had his own quarters in the Glebe Place annexe. Even here he was not safe from her and complained that she used his study as a cloakroom for male guests when she held parties. This makes her sound inconsiderate to the needs of a writer but he was rarely there, much preferring to be abroad with Haxton. It is hardly surprising that they had rows when he was in England, for which he blamed her, but under the circumstances she was astonishingly patient. If she had not loved him, she might not have put up with his neglect for so long, but she was proud, put on a cheerful front and confided her misery only to close friends such as Nellie Maugham and Rebecca West.

Syrie had already established herself as a skilled hostess, a talent she had not been allowed to use as Mrs Wellcome because her then husband preferred to attend to all the details of the large parties he enjoyed organising. No doubt, though, she learned from him as he fussed over placements and flower arrangements. In the new house, despite its intimacy, or perhaps because of it, she contrived small dinner parties that were much envied and, by an ingenious arrangement of mirrors and lighting, she even convinced her guests that the passageway to the Glebe Place annexe was a small but perfect ballroom. Her guests often included Jack Buchanan, 'June' (Lady Inverclyde), Beatrice Lillie, Noël Coward, Thomas Beecham, Lytton Strachey, Oliver Messel, Victor Cazalet, Gertrude Lawrence, Maud Cunard (or 'Emerald' as she preferred to be called) and Mrs George Keppel, the ex-mistress of Edward VII.

Next door in Argyll House, Syrie had a wealthy rival who operated as a hostess on a grander scale; this was Sibyl Colefax, the greatest lion-hunter of them all. When she was left badly off by the death of her husband she emulated Syrie and became a successful interior decorator with John Fowler as her partner. Mary Borden (Lady Sears) wrote a sinister short story called 'To Meet Jesus Christ' about a hostess whose ambition finally drives her mad and causes her to arrange a dinner party at which the place of honour on her right is reserved for Jesus. Everybody guessed it referred to Sibyl Colefax but Mary Borden naturally said it did not. Willie, asked by Beverley Nichols if he had read it, replied: 'Of course, my dear Beverley, and I am quite sure it is absolutely true because dear Mary's powers of invention are not vivid enough to have created it.'

The Maugham marriage was now a charade played ostensibly for the sake of their daughter and with little conviction by either of them. Some sort of climax seems to have been reached at a weekend house-party in 1925 at the Villa Eliza to which Syrie invited Willie and Haxton. Beverley Nichols believed it was her final but doomed attempt to achieve a workable accord with her husband. In his book *A Case of Human Bondage*, which is about Syrie's relationship with Willie, Nichols gives the only extant account of the weekend by a guest. Syrie emerges as a Garboesque heroine stoically bearing the brunt of Haxton's gibes and Willie's disdain, while a supporting cast including Noël Coward, his boyfriend Jack Wilson, Kruger, the Swedish match millionaire, Lord and Lady Plunket, Doris de la Vigne, later Viscountess Castlerosse, and Gertie Millar, an ex-star of musical comedy and later Countess of Dudley, swirl about in the background. As an accompanying lament to Syrie's situation, Nichols gave a detailed description of his own discomfiture: indeed, the book was as much about Nichols settling old scores as it was about Syrie. He had been one of Willie's itinerant lovers and he loathed Haxton, partly one suspects out of envy for his unassailable place in Willie's affections and because he treated Nichols with amused contempt. Years afterwards he reluctantly admitted that Haxton had a sort of glittery charm, 'but he was evil, like one of those exotic plants that devour living creatures'.

In the early hours of Sunday morning, Nichols discovered Haxton lying drunk and stark naked on the floor of his bedroom surrounded by franc notes, his winnings at the local casino. Willie marched in 'looking like the wrath of 49,000 Chinese gods' and assumed the worst. The Haxton anecdote seems to be true but

Nichols omits another scene when he was discovered by Coward with his lover Jack Wilson in apparently compromising circumstances. Although Nichols claimed complete innocence in each incident, he must have had a busy night. What with one thing and another, the atmosphere was icy the next morning and, after lunch, Nichols told Syrie he would have to leave. She was still preoccupied by a petty row which had occurred with Willie over laundry bills and did not appear to register what Nichols had said to her, but then abruptly announced she would return to London with him. When he pointed out that she could hardly leave a houseful of guests 'just like that', she answered: 'I can and I shall – just like that.'

Recalling the sequence of events, Nichols built the picture of a woman torn by conflicting emotions, edging nearer and nearer to a nervous collapse. By the time they were having dinner on the train from Dover to London, she was barely controlling her hysteria and in a high-pitched voice she described the failure of her marriage in explicit detail, condemning Haxton as a liar, forger, cheat and a sexual pervert of the most horrible kind. Whether her monologue was exactly as Nichols described or was the amalgam of several outbursts from Syrie around this time we cannot know, but his attempt to engender sympathy for her plight was undermined by his running commentary describing the outraged reactions of a typically tweedy English couple sharing their table. This gave the situation an air of comedy rather than tragedy. Unintentionally, he lent credence to those who reported that Syrie gossiped around London about Willie's affairs with Haxton, so contradicting others who were impressed by her dignity and tact during the periods prior to and after her divorce.

# VI

## Alan and Fred

In 1928, Willie began an affair with Alan Searle who was to become the second most important person in his life after Haxton. He was born in 1905 at 12 Moore's Buildings in Gilbert Street, a minor road off Oxford Street, only a short walk from Grosvenor Square. His father ran a clothing shop and probably dealt in aprons, hosiery, shirts and other paraphernalia for male domestic staff. Little is known of Searle's life until his late teens or early twenties when he is alleged to have become a lover of Lytton Strachey who called him 'my Bronzino boy'. It is true that there was a certain resemblance to the artist's portraits of elegantly slim young men, but later he came to resemble the chubby Jesus in Bronzino's *Madonna and Child*, and finally, as Willie once wickedly observed, the fat Dutch burghers of Frans Hals. He seemed an unlikely lover for Strachey who preferred the classically masculine type but he had a soft feminine charm and an ingratiating manner which appealed to older men. He may have been one of the clandestine group of exclusive rent boys that operated in the West End and he could have met Willie earlier than 1928.

Searle was asked at the last minute to substitute for someone at an all-male dinner party given by the antique dealer Robert Tritton in honour of Willie. He was placed on Willie's right which suggests that he was engaged to be Willie's after-dinner entertainment. In the event he proved to be more than a one-night diversion and Willie saw him several times, finally asking him to go to the Mauresque for a holiday. Searle's mother might

93

have accepted her son's popularity with well-off older men but, with the shrewd instinct of the working class, she drew the line at trips abroad. He defied her and, when he returned, he proved her instinct correct by leaving home for good. He moved into a flat in Half Moon Street rented for him by Willie who also paid him a salary to act as his 'London Secretary'. Searle, now financially independent, rarely contacted his mother again.

Searle claimed to have worked for the Prisoners' Aid Society and if so was probably employed as a typist. Undoubtedly, he knew about life in prison and provided information for three of Willie's short stories: 'The Kite', 'Episode' and 'The Round Dozen'. Lord Glendevon was under the impression that he may have been an inmate of Wandsworth, a gaol for first-time offenders, about which Searle was particularly well-informed. At some point before he met Willie, he was helped by a prominent clergyman, probably William Temple, President of the Workers' Educational Society from 1908 to 1929. It may be due to this connection that he worked at the YMCA in York during the early 1940s when Temple was Archbishop.

It is impossible to assess the accuracy of the stories of his early life because he was reticent about it and there is only a mixture of gossip from others and romanticised odds and ends from him. His friendship with Lytton Strachey, for example, does not seem to have been substantiated by any member of the Bloomsbury or Cambridge sets. It is even possible that he did not first meet Strachey until after he had started his relationship with Willie. There was the occasion in 1931 when Strachey took him to stay with Oswald Balfour at his home in Thorpe-le-Sokon, Essex, at the end of June. Searle was bitten in the stomach by Balfour's bulldog and, in Strachey's view, was very tiresome by promptly having hysterics. This incident and the fact that Strachey received from his Bronzino boy a copy of *Cakes and Ale*, which he thought an amusing novel but marred by 'some curious lack of distinction', seems to be the sum total of the relationship as far as it is known. His claim in a letter of 26 January 1963 to Strachey's biographer, Michael Holroyd, that he introduced Maugham and

Strachey to each other is suspect, for Willie already knew many of Strachey's friends: Desmond MacCarthy, George Rylands, Sibyl Colefax, Clive Bell and Osbert Sitwell. In any case, Strachey referred in 1927 to a luncheon party where a fellow guest was Willie. Strachey thought he was rather 'a hang-dog personage', as if this may have been their first encounter.

In the late 1920s, Willie also became interested in another working-class boy, Fred Bason, from Walworth. A keen reader of novels, Bason wrote a semi-literate fan letter to Willie; intrigued, Willie replied and asked for a photograph of the writer. In May 1930, he had tea with Bason's family at 152 Westmoreland Road, ten minutes' walk from the Elephant and Castle station, and signed eight copies of his books which Bason had collected. The next year, when he was back in England, Willie took him to the South London Palace, a vast music hall by the Elephant which Willie knew from his student days. From then on he always met Bason when he was in London.

By sheer hard work, Bason saved enough to rent premises in Walworth and to open a second-hand book shop. When he produced the first bibliography of Maugham's work in 1931, though it was full of mistakes and omissions, Willie provided the preface. In 1933 Bason wrote to Willie about an enquiry he had received from a Californian collector who wished to buy some of his manuscripts. Astonishingly, Willie appointed him as his agent and promised him a commission of £1,000 on sales. From then on relations deteriorated as Bason, commercially ambitious, set up a deal with an American which Willie deplored as vulgar because it involved touting for business by advertising. He also tired of his protégé's continual requests to sign and inscribe books to alleged friends, particularly when he found this was a ruse to sell them on at high prices to collectors. He ended the association in a letter of 11 May 1936, saying that Bason had done very well out of him financially.

Why Willie took to Bason in the first place remains an enigma; it is said that he saw him as a source of material for a new slum novel, but Searle was equally able to provide introductions for this and did so, though the project was finally abandoned. The more obvious explanation is that he fancied him sexually, but Bason denied this. When he was invited to the Mauresque in the early 1930s he refused; an actor friend, Miles Mander, had warned him against going there because of Willie's homosexuality. Mander, then a minor player in British films, would have been familiar with the gossip that circulated round the West End and it is interesting that the Mauresque should have acquired a reputation so rapidly. But Bason's implied claim to sexual naivety stretches credibility; a sharp boy from the slums who worked in the street markets from an early age, he could not have reached his twenties without knowing the facts of life. Like a teasing London sparrow, he probably kept one hop away from physical contact while leading Willie on.

# Malice Aforethought

It was now inevitable that the Maughams would divorce because of incompatibility. The case, heard in the Nice court on 11 May 1929, received scant publicity in the press, much to the relief of the Maugham family, though it is possible that Freddie may have used his powerful influence to good effect. Syrie was given the London house complete with contents, the Rolls-Royce, a lump sum of £12,000, an annual allowance of £2,400 which was to cease if she remarried and £600 a year as support for Liza.

During this difficult time in his personal life, Willie completed *Cakes and Ale* which appeared the year after the divorce. Although regarded as his finest work, it is not always seen for what it is, a masterpiece in the English tradition of ironic comedy. Roughly based on the life of Thomas Hardy, it tells the story of Edward Driffield, a grand old man of English letters, admired as much for his longevity as for his talent. Within this framework Willie exposed the nonsense of the class system and satirised literary pretensions through a rich gallery of characters. Devotees of Hardy were infuriated by insulting parallels but seemed unaware of the provocative use of 'Driffield' which in Old English means 'a manured field'.

Even more malicious was Willie's cruelly funny caricature of Hugh Walpole in the guise of Alroy Kear, a successful, second-rate novelist. Walpole, a discreet homosexual who reigned in benevolent, queenly splendour over his vast following of readers, was known for his kindness to everyone, particularly to attractive young men. One of these, Peter Daubeny, first met him as a result of sending him a torrent of fan letters which Walpole always answered. Eventually he invited the fifteen-year-old schoolboy to lunch at his flat in Piccadilly. In 1971 Daubeny commented:

> That lunch was one of the most important events of my life. Nobody under forty can properly grasp the position Hugh Walpole held in the London of the early 1930s. Then in his middle fifties, he was the viceroy of the literary world, a figure of Victorian munificence . . . He was naive enough to enjoy his power and he guarded against its waning. Although a patron of the young, always championing the new and avant-garde, he did so out of a lonely fear of falling behind the times.

Walpole was astonished and deeply hurt by the attack from Willie whom he thought of as a dear friend, but the dear friend assured him that any resemblance was accidental. He even wrote a preface for future editions of *Cakes and Ale* to say so but in terms so unconvincing and disingenuous that it kept the story alive long after it would otherwise have been forgotten. Walpole never recovered from the effects of the attack and, although he pretended it didn't matter, he remained bitter as he saw his position as literary viceroy slip away and his popularity begin to erode. Eventually, when Walpole died, Willie admitted the truth, but no one knew why he had been so vindictive, unless it was genuine contempt coupled with jealousy of Walpole's success. A more likely answer is suggested by Eric Ambler in his autobiography, *Here Lies*. He was a guest at a dinner party in honour of Willie given by Alexander Frere in the 1950s in his chambers in

Albany; the other guests included Noël Coward and J. B. Priestley. Ambler noted that Willie was taciturn until Coward arrived, curtsied, went down on one knee and said, 'Maître!', which made the old man simper with pleasure. During dinner, Priestley, never noted for tact, remarked that Hugh Walpole had been helpful to promising authors. Willie put down his knife and fork and gloweringly said that he had known Walpole for many years and that he behaved disgracefully to several talented young writers, including one whom he knew personally and whose life he had ruined.

To Ambler the meaning was plain: this was nothing to do with a young writer, but referred to a stolen boyfriend. Priestley, missing the point, declared that Willie had been unkind to Walpole in *Cakes and Ale*. The old man, stammering to find words, finally exploded with anger. He had known some odious men in his time, he said, and one of the most odious was Lord Alfred Douglas, but odious though he was, he had always remained a gentleman. Hugh Walpole, he declared, his voice rising, was a 'cad'. In the silence that followed Ambler conjectured that none of those present, elderly though they were, had ever heard this word used with such virulence as an expression of hatred.

Willie also turned against another popular writer, his ex-lover Godfrey Winn, known as 'Winifred God', satirising him in *Strictly Personal* in 1941. The section had to be deleted from the British edition for fear of a libel action but Winn bore no ill will; instead, he continually eulogised Willie as 'my darling friend and mentor who taught me how to write'. As Winn's literary style was appalling, this was a greater revenge than if he had extracted heavy damages. After Maugham's death, he bought his writing table and would show this to visitors, saying that it gave him spiritual inspiration: 'I feel Willie is guiding my hand from beyond the grave.'

For all its intricately-woven themes and subtleties, *Cakes and Ale* has only one character worthy of serious analysis and that is Rosie, the first wife of Driffield. On the surface, she is a commonplace country-girl, plain, plump, with an agreeable vulgar vitality but little else. Yet men who have been barely aware of her existence can suddenly become spellbound and see her as a transformed creature of incandescent beauty who not only promises sexual pleasure but also has no inhibitions about providing it. Apparently warm-hearted, she is actually selfish, avaricious and deceitful and once she has used her lovers, she doesn't give a damn for them. Nor does she care what her husband suffers when she leaves him alone in their bed while she goes off to someone else's, nor give him a second thought when she finally walks out to go with Kemp, a loud-mouthed low-life.

At the end of the story when she is an old woman, an over-made-up, grotesque parody of her youth, Willie introduces a last-minute revelation. In the early days, while she was married to Driffield and living in lodgings, she had had a child who died a painful death. After the funeral she sits alone with her husband, acutely aware of his suffering, but needing to get away from him. She puts on a new dress and says she is going out, in a tone of voice that makes it clear that she doesn't want anything to do with him. She goes to the Strand to pick up a man for the night and chooses an actor friend from her past because he is fun to be with and good in bed.

Willie makes no attempt to steer the reader to a conclusion about Rosie but it could not be clearer that the only person she thinks about is herself; yet critics have ignored the evidence, preferring to see her as the archetypal whore with a heart of gold, 'whore', however, not being a word they cared to use. Leslie A. Marchand of the *New York Times* called her a guileless child of nature 'apt for love'. Ivor Brown in the *Observer* thought her 'unchaste' but kind and comforting, while J. B. Priestley in the *Saturday Review of Literature* described her as an easy-going, amoral woman who good-naturedly let friends use her body. Since that initial reaction, the real character of Rosie has been submerged in sentimentality and a smugly masculine refusal to accept her as Willie created her. He was not an author to comment on the interpretation of his work so we do not know what he thought about this. As he said of his plays, once his task was completed it was up to the public to make of them what they wished. He must, however, have been surprised, initially at least, that none of the commentators could see that Rosie is a distant cousin of Ibsen's Nora, determined to live life on her own terms and conditions, something not easy to do in the late 1800s. She leaves Driffield when he is becoming fashionable because she refuses to be trapped in the role of subservient wife or to be scorned by his new friends for her lack of education. Sexually, however, she is more emancipated than Ibsen's heroines and can use men for her pleasure while maintaining her independence.

In the final scene of the book, set in Rosie's garish but expensively furnished Yonkers home in 1928, when she is nearly seventy, she admits that the deceased Kemp was probably the only man she ever cared for. Asked what she saw in him, her eyes linger on an enlarged photograph of him dressed to the nines as if for a day at the races, the embodiment of swaggering sexual vulgarity, and replies that he was always a perfect gentleman. Some have seen this as an example of Maugham's cynicism, others as a final reference to the complex class system which he holds up to ridicule. But surely there is nothing obscure about the meaning. Kemp, behaving as a perfect gentleman, has treated Rosie as 'a lady' which no other man, including Driffield, has done. To them, she was little more than a whore; to Kemp, she was a woman who commanded respect.

A few days after publication, Beverley Nichols dined at the Garrick Club with Hugh Walpole who complained about the cruel caricature of himself in *Cakes and Ale* and asserted that the only character in the novel that was obviously fictitious was Rosie. Next day, Nichols passed this on to Willie who immediately enquired how 'Dear Hugh' had arrived at this conclusion. Instead of keeping quiet, Nichols blundered on: 'Because he said that there'd never been a Rosie in your life and never would be.' The implicit reference to his homosexuality angered Willie intensely and there was a long pause while he struggled for words. 'If you see Hugh again, you may tell him with my compliments that I am sorry that I was so nice to him.' This acidic response did not dismiss Walpole's contention: it left Nichols convinced that Rosie was a character born of Willie's creative imagination and there was no reason to think otherwise, for his name had never been linked romantically to a female of any kind prior to Syrie.

Inevitably, there were those who sniggeringly supposed that Rosie was based on a male lover or was a composite, perhaps, of Walter Payne, Gerald Haxton and Alan Searle, with a dash of Syrie mixed in to give the character veracity. Willie seemed unaware of the ribald comment that circulated in the gay pubs, clubs and cafés of the West End or, indeed, of the gossip that had surrounded him for years, and his friends apparently lacked the courage to tell him. It came as a considerable shock to be warned by Freddie on behalf of the powers-that-be that his homosexual activities during his trips to London were well known to the police and he was in danger of prosecution; he must consider not only his immediate family but also the wider family of Romers and Maughams and the effect of adverse publicity on them. Freddie knew, however, that the authorities were reluctant to drag well-known people through the courts and believed a warning would suffice. Cynics might say that Willie's fame and family connections almost guaranteed him immunity unless he behaved with Wildean stupidity, but it is conceivable that this warning started the germination of the paranoid fear of public exposure that developed later.

What he needed later for *Looking Back* was some sort of proof that he had always been heterosexual but this was hard to find. It was not until he wrote a new foreword to the 1950 Modern Library edition of *Cakes and Ale*, in which he confessed that Walpole had indeed been the model for Alroy Kear, that he mentioned that Rosie was based on a woman with whom he had been closely connected. He added that when he wrote the novel she was already dead. It seems probable that thinking of Walpole reminded him of the comment passed on by Nichols and he took the opportunity to settle an old score. He did not claim to have had an affair with the unidentified woman but left the reader free to make assumptions. By now, Rosie had become a sort of patron saint of ladies of easy virtue and he was able to describe her with complete accuracy as his most engaging heroine.

No more was heard of Rosie until 1961 when Richard Cordell, an American academic, published *Somerset Maugham: A Biographical and Critical Study*. He had been the author of a similar work in 1937 and claimed to know Willie well enough to count him as a friend, but admitted later that he had no idea that he was homosexual. He put it down to his own naivety – 'I was just a country lad'. But he had no need of excuse, for many people were unaware of the truth and would have been shocked if they had known. The ability to deceive was part of the gay man's armoury and Willie was an accomplished liar and actor on the page and off it. In the preface to his new book, Cordell thanked Willie and Searle for providing information, checking the accuracy of details and 'generously answering many questions'. It is interesting that Cordell was able to give the first description of the lady alleged to have been the model for Rosie a year ahead of Willie's detailed version which appeared in *Looking Back*. In neither case was the lady's real name given; for convenience, Cordell called her 'Nan'.

Rebecca West, putting two and two together, identified her as Ethelwyn Sylvia Jones, a moderately successful actress always known as Sue. In a letter to Beverley Nichols of 4 May 1966 about *A Case of Human Bondage*, West expressed surprise that he had not deduced this for himself. Sue's father was Henry Arthur Jones, the fashionable author of plays including *The Silver King* and *Mrs Dane's Defence*. He was as esteemed as his contemporaries Pinero and Shaw. Sue married Montague Leveaux, a theatrical manager, in 1902 but, following a divorce, married Angus McDowell in 1913 and retired from the stage. Her husband, second son of the Earl of Antrim, became a Tory MP in the 1920s and served as honorary attaché to the British Ambassador in Washington during the war. She died in 1948 and he in 1966.

In *Looking Back*, Willie claimed that he had had an eight-year affair with Sue from about 1905 and that, in 1913, he proposed to her because it was time he got married. Though he didn't love her, he liked her as well as anybody; he was astounded when she rejected him and married McDowell soon after. He described her as a promiscuous woman who had been to bed with all his friends, one of whom we may guess was Gerald Kelly, probably the model for the artist Lionel Hillier in *Cakes and Ale*, who paints an idealised, full-length portrait of Rosie. This, from the description, was almost identical with one executed by Kelly of Sue. According to Rebecca West, she was also the mistress of Ivor Back. West thought of Sue as a big, vulgar girl, but there may be an element of cattiness in this description as Sue was generally noted for her beauty and intelligence, attributes which served her well as a politician's wife.

There is no reason to doubt that Sue inspired the character of Rosie and there may have been more irony in the secondary title of *Cakes and Ale* than at first appeared, for she was truly *The Skeleton in the Cupboard* as far as Ivor Back and a number of other men were concerned. As for Willie's own involvement with Sue, there is considerable reason for scepticism, though, in his 1972 *W. Somerset Maugham and the Quest for Freedom*, Calder was able to quote Gerald Kelly who said that there was definitely a romance. Encouraged by this, Calder suggests Sue's rejection might mark a turning point in Willie's life and 'the bitter-sweet love affair' would need to be appraised in future studies. Garson Kanin, in *Remembering Mr Maugham*, recalls Willie's tears as he speaks with regret of what might have been if Sue had said yes. Even Ted Morgan, who cannot be accused of sentimentality, apparently accepts his version of events.

But can we believe that this eight-year affair was conducted in such secrecy that nobody else knew of it except Gerald Kelly? It has to be remembered that Willie and Sue were part of what today might be broadly classified as 'show business'. Yet there has not been a whiff of gossip, not even an innocuous remark about the couple in the hundreds of books written by and about their contemporaries. Can such a long-lasting affair ever have been attended by such discretion that even those who disliked the couple bit their tongues rather than comment? Apart from her enjoyment of sex and a physical similarity, there is nothing to suggest that Rosie is based exclusively on Sue. The description of Rosie on her first appearance in the novel could apply to his initial reaction to Syrie. He describes her zestful, child-like eagerness and her engaging smile with its hint of something akin to shyness. As the tale develops, Rosie proves to be as sly as he later accused Syrie of being in *Looking Back*. If Rosie is an enchantress whose magic conceals from her victims that she is a cruel, selfish bitch, then *Cakes and Ale* can be read as an act of revenge on Syrie and Sue Jones, the first for marrying him, the second for refusing to.

# Queer Interlude

It has always been difficult to categorise Willie's next novel, *The Narrow Corner*, published in 1932. According to Robin it was described by Willie as his 'queer' novel, adding, 'Thank heaven nobody has realised it.' At the time it received patronising reviews from the critics who dismissed it as entertaining but uninvolving. Gradually it has been seen to be rather more substantial than something to pass the time between dozing on a holiday beach.

Dr Saunders, who made a brief appearance in his short story 'The Stranger', is a passenger aboard a lugger; with him is a beautiful Chinese boy who prepares his opium pipes and, we guess, is his lover. Also aboard is Fred, an Australian six footer of twenty-one with dark curly hair and a sulky look which is transformed by a dazzling smile; it transpires he is on the run after killing a woman for hounding him. The captain of the lugger is Nichols, a cordial villain who suffers from dyspepsia and provides a little comedy to balance the impending tragedy.

The lugger puts into an island to shelter from bad weather and there we meet Erik Christessen, a beautiful Danish youth who is in love with the mysterious Louise, the daughter of a one-time

English teacher. Dr Saunders observes the attraction the two young men immediately have for each other but then Fred is seduced by Louise, and Eric, in despair at the betrayal, shoots himself. Later Fred also dies. Louise remains oddly detached and, though she is sorry, tragedy has given her freedom from commitment. This outline can convey nothing of the complexity of the characters or their interaction with each other.

Robin always hoped to produce a film version that would emphasise the bisexuality of the young men. He seemed unaware that the story had already been filmed with Douglas Fairbanks Jnr and Ralph Bellamy in 1933 by Warner Brothers in a fairly truthful adaptation. Three years later the studio used the story as a vehicle for Humphrey Bogart, calling it *Isle of Fury*, but it was so dreadful that he later pretended that he had not made it. Needless to say there was no hint of bisexual behaviour in either version. To be really brave Robin needed to take the story a step further and change Louise to a young man, for, as Willie wrote her, she is coolly masculine, an emotional primitive, without remorse and intelligent enough to ensure her own survival. Some might say she is a typical Maugham woman and this again raises the question, 'How many of Willie's fictional women were all or partly based on men he had known?'

# Services No Longer Required

Despite his successes, or perhaps because of his failures, Willie became steadily disenchanted with the theatre, but he had ideas for four plays and he decided to write them before finishing with it for good. The last of these, *Sheppey*, presented in September 1933, was based on his short story 'A Bad Example', published in 1899. The leading character, a humble barber, is nicknamed Sheppey, after the place where he was born. (There is an obscure joke here because the Isle of Sheppey, near Willie's childhood home at Whitstable, derived its name from the Anglo-Saxon meaning 'a place where sheep are kept'). When Sheppey wins a prize in the Irish Sweepstake, it seems that his family will be moderately prosperous, but he suddenly decides to become one of Christ's flock, do good and give all that he has to the poor. He invites a prostitute and a young male thief to live at his home; oddly, he shares his bed with the young man. His shocked wife and family conclude that he is insane, a view confirmed by the doctor quoting a specialist who contends that 'philanthropy in general can be ascribed to repressed homosexuality' and that, with the sensible education of the young, philanthropy could be entirely stamped out in England. Before Sheppey can be committed to an asylum, death, in the guise of the prostitute, intervenes to take him to the hereafter. He protests, but succumbs to the inevitable and, as they go, he switches off the light: 'No good running up an electric bill.'

Read today, the play comes off the page full of life, demanding to be reassessed in the theatre, yet it is counted as a creative failure. The attitude of John Gielgud, who directed it, may partly explain why. He found it an extraordinary mixture of styles, the first act reminiscent of Pinero, the second of Shaw and the third, 'tragic fantasy'. It is hardly surprising that his confusion resulted in a production that bewildered critics and audiences alike. Willie described it as a sardonic comedy written in a consistent style throughout but admitted that he was aware that the final scene might displease. But far from being tragic, it is extremely funny; indeed, the play is a precursor to the Ortonesque nuance and satire of some thirty years later. To be fair to Gielgud, he tried to discuss the play with Willie who, while charming, was 'oddly devoid of enthusiasm' and did not comment on what he had seen in rehearsal.

His last four plays, *The Sacred Flame* (a plea for euthanasia), *The Breadwinner* (a male version of Ibsen's *A Doll's House*), *For Services Rendered* (an anti-war polemic) and finally *Sheppey* were unexpectedly different and showed that he had changed with the times. The first two plays were relatively successful but the complete failure of the final plays was a sad end to thirty years as a playwright; the fault lay with others, not with him. Willie remarked philosophically that he was out of touch with the theatre-going public, and once this happened to playwrights, they were unwise to ignore the warning.

# VII

## Robin

Robin's childhood was safe but lonely. Like Willie, he was left in the care of servants and had little contact with his own age group. Also like him, he became very attached to a new nanny-cum-governess who arrived when he was seven years old. She was a gentle creature, unlike the termagants who had previously ruled his life. When a year later he was sent to boarding school, he was far more distressed at leaving his nurse than he was at leaving his mother. Probably because of the ill health that followed his birth, Nellie sometimes appeared to resent him and was often impatient and irritable. He once overheard her say she did not like little boys and, though this may have been a jocular reference to her own childhood when she was at the mercy of her boisterous brothers, Robin took it personally. He tried to be 'good' but often appeared stupid: as Honor put it, he was 'pathetically docile'.

Away from London at the country house, Nellie was far more relaxed and would play the piano to amuse him, as she had done for his sisters. One of their favourite songs was about a boy called Tommy who got up to all sorts of mischief. Robin became so intrigued by him that he wanted to know more and Nellie, who was a natural raconteur, wove stories of his wild adventures. She told them with such relish that he began to think that this boy, physically strong, excellent at games and completely fearless, was the type of son she would have preferred. Disconsolately, he decided that he could never emulate Tommy and he resigned himself to being a disappointment to her. But in a psychological twist, instead of hating his mythical rival, Robin made him his friend, a strong male figure like an elder brother in whom he could confide his problems and pleasures. In return Tommy would reassure him and tell him what to do. Instead of fading away during Robin's childhood until he was forgotten, Tommy remained partly occluded in his subconscious ready to return to his imagination years later.

Nellie might have seemed somewhat remote but Freddie was an unapproachable god isolated on his own Olympian peak. One of the family stories, however, suggests that his omnipotence was limited. He was strolling through the West End one morning when he saw a gleaming new yellow Fiat tourer in a show-room window. Instantly, like Mr Toad, he was enraptured; the fact that he already had a Rolls-Royce and a chauffeur was unimportant – he must have the Fiat. Undeterred that he had never even touched the steering wheel of a car, he decided to buy it straight away and take it down to the West Country where the family were staying at Hamswell House. In those pre-test days there was nothing to stop him, but it occurred to him as he wrote his cheque for £375 that it might be wise to learn how to drive it and he asked for a member of the staff to take him as far as Reading. There, satisfied that he now knew all that he needed to know, he gave the driver his fare back to London, plus a tip, and set off to complete the rest of the journey on his own. Like Mr Toad, he knew no fear and was not the least bit disconcerted when he drove too close to a lorry and stripped off the Fiat's left mudguard. The lorry driver, placated by the price of several beers and the name of Freddie's insurance company, helped to strap the mudguard back on and the journey continued without further mishap until he was beyond Bath. Here, he had trouble with the gears, swerved into a large car and stripped off the right mudguard. There was a repetition of the scene with the lorry driver and, the mudguard safely tied on, he was off again.

Triumphantly, he arrived at the gates of the house and drove up the drive under the astonished gaze of Robin and Diana who were playing on the front lawn. Nonchalantly, he waved a 'hello' at them and, forgetting to brake, ended up with the now battered

Fiat wedged into the stone porch. He was quite unperturbed by the undignified end to his journey or by the laughter of his children. Despite Nellie's pleadings, he refused to repent, continuing to drive erratically for years afterwards and pretending that he could never understand why family and friends were so reluctant to be his passengers. It amused Freddie to tell the story of his adventure with a dead-pan expression but Robin perversely gave it as an example of his pomposity when he wanted to picture Freddie as a latter-day Mr Barrett.

Another story illustrated Freddie's dry humour. Driving to London from Hartfield, he became confused about who had the right of way at a crossroads and drove into another car. He admitted he was in the wrong and the other driver, who was the only occupant, received a substantial amount from his insurance company. Some months afterwards Freddie received a letter from the driver complaining that his ankle still hurt as a result of the crash and suggesting a payment of £1,000 in further compensation. He replied: 'I am sorry to hear that your ankle afflicts you but I am glad to note that, at least, you have not lost your nerve.'

By contrast, Uncle Willie was always jolly and gave Robin a good tip when they met. Once he suggested that Nellie should bring him to lunch at the Savoy. Mystified, because he did not understand what the Savoy was, Robin, only seven, asked his French governess what happened there. She sighed, 'Ah! C'est la vie!' Robin, no wiser, asked, 'But what do they *do*?' Mademoiselle thought for a moment. 'They eat oysters and drink champagne.' After his mother had ordered, Willie turned to the child and began reading out the long menu. Getting no response, he finally said, in comic despair, 'Oysters?' 'Yes please!' chirped Robin eagerly. Willie stared at him in mock gloom. 'You would be unlike the rest of the younger members of your family if you did not prefer the most expensive.'

When he was eight Robin was sent to Highfield, a preparatory boarding school in Hampshire which was dedicated to toughening up small boys for the rigours of public school. Robin suffered all the fears of a single child. He had no siblings near his own age to help him and none of his father's athletic or scholastic promise. He was not even attractive enough to interest an older protector. But his 'pathetic docility' goaded his form-master, Mr Grove, to demonstrate his skill at bullying sarcasm. Physical violence was forbidden – only the headmaster was allowed to cane boys – but Mr Grove could achieve a longer-lasting effect with his voice. He had been a sapper during the war and referred constantly to his experiences in the trenches and to all his suffering for the likes of 'YOU, Maugham', his voice rising to a frightening shout. Suddenly he would order Robin to stand and repeat what he had just been telling the class, word for word, exactly as he had said it. Even without the chill of fear that impeded Robin's mind it is unlikely he could have complied. This delighted Mr Grove who now had an excuse to launch a diatribe of crude abuse which ended with a contemptuous 'Go and stand in the corner. You'll stay there, at attention, without moving until the end of class.' Mr Grove was a sad example of the after-effects of the war; probably shell-shocked, he was mentally unsuited to be in charge of small children. The effect on Robin was to induce 'hideous' nightmares which left him shaking with imagined dread.

When he was ten, a boy two years older than himself tried to introduce him to mutual masturbation but he was too scared to co-operate. It was the same boy who reported one of the masters, a Mr Merrick, for sexual misdemeanours with other boys, apparently out of pique because the man did not fancy him. Another form-master, a Mr Rudge, who also took the boys for rugger, bullied one of Robin's classmates unmercifully on and off the field. But after he agreed to have sex with him, he became, rather obviously, form favourite. Another boy, older than Robin, rather quiet and shy but attractive-looking, was given extra tuition by one of the masters in his room after the usual lights out in the dormitory. The boy always came back tearful and Robin could hear him trying to stifle his sobbing. When he asked him what was wrong, he replied: 'You wouldn't understand ... You're lucky ... He says you're too young.' Robin claimed that he had no physical contact with anyone at Highfield, though sometimes the beauty of other boys aroused him sexually; it was not until he went to Eton that he overcame his inhibitions.

In his autobiography, *On My Way to the Club*, Ludovic Kennedy, whose years at Highfield overlapped with those of Robin, agreed it was a loathsome place. He did not encounter any homosexual goings-on but remembered the scandal of Mr Merrick's sudden departure. He described him as slim, quiet and bespectacled but he could not endorse Robin's story of Mr Rudge, a florid-faced man, a Cambridge rugger blue in his youth, who smoked an evil-smelling pipe. He once slapped Kennedy's face without any given reason, which seemed in character. Both boys shared an ambition to write and Kennedy completed a two-thousand-word novel apparently with a patriotic flavour, for the last lines described a bed of massed tulips illustrating George V's face. Robin's effort, of similar length, concerned an Egyptian mummy, Princess Ioki, who came to life and terrorised everyone. His lurid story told in the darkness of the dormitory as a continuing nightly saga was banned when one of his listeners had convulsions.

Despite its avowed intent, Highfield singularly failed to prepare Robin for his new life at Eton. He was placed in Butterwick's House and, at first, everything frightened him and he again retreated into pathetic docility in the hope that he might go unnoticed; instead, his and his ineptitude at games made him a target for bullying and mockery. Added to his misery were his duties as fag to a senior boy that included preparing cooked teas, knowing that burnt toast or an overdone sausage could result in a ritual thrashing by the captain of the house. Caning for trivial misdemeanours was standard practice, apparently in the belief that it strengthened the character of those involved, but it was more likely to produce a breed of sadomasochists. As for homosexuality, the clandestine nature of the activities, coupled with the threat of expulsion if discovered, added a frisson of danger for those boys whose sex-drive could not be controlled. Many, of course, did not want or need to indulge and, of those who did, most would look back later and dismiss it as a 'phase' or deny it ever took place.

Robin gradually resigned himself to Eton but in the first year or so he frequently begged his parents to take him away. Freddie dismissed his pleas as a sign of weakness but Nellie was mildly sympathetic, though she was not impressed by temperamental displays of adolescent introspection. On one occasion Robin sat mournfully on the sofa, sighing theatrically and clutching his head – a fifteen-year-old Hamlet. 'I want something,' he moaned, 'but I don't know what.' 'I know,' retorted Nellie crisply, 'a dose of castor oil.'

Towards the end of a summer vacation, Freddie was smoking his pipe when the subject of advertising came up. Unusually he interrupted the family chatter and said that he had often thought the posters for his favourite brand of tobacco, Three Nuns, could be vastly improved.

> I see the use of their slogan 'None Nicer!' extended. The poster would read in very large letters, 'None Nicer, None Finer, None Purer.' In the background there would be the walls of a beautiful convent and in the foreground a gentle stream. In the middle ground, gazing into the water, would be three attractive young ladies in nuns' habits; at their feet, each would have a scroll which would read from left to right, 'Nun Nicer, Nun Finer, Nun Purer.' On second thoughts the scrolls might be better placed floating above their heads but that's a detail. You are welcome to utilise my idea and send it to Three Nuns.

Back at Eton with nothing better to do one Sunday, Robin got out his paint box and a piece of cartridge paper, executed a miniature poster using his father's idea and sent it off with a letter written on the usual printed notepaper with his housemaster's name and address at the top. Nearly two months went by and he had forgotten all about it when he was summoned to Mr Butterwick's study and asked to explain a parcel of tins of Three Nuns tobacco addressed to R. Maugham Esq. Was this an attempt to smuggle a banned product into the house? Robin protested his innocence; fortunately he noticed an envelope concealed between the tins. In its letter the tobacco company explained that, excellent though his ideas might be, they feared objections to it on religious grounds if they took it up. As a token of their appreciation they trusted Mr Maugham would accept the enclosed tins of tobacco. When Robin told the story Butterwick laughed and arranged for the parcel to be forwarded to Freddie who, apparently, accepted the gift as his due and quite understood why his idea could not be used. 'Very sensitive, nuns,' he observed.

Robin's unhappy life did not alter radically until an older boy found him sexually attractive; it was the first of a series of affairs which brought transitory affection, satisfied his lust and gave him a sense of self-assurance. A fellow pupil, Michael Pitt-Rivers, first noticed Robin when he saw him as Captain of the Lower Chapel Choir leading the procession of boys to their places. He struck him as odd-looking with a full, round face, startlingly strong eyes and an expression of such profound sanctity that he could not believe anyone could be so religious. Robin observed many years later that he had thoroughly enjoyed dressing up in his cassock and long white surplice, and carrying the cross because it satisfied his sense of the theatrical. Later, Pitt-Rivers spoke to him and they became close friends: 'He was never conventionally good-looking, but very striking, with the mobile features of a clown, capable of expressing great sadness, but, for most of the time, pure glee.'

When Pitt-Rivers was a guest at Tye House, he saw that Robin took after his mother who had a remarkable and infectious sense of humour. 'She spoke very rapidly and exuded energy, very like Cicely Courtneidge, that bubbly comedienne.' Freddie, by contrast, looked like a High Court judge about to pass the death sentence. 'Robin's nickname for him was "The Walnut" because he was dry and crabbed.' During breakfast, while the others chatted, Freddie, immersed in *The Times*, suddenly put it down and said with awesome solemnity: 'It is disgraceful the way people dash about in their cars. They shouldn't be allowed to exceed 20 mph. There ought to be a law.' Nellie and Robin burst into laughter while Freddie stared at them balefully. At the time, Pitt-

Rivers was unaware of Freddie's fearsome reputation as a reckless driver. At another meal, Robin was schoolboyishly boasting that there were two High Court judges and a famous writer in the family, to which Pitt-Rivers quipped: 'All working-class men, you might say.' Everyone chuckled except Freddie who stared at him, his usual baleful expression intact.

Robin never did well at games and was merely competent in class, though he did win a prize for literature in 1930 and developed a talent for music, winning the Harmsworth prize in 1932 and 1933. Freddie, far from being pleased, took this as an ominous sign and lectured him on the insecurity of music as a profession, pointing out that the plan was for him to go to Cambridge, then into law, and that this was irrevocable. Robin, who had no intention of pursuing a musical career, pretended to concede and let him think that he had won some sort of victory but prudently kept silent about his real ambition to be a writer like Uncle Willie. He had already taken the first step towards this goal by starting a school magazine that took its name from its cost, *Sixpenny*, and he sent copies to Willie who criticised frankly but, on the whole, favourably. He must have read with some wry reaction the advertisement his enterprising nephew had obtained for the Castle Hotel, Windsor, where he and Syrie had provided evidence for the divorce from Wellcome in 1915. It informed him that luncheon cost 2/6, dinner 3/6 and a bedroom with breakfast 9/6.

Robin's main contributions to the magazine were short stories; these showed talent and were written under the pseudonym Romer Marck. As editor, he was not afraid of controversy and in one issue Airey Neave, who was to be murdered by the IRA, argued against pacifism while Michael Pitt-Rivers put the case in favour. Commenting later, Pitt-Rivers said: 'For a time, the German leadership misled some of us into thinking its protestations of peaceful intent were sincere. But when war eventually broke out in 1939, we all joined various regiments: I joined the Welsh Guards.'

By the time he had passed the exams which gave him entry to

115

Cambridge, Robin had changed into a charming, amusing and lively young man with far more Romer than Maugham in his character. Much to his anger, Freddie made him stay on at Eton saying that, as he had won colours for fencing, he should apply his energy to getting colours for some other, more virile sport. It seems that the father was trying to relive his life through the son, but he soon accepted that Robin had no sporting prowess and allowed him to leave on 28 March 1934. Robin later said that for years he could never think of Eton, or even drive through Slough, without feeling physically sick. Pitt-Rivers observed drily that, while Robin made his point somewhat dramatically, hatred of Eton was 'common among boys of above average intelligence'.

Robin had six free months before going up to Cambridge and Freddie agreed that he could go to Vienna to learn German. Kate suggested that she go with him for a two-week sight-seeing holiday and she booked rooms at the Koenig von Ungarn. When Willie, who was in London, heard about this, he instructed Haxton to take a room at the hotel and make himself generally useful as a guide. He also took Robin to lunch at the Garrick to speak to him like a 'Dutch Uncle'. It was a source of irritation to Freddie that his brother appointed himself as mentor to his offspring, but where Freddie disparaged, Willie encouraged. Over lunch, he gave Robin a generous sum of money as an eighteenth birthday present and as a help towards enjoying himself in Vienna.

When Willie sent a note to Freddie explaining about Haxton, the effect was explosive. Under no circumstances must Robin meet him. It was bad enough that the ghastly man was in the same country, let alone in the same city and at the same hotel. After threatening to cancel the trip, Freddie calmed down and agreed it could go ahead on condition that Robin and Kate stayed at a different hotel. Kate, a sophisticated woman in her mid-thirties, must have thought her father's attitude absurd but, for the sake of family peace, she changed the hotel booking, knowing full well that Haxton would have no difficulty in finding them.

The relationship between herself and her father was close

although she once jokingly remarked that that she was a married woman with three children before she discovered he was human. The barriers had actually begun to crumble when she was a teenager and had taken up golf under Freddie's guidance. He once told his children that he was not prepared to discuss anything with them until they had reached the age of reason; now he appeared to consider that Kate was worth talking to and he took her with him on his holidays. She described him as an indefatigable sightseer who walked her off her feet in most of the capitals of Europe and she found to her surprise that he had an extensive knowledge of the arts. He also shared her keen sense of humour and she was able to make fun of him to an extent the others did not dare. He was far more modern in his outlook than she had ever suspected and she was probably the least taken aback of the offspring when he began an affair with a young woman which lasted for nearly five years.

Kate and Robin arrived in Vienna a week before his eighteenth birthday and Haxton traced them to their new hotel on the second day. As Willie's emissary he was charming, attentive, a good host and an excellent guide to Vienna. While they were at the Vienna races, Robin recognised Myles Hildyard, an ex-Etonian some two years older than himself. He had not met him socially but introduced himself, and so began a friendship which lasted until Robin's death. As Hildyard's friendship with Robin developed, he became a frequent visitor to Cadogan Square. His experience at meals was similar to that of Pitt-Rivers; Freddie did not join in the inconsequential chatter but sat glumly eating: 'He was rather a crosspatch and Robin made fun of his solemnity.' Speaking of the first meeting in Vienna nearly sixty years later, Hildyard said that he found Robin great fun; he was entranced by Kate and quite liked Haxton though there was nothing special about him that he could remember. He confirmed a story Robin was to tell in his autobiography. Haxton, true to his lecherous reputation, made a pass at Kate, much to her amusement, and, failing with her, turned his attention to Robin who politely declined. Haxton was not in the least put out and, when he left before the end of the month to join Willie at the Villa Mauresque, they kept in touch by letter. One of these gives clues to his character and, by implication, a glimpse of Robin's too:

> Darling Robin,
> Mea Culpa, Mea Maxima Culpa. I know I owe you letters. I know I'm in your debt. But won't you forgive me. We arrive in Salzburg on August 13th Hotel Europe. I hope we'll see you.
> Please say SHIT in seven languages to Nikita and tell him I want his address. AND you might say to him that none of us thought much of his friend at the Koenig von Ungarn.
> My love to Kitty (Kate) who owes me for long letter.
>            Love to you
>                        G. H.

Another view of Haxton came from Pitt-Rivers. When he was on holiday in Cap Ferrat in 1938, he telephoned the Mauresque and was invited to dinner by Haxton. When he arrived he found that Willie was away and that he was the only guest. After the meal Haxton relentlessly pestered him to have sex but Pitt-Rivers told him he was being impossibly ill-mannered and left. He found Haxton brash and superficial with an exaggerated opinion of his sexual attraction.

According to Robin, Haxton once invited him to spend a few days in Venice, all expenses paid. On the first night in their twin-bedded room at the Hotel Danieli, Haxton, much more drunk than Robin, tried to have sex with him but was rejected. Early next morning Willie allegedly telephoned and asked, 'And was the young man satisfactory in bed?' Robin conjectured that it amused Willie for his own lover to have his nephew, and that, once seduced by Haxton, he would more readily have sex with him.

Peter Burton, who worked on Robin's autobiography with him, often sensed that he was letting his imagination take over and queried this episode, only to get the standard reply, 'I should know, I was there.' But Burton doubts very much whether Willie either colluded with Haxton's alleged attempt at seduction or fancied Robin for himself. He maintains that it would have been out of character for Willie to behave to one of the family in such a manner. Aside from this, there were enough subsequent opportunities at the Villa Mauresque if Willie had been sexually interested but Robin never hinted at anything of the sort taking place.

After Robin had moved into a *pension* in Vienna for three months' stay, Willie wrote to him on 4 June suggesting that, if he needed any financial assistance or got into any trouble, he should contact him rather than his parents. He was, he explained, a hard-headed cynic with a greater tolerance for the follies of the human race than Freddie.

Later Myles Hildyard joined Robin in the *pension* also to study German. Robin began lessons in piano technique as well but found them tedious and gave up. Hildyard remembers him as a bubbly personality with a taste for Viennese night-life. There was one club which he particularly liked where a girl dressed in white tails and top hat sang in the Dietrich style. The two young men were frequently joined by Hildyard's friend, George Morton, whose stepfather and mother lived in a small castle at Klosternburg and they often went there to swim in the pool and laze in the sun. It was a happy, sybaritic existence and they were barely aware of the growing crisis between Austria and Germany. They were staying at Klopeinersee for a few days when Chancellor Dollfuss was assassinated by Nazi sympathisers on 25 July. Nellie's brother, General Sir Cecil Romer, Deputy Chief of the Imperial General Staff, warned her that war could break out any day and she tried to get in touch with Robin, but failed. In a panic, she cabled Willie for help and he and Haxton surprised Robin by arriving to take him to Bad Gastein to catch a plane the next day. It was after dinner that Willie remarked to Robin, 'You are quite an attractive boy. Don't waste your assets. Your charm won't last for long.'

Robin arrived at Trinity Hall, Cambridge in October 1934, firmly resolved not to be intimidated by the achievements of the Romers and Maughams who had preceded him, nor by the expectations of his father. He planned to do enough work to scrape through exams, begin a writing career and generally have fun. Socially his status was impeccable but he found it useful to exploit the additional cachet of being Somerset Maugham's nephew. He soon gained a reputation for his sense of humour and ability as a raconteur and, as he was a generous host, he never lacked an audience. He began as he intended to go on and Charles Fletcher-Cooke remembers the grand parties he held in large rooms he had moved to in Lensfield Road 'which literary figures from London such as A. A. Milne, Humbert Wolfe, Ann Bridge and his uncle Willie used to attend'. Fletcher-Cooke, who became President of the Cambridge Union, recalls that although Robin was a member he did not attend very often. This is surprising because Robin had a natural aptitude for public speaking and success in union debate would have been consistent with his desire for recognition, particularly as he had strong left-wing opinions to expound.

If he had inherited Mark Lemon's rhyming abilities, he might have been drawn to the Cambridge Footlights and their satiric revues, but instead he preferred the long-established Amateur Dramatic Company. Here he found a new, ready-made social set which included a few effeminate young men who prettied themselves up with cosmetics. This was hardly new: ten years before there had been a minor furore when a national newspaper, the *Daily Sketch*, fulminated under the headline 'The Girl Men of Cambridge': 'Nowhere else in Britain except in London, or perhaps Oxford, will you find so many soft, painted, be-rouged youths.' The sight of two of the boys visiting Robin's rooms with the ADC crowd so enraged a senior member of Trinity Hall Boat Club that he threatened to get a posse together to smash the rooms up unless these 'perverts' were barred. Not for the last time Robin wondered if some heterosexual men saw effeminacy as an assault on their own, presumably shaky, sexual identity. Gambling that his tormentor would have spurned fencing as a sport too delicate for his image, he went up to him in the street, slapped him across the face with the back of his hand and challenged him to a duel, adding that, as the insulted party, he had the choice of weapons and nominated sabres. His 'opponent', surrounded by hearty friends, was dumbfounded and outmanoeuvred; panic-stricken, he went to the Senior Tutor, Dr Owen Wansburgh-Jones, who summoned Robin and told him that he must not go around challenging senior undergraduates to duels. The matter would be settled by mutual apologies and a handshake. 'And now,' he said, 'shall we take a glass of sherry together?'

During the winter term, while he was rehearsing, Robin received another summons to see the Senior Tutor.

I put on my cap and gown and appeared very promptly. The Senior Tutor was sitting at his desk smoking a pipe. 'Good morning, Maugham, I have something to tell you. It is not so much that each night when you illegally climb into college that I fear you will fall and maim yourself for life; far more important is that the place you have elected to climb in at is directly beneath my windows – and it disturbs my sleep. So I would be grateful if, in future, you will ask me for an exit permit for your rehearsals which will be readily granted.' Then he smiled and added, 'Good luck with the play.' From that moment my whole attitude to authority changed. I couldn't believe after the misery of Eton I could find such happiness in Cambridge.

Robin wrote a thriller for the ADC called *Thirteen for Dinner* which was produced on 11 February 1935 for a week and played to full houses. Nellie took a party of six to see it but later said that she was pleased that Freddie had been unable to join them, as the line 'Let's face it, your father may live for years and years and years' produced spontaneous laughter from their row. She thought the play interesting in parts but immature. At the final-night party Robin gave extravagant presents to the large company: silver powder compacts for the girls and solid silver cigarette cases for the men, all engraved with his signature. Robin congratulated himself that, after only a few months, he had made an impact on Cambridge life. He followed up his success by directing his own one-act play, *The Walking Stick*, which featured in an ADC evening at the Duke of York's Theatre, London, in December 1935. Willie attended initial rehearsals for this and suggested several cuts and alterations which sharpened the piece considerably.

Included in the party to see *Thirteen for Dinner* had been G. B. Stern, one of Willie's favourites, known to close friends as 'Peter'.

A popular novelist, she was best known for her sagas of Jewish life, typified by *The Matriarch*, dramatised in 1929 with Ethel Irving in the lead. Peter was a bun-faced woman with a lumpy body and a mannish haircut which did nothing to flatter her. She had no dress sense and Noël Coward may have had her in mind when he described a woman who looked as if she had been upholstered by Maples. Although she was well off and lived in style in Albany, she had a mean streak; Robin and Pamela Frankau usually took a bottle of wine when they visited her but it was never opened. 'Another one for my store,' she would crow delightedly or 'Oh dear, I've mislaid the corkscrew.' After experiencing this several times Pamela Frankau produced a corkscrew from her handbag, opened the bottle she had just brought and said, 'Glasses?'

Pamela Frankau, the daughter of Gilbert Frankau and an accomplished novelist in her own right, was one of the set of literary figures who were friends of the London Maughams. Her grandmother Julia was a friend of Willie's, but he was not always the only linking factor. Nellie and Freddie got to know Arnold Bennett as a neighbour in Cadogan Square and in a similar way became friends with A. A. Milne and his family who lived at Cotchford Farm near Tye House in Hartfield. Diana remembered Christopher Robin as a tough little boy determined to win at games and felt sorry for him growing up in the shadow, as it were, of Winnie-the-Pooh. She often played golf with his father who was also determined to win and unwilling to concede the smallest advantage. He had a reputation for aloofness but there was no reserve when he was with the Maughams and he was particularly fond of Nellie: 'a visit from her, or to her, was a tonic for any depression of weather or spirits,' as he put it.

By this time Kate was established as a moderately successful author. Her fourth book, *Tory Blaize*, evoked a long, handwritten letter from Willie asking why it was not better. He went on to tell her that she made her novels out of her daydreams and her daydreams were extremely commonplace. He reassured her that she had gifts but they would never be of use unless she applied them to observation enriched by experience and active, vivid, imaginative invention.

At some point in her literary progress Kate became friends with Humbert Wolfe who worked as a civil servant at the Ministry of Labour but was also an established poet. He was noted for his bons mots: on one occasion he took Leon M. Lion, the actor manager, to one of Kate's parties and, as she left, Lion said, 'Goodbye, Mrs Bruce. I don't know when I enjoyed a cocktail more.' Wolfe flashed back, 'You mean you don't know when you enjoyed a cocktail more often.' It was Wolfe who introduced Pamela Frankau to Kate who learned later that Pamela was his mistress. His wife Jessie had refused to divorce him and the affair which lasted many years was conducted in great secrecy in a series of service flats. Pamela was in bed with him when he died in his sleep in 1940 aged fifty-four. As she told her nephew, Tim d'Arch Smith, she was advised by a friendly doctor to clear the flat of all evidence of her presence – 'Do not leave a hairpin.'

In 1935 Kate and her husband Bob bought the lease of 79 Cadogan Square, three doors away from her parents' house. Some friends suggested to Bob that this might be a rash move and reminded him of ancient music-hall jokes about mothers-in-law, but it worked out well, though sometimes it was difficult to decide if No. 79 was an annexe to No. 73 or vice versa. The Bruces' move to such a large house from a much smaller one in Kensington Square was prompted by Bob's inheritance of a collection of Chinese jades and ceramics begun by his great-uncle, Sir Frederick Bruce, in 1850. His father, Lord Elgin, had been minister in Peking and many of the pieces came from the Summer Palace. This collection, added to the one Bob had built up himself, needed space to display it. The new house also gave them room for mammoth parties as well as intimate ones and No. 79 became a popular salon for the likes of H. G. Wells, Baroness Budberg, Ivor Novello, Elinor Glyn, Hugh Walpole, Noël Coward, Violet Loraine, Mary Ellis, Willie, when he was in London, and Syrie when he was not.

It was at one of Syrie's parties that Kate first met Elinor Glyn, the writer who had scandalised and delighted the Edwardians with *Three Weeks*, and introduced 'It' into the vocabulary as a euphemism for sexual attraction. 'I have a message for you,' she once announced to Kate who, knowing of her interest in the occult, waited expectantly for a communication from the spirit world. After a long, dramatic pause, she continued solemnly: 'If you laugh less often, speak lower, spend less time with women and put more ice into your expression, you will see the look you want to see in men's eyes even when you are sixty.' She delivered her epigrams and aphorisms with an inscrutable expression on her face and nobody quite knew if she was serious. Beverley Nichols decided that she was making fun of him when she declared that, in a previous life, he had been a horse. She once exclaimed to him that she had never let sex touch the hem of her garment but she gave a different impression when she talked to Kate about her youth. 'House parties were so different in those days. Then, there was always a bachelor next door to you: nowadays there's always a bathroom.'

In 1934, Freddie had been appointed to the Court of Appeal by the Prime Minister, Ramsay MacDonald, to fill a place left vacant by the resignation of Lord Justice Lawrence. In 1935 he was made a Lord of Appeal in Ordinary to fill another vacant place, caused by the death of Lord Tomlin. This meant being made a Life Peer and sitting in the House of Lords. On 26 September Nellie recorded her excitement in her diary in red ink to highlight the occasion. On 20 January 1936 she noted the death of King George V and the following day the summons of Freddie to St James's Palace to meet the new king.

On 7 March she wrote about the occupation by Hitler of the demilitarised Rhine with 60,000 troops and of everyone's alarm but the crisis did not last and tension relaxed. Confident of the future, Kate and Bob bought a large house, Sandcroft, built by Lord Gladstone's son, on the front at Littlestone. The main attraction was the golf course and the Bruces entertained parties of players though sometimes a non-golfer was included. When Noël Coward stayed with them, Freddie enquired if he played. 'I used to,' Coward replied, 'but I had to give it up; it made me cry so terribly.'

In July 1936, Liza married Vincent Paravicini, son of the Swiss Minister to the Court of St James, at St Margaret's Church by Westminster Abbey. It was one of those society events that delight the press, and typical was the *Daily Express* in which the William Hickey column eulogised: 'Was it the opening night of a C. B. Cochran show? No, it was an entire issue of *Vogue* come to life! Liza, dressed by Schiaparelli, was "the bride of the month".'

Although Willie and Syrie sat together she afterwards complained that he contrived to ignore her and refused to be photographed with her. The guest list was impressive: apart from Grandma Barnardo, Nellie, Freddie and other members of the family, there were many diplomatic representatives, a scattering of minor royalty, members of the aristocracy and 'names' including Osbert Sitwell, Marie Tempest and Elsie de Wolfe. At the reception held at the Swiss Legation the cake, 'created' by Oliver Messel the stage designer, made a suitably elegant centrepiece. The presents were also suitably elegant but the most practical was a gift of shares from Willie together with the lease of No. 15 Wilton Street, off Grosvenor Place, which Syrie decorated for the couple. They left for the Villa Mauresque which Willie had lent them for their honeymoon. In the meantime Haxton and Willie went off to Bad Gastein for the cure, followed by several hectic days in Budapest and Vienna, which undid its effects.

That year Robin and Honor went to Salzburg for the opera and Haxton arrived to take them both to *The Meistersingers* as his guests. He was his usual charming, solicitous self but inevitably he tried to persuade Honor into bed with him, as if his reputation as a seducer might suffer if he did not at least try. He refused to admit defeat and almost forced his way into her bedroom with a drunken story about losing his camera. The sight of this middle-aged man behaving as if he was irresistibly attractive was not amusing. Robin managed to coax him away under the icy surveillance of Honor. Within minutes he had recovered his poise and insisted on taking Robin with him to a beer hall where elderly men in lederhosen eyed young hustlers similarly but rather more alluringly dressed. They were joined at their table by a pretty youth with pale blond hair that flopped over his blue eyes. Haxton, with a few ribald comments and a grope under the table to make sure 'it was as good as ever', introduced Dieter as a Viennese factory worker who spent his spare time on the game. In turn they were joined by Felix who looked about fourteen and had a cheeky smile for his 'Onkel Gerald'. Shortly after, they went off together leaving Robin and Dieter alone. After buying a bottle of kirsch they walked a little way to a hilly open space where they sat talking until sunrise. Although Robin gave him money, they did not have sex, but Dieter related the story of his life.

Nearly fifty years afterwards Robin included Dieter's story in his autobiographical *Search for Nirvana*, by which time it had become an overblown mixture of sentimentality and crude sexual detail. Essentially it was the hustler's tale of hardship, thwarted love and a noble heart that has probably changed only slightly since it was first used by rent boys when market forces became a reality at the dawn of civilisation. At the age of twenty Robin might be excused for his wide-eyed naivety and gullible acceptance of a concoction of lies and half-truths. Unfortunately he went on being naive and gullible, ready to welcome the next slick operator who had a glint of sexual promise in his eyes.

In the late summer Robin was invited by Willie to stay at the Villa Mauresque for the first time and Freddie made no objection, apparently deciding that there was no danger now that Robin was unofficially engaged. He had met Gillian Dearmer, the daughter of Dr Percy Dearmer, a Canon of Westminster Abbey, at G. B. Stern's chambers in Albany. 'Peter' had engineered the encounter between her two 'protégés', as she called them, and was delighted with the resulting mutual attraction. It was a case of first love and, as Robin put it, 'We would dine at some country inn and then walk through the soft, misty fields hand in hand.' On holiday with her and her brother in Berlin, he bought her a modest ring to seal their love until he could afford to buy her a proper one when they became officially engaged. In time the romance faded though they remained good friends. Early on, she had been introduced to Willie at one of Humbert Wolfe's parties and immediately sensed the hostility in his appraising stare. Apparently she did not fit in with his preconceived ideas of the type of woman Robin should marry.

Although Robin had heard accounts of the style in which Willie lived, none of them measured up to the actuality and it is easy to understand the general effect of opulence on an impressionable twenty-year-old. But only the year before Willie had very nearly sold the villa and moved permanently to London after a difficult time with Haxton, whom he alleged was increasingly addicted to alcohol. The plan had been to settle him in the Paris apartment at 65 Rue La Fontaine, but some sort of compromise had been reached and Haxton had been on his best behaviour. As Robin discovered, the running of the villa was in Haxton's control and he made an excellent job of it.

Soon after he arrived he was invited with Willie and Haxton to a lunch party. The other guests included Elsa Maxwell and the writer Dorothy Parker, but for some reason Miss Parker had not arrived by the time luncheon was announced. Robin, trailing in the wake of the other guests, noticed in an alcove behind a screen a table on which a cocktail-shaker of daiquiri and glasses stood in reserve. Needing, he told himself, more Dutch courage, he moved stealthily behind the screen and reached for the cocktail-shaker. At that second a small, thin hand also reached out and an American voice said: 'Mine first, I think.' It was Dorothy Parker who had only just arrived. 'Let's finish it,' she suggested sensibly and they quickly emptied the shaker.

Over lunch, at which the latecomers were placed next to each other, Elsa Maxwell, who knew the details of 'Dottie' Parker's background, told a series of anti-Jewish jokes. Aware of Robin's discomfort and distaste Maxwell, in her parade-ground voice, observed: 'You don't seem to appreciate my jokes, young man.' Robin, flushed with embarrassment, said: 'I don't appreciate anti-semitism.' In the silence that followed Parker laid her small hand on Robin's and gave it a tiny squeeze of approval but said nothing. The conversation, hastily resumed by the hosts, moved to safer topics and much later someone mentioned Augustus John, the painter, whom Willie had known since 1914. Seeing her chance to take the floor again Maxwell boomed: 'Augustus John is one of my dearest and most intimate friends.' Instantly Parker's voice interposed: 'Elsa knows Augustus John so intimately that she calls him Augustus Jack.'

The rest of Robin's detailed account of this visit given in *Escape from the Shadows* has to be treated with caution. By the time he wrote it in the early 1970s, he took a gleeful pleasure in shocking people with revelations of his homosexuality and, where memory failed, his imagination took over. He began with an account of a visit with Haxton to a brothel in Nice. This had been proposed by Willie who regarded his love for Gillian Dearmer with derision. 'You just want to go to bed with her. You're a vigorous young man. You need a romp.' After a tour of various louche bars and bordellos, Robin ended up with a young girl of his own age who told him she was really a stenographer in Paris, but she worked in the brothel two nights a week to pay for her holiday. This unlikely story made the transaction seem less sordid and he enjoyed the 'romp' as prescribed.

The next evening, according to Robin, Haxton took him to his yacht moored at Villefranche, introduced him to a pretty, golden-haired youth called Laurent, and left them together. They had sex and the next day Robin declared that he and Laurent were wildly in love with each other. Disillusionment followed when Willie announced that Laurent was a male prostitute whom he had employed to sleep with Robin. Willie contemptuously dismissed talk of love and said that Gerald would pay Laurent off and he would not be seen again. Laurent was actually Louis Legrand, nicknamed 'Lulu', who was one of Haxton's boyfriends and was known as such to gay visitors to the villa.

On 27 September, Harold Nicolson arrived to stay and was immediately attracted to Robin. It was the start of a friendship which deepened with the years.

When heterosexual guests were present, Haxton and Willie behaved circumspectly, although Haxton sometimes forgot himself and inadvertently called Willie 'ducky', or, if he was drunk, said something outrageous. The atmosphere was entirely different when the party was completely composed of gay or bisexual men. Willie spoke in a manner which would have shocked his straight friends and there were occasions when his uninhibited behaviour would have disgusted them.

Robin returned to Cambridge bursting with excitement at the freedom and sybaritic style of living at the villa. He had been flattered, pampered, encouraged in his dream of becoming a famous writer and had his homosexual propensities condoned. No doubt it amused Willie to play the over-indulgent uncle as a counterpoint to Freddie's strict father but later, when he criticised Robin's behaviour behind his back, he conveniently forgot that he had been a major influence in the way he developed.

# VIII

## Lord Chancellor

In October 1936, Freddie's second book, *The Tichborne Case*, was published to good reviews. He had spent many months researching it, reading over five thousand printed pages of notes in the civil trial, over four thousand in the criminal trial, and a mass of letters and other material. The summing up to the jury in the second trial alone took twenty days and all this Freddie conscientiously absorbed before beginning to write his epic treatise. It discussed the legal niceties of this famous case of attempted fraud in which a fat, uncouth butcher from Wapping claimed to be the elegant, French-born Sir Roger Tichborne, the missing heir to immense estates and wealth in England.

Freddie was in his element with such a scenario and it is not surprising that Robin later used it as a basis for a novel and a play. Willie praised his brother for his lucid exposition but it was a disappointment after the originality of his first book, *The Case of Jean Calas*, which had appeared in 1928. This dealt with the notorious trial of Calas for the murder of his son Marc-Antoine in 1761 at Toulouse, the verdict of guilty, his execution and eventual rehabilitation due to the efforts of Voltaire. Freddie had been intrigued by a legal study, *Les Grands Procès de l'Historie* (1925), which argued that Voltaire was mistaken. Freddie investigated all the available documentary evidence for himself, finally ending his research in Toulouse. His startling conclusion was that the son had committed suicide by hanging; moreover, he presented an imaginative reconstruction to show how this was technically possible.

The London Maughams saw little of Syrie after her divorce
but they could not miss evidence in the press of her unquenchable
ability to combine an active social life with a shrewd sense of
business. In 1932 she had worked for Mrs Wallis Warfield
Simpson at her home in Bryanston Square and became sufficiently friendly with her to be lent her flat in Brighton when she
was recovering from an illness. By the time Mrs Simpson was
embroiled in her affair with the Prince of Wales, Syrie was one of
the large group who could be trusted to keep silent. She supplied
Mrs Simpson with furniture for her new house at 16 Cumberland
Terrace in 1936 and also carried out a decorating commission at
the prince's home, Fort Belvedere. It was here, it is said, that the
three of them found themselves trapped in a lavatory and the
prince burst into the vulgar song about three old ladies in a
similar predicament; the women shrieked with laughter until
servants released them.

The British press, with the staggering restraint of the time, said
nothing about the royal affair but it was widely reported abroad
and rumours filtered back. Then, on 3 December, the British
papers were at last full of the news that the recently acclaimed
King Edward wished to marry Mrs Simpson. The general public
was stunned at the thought of a divorced woman becoming queen
and, as Freddie punningly put it, 'Consternation reigns'. All the
royals cancelled their duties and social commitments, and the
King retreated to Fort Belvedere. On 10 December Edward
abdicated and two days later Freddie was once again at St James's
Palace to be sworn in with the Privy Council before the new
King.

The following year, on 12 May, Freddie and Nellie were in
Westminster Abbey for the Coronation. They arrived at seven-
thirty and separated; Nellie was seated on the right of the altar
between Lady Roche and Lady Kennett, and Freddie with his
peers in Poets' Corner. The King arrived at eleven-fifteen and,
after nearly five hours' wait, the ceremony began. Nellie described
it as quite lovely and impressive. Afterwards they lunched at the
House of Lords – 'abominable' was Nellie's comment on the

meal. They eventually got away in their car at seven, having waited from three-thirty standing under an awning that let in the rain. Others, she discovered, were still there two hours later. That night they had twelve guests to a late supper and five days later they were guests at the Royal Ball at Buckingham Palace.

On 21 May they set off with Kate and Bob on the 'Coronation Cruise' to watch the Review of the Fleet by the King aboard the *Victoria and Albert*. At ten that evening all the ships suddenly lit up and there were fireworks until midnight. Nellie wrote in her diary that Commander Thomas Woodruff who intended to give a commentary for wireless listeners had evidently taken the order to 'splice the mainbrace' too enthusiastically; he kept repeating 'the Fleet'sh lit up' until he was removed. The phrase passed into the language and was used as the title for the next lavish George Black 'musical frolic' at the London Hippodrome. To be 'lit up' became slang for being drunk.

Robin's Cambridge career ended a few weeks later with only a second in the English tripos and the same in law. Freddie was disappointed by the results but Robin believed the work he had contributed to *Granta* far more important to his future than qualifications or evidence of sporting prowess. Freddie thoroughly disapproved of his writing, so it had become a secret which the family kept from him with some difficulty. Once, when Freddie and Nellie had arrived unexpectedly in Cambridge on a visit, Robin had had to divert attention away from posters for *Granta* which included 'New story by R. Maugham'. He was aided by Nellie who burst into fevered conversation to distract Freddie as soon as she spotted one of the posters. In his final year Robin had become editor of *Crescent*, the Trinity Hall magazine, but dared not take on *Granta* when he had the opportunity.

Robin's conversion to socialism followed his experience of working in the Cambridge Juvenile Employment Office. This had been at the instigation of one of his tutors and he was shocked by countless examples of the exploitation of children. His convictions were strengthened when Honor took him with her to London's

East End where he could hardly believe the conditions he saw in the homes they visited.

In 1931 Honor had become a 'school care-committee secretary' for a school in Limehouse. Most of the fathers were dock workers who had no guarantee of employment from one day to the next and their poverty was reflected in the children's health, categorised by the school doctor into nutritional grades. Honor never saw a child graded as 'satisfactorily nourished'; most were graded 'borderline starvation'. This, and what she learned on visits to their homes, made her tackle the members of Parliament she knew socially. When they patronised her with clichés like 'There will always be rich and poor, my dear', she frequently lost her temper. The frightening fact was that conditions had not changed fundamentally since Morrison wrote his books during the 1890s and Willie had described the slums south of the Thames in *Liza of Lambeth*.

Honor was particularly appalled that modern techniques were not used to eliminate the suffering caused to women by constant child-bearing and the resultant misery of bringing up large families in the slums on next-to-no income. She discovered that hospitals warned women in poor health of the serious consequences of further pregnancies, but without giving guidance on how to avoid them. Birth control was not considered to be a fit subject to discuss with patients. Indignant at this antiquated attitude, Honor went to see her friend Dr Marie Stopes, the pioneer of modern birth control. With the co-operation of a sympathetic district health visitor, it was arranged that women badly in need of help would attend the Marie Stopes Clinic. The clinic was free but Honor started a fund to pay for other expenses such as fares and the cost of baby minders. Medical checks at the end of a year showed that the health and well-being of the women had greatly improved, and none of them had conceived. The findings assisted Dr Stopes in her campaign to overcome prejudice among medics. In 1992 Honor said: 'Few women in this century have done so much for the welfare of their own sex.'

Diana was to make her own discoveries about life in London's slums. In 1932 she had married Kenneth Marr-Johnson, who was later to become a senior partner in Cluttons, the chartered surveyors. At first they lived in Cadogan Street and then moved to a newly built home at 8 Porchester Close in Bayswater. Much of the area had lost its Victorian grandeur but Westbourne Grove, once compared to Bond Street, still retained traces of elegance. At Whiteleys, the first purpose-built English department store, a small orchestra in the balcony restaurant played soothing selections while waitresses served dainty meals to ladies in hats and mannequins strolled between the tables modelling the latest fashions. On the ground floor, the magnificent food hall with its elaborate displays rivalled those of Harrods.

At the other end of Westbourne Grove, Bradleys of Chepstow Place still claimed to be the leading London couture house for furs and clothes. It was here at Bradleys Corner, as bus conductors called it, that Freddie had regularly bought exclusive items for Nellie; one year for her birthday an evening gown, another an opera cloak, and one Christmas a fitted dressing case. It was a store for the well-to-do only, but not far to the north of Westbourne Grove, behind the still-pretty façades, houses had become festering slums where people almost starved to death.

Diana was asked to join the Paddington Housing Council, a voluntary body dedicated to improving conditions. There was endless discussion under the chairmanship of Sir Edgar Bonham Carter but in practice little could be done except to lobby the authorities. When Diana began regular visits to houses, the shock was total. Inside, the buildings were crumbling, toilets were frequently blocked, taps broken, roofs leaking, walls sweating damp and, over all, there was the stench compounded of wet rot, dry rot, mice and bugs. Yet the women, old before their time, fought for their families who were crammed into one or two rooms without the most basic of amenities. At first Diana thought her visits might be resented and seen as gross impertinence but she was welcomed with cups of tea, sweet and sticky with condensed milk, as the women told her their troubles. Even when they realised she had no authority to alter their conditions, she was still welcomed.

Horrified when a baby was attacked by rats, she began to campaign, but, whoever she spoke to, the reply was always the same. Sometime in the future, but nobody knew when, all the property would be demolished and replaced with splendid new homes. But surely something could be done now, she argued. What about getting rid of the bugs for a start? Patiently it was explained that, as cyanide gas was needed, the houses had to be evacuated for two days and where would the people go? As for lists of essential repairs, why bother when there was the plan for new homes? It was circular argument which got nowhere, but gradually Diana and her fellow committee members, by making themselves tiresome to the powers-that-be, managed to get some of the problems alleviated. Once she was asked to speak at a public meeting at the local Town Hall; she had never done anything like it but, as she discovered, anger was a powerful antidote to shyness. After the meeting, the youngish, red-headed MP for North Paddington, Brendan Bracken, offered to help, and became a powerful ally.

Bracken was a close friend of Winston Churchill to whom he was later appointed Parliamentary Private Secretary before becoming Minister of Information and, finally, First Lord of the Admiralty. His business interests were in publishing and he became Chairman of the *Financial Times*, among other activities. Churchill's wife Clementine disliked him and Randolph resented his influence on his father. So close were the two men that gossip, completely unfounded, had it that Bracken was his illegitimate son. There even were those who suggested that the initial attraction might have been sexual. This speculation may have been a legacy of the allegations made about Churchill's homosexual activities while he was at Sandhurst. The story was widely publicised but he brought an action in the High Court which was settled in his favour. Robin, who knew both men, believed the idea of a liaison between Bracken and Churchill completely ludicrous.

At seventy-one, Freddie was reasonably content with life and assumed that his position as a Lord of Appeal in Ordinary would see him to retirement. When Nellie told him of rumours from the wives of legal men that he was likely to be offered the Lord Chancellorship he thought these were nonsense. It was a political appointment but, although he was a staunch Tory, he had no practical experience of the party that qualified him for it. It struck him as typically stupid of the press when it picked up the rumour and took the possibility seriously. It came as a complete surprise when he received a telephone call from No. 10 Downing Street requesting his attendance the following morning, 9 March 1938. He had never met Neville Chamberlain and found him stern and scrupulously correct as he discussed and then formally offered him what had once been the most influential role in the English Constitution. Freddie, with equal formality, accepted. Before he left he attempted an anecdote from the Latin about a humble soldier promoted to a senior command by Julius Caesar. When the soldier's colleagues later expressed surprise he retorted: 'Why should I doubt whether I am fit for the job if he thinks I can tackle it?' Chamberlain smiled for the first time since they had met. 'Much worried and greatly tried' was Freddie's verdict on him.

Nellie had collected as many of the family as she could to drive to Downing Street to be there when Freddie came out. They were all delighted when he told them the news and then stood back while reporters and photographers surrounded him. He maintained his usual phlegmatic calm and, as soon as they had finished, went off to spend the rest of the day playing golf as he had previously planned to do. Nellie, by contrast, spent the afternoon excitedly telephoning relatives and friends to chat about everything. In the evening she and Freddie had dinner with Kate and Bob before going to the cinema. In her diary Nellie described it as the most thrilling day of her life. The congratulations began to arrive by every post and within three days Freddie had received over four hundred letters and Nellie over a hundred. On 9 March, the appointment was officially announced and five days later, after an audience with the King, he went to the Law Courts where the family watched him sworn in. The following day, he took his seat on the Woolsack as Speaker to the House of Lords.

For historic reasons the Lord Chancellor has precedence in the royal presence and in public functions over all the peers and commoners in the land with the exceptions of the royal dukes and the Archbishop of Canterbury. Freddie found this tradition extraordinary but Nellie enjoyed the position it gave her, only a little lower than the female royals, and both agreed it had its comic side. For Freddie to follow in the steps of the great Cardinal Wolsey and Sir Thomas More (without the risk of having his head chopped off) was a singular honour and, although he never actually said so, it must have given him amused satisfaction to have reached an eminence which Willie could never emulate.

On 13 March Freddie telephoned Nellie to tell her that they had been 'commanded to spend the night at Windsor Castle'. That afternoon he bought a tiara of diamonds and pearls as a surprise celebration present for her to wear on their visit. In her diary she wrote excitedly about it. They arrived by car just before five o'clock, were shown to their rooms in the Edward III tower and went on a brief tour before sitting down to tea. After bathing and dressing they were escorted to dinner at half-past eight. Freddie sat next to the Queen and Nellie to the King; Mary, the Queen Mother, was there too. Afterwards they all watched *The Drum*, a patriotic film about the British army helping an Indian prince to overthrow his usurping uncle. At a dramatic climax, when the bagpipes played, the Queen delightedly took the King's hand and seemed to Nellie to be as excited as a young girl. Then the party returned to the Red Drawing-room for sandwiches, hot punches and pots of tea. The royals retired just after midnight; characteristically Nellie was far too excited to sleep properly.

Six months later it seemed Europe might be on the brink of war. On 14 September Freddie took Nellie to dinner at the Athenaeum and said that he had an astounding secret which he had to keep until nine o'clock when there was to be a public announcement. With ten minutes to go he could not contain himself and told her that Chamberlain was to fly to Munich to meet Hitler at Berchtesgaden the following day.

As a member of the Cabinet Freddie endorsed the effort of Neville Chamberlain to prevent a war. Throughout Europe fear was almost tangible and daily events did nothing to disperse it. Those old enough to remember the horrors of only twenty years before suffered terrible dread, their apprehension fed by the press and by scenes of the Spanish Civil War on cinema newsreels. Only the foolhardy or stupidly patriotic could be under any illusions about the effects of intense bombing and poisonous gas.

The crisis staggered on and then Hitler agreed to a meeting with France, Italy and Great Britain. The House of Commons cheered when told this on 28 September and the next morning the entire Cabinet including Freddie, accompanied by Nellie, went to Heston aerodrome to see Chamberlain off to Munich. The next day the agreement announced by the four powers meant there would be no war, and Chamberlain came back to a hysterical hero's welcome. *The Times* said: 'No conqueror returning from victory on the battlefield has come adorned with nobler laurels.' Nellie, Kate and Robin watched Chamberlain's arrival in Downing Street from a window at the Privy Council. As the cheering crowd mobbed his car, Kate voiced her sense of foreboding: suppose Hitler was bluffing?

The widespread abuse of Chamberlain following the Munich Agreement outraged Freddie's sense of fairness. He was unfamiliar with the cynical opportunism of politicians and he was incensed by the hostile attitude of those who had previously supported the Prime Minister's action. He published his 'reply' in 1944, *The Truth About the Munich Crisis*, and stated the facts with legal clarity. Whatever the arguments for or against the Munich Agreement, Freddie's unique position as an insider and as a non-politician makes his view of events essential to any serious assessment.

Public opinion which had been against war now gradually changed as it accepted that confrontation with Hitler was inevitable. Kate said that the months following Munich were among the most painful of her life. When people, knowing whose daughter she was, criticised the government and poured abuse on Chamberlain she had a vicarious sensation of guilt and frequently walked out of social events in tears. Robin, the angry socialist, had no time for the Tories and was so appalled by events that he swung from pacifism and joined the tank section of the Inns of Court Regiment to express his protest. When Chamberlain came to dinner at Cadogan Square Robin could barely contain himself and sat sullenly manufacturing a verbal hand grenade to throw into the complacent calm of the small talk. When the opportunity came, he began loudly, 'Speaking as a member of the middle class—' but his father cut in, 'Speak for yourself!'

Robin refused to accept a commission in the Inns of Court Regiment because he lacked the confidence to be an officer.

I thought I would be so inefficient that I would lead my men to certain death! I was a trooper for a year and I had the most enchanting time. I discovered to my amazement that the love of one boy for another or one man for another wasn't at all limited to the upper-middle class to which I belonged. Subsequent experience and enquiries have convinced me that homosexuality is rife in what is called the lower income group – manual workers and miners for instance. Next comes the upper class or aristocracy and the upper-middle class, equally as free, but then in the middle and lower-middle classes there is an intolerable prejudice against homosexuality which has never ceased to shock me. Many lives have been ruined by the kind of London surburban attitude of parents to all sex, which has thwarted the natural instincts of their children and made them into unhappy, neurotic wrecks.

## Robin was miserable studying law:

I had to go to a crammers and I shall never forget the boredom of catching the nine o'clock tube train to Chancery Lane and the walk to the building, knowing you'd be there all day and you'd get back, weary and tired, with homework to do and no proper life at all. Uncle Willie shone like a meteor in the dreariness of my existence and on one occasion gave a dinner party in my honour and there were E. M. Forster, Osbert Sitwell and Christopher Isherwood – to whom I took an immediate and very strong liking. Willie once said that Isherwood held the future of the English novel in his hands; he never said anything like that about me!

He enjoyed life more when his father got him the temporary job of judge's marshal, a sort of secretary-assistant, to Mr Justice Macnaghten at two guineas a day. Gillian Dearmer heard that Robin was 'the life and soul of the judge's circuit' and kept everyone in fits of laughter behind the scenes. As a reward for this stint his parents funded a trip to Mexico and the USA. It was while he was staying with Bert Alanson and his wife at their home in San Francisco that he met Marshall Dill Jnr at a party. The young men were instantly attracted to each other but were not to meet again until the war when Dill, then in the US Navy, was posted to England.

After Robin passed his Bar exams in February 1939, Willie sent him a letter of congratulation to which he added a warning about drinking too much. It had no effect because, like most young men, Robin could see no danger in getting 'lit up' occasionally and thought it impossible that he could ever become dependent on alcohol. He had no immediate plans for work until Humbert Wolfe got him the post of Private Secretary to Sir Herbert Morgan, the newly appointed director of the National Service Campaign. Robin decided that its efforts were too feeble and wrote a memo dated 15 May 1939 proposing a more positive approach. It was socialist in tone and in places naive but at its core lay the covert accusation that the country lacked leadership. By roundabout means it was brought to Winston Churchill's attention and Robin was invited to Chartwell one Sunday to have tea and to discuss it.

At this time Churchill was still regarded with suspicion by Freddie and fellow Tory grandees, who thought he was conniving, opportunistic and a dangerous warmonger who should be kept firmly in the political wilderness. At the Constitutional Club the previous December Freddie had attacked him in a widely reported speech, demanding that politicians who advocated war without considering the probable results should be impeached. It was the supreme insult, implying treason against the State. But

Robert Maugham, lawyer
and 'Father of Legal Journalism'

Edith Maugham.
Willie kept this photograph
as a reminder of her beauty.

Willie, aged eleven

Willie in Heidelberg, aged seventeen

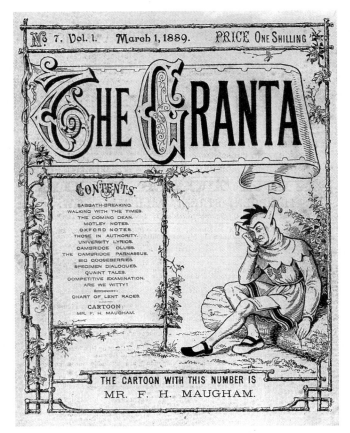

Freddie in thoughtful mood
on the cover of *The Granta*, 1889
Harry Maugham, writer and poet

THE "TIVOLI" STRAND : THEATRE AND RESTAURANT : WALTER EMDEN, Architect

The Tivoli Theatre, Strand,
where Willie often spent Saturday afternoons

Charles Frohman

A worried Shakespeare in front of Maugham posters

Billie Burke starred in *Mrs Dot*
and *The Land of Promise* in New York

Ethel Irving in Willie's first
dramatic success, *Lady Frederick*

Gladys Cooper,
Willie's favourite leading lady

Constance Collier, who praised
Willie for his kindness to her

Mrs. Syrie Maugham
in a Louiseboulanger
dress

Syrie, the epitome of fashion,
drawn for *The American Sketch*, January 1929

Syrie, Liza and Willie at the Villa Eliza, 1925

Gerald Haxton

Beverley Nichols

Cyril Butcher

The Villa Mauresque.
Note the sign against evil over the front entrance.

Freddie Maugham, Robert Bruce, Kate Mary Bruce,
unknown and Noël Coward on a golfing weekend at Littlestone

Freddie had failed to understand that Churchill's demand for action against Germany when he knew how ill-prepared Britain was for any form of military adventure was in fact no more than political gamesmanship within Parliament.

Robin intended to keep his visit to Churchill a secret but Freddie, sensing he was up to something, cross-examined him and under pressure Robin told him of his invitation without disclosing the reason for it. Freddie stared at him solemnly and then observed tartly: 'There is no accounting for taste.'

Churchill greeted him with: 'And how is your sainted father?' Over a whisky and soda he listened intently while Robin explained the situation that had prompted the memo. The information probably only confirmed what Churchill already knew and it is doubtful if he would have bothered with Robin at all had he not been the son of the Lord Chancellor. Significantly, he suggested that Robin contact him immediately if he discovered further matters of interest. At this stage Churchill could only guess how long the uneasy peace might last and information from Robin, however unimportant in itself, could add to the knowledge he gleaned from other sources to be used in his campaign against Chamberlain. Robin, flattered by his attention, did not realise that he had been recruited as one of Churchill's many undercover informants: instead, he believed he had simply made a friend of a man he admired. Nor did it occur to him, as it must have done to Churchill, that his story of Whitehall incompetence might have been better told to his father who, as a member of the Cabinet, was in a better position to do something about it.

The most powerful of Churchill's circle of informants was William Stephenson, a Canadian-born millionaire businessman. While in Germany to purchase steel for car manufacture, Stephenson discovered that almost all production had been switched to clandestine preparations for war. As the British government seemed indifferent he formed an alliance with Desmond Morton, a special assistant to Churchill. The upshot of this was the formation of an unofficial, secret group responsible for sabotage and assassination in war. After the fall of France,

Willie was to work for Stephenson who became vital to the organisation of American Intelligence, the OSS in particular.

In late July, Robin went on holiday to the Villa Mauresque where relations between Willie and Haxton were amicable, and plans to separate postponed indefinitely. Not surprisingly a second attempt to sell the villa had failed as it was generally assumed that Mussolini would invade France if war broke out. Earlier that month Willie had been told by Freddie that this seemed inevitable but the timing would depend on Hitler, whose claims on Poland might provoke another crisis in 'several years' time'.

This sanguine attitude stemmed from Chamberlain and explains why Freddie and Nellie sailed for Canada in August in the *Empress of Britain* to fulfil a programme of official engagements at the invitation of the Canadian Bar Association. Chamberlain considered it important that Freddie should behave as if times were normal but requested him to put the official British view whenever possible. This he did in talks with the Canadian Prime Minister and other officials. Escorted by the Under-Secretary of State, Freddie and Nellie fulfilled a hectic schedule of lunches, dinners, garden parties and entertainments specially staged for their benefit. On most of these occasions Freddie was expected to speak on legal or topical subjects. In Quebec they were guests of honour at a dinner for 800 and in Toronto he opened the Canadian National Exhibition. His voice shaken by patriotic emotion he described the event as symbolic of the unity of the British Empire.

The visit was like a royal progress and he found it exhausting, but Nellie was in her element and she was very disappointed when Freddie, disturbed by news of the non-aggression pact between Hitler and Stalin, cut the visit short by ten days; sanguinity had proved misplaced. Before they sailed, news came through that Britain had signed a Treaty of Alliance with Poland and he was besieged by reporters asking for his view of the situation. They arrived home on 31 August exhausted. In the early hours of the next morning Freddie was awakened by a summons to attend a Cabinet meeting immediately.

At Downing Street, members learned that Hitler had invaded Poland. Chamberlain was reluctant to take action but while he prayed for a miracle, the Poles were being bombed and massacred. He finally gave in to pressure from his Cabinet colleagues on Sunday morning, 3 September, when he sent an ultimatum giving Hitler two hours to cease military operations. There was no reply and, at eleven, Britain and Germany were at war. The following day Freddie resigned as Lord Chancellor.

Winston Churchill now joined the Cabinet as First Lord of the Admiralty and, in a preliminary discussion with Chamberlain, had made it a condition that certain people should go: Freddie was an obvious candidate for his blacklist. Even if Churchill had forgiven him, it is impossible to believe that he could have lasted after Chamberlain ceased to be Prime Minister in May 1940. In his autobiography Freddie said that he had considered giving up his office in the event of war, not because he thought himself incapable of carrying on, but because 'ordinary people' would think he was too old at seventy-two and should give way to a younger man. This reference to age was ironic; Chamberlain was seventy, Churchill sixty-five. Freddie went on: 'And I personally to some extent welcomed a resolution of the Cabinet which involved my retirement.'

In replying to a letter of sympathy from Lord Simon who had previously written to him to congratulate him for 'the trouncing of Churchill' he was more explicit, suggesting that his political conduct and speeches had 'not altogether pleased some of my colleagues' and he added: 'I am a little sad at leaving my great position so soon and should be sadder if I thought it was perhaps because I had done my job badly.' Far from doing his job badly, he gave to it an honest detachment above the usual party interests.

In acknowledgement of his services Freddie was offered an hereditary peerage but, before accepting, he discussed the implications with Robin. At first Robin was not keen because a title of any kind offended his socialist principles, but then reluctantly gave Freddie his support. When, in 1958, Robin became Viscount Maugham, his reservations had completely faded and he relished the title; as Myles Hildyard put it: 'He loved being a Lord and being Lordly.'

# IX

## Cry Havoc

At the beginning of the war, Willie was commissioned by the British government to write a series of propaganda articles about France and he toured various locations, including the Maginot line. The job was actually a cover for the important task of assessing French fighting resolve. His secret reports were sent disguised as personal letters to Freddie who then passed them to the appropriate intelligence-gathering section in Whitehall. This may give a clue to the war work Freddie did at Westminster in addition to his role as a Lord of Appeals in Ordinary. In 1941 he also joined a working group under Lord Salisbury to oversee and advise on the conduct of the war.

When Freddie was invited to take on the time-consuming task of Treasurer of Lincoln's Inn, he said that he would accept the role, but his availability would be subject to the demands of his work at Westminster. This displeased his fellow benchers, who anticipated an enthusiastic acceptance without conditions, and they looked elsewhere. In 1946 he again refused the post of Treasurer on the plea of public duties, to the bewilderment of friends, who could not understand why he had turned down an opportunity of serving in an office so highly esteemed.

The 'phoney war' ended with the German invasion of Denmark and Norway in April 1940 and events moved with frightening speed, culminating in the Dunkirk evacuation in May and the fall of France in June. Willie, leaving Haxton and Legrand in charge at the Villa Mauresque on 16 June, went to Cannes where he managed to get a place aboard a collier, the

*Saltersgate*. The ship, designed for a crew of thirty-eight, was crammed with some five hundred refugees who had to live in the filthy coal holds. There was no bedding, no proper lavatories, the supply of water was strictly rationed, washing forbidden and the only food was corned beef, rough biscuits and tea.

In sensational headlines the British and American press reported that Willie had vanished, and speculated about his fate. Freddie was inundated with enquiries and tried to get information from the Red Cross and the American Embassy but they knew nothing. Meanwhile, the *Saltersgate* travelled with a slow-moving convoy via Gibraltar, where Willie managed to get a telephone message to Nellie who was beginning to accept that he might be dead. A week later the ship docked at Liverpool and Willie arrived at the Dorchester Hotel, London, on 8 July. For three weeks he had not been able to wash or take his clothes off and he stank, but before having a bath he telephoned Nellie and arranged to go to Cadogan Square the following day. He kept a duplicate wardrobe at the hotel so he arrived as well-turned-out as ever, but Nellie and Freddie were horrified by his emaciated condition. He was in good spirits, apparently none the worse, and gave them a graphic account of his journey on the 'hell-ship'.

He also told his story on BBC radio and recorded other talks, including one to France to counter the Vichy government's anti-British propaganda. Speaking of his escape, Willie made the point that the voyage began with a chilly division of the classes and ended with a thoroughly democratic mix-up. Brian Howard, the journalist and poet, who escaped on an English collier from Cannes on 24 June, had precisely the opposite experience which he told in a series of articles for *Horizon* at the end of 1940. To begin with, he said, everyone intermingled, but then quickly separated. 'Thus were the social levels, at the last, so mercilessly mapped out that one was able to find any given person within a minute. And that is why I find Mr Maugham's experience so very surprising.'

There had been a curious encounter between Willie and Howard just as war was declared. Haxton and Willie were searching for a new mooring for their yacht *Sara* after Ville-franche was taken over by the French navy, and they sailed into Bandol, a small port west of Toulon. Here they met Howard who was very worried about the fate of his German lover Toric who had been put into a local internment camp after an indiscriminate round-up of all male Germans up to the age of sixty-five. Many of them were anti-Nazis who had fled to France, including Lion Feuchtwanger, the author of *Jud Süss*. Howard himself had been forced to leave Germany in 1936 after writing a series of anti-Nazi articles that had begun in 1933 with one in the *New Statesman*. Klaus Mann's sister Erica described him as the first Englishman to foresee what was to come and to express his fears for others to read.

Howard, it is believed, was the model for Ambrose Silk in Evelyn Waugh's *Put Out More Flags* and Anthony Blanche in *Brideshead Revisited*. Although he was often dismissed as a flibbertigibbet, the facts show differently. Willie knew him and his family well, but when Howard appealed to him to use his influence over the matter of the refugees, he adamantly refused and was so angered that he referred to Howard in *Strictly Personal*, without naming him, as an averred coward. Howard, who volunteered for the RAF and worked for MI5, was to remark: 'That was a grinding time at Bandol when I visited Willie Maugham on behalf of the refugees and later had my conversation falsified for my pains in that unfortunate little book of his.'

The reason for Willie's anger was fear of being associated officially with someone who was openly proud of his homosexuality. He was to react in a similar manner when asked for his moral support in protesting against the British government's hounding of gay men in the 1950s, but his extreme reaction to Howard so much earlier was symptomatic of his growing paranoia.

Willie was determined to get a war job and spoke about it to his friend Duff Cooper, the Minister of Information, who had moved into the Dorchester because it was supposed to be bombproof. It was agreed that Willie should go to the USA as a propagandist and he told Freddie and Nellie in strict confidence because ostensibly he was going to join Liza, already living in New York. Plans were made for his departure on 10 September and Nellie had a farewell tea with him at the Dorchester the day before. The American authorities, however, suddenly refused to issue the necessary papers; supposedly they had got wind of his mission which, as a neutral country, they could not endorse.

During the delay Willie saw as much of his family and friends as possible. When he went to spend Sunday with Freddie and Nellie on 15 September he mentioned that a bomber had been brought down in St James's Park and was displayed in the forecourt of Victoria Station. After lunch, between raids, Nellie persuaded them to take her to see it and they joined a seething mass of sightseers to peer at the wreckage. Although a minor incident in itself, it added to the stock of stories Willie was able to use in America.

Train travel was hazardous but Willie managed to visit York to spend several days with his lover Alan Searle who was working at the YMCA hostel. Their affair had now lasted for twelve years, secretively in England but more openly when Searle visited France. Now they faced the possibility that they might never meet again as it was out of the question for Willie to take him to America. On the way back from York he stopped at Kettering to visit Robin and his son-in-law, Vincent Paravicini, whose regiments were stationed in the area.

Willie also visited old friends including Sibyl Colefax who had been forced by a reduced income to give up Argyll House and move to a tiny Georgian house at 19, Lord North Street, Westminster. It was across from Brendan Bracken who had been largely responsible for the street becoming fashionable after decades as a slum and for the addition of 'Lord' to the name. (This was not a happy idea as Lord North was the Prime Minister who lost the American colonies.) Sibyl Colefax continued to entertain the famous as she had done in the past but as the dining room was so small she often held her dinners at the Dorchester when the guests cheerfully paid the accounts she sent to them afterwards. Willie, enclosing a cheque, remarked in a letter that he had eaten and drunk much more than one pound four and sevenpence worth and that she would never make ends meet that way. During a lunch party at Lord North Street there was an air raid, but H. G. Wells refused to take shelter. As a compromise the blackout screens were put up at the windows to stop flying glass and lunch was finished with the lights on. Bruce Lockhart, a fellow guest, recorded in his diary that Wells held forth for almost an hour on God and his stupidity and how people did not read their Bibles properly. Willie sat chewing the cord of his eyeglass in a state of palpable boredom. On another occasion Wells told Willie that he could not write unless he had sex with a woman after lunch and before dinner every day. 'And what do you do after tea?' Willie enquired drily.

Among the many friends who visited Willie at the Dorchester was Beverley Nichols who envied his going to America and complained that his own attempts to get a proper war job had been snubbed. Another was Osbert Sitwell. (In a letter of 6 September 1941 to his lover David Horner, Sitwell was to speak about Searle's news of Willie, by then in California. He had decided not to return to England until the war was over. 'Really, these patriots!' exclaimed Sitwell.)

Willie made no attempt to contact Syrie but by chance met her in the hotel where she was lunching. She told him she was going to join Liza in New York and confessed her fear of drowning if the ship was torpedoed. Willie, who had spoken to a doctor about his own dread of drowning, passed on his advice without preamble: 'Don't struggle, open your mouth and you will drown quickly.' Syrie, mistakenly thinking this was further proof of his disregard for her, promptly burst into tears.

Finally, after much string pulling, Willie got away on 2 October, three weeks after the start of the Blitz.

The Maugham women took on full-time voluntary work as a matter of course. Nellie was already on the Board of the Elizabeth Garrett Anderson Hospital for Women as well as working for other charities. She now became chairman of the Soldiers', Sailors' and Airmen's Families Clothing Depot where she organised teams to sort out gifts of clothes for the victims of bombing. Kate helped when she was not working at the Cheyne Hospital which had become a hostel for European refugees. Later Kate was invited by the British Council to be Director of the Free Polish Forces Club, Oznisko Polski (Polish Hearth), set up initially at 55 Prince's Gate and then moved to Belgrave Square. She worked long hours despite increasingly poor health and Nellie felt it was too much but Kate refused to give it up.

In winter, Nellie always wore cloaks instead of furs and as the war dragged on they became more and more threadbare. The clothing ration was not enough to make such a voluminous garment but then she remembered Freddie's discarded cloak from his days as Lord Chancellor. This was a magnificent affair in heavy black cloth, lined with satin, with a rich velvet collar and large gilt buttons, ideal for cold winters. She was wearing it at a charity bazaar when she came face to face with Queen Mary, whose smile changed to a frown of displeasure and reproach when she recognised it by the distinctive buttons.

Diana continued doing what she could for the Housing Council; it occurred to her that it might help if the women could escape from their dreadful surroundings to some social meeting place. She found a large, empty property on the Harrow Road called Beauchamp Lodge, reputedly once a home for the French Ambassador and where Katherine Mansfield had lived for a while when it was a hostel for students. Following the example of her mother in the General Strike, she obtained keys and took it over, persuading the somewhat bemused owners, the Paddington Estate, to give it to her rent free. Then followed months of preparation to get the place cleaned up and furnished to open as a club, membership to be twopence a week. But in the meantime she was also enlisted to help with refugees from Nazi Germany and Austria.

The club finally opened in June 1940, but during the Blitz its importance to the local community changed dramatically. It was no longer simply a refuge for women but a day nursery, a youth centre in the evenings, a place for hot meals, and a sort of unofficial advice bureau. Diana worked long hours with volunteer help but it soon became clear that she needed paid staff as well. Brendan Bracken made time in his hectic schedule to help solve problems which might otherwise have been strangled with red tape and the club was given War Charity status. Diana also opened a depot at the back of the club to receive clothing for bombed-out victims. When she discovered that homeless families had been put into derelict houses in Westbourne Terrace which had no basic facilities, she took the law into her own hands, moved them into Beauchamp Lodge, went off to Whiteleys with Nellie to buy blankets for them and then persuaded the authorities to find them proper accommodation.

Honor worked as a waitress in the canteen of General de Gaulle's HQ in Carlton House Terrace and then as an assistant to the government department organising National Savings Groups. She also gave regular talks on painting and drawing at Stoke Mandeville Hospital where soldiers were sent for long-term treatment for bone injuries. To illustrate her theme she sketched portraits of the wounded men to give to their families.

As American troops arrived in Britain, it was proposed to Honor that she paint portraits to represent the variety of races who made up the population of the USA. The resulting exhibition, called 'We are the Americans', was sponsored by Selfridges and opened by John Winant who had succeeded Kennedy as ambassador. It aroused so much interest that it was toured around the UK under the joint auspices of the British and American authorities. Honor was invited to follow up her American exhibition with one representing servicemen from every part of what was then known as the Dominions and Colonies. It opened in 1944 with a title that Honor thought far too grandiose: 'Warriors of the Empire'.

Before the war Honor had been appointed an 'official visitor' to the girls' Borstal establishment at Aylesbury. Lady Ampthill, who interviewed her initially, began by telling her not to wear make-up on her visits. Honor later confessed that she felt sorry for Lady Ampthill who seemed to assume that she must be the 'right sort of Conservative' because Freddie was Lord Chancellor. Honor was far from being 'conservative' in her attitude to punishment. She regarded the prison regime as often unnecessarily harsh as well as unintelligent and frequently said so, to the chagrin of the Borstal authorities. Later she applied to become a prison visitor to Holloway gaol and was accepted. She was prompted to do this when so many of the girls 'graduated' to a women's prison when they became adults. It made her question the system, especially when, over the nine years she visited Holloway, a hard core of the inmates returned time and time again, mostly convicted for petty theft and prostitution.

Honor discovered that there was class distinction even among prostitutes. Ruby, for example, proudly described herself and some other inmates as 'West End girls' because their beat was in the Piccadilly area, as opposed to main-line stations or the docks. She specialised in kinky sex and Honor was enthralled by detailed descriptions of what Ruby did to satisfy her clients: 'The only time I ever managed to interest my uncle Willie in anything I said was when I told him of some of Ruby's experiences.'

In 1941 she founded 'The All Nations Voluntary League' with the aim of changing the attitude to refugees still treated with suspicion because most of them came from Austria or Germany. They were only permitted to work as domestics and even forbidden to do voluntary war work. Honor thought it ridiculous that highly qualified doctors and surgeons should be scrubbing floors. She won the active support of prominent figures in the Jewish community and an impressive list of patrons including Sir Julian Huxley, Lord Horder and Lady Violet Bonham-Carter.

She was also asked to join 'The 1941 Committee', a sort of think tank for 'planning the future', which included J. B. Priestley, H. G. Wells, Kingsley Martin and Richard Crossman.

They met regularly at Edward Hulton's Mayfair home for supper and discussion.

> We were all passionately dedicated to reform in our different ways but few of these high-powered gentlemen seemed to understand what the others were driving at, and would get into furious rages with each other through pure misunderstandings.

Honor added: 'I greatly enjoyed these evenings. They were a most pleasant light relief in the blackness of war.'

Apart from their voluntary activities, Nellie and her daughters had ARP duties on top of coping with the problems of running homes often shattered by bomb blast or without power or water. Nellie and Freddie slept soundly during one of the most severe nights of bombing on 10 May 1941. Their senior maid woke Nellie at 2.30 a.m. to say: 'Sorry to disturb you, m'lady, but the houses on each side of us are on fire.'

Throughout the war, the Maughams, the Marr-Johnsons and the Bruces kept open house for friends and acquaintances, many of them in the armed services. Parties planned and impromptu were the order of the day; this may have been in the Romer tradition of hospitality but it also typified the universal camaraderie of the war years.

In February 1940 Robin was invited to Mary Churchill's coming-out dinner at the Queen Charlotte Ball. He was unable to change into a dinner jacket and wore his uniform, but as he was not commissioned a flunkey stopped him imperiously and pointed to a notice which announced that the hotel was 'out of bounds to other ranks'. Robin demanded to see the manager and told him what he thought of reserving hotels for officers only during a war for democracy. The manager signalled to his minion to call the Military Police but Robin pushed him aside and went through to the ballroom. Indignantly the manager followed him but stopped short when he saw him go up to the Churchills' table. A few minutes later, Robin waltzed past him with Mrs Churchill in his arms.

Most of Robin's initial training took place at Sandhurst,

followed by a course in tanks at Bovington where the troopers were housed in old huts which had been out of use since 1914. One of the sergeant instructors, a man in his forties, meeting Robin off duty in a local pub one evening, became surprisingly friendly. When he suggested they continue drinking in a room upstairs which he 'rented occasionally', Robin went with him, curious to see how the situation might develop. After a few more drinks the sergeant moved closer to him and said that this was the room where T. E. Lawrence, then at Bovington under the name of Shaw, had invited him. A lance-corporal in those days, he had been persuaded to whip Lawrence before buggering him. As he described this he became sexually aroused and Robin had to talk his way out of the situation without offending him. He dismissed the story as unlikely but wondered how many callow young soldiers the man had seduced with it.

Later that year, now commissioned in the 4th City of London Yeomanry, he was invited to lunch at Chequers where there was talk of the German invasion, expected any day. Churchill asked if morale was high in his regiment. Robin told him it was. Then Churchill asked if the tanks were ready to advance to repel Hitler's forces on whatever beach they might land. There was a deathly silence when Robin answered that they were not. Stony-faced, Churchill asked why. Because, Robin told him, not one of the tanks was capable of movement. Churchill banged on the table and demanded an explanation. Professor Frederick Lindemann (later Lord Cherwell), Churchill's scientific adviser, made frantic warning signs but Robin ignored him and explained that the small springs which held the track pins in place were missing from all the tanks: consequently the track plates fell to pieces if the tanks started any movement. Churchill erupted in fury, lunch was forgotten and Private Secretaries were sent to make frantic phone calls. The regiment received a special delivery of the springs within twenty-four hours.

Robin, telling this story years later, commented that Churchill's habit of gathering young officers around him was precisely to get at truths which others might try to keep from him.

# One of the Bravest

In the summer of 1941 Robin was given a few days' leave before going overseas. Nellie and Freddie threw a cocktail party for him on his last evening. Mary Churchill and a few others stayed on for dinner and on 6 August he left.

Robin's regiment, the 4th City of London Yeomanry, formed part of the 22nd Armoured Brigade which set sail for a secret destination. Most guessed it was Egypt. The troop ship, a luxury liner in peacetime, had been converted with minimal structural alterations. The officers travelled first class complete with white-coated stewards to wait on them. In the restaurant there was a semblance of pre-war haute cuisine only possible because provisions were taken on board in unrationed South Africa. Non-commissioned officers enjoyed similar luxury, but the rest were crammed down below into the hold which had never been intended for human habitation; here they ate, slept and spent most of their time. Ventilation was inadequate and the stench so appalling that Robin and his fellow officers were nearly sick every time they went on inspection rounds.

One of Robin's duties was to read the men a lecture called 'The Common House Fly as a Carrier of Disease' but neither he nor they had any concept of these pests in the desert, fat on the corpses of the dead, swarming over the bodies of the living. As for the desert itself, he had only the vaguest idea culled from Hollywood films, where beautiful men performed heroic deeds and Marlene Dietrich, looking seductive in flowing chiffon, was ready to kick off her high heels and follow her lover into the soft, clean, yielding sand. Disillusionment came rapidly when they landed in Suez, made camp on dirty, stony wasteland and a sandstorm blew up, stinging the eyes, coating the body and getting into every orifice.

Robin's socialist conscience was constantly offended by the artificial gulf between officers and men dating back to a time when the former were 'gentlemen' and the latter pressed into service from the peasant class. To a tank crew of four, who had to work and live in intimate conditions beyond anything in their experience, such distinctions were ludicrous. During the heat of the day they were crushed into the confined space, body to body, pouring with sweat, and at night they huddled together against the cold.

In his novel *Enemy*, published in 1981, Robin wrote:

> Their bivouac was made from a tank tarpaulin stretched out to form the sides and top of a low tent about three feet high. The sides were supported by wireless poles and a disused lorry hoop placed over a dug-out two or three feet deep, so that they slept below ground level, which kept out the sand. By day one side was left open. They got in at night by crawling under the tarpaulin to avoid showing the light outside, and slept stretched out in one long row. The bivvy was lit by an oil lamp. There was very little room to move. At this moment the men were leaning against their packs, equipment and bed rolls, which had been unrolled because they would be putting out the lights soon and opening the tent a bit to let out the stale air and tobacco smoke.

As troop commander Robin had three to four crews under his control plus six men in reserve who travelled in supply lorries. He believed that the necessary ingredients for harmonic balance included a sense of humour, tolerance and a mix of sensual affection and sentimental regard, but he found it difficult to achieve this when men disliked each other for instinctive reasons that defied logic. But, ill-matched through a crew might be, the need to survive under fire welded them into an efficient unit.

In the early weeks the men carried out exercises to learn how to control their tanks on a terrain of extremes, from hard rock to soft sand as treacherous as a bog. They clubbed together to buy extras to make desert life more bearable and embellished the interiors of their tanks which they believed to be almost indestructible. In the first taste of battle they learned the bitter truth. Robin never blocked out the memory of men, clothes blazing, scrambling to escape and the screams of those trapped and burning to death. He had four tanks shot from under him but suffered only a few cuts and bruises. For a while, he was convinced that he had a charmed life, until a recurring premonition of personal disaster began to haunt him.

By January 1942 Rommel had driven the Eighth Army back to

a new defence line, Gazala-Bir Hacheim, and there was a lull in the fighting while both sides re-equipped. The British created a series of defensive strong points or 'boxes' linked together by minefields. They seem to have forgotten that the Italians' use of a similar scheme led to their defeat in 1940 when they were outflanked. But Rommel had not forgotten.

During this period Robin was appointed an Intelligence Officer and his duties included making regular sorties in his scout car to assess enemy preparations. The hazards were minimal compared to a battle situation but the desert had its own perils and a compass was essential to safeguard against disorientation. All in all, life was relatively enjoyable, made more so by his driver Jim, a good-looking, fair-haired twenty-year-old. Robin was not sure his feelings were reciprocated until they bivouaced overnight and the boy made the initial move. This was probably the first significant homosexual affair of Robin's adult life and, as memory idealised it, he became trapped by the need to duplicate the experience with future lovers. These he preferred to be men who looked and behaved in a masculine manner, came from the working class, were educationally inferior and had a low income or none at all so that he could play benefactor.

On the evening of 26 May Rommel's forces attacked. In the account published by the British government it was tacitly admitted that the battle was an unmitigated military disaster, but as Rommel's plan to capture Tobruk was delayed for several weeks, albeit at frightening cost, it was conveyed as a victory of sorts. Subsequent accounts of the battle make it clear that there were fundamental errors of judgement; communications between various elements of the army broke down and the situation became chaotic, as Robin discovered.

There was nothing for Robin to do but try to stay in visual contact with his colonel's tank and hope that the scout car would not be blasted out of existence by enemy shells. He was angrily cursing his inability to do anything positive when through the clouds of swirling sand he spotted a crew huddled behind their wrecked tank. On an impulse he ordered Jim to get over to them without any clear idea of what he could do. They found one of the men was seriously injured and they laid him on the passenger seat while Robin, perched precariously on the back, set compass course for 'Knightsbridge'. This, the key position that commanded the supply routes, was held by the Guards Brigade and had its own medical station and airlift facilities to take the badly wounded to Tobruk.

The battle situation changed with such rapidity that on the way back they nearly joined a line of tanks until, at the last minute, they realised they were German and streaked away to safety bumping over ruts and camel grass and swerving to avoid old slit trenches. With the help of the compass and a degree of guesswork Robin eventually located his regiment in new positions following a forced withdrawal. The colonel had been injured just above the spinal column and Robin took him to Knightsbridge to get the wound properly dressed. While they were there the Germans began massive shelling and Jim drove out by the last open track before the Guards sealed it up with coils of wire and land mines. This was the prelude to the battle for the Knightsbridge Box, soon to be renamed the Devil's Cauldron.

From his position on the fringe of the action, Robin saw a sheet of flame sweep over a tank and the crew jump out and hurl themselves on the ground while the enemy raked them with machine-gun fire. Without thinking, he shouted at Jim who drove into the action and somehow all four crewmen clambered on to the scout car which lumbered away, slowed down by the extra weight. Incredibly nobody was hit by the machine-gun fire that followed them.

That afternoon Robin was standing by the scout car observing through his binoculars when he was struck in the chest by a flat piece of flying metal; it felt as if he had been punched by a giant's mailed fist. The wound was not deep but bled profusely and Jim drove him to a medical unit to have it treated. There they found he also had several broken ribs which they strapped up in plaster. As he rested outside in the shade of a truck he could see Stukas dive-bombing Knightsbridge three miles away. In spite of the continuous noise, he dozed off. Suddenly he was woken by the deafening roar of a plane and the staccato cracks of cannon fire. Involuntarily he sprang to his feet and simultaneously something hit his legs and head. As the plane zoomed away Jim staggered towards him, his head split open and one side of his face sheared from the bone, the flesh hanging down, flopping with blood. He seemed to try and say something before he collapsed and died. In agony from his own wounds Robin lost consciousness and fell beside him.

For the weeks that followed, time was divided into segments by the strict routine of a military hospital, but otherwise had no significance. For most of it Robin was unaware of anything outside his own mind; dreams sometimes became journeys of escape that would twist into nightmares, while hallucinations took him into greater dimensions of horror in which doctors and medical orderlies became torturers who had to be fought off. And dominating his turbulent mental state was the image of that mutilated face.

Gradually, as his wounds healed and as drugs were reduced, mental order returned and he remembered something of what had happened since Jim's death: the journey in an ambulance to Tobruk, the screams of the wounded lying on stretchers in a vast hall, the smell of disinfectant and gangrene, the sea journey and the jolting train to this hospital near Cairo.

He had been wounded in both legs, and in the right arm which had nearly been amputated until a doctor had insisted on trying one of the new antibiotics and saved it. The wounds to his head and chest appeared to be relatively superficial and his ribs had healed. It seemed that he had escaped any long-term consequences and he was eventually discharged and given sick leave. The only problem was a persistent headache that could flare into severe pain, but he was assured that this was temporary and in time would vanish.

During the final weeks in hospital he had tried to come to terms with the death of Jim and he mourned for what had been and for the promise of a future unfulfilled. Common sense told him that the relationship might not have lasted but this did not ease the shock of its abrupt ending. There was no one he could discuss these feelings with and outwardly his disposition appeared unchanged, as hail-fellow-well-met as ever, but inwardly fundamental changes were taking place. Paramount among these was the resolution never to marry, for he was now convinced that his nature was predominantly homosexual. Speaking of this decision in an interview in 1977 for an American gay newspaper, he admitted that marriage could work if the wife accepted the situation but he added:

> I've seen so many marriages between a bisexual man and a girl which go all right at first but eventually, when he becomes unfaithful, there is terrible unhappiness for the woman and a kind of guilt feeling in the man which makes him rather cruel to his boy friends as a consequence . . . one can only generalise very vaguely in these matters but be specific in one's generalities.

In Cairo he stayed at Shepheards Hotel where life continued, for those who could afford it, with only the slightest acknowledgement that a war raged in the desert. His old friend Alec Waugh was there too; they went to the cinema almost every afternoon and often ate in one of the many excellent French or Greek restaurants and drank at the Turk Club or the Mohammed Ali. In fragmentary recollections of Cairo, Robin spoke of the absence of rationing, the superb wines still to be found and the greedy enjoyment of large cream pastries and coffee at Groppi's, pleasures long vanished in London. But he criticised the class distinction that forbade him from taking a non-commissioned friend into Shepheards for a drink; this relic of an unacceptable tradition symbolised the antithesis of his socialist convictions.

While he had been in hospital, his commanding officer, Brigadier Bill Carr, had written to his wife of Robin's bravery and she had copied the paragraph and sent it to Nellie. It read:

> There are two kinds of bravery. One is sheer guts and lack of imagination and I don't call this real bravery because it does not take any real effort. The other is bravery forced on and on by one's own

pride. Pride may be in one's breeding, one's regiment or even pride in one's own self-control. I think Robin Maugham is one of the bravest men I will ever see.

Robin spent part of his convalescence with Major-General Sir Edward Louis Spears and his wife Mary Borden, the novelist, at their summer residence in the mountains above Beirut. As Robin somewhat disingenuously puts it in *Escape from the Shadows*, 'Thus I was "drawn" into intelligence work,' but he never explained Spears' importance to British aims in the Middle East.

Spears, an old and trusted friend of Winston Churchill, had been his representative to the French government from 1940 and at the surrender of France had heroically rescued General de Gaulle from arrest and possible execution. Nothing explained de Gaulle's subsequent betrayal of Spears' friendship or his petulant anti-British stance, unless he resented the debt he owed Britain. From 1942 Spears was British Minister to the Republics of Lebanon and Syria. Independence for Syria, with elections in 1942, was essential to his strategy but de Gaulle, once in favour, now opposed him. Indeed, de Gaulle became so illogical, unpredictable and a danger to the war effort that the British considered deposing and, if necessary, imprisoning him. Meanwhile the Syrians were growing increasingly impatient with French rule, particularly as the Germans had also offered them independence. As Sir Alexander Cadogan noted in his diary for 23 April 1942, there was a possibility that the Germans might attack through Syria as the prelude to a fresh attempt to conquer the Middle East.

This then was the situation when Robin was promoted to captain, joined the Middle East Intelligence Centre in Cairo, and was immediately sent to report to Spears in Damascus. In his account of events published less than five years later, entitled *Nomad*, Robin was legally constrained from telling the entire truth and so diverted attention from obvious questions with a rather unconvincing display of verbal legerdemain. We never learned why he joined Spears or what the purpose of the training programme devised for his benefit really was. It began by him being assigned to Major Ernest H. R. Altounyan, MC, one of the most important secret agents in the Middle East. Altounyan, educated at Rugby and Cambridge, studied medicine at the Middlesex Hospital and was officially with the Royal Army Medical Corps, but on attachment to GHQ Cairo. It was of him that T. E. Lawrence had written in one of his last letters: 'An Armenian called Altounyan is one of the three I most care for.' He was actually half Armenian, half Irish. He gave Robin an intensive course on the political realities of Arab and Jewish problems after which Robin was attached to General Staff Intelligence, Damascus where he studied to improve his basic knowledge of the Arabic language and of Arab traditions and history.

It is at this point that Robin's version of events in *Nomad* begins to look suspect. According to him he conjured up a Lawrence-like scheme for British officers to train and organise small units of Arabs to continue the fight against the Germans, should the Middle East be conquered. As this became increasingly unlikely following the victory at Alamein in October and Allied landings in Morocco and Algeria in November, the scheme was scrapped. Instead he devised a plan for the education of British officers in Arab studies so that they could be useful to self-governing states in peacetime. This appeared straightforward enough but excited such a degree of interest that one wonders if it was as simple as Robin asserted.

If there was a controversial and secret aspect for the plan, we are unlikely ever to know what it consisted of, but Spears' suspicions of the French may have influenced it. The final document, drafted under advice from John Adam Watson, second secretary at the British Embassy in Cairo, was reproduced in heavily edited form in *Nomad*, but a reader searching today for significance will be disappointed unless he finds the underlying assumption that the British would automatically dominate the entire Middle East after the war more than a touch provocative. But at the time the assumption was a normal constituent of British policy. The plan was approved initially by Spears and Colonel Elphinstone of Intelligence, Damascus, then by Brigadier

Clayton, Head of Middle East Intelligence, Lieutenant-General John Glubb, founder of the Arab Legion, and Field Marshal Sir Henry 'Jumbo' Wilson, Commander in Chief, Persia–Iraq Command. This was heavyweight endorsement to the point of excess but Robin was sent to Jerusalem to obtain further approval from Sir Harold MacMichael, High Commissioner of Palestine, and to Baghdad to get agreement from the British Ambassador to Iraq, Sir Kinahan Cornwallis. This was not all: the plan was seen by Churchill who summoned Robin to the embassy in Cairo where he was staying after visiting Turkey for the Adana Conference. Churchill apparently gave it his blessing but no action followed, though Robin claimed that the Middle East Centre of Arab Studies, established several years later, was based on his idea. True as that may be, it beggars belief that a junior officer obtained access to some of the most powerful men in the Middle East, not to mention the Prime Minister, to gain approval for a plan apparently of such minor importance, while the biggest war in history raged round the world. It seems that we will never know the truth behind this time-consuming exercise any more than we will know the reasons for Robin's return to Cairo three years later on another mission.

Churchill was in a jovial mood at the embassy and after dealing with official business over several whiskies, gossiped about their respective families. He told Robin with much amusement that Freddie was carrying out a study of tank production and had been seen test-driving one of them which at the age of seventy-seven was quite a feat. Robin later learned that Lord Beaverbrook had asked Freddie to investigate the problems connected with the 'Churchill' tank and he had taken on the task with the gusto of a twenty-year-old; no doubt its name added a touch of piquancy to the task. In his report Freddie recommended several important changes to the design including the replacement of the existing gun with one of heavier calibre. His findings were incorporated into an appraisal by Sir Stafford Cripps and subsequently implemented, making the Churchill a more efficient fighting machine. Freddie was somewhat put out when his success did not bring acknowledgement or further jobs of a similar kind. He had thoroughly enjoyed careering round the testing ground at Luton in a tank.

When he saw Churchill, Robin was recovering from a bout of jaundice which he was unaware of until friends drinking with him at the Continental Hotel remarked on his peculiar yellow complexion. They thought it rather a joke and suggested a slap-up last supper with plenty of wine before his supply of booze was cut off by the medicos. He woke next morning with a thundering hangover in the fifteenth General Hospital without any idea how he got there and learned with wry amusement that it specialised in head injuries. Major Michael Kremer, the senior neurologist, became more interested in Robin's story of his head wound than the jaundice and began a long examination. For the first time since Knightsbridge, X-rays were taken and these showed two slivers of metal embedded in his skull so delicately and dangerously positioned on the brain that an operation to remove them was out of the question. This meant that not only were the blinding headaches he had tried to obliterate with a mixture of pain-killing drugs and drink to be a permanent feature of his life, but there was also a possibility of damage or death if the metal moved.

So far he had dealt remarkably well with his wounds, though he had developed an incipient stammer and limped slightly; nobody knew of the sorrow of Jim's death, buried deep away from detection, but the new revelation was a terrifying climax to a series of shocks. He later joked about 'my own personal sword of Damocles' but he also confessed: 'The fear of death? That does not disturb me so much as the fear of being maimed in body or spirit. That's the fear that drenches my sheets with a chilling sweat.'

Robin was advised that it would be best if he returned to the UK. He arrived at Liverpool on 16 June 1943 and telephoned his mother from the Adelphi Hotel. She was not sure what to expect when she saw him the next day, as a well-intentioned letter from Lord Croft at the War Office three months previously had alarmed her. But he did not look as ill as she had feared and was as ebullient as ever. Freddie opened champagne to celebrate and various friends dropped in, including Mary Churchill. Robin took them all along to Kate's home where the celebrations lasted until the early hours. It was too much for him; he became ill and was told to rest undisturbed in bed, but Nellie found it difficult to obey the doctor's instructions as people kept arriving to see him.

He was eventually discharged from the army in 1944, classified fifty per cent disabled, and given a small pension. In the meantime he was attached to the Army Bureau of Current Affairs and, with the blessing of its director, W. E. Williams, and the co-operation of William Collins, the publisher, he launched a new magazine called *Convoy*. Its purpose was to bridge the gulf between the Services and civilians by explaining the effects of the war on each of them. The first issue of *Convoy* sold out its run of fifty thousand copies but its success did not bring in the written contributions Robin had expected and, to get stories, he worked as a miner in the North Walbottle Colliery for two weeks and flew with the RAF on submarine patrol over the Atlantic. He also persuaded others to help out, among them Pamela Frankau, G. B. Stern, Harold Nicolson's son Nigel, S. P. B. Mais, Alastair Forbes, Mary Ellis, Charles Fletcher-Cooke, Ronald Searle, Hermione Gingold and Richard Mason. But the magazine's reason for existence vanished with the end of the war and it finally ceased publication in 1947.

Robin's most interesting piece of writing was not for *Convoy* but a novella of fifteen thousand words, *The 1946 Ms*, for the War Facts Press which published authors with 'something to say about tomorrow'. Due to the wartime shortage of paper only a limited number of copies was printed in 1943 but it was rescued by James Drawbell, the editor of the *Sunday Chronicle*, who bought serialisation rights. At the last minute it was withdrawn by the proprietor, Lord Kemsley, who thought it too controversial. Outraged by this slur on his judgement, Drawbell fought back and it was reinstated the following week. This was Robin's first attempt at a novel and its appearance in a major Sunday newspaper assured him that his decision to be a writer was justified.

The manuscript of the title is supposedly written by a young anti-Fascist freedom fighter in hiding who records the events that have led to a totalitarian Britain under the dictatorship of a famous army general. The idea for the story came from rumours of a military putsch to take the country over after the war and install a government headed by Field Marshal Montgomery. Copies were not allowed to reach the Middle East because some of the story was set during the desert campaigns of 1942 and it was feared it might have a detrimental effect on morale.

Robin was not so lucky with his first professionally produced play. In the spring of 1944 a company headed by Lawrence Payne took over the Chanticleer Theatre in South Kensington. Robin's piece, *He Must Return*, opened on 3 May; it is a disjointed tale in three acts of a famous pianist, John Ross, who has retreated to a mountain hut east of Beirut to avoid the war. When four servicemen on leave discover his hide-out they persuade him by argument that he must fight. A year later in the western desert Ross is killed in a tank battle and, in the last scene, the men wait in their bivouac for Rommel's next move. Robin crammed the dialogue with many of his own views on freedom, unemployment, the meaning of war and the future after victory. Although deeply sincere, his lack of skill made it sound superficial, but when he wrote about ordinary soldiers his dialogue was authentic and the play came to life.

In view of the size of wartime newspapers, with an average of only six pages, the play received surprisingly wide critical coverage, presumably more because of Robin's connections than its merit. The *Stage* advised him to pay greater attention to motive and psychological effect and less to propaganda. The *Observer* said much the same and *Punch* remarked: 'Captain Maugham has yet to master his uncle's technique or sharpen his dialogue to the razor's edge.' Although *He Must Return* was a failure, bits of it kept reappearing in new guises, an example of Robin's facility for taking rejected material and recycling it.

He invited Sergeant 'Buck' Ryan and Corporal George Langfield, MM to see the play. Both had been with him when their tank was blown up and, interviewed by the local newspaper, they agreed that the desert scenes were 'just like the real thing'. Peter Noble who played a character based on Langfield said:

> Business was terrible. Robin was around most of the time and we often drank with him in the local pub. He was great company and kept cheerful however bad the box office receipts were. We guessed he might be queer when he took rather an interest in one of the lads in the cast, but otherwise there was no hint in his manner. I remember him being terribly embarrassed when a very camp friend turned up in the pub after the show.

Robin could never relax in the company of effeminate men in public unless he was too drunk to care. Like Willie he did not understand why some homosexual men felt compelled to behave flamboyantly to challenge total strangers with their brand of sexuality. Camping about with friends in private was a different matter, though he never felt entirely at ease with this, but to be anything other than masculine in public was a betrayal of the male ethos.

He was delighted when Marshall Dill from California, now an officer in the US Navy, was posted to London. He showed him the sights, took him to the best night spots and introduced him to his friends. When Harold Nicolson had dinner with them at the Garrick he recorded the gist of the conversation in his diary of 8 November. Apparently Nicolson gave them pause for thought when he delivered a Wildean rationalisation to the effect that he did not regard his own acts of self-indulgence as real vices. The Maugham clan all entertained Dill but he was amused to find that Nellie did not approve of the behaviour of GIs in London who, as the popular saying of the day put it, were 'overpaid, oversexed and over here'.

At one of Kate's dinner parties Dill was seated opposite Pamela Frankau: 'She was so effervescent and such good fun and I couldn't take my eyes off her.' For both of them it was a classic case of falling in love with the idea of being in love and it became a typical wartime whirlwind romance. They married at St James's Church, Spanish Place. The reception was held at Kate's house and there were over a hundred guests. Dill was bewildered by the large number of celebrities from Pamela Frankau's world.

> I remember meeting G. B. Stern, Beverley Nichols, Rebecca West, Jack Hylton the theatre impresario and Alexander, First Lord of the Admiralty; after that, everyone merged into a haze. Robin said to me: 'You've met half London. Come next week and you'll meet the other half!' Those Maughams were so kind and, of course, I adored and admired Robin.

Pleased as he was to see two of his closest friends so happy, Robin commented to Kate: 'There's a marriage doomed to disaster,' and he was proved right when it broke up a few years later.

All this time Robin was aware of his weak physical state, but blocked it out with drink. While staying at Chequers with the Churchills he passed out, and Noël Coward, who had been a lunch guest, drove him back to Cadogan Square. A few days later he passed out again and was taken by ambulance to the Hospital for Head Injuries in Oxford where Dr Michael Kremer was now working. He recovered after rest and medication but a far more alarming complication developed when he began to suffer from bouts of amnesia which lasted for anything up to twelve hours. During these he behaved rationally and appeared to have a heightened awareness and sharpened lucidity of speech. This phenomenon might have been the result of Robin combining drugs and alcohol, bearing in mind that little was known about the side effects of the newer medicaments, with or without alcohol. As far as he was concerned the mixture relieved his pain and gave him a wonderful sense of well-being, but once the effect began to wear off he felt terrible and the cycle began again. Robin could not know then that he was trapping himself on a treadmill of addiction from which eventually there would be no escape.

# X

## Gerald Haxton: Appearance and Reality

Willie had every cause to be grateful to the British government for giving him a valid reason to spend the war years in the safety of America, though, as he intimated to Glenway Wescott, he would probably end his days there as he did not think he would ever see the Villa Mauresque again. He lived at the Ritz-Carlton Hotel, New York in the spring, spent the summer at the Colonial Inn, Edgartown on Martha's Vineyard, and the winter at Parker's Ferry in a house built for him by his publisher, Nelson Doubleday, on the family estate near Yemassee, South Carolina. His official brief was to counter the isolationism endemic in the States prior to Pearl Harbor and afterwards to increase understanding between the two nations. He lectured extensively, broadcast, wrote features for the press, sold war bonds and, as he had celebrity as a 'grand old man of letters', never lacked invitations. Cecil Roberts in *Sunshine and Shadows* said that he was astonished at Willie's fluency and ease as a public speaker; there was no sign of his stammer, but he carefully avoided words that might give him trouble. As further 'payment' for his safety he also advised Washington on intelligence matters when William Stephenson began operations.

Willie's financial agreement with the British Treasury over dollar holdings and earnings appears to have been flexible, but out of his dollar allowance, estimated at figures ranging from $12,000 to $24,500 per annum, he gave Liza regular sums and paid Syrie her alimony. If he ever ran short of funds he could fall back on Bert Alanson who had access to Willie's stocks held in nominee names. Foolishly, Cecil Roberts, passionately dedicated to the war effort, lived off money borrowed from a friend and off earnings made in the States. At the end of the war, despite an impressive dossier of unpaid work for the British government, he was told he could be prosecuted for using undeclared dollars and advised that the only way to solve his financial problems was to emigrate. Even Noël Coward, working under government auspices, was subjected to two court cases for spending money from his dollar account to finance work for the Ministry of Information and was fined a total of £1,800.

In 1941, Willie published *Up at the Villa*, a novel expanded from an unused short story written over twenty years before. It was feeble and the critics said so, but it was not nearly as bad as *The Hour Before the Dawn*, a novel intended to give America a contemporary picture of Britain at war. Apart from a brief sequence based on his experience of the Blitz it was so out of touch and so awful that he refused to allow it to be published outside the States, and later withdrew it from his canon. It tells the story of a patriotic upper-middle-class family with a mansion in Sussex who employ an apparently delightful Austrian refugee as a quasi-domestic. She marries the pacifist son who has caused grief to the family by his refusal to fight. He is horrified to discover that she is a Nazi espionage agent who signals to enemy bombers by lighting slow-burning matches at the bedroom window of their cottage to guide them to a secret airfield being built on the estate. (This is so secret that the upheaval caused by workmen, bulldozers, cement mixers and so forth has gone unnoticed by the local population!) Shocked into belated patriotism, he strangles her and shoots himself, thereby restoring family honour. As a final touch the authorities conspire to cover up both murder and suicide. The ludicrous plot was emphasised by the stilted characterisation of the family who spoke and behaved as if it were 1915. Astonishingly it was filmed by Paramount in 1944 with a solemnity that only highlighted its absurdity, compounded by casting the glamorous and unmistakably American Veronica Lake as the Nazi.

Gerald Haxton joined Willie in America at the end of 1940 and resumed his important role of organising Willie's life. For a while they rented a house in Beverley Hills where Willie cross-examined Christopher Isherwood, Aldous Huxley and Gerald Heard in preparation for his long-planned novel, *The Razor's Edge*. They were leading figures in the California Vedanta movement which teaches man to recognise the secret divine nature within him by means of meditation.

Once Haxton had helped to furnish the house at Parker's Ferry he had little to occupy him and, according to Willie, as soon as America entered the war he left for an assignment with the OSS in Washington. This was followed by a brief period in New York before he returned to a permanent staff job with the OSS. In April 1944, he became ill from what transpired to be tuberculosis. He died in New York on 6 November.

Had Haxton not existed, Willie might only be remembered as a once-fashionable playwright and the author of a few books. Willie's best work was produced while Haxton was with him: the most successful plays, nearly all the short stories and the novels, from *The Moon and Sixpence* to *The Razor's Edge*, all show the importance of his influence. In a typically tight-lipped way Willie paid scant tribute to him in *The Summing Up*, thus depersonalising their intense relationship. He admitted that he had a 'companion' with him on his foreign travels who had the social gift of making friends very quickly and the investigative skills to persuade people to talk about themselves; this provided much of the material that he fashioned into his stories.

It is said that Haxton was blunt when Willie asked him what he wanted from life and replied: 'To be looked after', but, as so often happens, the kept younger man became the older man's keeper. Willie paid the bills but Haxton ran the Mauresque, played host, organised their travels, found the young men for Willie's bed and made life smooth and free of complications so that the writer could concentrate on writing. Yet what we know about Haxton amounts to very little and assiduous research has not been of much help. However, with the help of Lord Glendevon and from odds and ends, aided by speculation, it is possible to put together the picture of a man who must have been more important than his critics would have us believe.

His real name was Voss. Sara, his mother, was English and his American father probably of German origin. Soon after his birth in San Francisco in October 1892 his parents' marriage failed and Sara returned to England taking him with her. In time she married Henry Haxton, a writer. Rebecca West retained a hazy recollection of him in connection with the *Encyclopaedia Britannica* and thought the family lived in Manchester.

We know nothing about the boy's first twenty-two years; whether, for example, he was educated in England or America, or a combination of both. In 1914 he volunteered to work for the ambulance corps when there was no obligation for him as an American citizen to do anything. Was it heroic bravado or to satisfy his inherent British patriotism? Perhaps it was both, spurred by his need to be with Willie with whom, gossip suggests, he had begun an affair in London before the war and before Syrie entered the scene.

In 1918 when Haxton was freed from a German prisoner-of-war camp, he made his way to England to see his mother and to be reunited with Willie but was forbidden entry. Pleas made on his behalf at the highest level were turned down and he was not even allowed restricted entry to visit his mother when she lay dying at her home in St John's Wood or to attend her funeral in 1923. Why remains a mystery and it requires a feat of considerable imagination to conjure up a reason of such gravity that the might of the British Empire was so challenged that this young Anglo-American was forbidden to set foot in the land of hope and glory for the rest of his existence.

Attempts made over the years to persuade the British Home Office to reveal the information contained in the secret Haxton files, numbers 303705 and H2885, have failed. Enquirers were told that the files remained under an embargo until the year 2019 but even then there was no guarantee that the truth would be available because a future Home Secretary might in his wisdom extend the embargo for another hundred years.

Robin, by then Lord Maugham, was rebuffed by the Home Office in the 1960s but Ted Morgan did rather better when he approached them a decade later. The departmental official, a Mr H. G. Pearson, disposed of the widely held belief that the charge of gross indecency in 1915, of which Haxton was acquitted, had a direct bearing on his case; instead, he insisted that the decision came into the area of 'security or other grounds'. This confirmed the possibility that Haxton was a spy of some sort, a theory that had persisted since World War I. But to accept this means stepping into the realm of espionage which requires a suspension of agreement on what is normally held to be real, for nothing may prove to be something and something be revealed as nothing.

It was said that Haxton spied for the Belgians but 'gallant little Belgium' was an ally so why should this offend the British? He was also thought to be an American agent which, in some ways, was more likely to upset Whitehall grandees to whom America was still a colony in revolt.

Alan Searle later accused Haxton (out of Willie's hearing) of collaborating with the enemy while he was a prisoner of war in Germany. To give credence to the story he would say: 'Ask John (Glendevon), he knows all about it.' When Lord Glendevon was questioned about this in 1993 he denied all knowledge of it, adding that he did not even know that Haxton had been a prisoner of war.

Was the Home Office ban perhaps intended to provide credible cover for Haxton in the role of double agent working for the British while also in the pay of the USA? The idea of Haxton, the social decadent, convincingly urbane, as the real-life counterpart of fictional secret agents may test belief, but Willie, who was himself in intelligence, created Ashenden in his own image and perhaps he moulded Haxton into a fellow spy. The two made a good team, the older man increasingly inscrutable and the younger arranging meetings in circumstances where secrecy could be maintained. As they travelled around the world, particularly the Far East, they were like an odd couple from a Warner Brothers espionage movie.

In Europe the Villa Mauresque, isolated in its own grounds away from prying eyes, was ideal casting as a clearing house for the checking and exchange of information. Its increasing popularity with café and literary society as a place of pilgrimage distracted attention from the anonymous visitors who met in conference under the aegis of its two masters, Willie and Haxton. After the war Alan Searle, who became chatelaine of the villa, was annoyed when he was excluded from these mysterious gatherings, being told by Willie that it was better that he did not meet these visitors or know what was discussed.

Once a spy always a spy, so it was unremarkable that Willie should continue his work in America during the war under the aegis of William Stephenson, or that Haxton should be employed by the Office of Strategic Services in Washington. This organisation, modelled on Stephenson's British Security Coordination based in New York, was set up by Colonel William J. Donovan who was selected by President Roosevelt and Stephenson in cahoots. Its first task was to collect data and even if Haxton had not already worked as an agent, his knowledge of Europe and the Far East would have been of value. It is very likely he was introduced by Willie, who advised the head of Viking Press, Harold Guinzburg, on staffing the new agency. (It is probable, of course, that Haxton was already known.) After a period in Washington Haxton left in April 1943 for New York where he worked as a manager for Willie's publisher Nelson Doubleday, running a commissary which sold groceries to staff at wholesale prices. This may have been a cover, his real job being with Stephenson's BSC at the Rockefeller Center. At the end of October he returned to Washington in a permanent position with the OSS. While this was happening, Willie, in letters to Robin, Karl Pfeiffer and Bert Alanson among others, mocked Haxton's new independence, describing him as 'very small fry in a minor office' and expressing relief at being shot of him at last. The effect of this was to diminish Haxton and forestall curiosity in what he was doing in Washington.

What came as a surprise was his transformation from ageing playboy to sober executive. Sober seems discordant applied to Haxton, whose detractors prefer to think of him as a hopeless alcoholic, but this reputation had a dubious basis and Willie, who promoted it, had a cautiously dainty approach to alcohol. It suited Haxton's cover to play up to the reputation and though a hearty drinker to the point of stupidity he always contrived to be sober when duty required. In his final illness doctors found that his liver was perfectly normal – in contradiction to the myth.

Relaxing away from Washington he once indiscreetly mentioned a task he had just completed, but his acquaintances treated it as a drunken joke. Could Haxton have interrogated a high-ranking Nazi prisoner of war, as he claimed? Investigation was Haxton's strongest skill and his knowledge of Germany, his fluency with the language and his personal charm combined to give some credence to his claim.

A vigorous athlete in bed and out of it, he enjoyed the social whirl of wartime Washington and the opportunities it offered, relishing the novelty of leaving others to organise Willie's life. His health was good and he had every reason to suppose that he had a long life ahead of him. Typically he hated petty ailments and refused to take them seriously which explained his neglect of what started as a chest cold, appeared to become pleurisy and transpired to be advanced tuberculosis.

It took him six months to die, during which time Willie spent long hours at his bedside and made sure that every effort was made to save him. In periods of extreme anger Haxton attacked Willie verbally, accusing him of infecting him with the disease that was destroying his body. At other times he tried to be cheerful and optimistic but, as he wasted away, he lost hope. After an operation he rallied slightly but slipped into a coma and died on 7 November 1944. He was buried in Ferncliff Cemetery, Hartsdale, New York after a service at the Episcopal Church of St James on Madison Avenue. He was only fifty-two.

The British Home Secretary was approached in 1993 in the hope that recent relaxation in the matter of secrecy might extend to the Haxton files. If these gave basic details it could be possible to find more about his early years in England or America, but it seemed unlikely that the reason for his exclusion would be readily disclosed. After a prompt acknowledgement it took nearly three months to receive the following reply from the Head of Record Management Services.

> I should first explain that the general policy, relating to immigration personal records, is that few, if any are selected by the Public Record Office for permanent preservation, and the vast majority are destroyed. I am afraid that the immigration files reference 303705 and H2885, which related originally to Gerald Haxton, fall into this latter category and have been destroyed in the course of normal review procedure.

In a telephone conversation, it was said that the papers appeared to have been disposed of in the early 1980s. This was curious, to say the least, coming as it did shortly after Ted Morgan's meeting at the Home Office. What had so radically altered the situation that files designated as secret until the year 2019 and kept for over seventy years should suddenly be destroyed in the course of a 'normal review'? What had happened during previous 'normal reviews'? Was it now realised that the reason for the Haxton ban was trivial and unjust, or so dramatic, involving a person or persons with descendants in high places, that the truth should never be known?

The result of enquiries in Washington was disconcerting: men who had worked with the OSS in its early days could not recollect anyone called Haxton or Voss: he was not listed in the records of the Veterans' Association nor in those of the National Archive nor in certain personal files now held by the CIA. It later transpired that early history of the OSS was either lost or still remains top secret. William Colby (at one time Director of the CIA), who began his career with the OSS, was not surprised at the complete lack of information about Haxton. In the early days, he explained, the organisation was a little chaotic and, to add to the confusion, it was not unusual for staff to use false names. Real identities were on a 'need to know' basis.

To what extent Haxton was involved in espionage activities remains a question that may never be answered. Nor is it likely that Willie's record in intelligence will ever be fully revealed.

# Prospects of Peace

The final novel of the Haxton years, *The Razor's Edge*, was an instant bestseller when it appeared in April 1944. The theme of a young man seeking spiritual enlightenment struck a deep chord with the public who, after long years of war, were in a mood to think about such matters. At the time the lack of substance in the central character went unnoticed, but the years have exposed Larry Darrell, the good young man, as a tiresome bore. Willie's use of Vedanta philosophy and Chinese mysticism fail to convince, probably because his own inherent scepticism undermined his attempts to give Darrell credibility. Fortunately, to compensate for the void at the centre of the book, there are other pleasures. Elliott Templeton, a punctiliously elegant, viperish, snobbish old queen living in splendour on the Riviera, is the nearest Willie dared to go in portraying an obviously gay character.

To Willie's surprise, 'Chips' Channon unexpectedly called on him at the Ritz-Carlton to ask if it was true that he was the model for Templeton. Willie, who had not met Channon since a luncheon at Lady Cunard's Grosvenor Square house in 1935, and faced with a possible libel suit, blustered his way out by saying that Channon had influenced no less than three of the characters: the saintly Darrell, the narrator and Elliott Templeton. Sublimely vain, Chips was deeply flattered and proclaimed the novel to be a masterpiece.

Chips Channon was charming, good-looking, bisexual, well-off and generous. It may be concidence that his nickname 'Chips' was the term used for a ship's carpenter (his grandfather owned a shop in Chicago which supplied ships on the Great Lakes) but more likely it referred to his readiness to stake his friends when they were low in funds. A grotesque seeker after status and therefore a brilliant chronicler of his own progress, as his diaries attest, he resolved to reinvent himself as an English gentleman, a task to which he devoted himself for the rest of his life. At Oxford, during their brief affair, he told Beverley Nichols that he would marry an heiress, go into politics and gain a title, all of which he did, not giving a damn for those who mocked his snobbery. Though he was betrayed by a weakness for forms of vulgarity that only money can buy, his masquerade was harmless and he was a popular if slightly comic figure.

By the time of this meeting with Willie in New York his marriage was effectively over and he had accepted his homosexuality. Apparently the two got on well and when Willie returned to the Mauresque after the war, Chips was a welcome guest; presumably he revised his verdict of 1935 when he noted in his diary that Willie was not a gentleman.

Probably Willie used elements of Chips in the character of Elliott Templeton, but it is also the closest he came to a self-portrait, not the penny-plain version generally on display but the twopence coloured kept for close friends and secret thoughts. Like Elliott, Willie was waspish, a snob, a shrewd collector of works of art, as pernickety about his own appearance as the look of his house, a devotee of fashionable health-giving injections and completely preoccupied with himself, although capable of kindness. Unlike Elliott, he did not build a church to shelter his remains but, going one better, wished to be buried in the premier cathedral of England.

When Twentieth Century-Fox bought the screen rights of *The Razor's Edge*, George Cukor, assigned to direct the film, wanted Willie to write the screenplay. The studio boss, Darryl F. Zanuck, had already paid Lamar Trotti for a screenplay and was loath to spend more, but then Willie offered to do it for nothing. He moved into Cukor's home in Beverley Hills to work. The house was a Tinseltown version of the Villa Mauresque: it had acres of gardens and a secluded swimming pool where, as at the villa, the guests could swim in the nude without fear of peeping Toms.

Like Willie, Cukor feared that his homosexuality might become known to the general public, but within the Hollywood community his tastes were tolerated and the system controlled by the studio bosses conspired to protect him. For six days a week he was obsessively discreet but on the seventh he held swimming-pool supper parties for gay friends with a selection of Hollywood's most beautiful young men as decoration. Not all of these were gay but some provided sexual favours in return for reward. Cole Porter held similar parties at midday and it was considered the height of social success to be invited to both. Porter's song 'Love for Sale' neatly sums up one aspect of these occasions.

Willie was thoroughly at home in this milieu; old age had not impaired his sex drive and he continued to enjoy a mixture of brief affairs and one-night encounters. Dorothy Parker once said with more acidity than wit that she spent three boring weeks at Parker's Ferry hoping for scintillating conversation but got instead 'that old lady' Willie Maugham and a set of young men who were not interested in 'real women'.

Willie completed the screenplay and, as a token of his appreciation, Zanuck gave Willie a Pissarro worth some $15,000. In the event Cukor was unable to direct the film, so Willie's work was quietly shelved and the more commercial version used instead, directed by the equally gay Edmund Goulding. Trotti's screenplay softened the theme with lavish scenes of high society that suggested all concerned were about to break into a big musical number. Tyrone Power did what he could with the feeble Larry Darrell, Gene Tierney looked stunning as a cold-hearted beauty and Anne Baxter won an Oscar for her performance as a man-mad dipsomaniac, but the film was stolen by Clifton Webb as Elliott Templeton.

Willie was grief-stricken by Haxton's death and expressed his emotion in letters to England that contrasted sharply with those he had written earlier to Robin and others. It seemed there was no one in the States among those who regarded themselves as close friends to whom he felt able to turn. If there was ever an opportune moment for a reconciliation with Syrie this might have been it, but while like Barkis she was always willing, he was too imbued with antagonism for the thought even to occur to him. Liza could have given him support but with the war entering its final phase she had returned to England with her children.

In July 1944 Willie had suggested that Robin visit him and also see a New York specialist about his head wound, but permission was refused by the British authorities until Brendan Bracken intervened. Robin eventually reached Parker's Ferry in mid-December where he found Willie virtually a recluse and in a bad state of depression following Haxton's death. Although he could understand Willie's state of mind, Robin had become inured to death and he suspected that Willie's grief, genuine though it might be, was overlaid with self-pity and nostalgia. Maudlin sympathy was the last thing the situation needed so he remained detached and listened while Willie, between bouts of sobbing, talked the emotion out of his system.

Gradually, as he became more stable, Robin steered the conversation away from Haxton. At one point, he chatted about the success of *The 1946 Ms* and the work he was doing on a new book based on his war experience. When he elaborated on his future as an author Willie, getting back to form, pooh-poohed the idea. 'You'll never make more than £300 a year as a writer. Emerald Cunard and I will find you an heiress – the rest is easy.' There was nothing wrong with this advice which followed the tradition of titles marrying money but, unlike other bisexual men Willie had known, Robin lacked the cynicism needed to take it. Earlier in the war, when Robin was serving in North Africa, Willie told Glenway Wescott how worried he and Freddie were about the danger he was in. Both shared great hopes of him as the one to carry on the Maugham name and believed that from a career in law he would become a member of Parliament and then take his place in the House of Lords when he succeeded to the title. To them it seemed obvious that he had a vocation for government but, plot as they might, all their efforts were defeated by Robin's determination to become Willie's successor, a fusion of the writing talents of the Romers and the Maughams.

Willie improved sufficiently to accept an invitation from the Doubledays for Robin and himself to dine at 'the big house'. This was his first step back into a social life and it went well enough for him to accept another invitation for New Year's Eve. This also went smoothly until the moment came for 'Auld Lang Syne'. Robin saw dismay in Willie's eyes at the thought of physical contact with the two women ranged ready at his side. But Willie was prepared: 'When on New Year's Eve,' he announced, 'I hear people singing that song in which they ask themselves the question "should old acquaintance be forgot?" I can only tell you my own answer is in the affirmative.' With this, he backed away and, catching Robin's eye, winked.

Shortly afterwards Robin wrote a long account of the scene in the garden when the guests gathered to listen to the black employees sing spirituals. Implicit in his description is his dislike of the discrimination between the two groups. On the terrace were the white women proud in their expensive gowns and glittering jewels, while their cigar-smoking men hovered uneasily around them. Ranged on the grass below in the light from a huge bonfire, the black employees, modestly dressed, waited for the signal to sing.

With a nod from Nelson Doubleday they began. At first the group on the terrace chattered and laughed, but gradually they fell quiet, overwhelmed by the purity of sound and the simple message of the old spirituals. When the singing ended some of the white women rushed off to repair their tear-ravaged make-up while the men, self-consciously jocular, went to get fresh drinks.

Telling the story when he returned to England, Robin posed the question: 'Which of the two groups enjoy real happiness?' It would be too easy to dismiss his reaction as sentimental until it is remembered that this was some twenty years before African

Americans found their political voice. In South Carolina in 1945 it was as if the American Civil War had never happened; legally the slaves had been freed but equal status with whites was still a dream. Robin's question may have been indicative of his own striving towards some kind of personal philosophy which could surmount the barriers of race, colour and creed.

In January Robin spent time in New York consulting Max Wolf, a disciple of Dr Paul Niehans who believed in the curative properties of injections made up of enzymes and other ingredients. In 1942 Wolf had successfully treated Willie for a benign tumour and persistent malaria symptoms with his special injections and a massive dose of quinine. Robin, however, returned to Parker's Ferry after treatment feeling so ill that he took to his bed. In a letter to the London Maughams, Willie explained that Robin was not suffering from his wounds after all but from 'neurasthenia', in other words nervous debility. Wolf believed that this arose from an inferiority complex occasioned by having a famous father and uncle. Once implanted, the idea of inferiority became another mental burden and Robin convinced himself that he would always be overshadowed by Willie and Freddie, thus providing an alibi for failure.

After Robin returned to England in May, Willie, in a letter to Kate, commented that Robin's charm was due to the need to be the centre of attention. Everyone interviewed for this book, relations, lovers, close friends, colleagues or acquaintances, have referred to his charm as a natural component of his character, but some who knew him well concede that, however ill or depressed he felt, he could put on a social show when required. If Willie detected a false note, it stemmed directly from the effort Robin had to make to overcome his own emotional and physical problems and to deal with Willie's maudlin self-pity and grief.

Haxton's death made Willie more determined than ever to have Alan Searle live with him permanently but there was no legitimate reason why the authorities should provide the necessary permits. Then Willie offered the manuscript of *Of Human Bondage* to the Library of Congress and cunningly nominated Searle as the courier to bring it across the Atlantic. After a deal of string-pulling Searle arrived in the States and quickly settled down to become Willie's secretary, companion and live-in lover, in succession to Haxton.

In London, the V1 flying bombs had been superseded by V2 rockets. The Maugham homes all suffered damage and the family had some miraculous escapes. Kate worried constantly about her sons in the army. David had been injured in action twice; on the most recent occasion he was brought back from France and sent to the Horton Hospital. When she and Bob visited him he was more cheerful than they had expected. He pointed to a Polish officer who had had both legs amputated. When he had come round from the anaesthetic he had asked the surgeon: 'How am I for the womens?' On being reassured that everything in that area was intact, he heaved a sigh of relief and fell asleep.

On 2 April the Bruces received a letter from their other son John to say he was coming home on leave. They had not seen him for a year and arranged a big party. When he did not arrive, Kate went to Victoria Station expecting to meet him off the last train but there was no sign of him. Next day they were told he had been killed in a car accident. Two days later Diana had a baby son and, as John was to have been his godfather, it was decided to name the boy after him.

A week later the family attended a memorial service at St Peter's, Eaton Square at which John's name was read out with those of other Grenadier Guards. Kate was determined that there would be none of the consequences of bereavement she had seen in the 1914–18 war with mothers giving up the living to mourn the dead. She coped with grief by avoiding being alone and keeping up an appearance of cheerfulness. This façade was severely tested on 8 May when peace in Europe was officially declared and, as in 1918, London 'went mad' in celebration.

Robin's first novel, *Come to Dust*, published by Chapman and Hall in 1945, a lightly fictionalised version of his experience of desert warfare, acted as a coda to recent events. Its sales benefited from the public mood of sober reflection that followed VE day.

Graham Greene, not given lightly to praise, said of it: 'I know of no other book which gives to the outsider so vivid and particularised a sense of this form of fighting.' Excellent reviews came from Howard Spring and Peter Quennell but perhaps the *Observer* was the most perceptive, describing it as visionary, tough, tender and 'disclosing again and again the compassion and brotherly love that deepen as men get closer to combat'.

At the end of May the Labour Party ended the coalition which had governed the country and a general election was called for 5 July, with a delay of three weeks before the result was known to allow for the votes of servicemen overseas to be collected and counted. Robin did not believe the Labour Party was fit to govern on its own and hoped that Churchill would continue to lead the country, so he gave his active support to the National Labour Party which allied itself with the Conservatives. He spoke at public meetings for Harold Nicolson who had represented West Leicester since 1935 and for Honor's husband, Sebastian Earl, who stood for this small party at Wednesbury. They found universal confusion about Churchill's future role; people believed that, whatever the outcome, he would still be the national leader.

On 25 July, the day before the election results were to be declared, Robin was invited for late-evening drinks with the Churchills at the annexe of No. 10 Downing Street. Churchill was in an optimistic mood having heard stories that the voters had turned against the Labour Party. His son Randolph was pessimistic but Mary shared her father's view and invited Robin to go out with her the following night to celebrate the Conservative victory. However, by noon the next day it was clear that the Labour Party had won and Robin telephoned Mary who asked him to call round after dinner. He arrived with a mutual friend, Michael Parrish, and they found a sad little group in the sitting room of the annexe: Churchill's brother Jack, Diana and Duncan Sandys, Brendan Bracken and Mary. The door opened and Churchill appeared dressed in his famous open-necked boiler suit and embroidered slippers. He looked stricken. No one spoke and then Robin crossed to him. 'Good evening, sir. I'm so very sorry about what has happened.' Churchill smiled. 'So you are sorry! And your farther, is he sorry too?' 'Yes, sir, he is sorry too.'

Churchill sat down and beckoned Robin to sit at his side. There was general talk about MPs who had been defeated and Harold Nicolson's name was mentioned. 'The house will be a sadder place without him,' Churchill said and, after a pause, added, 'and smaller.' (Nicolson was greatly pleased when Robin telephoned him to report this comment a few days later.)

Suddenly Anthony Eden, the deposed Foreign Secretary, breezed in, debonair as ever, looking fit and bronzed, the antithesis of defeat. He stayed for only a few minutes and, as he left, Churchill said meaningfully: 'I expect I shall see you one of these days.' 'I don't think it's as bad as all that,' Eden replied calmly.

Conservative seats had fallen from 585 to 213 with Labour having a majority of 146 over all other parties and Churchill doubted if he would be asked to remain leader of the Tories. In the circumstances Eden's attitude was mystifying and remained so to those who were shattered by the extent of the party's humiliation. Others, taking a more objective view, could see that events might work to his advantage. As Bruce Lockhart noted in his diaries, for Eden the defeat was 'like a gift from Providence'; it freed him from Churchill and gave him time to prepare for leadership. (When the Tory Party was re-elected in 1951, however, it was with Churchill as leader, not Eden.)

After Eden had bounced out smiling, Churchill talked of the grim future and of the huge debts owed to America, India and the Middle East. He turned to Brendan Bracken:

We must be fair to the Labour Party. They have inherited terrible difficulties. We must lay off them for a few months and give them a fair chance. But if they start tampering with the Constitution, then we must go out on the streets and protest ... They may send me to a factory. They may conscript me where they please, but they will not induce me to work in the mines!

After an awkward pause Michael Parrish said, 'Well, at least, sir, you won us the race.'

Churchill brightened up and smiled. 'I won the race but now you've warned me off the turf!' Then with an effort he rose and moved slowly towards the door, each step heavy with weariness. He stopped. 'I have no regrets.' His eyes filled with tears but then the old statesmanship reasserted itself and he turned. 'I have no regrets,' he repeated firmly. 'I leave my name to history.'

And he was gone.

When the war finally ended with the surrender of Japan in August 1945, the British believed they were entitled to be rewarded for their sacrifice in standing alone against Nazi Germany. This belief was destroyed by the abrupt ending of the US Lease–Lend programme and by the cruel conditions demanded by America for new financial aid. Most people were unaware that Britain was being treated more as vanquished than victor and, when a period of austerity worse than any they had suffered during the war had to be imposed, they blamed the Labour government.

When the army handed back Tye House, Nellie decided that it was too costly a responsibility and it was sold. Kate and Bob moved back into their home at Littlestone when the navy departed. Honor and Seb found a cottage at Chilland Ford on the River Itchen, while Diana and Kenneth left central London for a country house near Maidstone.

The sisters were now determined to resume their careers. Diana, bringing up her young family and coping with the demands of a farm, began writing short stories again. Her first full-length post-war novel, *Bella North*, came out in 1954. Kate published *Daughters* in 1949 but before this, in 1946, she believed that her career would be transformed when she sold a play, *The Rocking Horse*, to Peter Glenville. It went into immediate production directed by Henry Kendall. The leading lady was Mary Ellis who had played in several Ivor Novello operettas and had appeared at the Old Vic and at Stratford-upon-Avon. The play was to be tried out at the now defunct Q Theatre near Kew Bridge before moving into the West End. Suddenly Kate was taken seriously ill with diabetes. The specialist at King's College

Hospital told the family that there was 'a fair hope she would live'. After two days in a coma she came round and slowly began to recover. When she was well enough to go to rehearsals she sat mortified as it dawned on her that *The Rocking Horse* was fundamentally bad and the efforts of Henry Kendall, Mary Ellis and the company could not save it. To her dismay Willie insisted on attending the first night and afterwards she asked him what was wrong with it: 'Surely you must know by now. Anyway, it's not as bad as some I've seen.'

Mary Ellis wisely omitted *The Rocking Horse* from her autobiography, *Those Dancing Years*, but she spoke fondly of the Maughams and of their hospitality at both Cadogan Square homes; of Kate's house where she met among others H. G. Wells, whose unexpectedly high-pitched voice she found startling, and of Freddie who enjoyed singing old songs with her after a supper of kippers and champagne.

Unlike her sisters Honor had been able to continue her career during the war. She now needed to resume her work with children and famous personalities; consequently she was delighted when, in 1947, she was commissioned to do a series of portraits for MGM in Hollywood. Her association with America had started in 1938 when she held an exhibition in New York. (Included among portraits of children was one of Edward, the youngest son of Joseph Kennedy, the American ambassador in London.) The press ignored the exhibition and the attendances were poor until Lord Duveen, the art dealer, went to it. Word of his favourable reaction spread, and resulted in sales and commissions, so saving the event from disaster. Lady Duveen seemed to be less taken with Honor's work than her husband. When a young woman told her that she was the model for one of the paintings of nudes, Lady Duveen looked at her in consternation: 'Oh, my dear,' she said, 'you won't tell anyone else, will you?'

While she was working in Hollywood, Honor stayed with Andrew Marton and his wife Jarmila whom she had met in the 1930s. Marton, a distinguished director in Europe before the war, was still low down the Hollywood pecking order. Before she left

Los Angeles, Honor asked her hostess if she might hold a farewell party for the various MGM people she had met. Mrs Marton warned her that, as Andrew was a minor director, it was not done to be 'seen' at their house. Honor could not believe this and went ahead. Her invitations were formally accepted, but on the night only one guest arrived. This confirmed that MGM, like other major studios, exercised a rigid control over its stars' lives. Later she maintained that it was impossible to exaggerate the effect of the fear and apprehension generated by Louis B. Mayer's cruel dictatorship on the people who worked for him. When she carried out a similar commission at Ealing Film Studios she was astonished by what she described as 'the most fantastic contrast to MGM that could be imagined'. No one appeared in the least apprehensive, nor was anyone afraid of Sir Michael Balcon, the head of the studio.

In December 1946 Freddie and Nellie had celebrated their golden wedding with a champagne party for nearly a hundred guests. After a family dinner at the Bruces' house they entertained each other doing what Kate described as 'our stunts'. Finally Nellie played and sang the old songs that transported her children back to nursery days. When she stopped, saying her fingers were too tired, they all begged for just one more tune and she sang 'Just a Song at Twilight'. This was the last occasion when the family were 'all together in a floral dance', as Robert Bruce described these gatherings.

# XI

## Return to the Villa Mauresque

Willie and Alan arrived in France in June 1946 and were shocked by the extensive damage to the Villa Mauresque. In the order of priorities the restoration of the property ranked at the bottom of the list of urgent work to be done in war-shattered France but Willie was prepared to pay black-market prices for labour and materials for it to be carried out. An army of men took twelve weeks to repair and redecorate the house and replant the gardens. During this time he and Alan stayed at the Voile d'Or hotel, and then Willie accepted an invitation from his old friend Bill Sherfesee for both of them to live with him at his home, the Villa Bontoc, only ten minutes' walk from the Mauresque. Willie got on very well with his host but then fell out with him over a young man they both took a liking to. They made up later, but Sherfesee became sensitive about young male guests whom he went to some trouble to keep away from Willie. Colin Spencer recalls staying at the Villa Bontoc in 1957 and being told to remain out of sight by the swimming pool when Willie arrived for tea one afternoon. Being unaware of the reason, he was furious at what he took to be a snub though, as he admitted, 'I was also then not an admirer of Maugham's work, thinking in my arrogance that it dealt merely with the surface of life.'

Relations between Willie and Sherfesee remained erratic after their first jealous tiff but Willie was grateful for the generosity shown to Alan and himself, although not generous in his comments. He remarked to Beverley Nichols that 'Sherfesee was not nearly such a bore as one imagined'.

Sherfesee, who was an old friend of Nichols, once told him the story of the work done on the Mauresque in 1946. According to this, Willie was prepared to use any stratagem from string-pulling to bribery and even blackmail to get what he wanted. Nichols had not known this when Willie complained of the exorbitant cost of the restoration. In response Nichols, who was restoring a large country house in Surrey, had observed reprovingly that, in austere post-war conditions, English government controls prevented the equivalent of the French black market. There had been no reply.

Willie admitted the truth in *Purely for My Pleasure*, the book about his collection of paintings published in 1962. He also described returning to France after a shopping spree in New York with twelve huge crates packed with every conceivable necessity: bedding, towels, pots and pans, china, glass and silverware. The customs inspectors were so staggered that they sent for their head man who asked to see Willie's passport. Recognition dawned: 'Ah, you wrote *Gone with the Wind*, didn't you?' Willie, restraining the impulse to tell him the truth, gave the sort of shy, deprecating smile which an author reserves for the giver of a fulsome compliment. The twelve crates, packed with riches beyond the imagination of war-weary European housewives, were allowed through without further question.

By early August the house was habitable; Annette Chiaramello, his cook from pre-war days, once more took charge of the kitchens and he was able to find attractive young men to work as servants. The finishing touch to the interior of the house was the re-hanging of the pictures which were said to have been stored by Lady Kenmare in her villa, La Fiorentina. A close friend, she was a great beauty in her youth and had a deceptively grave demeanour and could startle by telling a bawdily scandalous story. Willie was particularly fond of her gay son Rory Cameron who was a frequent caller at the Mauresque and confided the problems of his love life to him.

Willie's story of the pictures has always seemed unlikely, however, as La Fiorentina was ransacked and half destroyed by the Germans. It transpires that Gerald Haxton arranged for the French authorities legally to take over the pictures and certain valuable items of furniture and, in recognition for saving them from the Germans, they were promised a bequest of paintings. They kept their side of the bargain, but it seems Willie did not.

Finally, new Pekinese dogs were purchased to replace those left behind in 1940. When one of the staff was asked what had become of them, he replied: 'They were eaten long ago.'

Willie returned to the routine devised by Haxton: work in the mornings, drinks before lunch, swimming and tennis in the afternoon, a bath before dressing for dinner and, afterwards, bridge or music, then to bed, usually to read popular detective fiction. Only the absence of Haxton indicated any change. Alan Searle could not replace him but he provided instead a comforting presence, a little like a reliable nanny.

Although Cap Ferrat had suffered from entrepreneurs and lost much of its unique quality, Willie maintained a court which retained the atmosphere of the thirties. In what Noël Coward dubbed 'the other Vatican', Willie received a steady flow of guests, either to stay or to have lunch or dinner, but above all to pay homage. Kitty Black, who became a regular visitor when she worked for Curtis Brown, Willie's literary agent, admired the food, particularly the avocado pears gathered from trees in the garden.

Avocado ice-cream was one of Willie's favourite puddings and he had grown the trees from stones he had smuggled into France. English visitors, to whom avocado pears were a rarity, were asked to guess what the confection consisted of. Few succeeded, probably because the dominant flavour was that of the Barbados rum which Annette used in it.

Cyril Butcher said that he and Beverley Nichols were not so enamoured of food at the Mauresque as others appeared to be. 'We put it on a par with good hotel food – bland and safe. But as Willie gobbled his food so quickly, and smoked incessantly, I don't suppose he noticed how dull it was. As for the avocado ice-cream, it was tasteless!'

Kitty also recalled that the Pekinese dogs were allowed into the dining room when coffee was served, and then fed biscuits which were kept specially for them. In her memoir, *Upper Circle*, she mentioned that, of the older clients of Curtis Brown, Willie was probably the most lucrative.

Peter Quennell remarked that a visit to the Mauresque was always interesting rather than wholly enjoyable, and much depended on Willie's mood:

> He imposed a strict regime and demanded a standard of behaviour that his guests neglected at their peril. He was always kind to me; he even flattered and encouraged me but I was never entirely at ease in his company. Once, when he heard that I had remarried, he offered his congratulations, asking: 'Happy now, Peter?' I answered cautiously: 'Not unhappy,' which brought the gloomy response: 'Well, that's something, isn't it?'

According to Quennell, Willie's opinion of the human race was low and he found very little to say about its virtues. He applauded the success of fellow writers and those with the gift of making money, citing Godfrey Winn who had safely invested a large sum in the soundest stocks before he was forty. He was impressed by social rank and was surprised when a female guest whom he had always thought raucous and common remarked, apropos of a tiff with a neighbour: 'I hear she says I'm just an old German bitch; et, après, je suis certainement Princesse de Schleswig-Holstein.' As soon as she had left, Willie sent Searle to fetch the necessary reference books, remarking how pleasant it was to be able to look up a departed guest in the Almanach de Gotha.

Peter Daubeny, when a struggling theatre producer, was invited to stay after a well-received but unsuccessful revival of *Our Betters* in London in 1946. Full of expectations of luxurious living in France in contrast to the austerity of Britain, he was disappointed by the gloom of the house but amused to be warned by Searle that the mirror in his bathroom was two-way. While on a stroll along the corniche, a car roared by with a perambulator strapped to the roof and a holiday family crammed inside:

'That's what you'll be doing a year from now,' commented Maugham, chuckling and slipping his hand into mine. I had just become engaged to be married and had broken the news on my arrival. There was something faintly suggestive in his tone of voice, and in a reflex I pulled my hand away. I immediately sensed that I had done something foolish and gave him an uneasy smile. It was met by a face of freezing scorn and hostility. The walk continued in ominous silence. It had started to rain.

From then on the week was pure disaster. At dinner, and every subsequent meal, Maugham made desultory conversation but with an icy, withering malice, bitingly disparaging of anything I had done in the theatre and scornfully implying that I was incapable of doing better. A failure to reply brought silences which fell even more glacially.

One day a young man, who had been introduced to Maugham by Robin, came to lunch. As they sat in the salon awaiting his arrival Daubeny sensed a particularly bad atmosphere. The young man was nervous and received no help, except from Alan Searle who made a great effort without losing his sense of control or humour.

Lunch was announced and we followed Maugham into the dining room. After what seemed an endless silence, Maugham adjusted himself like some predatory animal about to crush his victim before devouring him. He settled his beak into his helpless guest. 'Why,' he said to the young man stuttering badly, 'did you come to the South of France?' There was just the sound of the rain filling in the gaps as the vulture poised for the kill. 'I felt I wanted to come when you wrote that marvellous play about the South of France,' the young man eventually replied. This was followed by total silence. 'But,' Maugham then continued, focusing on his target, 'I have never written a play about the South of France.' The young man looked at me in desperation. 'Didn't you write about it in *Lady Frederick*?' I chirped up gallantly, sensing immediate but inevitable disaster. Maugham took no notice and after one or two munches of boeuf à la mode he reconsidered his young guest, who was on the point of expiry. 'If you have come (stammer) to the South of France because (stammer) I mentioned it in a play, I feel (stammer followed by gulp) very sorry for you.'

Later, when his guest had left, Maugham gave a sort of spit into the air like a witch and accompanied it with the most ungracious exclamation I have ever heard. 'That little Welsh tyke will never come here again.'

Daubeny's unhappiness was accentuated by a feverish sore throat. Searle was sympathetic but warned him to keep his condition secret from Willie who hated illness of any sort. He stayed out of his way but could not avoid him at mealtimes. 'Maugham met me with total indifference, the most offensive of all weapons. There seemed nothing to do but pretend nothing had happened and it was still trying to pretend under the hooded stare of those cold, savagely hurt old eyes that I miserably made my escape.'

Cecil Beaton described life at the house as ideal for a semi-invalid but added:

At the Villa Mauresque everything is arranged with military precision. Woe betide anyone who puts a spanner in the running order so that an appointment is delayed; a guest who is late for a cocktail on the terrace learns not to be late a second time. My darling Lily Elsie, the original 'Merry Widow', now, like so many of us, past middle age, found the foreign currency restrictions made her holiday seem alarmingly expensive. Willie invited her to lunch at the Villa Mauresque but omitted to send his motor car for her, deciding that she could hire a taxicab from her Monte Carlo hotel. But Lily Elsie decided to save her precious francs by taking a bus which deposited her at the bottom of the Cap Ferrat hill. Unfortunately the bus was late and the great heroine of musical comedy who, in the phrase of the time, 'had all London at her feet', arrived distraught, sweating and tired, twenty minutes late. Willie was furious that lunch was kept waiting. 'She was always a stupid woman,' he said.

John Gielgud found: 'He was always most courteous and enthusiastic but I was rather in awe of him and his rather abrasive manner.'

Other visitors included Elizabeth Russell (of *Elizabeth and Her German Garden*), Moira Shearer and her husband Ludovic Kennedy, George Cukor, Cyril Connolly, Evelyn Waugh, his brother Alec, Daniel Farson, Arthur Marshall, Noël Coward, Artur Rubinstein, Winston Churchill, Raymond Mortimer, Robert Boothby, Ian and Ann Fleming, Lord Beaverbrook, Desmond MacCarthy, Jean Cocteau, Chips Channon, the Duke and Duchess of Windsor and, of course, members of the Maugham clan.

Willie was particularly fond of Desmond MacCarthy whom he had first met when they worked together for the Red Cross in 1915. A genius as a literary and dramatic critic, MacCarthy played an important role in Willie's life, providing the intellectual stimulus for which he hungered as an antidote to the repetitive tinkling of Riviera small-talk and London gossip. When MacCarthy died in 1952 Willie wrote to his wife Molly that never again would they know such varied and brilliant conversation.

Another visitor who did not fit in with the usual crowd was Ronald Howe, a barrister who made his career at Scotland Yard and became commissioner; he was also the British delegate to the International Police Organisation (Interpol). Little is known about their friendship but it seemed to be based on their mutual links with the intelligence network which probably began during the 1914 war when Howe served in France and was awarded the MC.

In September 1946 Willie left the smell of new paint at the Mauresque and arrived in London for the first of his annual post-war trips lasting ten weeks or so, which continued until the scandal of *Looking Back*. Before the war he had stayed at the then new Dorchester Hotel and now he took a large suite where he and Searle could live in luxury – a home from home.

His visit coincided with a ban in Russia of *The Circle*, lavishly staged at the Moscow Theatre of Drama earlier that year. Reviewing the production in *Theatre World* in April, Nikolai Volkov noted that it 'stresses the drawing-room character of the play' and mentioned the lyric acting and the newly composed lyric background music. It seems the satire was smothered and may explain the official reaction to this and another Maugham production, *Penelope*: 'bourgeois reactionary ideology and morality calculated to poison Soviet minds', as the London *Evening News* reported on 4 September. The ban had no lasting effect on Willie's enormous popularity in Russia.

In London it was as if 1946 was dedicated to a mini-festival of Maugham drama: *Lady Frederick*, *Our Betters*, *The Constant Wife*, *The Sacred Flame* and *For Services Rendered* all received new productions, and Willie himself was as much in demand at seventy as he had been forty years before. He could only cope with a selection of the avalanche of invitations for public and private events which typified this and future visits. In between seeing the latest Coward, Novello or Rattigan production, there was a little gentle shopping to be done, though retailers would often be summoned to the Dorchester to parade their wares. He entertained frequently in his suite, spent time with the family and often went away for weekends with old friends such as Lady Juliet Duff at Bulbridge House. In 1950 Chips Channon, a fellow guest on one of these occasions, noted that he was growing gentler and more mellow.

Among the invitations were always some to male-only gatherings; these were completely homosexual. At first sight the guests might have been a collection of respectable businessmen except for a leavening of attractive young men and a few guardsmen in their scarlet rig. These parties were often dull until drink, drugs and music enlivened the atmosphere. At some of them, entertainment was laid on later. This varied, but basically consisted of a demonstration of sexual prowess by the guardsmen or others hired for the night, often with the ready assistance of volunteers from the audience. Illegal and highly dangerous, it was impossible to keep these occasions a secret and stories circulated around the gay community about what went on and which prominent personages were said to be there. In the fifties a story circulated about a party at which a young guardsman was drugged and badly abused. Willie was alleged to have watched the proceedings from his armchair but shared the general panic when the soldier passed out and could not be revived. The man was smuggled away from the host's Mayfair home, dumped in Hyde Park still unconscious and the authorities tipped off. In the subsequent cover-up anonymity was preserved but Willie and others had a narrow escape from scandal. It seems astonishing that he ever ran such risks, but of course the story may not be true, at least in its more lurid details. Stanley Millar, Billy Milton and Cyril Butcher, who had each heard versions of it, conceded that it may have become exaggerated.

Willie enjoyed being fêted while in London, but he could be a difficult guest. Ludovic Kennedy recalled in *On My Way to the Club* that he and his wife held a drinks party at their home for Willie, and carefully chose a group of mutual friends including Sacheverell Sitwell, Kenneth Clark and his wife. Because, apparently, none of them encouraged him to play the Grand Old Man of English Letters, he left after ten minutes looking glum, saying that he was sure their 'little party' would get more and more uproarious.

Eric Ambler and his wife had a rather worse experience. Willie was due to arrive for dinner at eight but appeared at seven demanding food, having left a cocktail party at Scotland Yard early because he was bored. He had specified an Indian dinner and the Amblers had engaged a chef to prepare it. While waiting for the other guests to arrive, he sulked and refused a drink. At dinner he said he did not want wine, he wanted beer. When that was brought he ignored it and asked for wine. At last, when he left, he gave a thin smile and said he had enjoyed himself. The Amblers had not: 'It was a ghastly evening.'

At home in France Willie could be an equally difficult guest if the mood took him. Robin told the story of a trip to Monte Carlo to have lunch with Maud Marriott, the daughter of Otto Kahn. During the war, in Cairo with her husband Brigadier John Marriott, she had entertained as lavishly as she had in pre-war London, Paris and New York. Worldly wise as she undoubtedly was, 'Momo' was put off her stride when Willie refused to cross the threshold of her home unless she stripped down to the nude: 'There's only one excuse for plump women like you and that is that they should have no clothes on.' She recovered her poise and blithely assumed this to be a witty aside, but Willie would have none of it until Searle told him to behave himself. During lunch Willie kept Momo on tenterhooks in case he said something outrageous to her other guests but he was at his most benign, his bad behaviour presumably having served its purpose.

One of Willie's neighbours was Eric Dunstan, who lived at the Villa Flore, and they quarrelled intermittently. Beverley Nichols decided Willie was jealous because people found Dunstan fun and preferred his company. During a period of reconciliation Dunstan held a lunch in honour of Willie, but a fellow guest, Billy Milton, recalled that at one point he asked loudly, 'Whatever happened to Eric Dunstan?' Similarly, at a lunch at the Mauresque, Willie, having been pleasant enough, suddenly gave Dunstan a piercing look and said: 'Tell me, whatever happened to that swine Eric Dunstan?' Some saw these instances as signs of increasing madness and some as an old man getting malevolent amusement from the discomfiture of others.

In February 1947 Freddie and Kate went to stay at the villa with Willie; also there were Alexander Frere and his wife Pat, the daughter of Edgar Wallace. During dinner one evening the subject was 'bricks dropped' or 'faire une gaffe'. Willie recalled an evening at Bayreuth when a squat, elderly woman in a cloche hat and a long, brown coat rushed up, embraced and kissed him and said, 'How lovely to see you.' He stared at her blankly. 'You don't recognise me. What a humiliation!' 'But how could I be expected to recognise her?' Willie asked. 'I was only used to seeing her dressed in white satin and diamonds.' It was Dame Nellie Melba.

After dinner Alan put on gramophone records; Beethoven, then Ezio Pinza singing 'Some Enchanted Evening' and finally Willie's favourite song, 'Diamonds Are a Girl's Best Friend'. (At all gay gatherings, it is said that Willie would mime to this.)

On another occasion, at a lunch where the guests included Prince Pierre of Monaco and Nadia Boulanger, Freddie remarked that the English were more emotional than they used to be. Willie said that they had always been an emotional and sentimental people until the Victorian era when Prince Albert invented the stiff upper lip.

In his autobiography Robin stressed the incompatibility of the brothers and the coldness between them but Kate saw no sign of it at the villa. They both used ironic humour to tease each other and anecdotes about them indicate that they were very similar. One evening they were chatting when Willie mentioned that he thought a mutual friend was very common. Freddie said nothing but smiled. 'What are you smiling at?' demanded Willie. 'I was only thinking that I know many more common people than you do.' After a second's pause Willie retorted indignantly: 'But almost *all* my friends are *terribly* common!'

# XII

## *The Servant*

Robin had been called to the Bar in 1945 but he had no intention of following a legal career. In September of that year he made a series of visits to Whitehall departments and on 12 December he was airborne for Cairo. According to his account, General Paget, Commander-in-Chief, Middle East, 'suddenly' sent him a secret invitation to work as a journalistic 'observer', but of what he did not say. In those days of complicated restrictions no one could simply pack a bag and board a plane for Cairo without the necessary permits; his trip was in fact under the auspices of British Intelligence. Following discussions with General Paget and his senior staff, Robin was assigned to work with Major Altounyan and Glubb Pasha as he had done before. Subsequently he gave differing written versions of events but in each one, just as he appeared to be on the brink of a coherent explanation of his mission, he scurried away down a verbal cul-de-sac either to give the reader a snapshot of Arab life or to meet entertaining characters he beguilingly admitted to be fictional.

Glubb Pasha, dismissing Robin's phoney journalistic cover as farcical, put him into the uniform of a captain in the Arab Legion and supplied documentation enabling him to travel freely through British army checkpoints. In all he visited five countries and it is possible to deduce, despite his evasion, that his mission was to test Arab opinion on British policy in general and the Jewish question in particular.

The new Labour government, strongly supported by the United States, had agreed to allow Jewish refugees free access to

Palestine but the logistical problems this created were overwhelming and restricted entry had to be introduced. The resulting frustrations and growing nationalism bred Jewish terrorist groups set on forcing the British out. The Arab view was simple: the British had no right to give away what they did not own. Robin returned to England sometime in April 1946 and reported to his superiors; then on Easter Sunday, 21 April, he went to Chartwell to see Churchill who, although out of office, still maintained his sources of information as he had in the thirties.

When *Nomad*, in which Robin told his story, appeared in 1947 nobody commented on the lack of specific information but treated it as a sort of travel book. The *New York Times* commented that he started his journey a little like the Lone Ranger and ended up as a minor philosopher-cum-statesman, and that some of the mystic quality of T. E. Lawrence was evident in his reflections. Harold Nicolson not surprisingly gave him a warm review in the *Daily Telegraph*, describing him as a heroic young man with a nimble pen and romantic impulses.

Robin claimed impartiality, but it is clear from the book that his sympathies lay with the Arab people. In a strongly-worded attack he accused European Jewish refugees of importing fascist totalitarianism into Palestine and of poisoning the pure stream of the Jewish religion. In later years he believed that he was marked down for assassination by extreme Zionist groups but this seems unlikely, if only because time had lessened his importance. In conjunction with *Nomad* Robin published a pamphlet, 'Approach to Palestine', in which he propounded solutions which seemed viable but required a level of moral and financial commitment by the major nations that only an idealist could imagine them giving.

Among the Arabs Robin had found a relaxed attitude towards homosexuality which coincided with his own views. Although he enjoyed sleeping with women, he also enjoyed sleeping with his own sex and was baffled by the British attitude towards what seemed no more than an ordinary activity between males. He knew the religious arguments, but he could not understand why Christians clung to rules of behaviour originally made for Jewish tribes intent on surviving by increasing their numbers; what made perfect sense at that time hardly applied in the modern world. But in Britain the confusion was compounded by the equation of sexual enjoyment with sin as defined by decades of Christian theorists who preferred to ignore Christ's teaching in favour of their own guilty obsessions and bigotry.

After failing to get a contract to write on Middle East politics, he went to Egypt as a freelance journalist hoping that something might turn up. Money was short but Eric Duke, whom he had met during the war, invited him to stay at his penthouse apartment in Alexandria. He eventually sold several articles to the *Spectator* magazine which illustrated his political viewpoint. Similar work also appeared in *Contact*, a lushly produced series of magazines edited by George Weidenfeld, later Lord Weidenfeld, with Nigel Nicolson as his deputy.

At the suggestion of David Astor, Robin set out to find Michael Davidson, the special correspondent of the *Observer*, who was based in Tangier but from whom the paper had not heard for some while. Colourful stories about Tangier had not prepared Robin for the reality and his initial reaction was one of stunned disbelief. For decades its sex industry had attracted Europeans and Americans whose tastes could be described euphemistically as exotic or alternatively as repellent. There were over a hundred brothels, among them a high proportion offering young boys, as well as exhibitions of a particularly brutal kind. Robin, taken to a selection of these places in the Petit Socco, was horrified at his new English expatriate friends who dismissed revolting cruelty to small children with a joke. Robin later discovered that children often died from the injuries inflicted during these sessions.

Robin believed that he was hardened to perversion in all its variations but he had been mentally sickened by the sex exhibitions he had seen, yet simultaneously aware of an insidious stimulative effect. He felt degraded, alarmed at the attrition of his compassion and deeply guilty. He rarely spoke of this experience, as if he could not face the memory; instead, he tried to exorcise it through his writing but this, far from freeing him, seemed to trap and overwhelm him.

In his search for Michael Davidson he went to the notorious Dean's Bar where one of the regulars explained that Davidson was confined to a male brothel for non-payment of his bill. The proprietors had taken away his clothes and typewriter and pawned them to get some of their money. In the meantime, they kept him locked up in the hope that someone might rescue him and pay off the rest of the debt. Robin paid and also recovered Davidson's clothes and typewriter. He was so beguiled by this strange man who looked like a humorous camel that, over dinner, he suggested that Davidson accompany him on a trip around Morocco.

Michael Davidson was about fifty when Robin met him. Educated at Lancing College, he was an officer in World War I and, after a spell farming in Africa, became a junior sub-editor on the *Eastern Daily Press* in Norwich. It was here that he met the sixteen-year-old Wystan Auden: 'there began a poetical relationship which for two years or so absorbed me'. He then worked in London but was given four months in prison for a minor sexual offence. After this he ended up in Morocco teaching English and, during the war, worked for British Intelligence. Back in London he was taken on by the *Daily Express*, followed by Reuters, and was then recruited by the *Observer*. He was a vivid personality with an irrepressible sense of fun, always on the verge of poverty from which he was rescued by friends. Robin said: 'His trouble was that he had an incurable passion for the pursuit of boys. I've never known anyone devote so much energy to it. He did things that I myself might like to have done but which I was too afraid or too nervous to do.' Unfortunately he proved to be a corrupting influence on Robin who was still, in many respects, an innocent and highly impressionable.

While he was living in the Middle East Robin, with assistance from Davidson, completed a short novel which he dedicated to Eric Duke. He entitled it *The Servant*; it was to become his best-known work. The experience that suggested the plot of the novel occurred when he was living in Chelsea just after the war. As he explained in an interview for the American magazine *Gay Sunshine*:

> My mother bought me a little house in Chelsea . . . and installed this manservant who, in the novel, I've called Barrett. He was the perfect manservant and he looked after the house beautifully, cooked terribly well and kept everything very clean. But somehow he gave me the shudders. Something about him frightened me. But it seemed too ridiculous to dismiss the perfect manservant merely because he worried one by his presence.

Robin recalled how he arrived home with Mary Churchill after a trip to the cinema and went down to the kitchen to fetch lagers from the refrigerator. As he passed Barrett's bedroom he saw through the open door a naked young boy spreadeagled face down on the bed.

> His hair was fair and curly, his skin was immaculate and his figure was lovely. While I was staring in wonderment at this beautiful creature a voice behind me said: 'Good evening, sir. I see you are admiring my nephew. Perhaps you would like him to come up later to say goodnight to you?' And at that moment I saw the portals of blackmail and the gates of prison yawning open before my gaze. I pretended I hadn't heard. When I got into the living room Mary Churchill stared at me and said, 'Whatever happened to you? You look as white as a ghost.' And I said, 'Yes, I've just seen one.' But I never told her the story.
> A few weeks later when I was down in the country, I was telephoned by the police who told me that Barrett had been caught trying to pawn all my clothes. I was asked if I wanted to bring an action and I said no. I just wanted him out of the house and never to see him again. And I never have.

Robin asserted that the novel was not autobiographical but he projected three aspects of himself into the main male characters: Richard Merton from *Come to Dust*, who acts as narrator, exhibits the best in him; Tony Williams, the tough veteran of war in the Far East, personifies his sexual vulnerability; and Barrett, the tempter, epitomizes the depraved aspect of his personality.

It was impossible at that time to publish an overtly homosexual novel in Britain, so the young boy became a teenage girl. Robin based her on a girl he had met in the country soon after his demobilisation. She was a good-looking blonde of about sixteen whom he had first seen galloping across the fields on a coal-black horse. Once, after they became acquainted, they were strolling through the woods when they came to a grassy bank. The girl lay down and told Robin that this was where her riding master had seduced her two years previously when she was only fourteen. 'So, you see, you needn't worry,' she said, sensing Robin's desire. Then she held out her arms to him.

Whether this story is true or false it bears a strong similarity to another Robin told about an experience he had when he was eleven years old. Once again the setting was a wood but this time the grassy bank overlooked a stream. The girl, the daughter of a neighbour, suggested playing at dressing up. They exchanged clothes, he pretending to be her and she him. When this palled she stripped off the clothes and jumped into the stream. Shyly he did the same and then she rushed up the bank, grabbed all the clothes and ran off. When he caught her they wrestled until, exhausted, they lay naked in each other's arms.

The action of *The Servant* covers two years from 1945 and in only ninety-four pages Robin depicts subtle and intricate relationships between protagonists motivated by love, sexual envy, lust and greed. Tony is loved by his childhood sweetheart Sally and it is assumed that they will marry, but she realises that, while he admires her beauty and enjoys showing her off, she has no physical attraction for him; consequently she leaves him and marries someone else. Tony is also loved by Richard and despite a disclaimer in the text it is clear that in the past there has been a fusion of mutual attraction which still lingers. Richard suggests they go away together. 'I'll do all I can to make you happy.' Tony stares at him, eyes filled with tears. Then Barrett calls him and, as if mesmerised, he turns away from Richard.

Barrett has made Tony dependent on him by detecting his weakness and satisfying it. Early on in the story he brings a young girl into the house whom he says is his niece. Ostensibly she is there to help with the work but her real task is to seduce Tony and then to reveal that she is underage and has been a child prostitute for several years. Blackmailed, but at the same time cosseted by Barrett, Tony succumbs to a routine dominated by alcohol, drugs and group sex with female children and Barrett himself.

Robin handled the sexual details with considerable skill and left much to be read between the lines, as he could not be explicit for fear of the Obscene Publications Act. It was to be some sixteen years later, after Penguin Books were exonerated for publishing D. H. Lawrence's *Lady Chatterley's Lover*, that writers had complete freedom to express themselves. Bearing this in mind, Robin achieved a result which, in its way, remains a minor classic of its time with some of the resonances of *The Picture of Dorian Gray*. The *Times Literary Supplement* praised it and the *New York Times* called it 'a masterpiece'. Its success set the pattern of his future novels in which he examined the themes of sexual ambiguity, guilt, fear, repression and hopeless despair. Unfortunately his ambitious intentions exceeded his ability to deal with them.

From the beginning Robin saw *The Servant* in terms of cinema and he submitted a version to the censor, edited in anticipation of objections. Some weeks later he received a letter saying, 'I have been through it most carefully and so has my assistant. Never in our lifetime can *The Servant* be made into a film.' In 1958 a stage version was tried out at the Connaught Theatre, Worthing, but it did not work satisfactorily because the Lord Chamberlain's Office controlled the theatre by a rigid set of rules which could only be evaded with an experienced cunning which Robin did not possess. Even so, the play had impact and there was a shocked reaction by elderly season-ticket holders on the first night. In one scene the girl, now older to comply with the legal age of consent, knelt down in front of Barrett and put her arms round his waist. It looked as if she was about to mime oral sex and there was a sharp intake of breath from the grey-haired brigade followed by the banging of seats as some of them trooped out in protest, 'in a great whiff of mothballs and a clatter of bangles,' as Robin put it.

Robin made extensive revisions and the play was tried out again in 1966 at the Yvonne Arnaud Theatre, Guildford but still it did not work. For reasons now forgotten Robin set both dramatisations in a time vacuum conveniently labelled 'the present', but tearing it away from its 1945 setting destroyed its essential post-war flavour and left the behaviour of the characters confusing. By 1966, twenty years adrift, it merely appeared anachronistic and nothing to do with the 'present time' of the swinging sixties. In his highly praised revival at the Birmingham Repertory Theatre in 1995, Bill Alexander set the play firmly back in the late forties and gave the audience an opportunity to judge the complexity of the story and to react to the emotions it invited them to share.

Robin hated the screen version, released in 1963, though it had a brilliant script by Harold Pinter. Tactfully he said nothing adverse in public but in private referred to it as that 'fucking film', often remarking, 'I took the money and ran.' But this was later. While the film was being made Robin was on good terms with everyone. Joseph Losey, the director, often stayed at Robin's Seaton Street house. 'I can't remember how many breakfasts I'd have and then think "The Gainsborough's gone!" But Joe had whipped it off for the film.' Losey also used much of Robin's furniture because he believed it provided authenticity. The items included the convex mirror used in the well-known shot of Barrett dusting, while Tony looks on.

Losey had been blacklisted in America as a suspected communist in 1951 and was struggling to make a living in Britain while trying to come to terms with its complicated social structure. Harold Pinter, who had made his name as a dramatist with *The Birthday Party* (1958) and *The Caretaker* (1960), came of a Jewish East End working-class family. Between them, Losey thought, they could look at aspects of England that probably no others in the world could do.

Losey, updating the story to the sixties, apparently believed it was about the English class system, a thought that had not occurred to Robin. Unfortunately Losey was a stranger to the upper-class milieu and characters of Robin's story, and did not understand them. Losey also failed to comprehend the complexities of bisexuality which may explain why he completely overlooked the interlinked sexual significances and why the vital character of Richard Merton was eliminated. This led to unavoidable changes to disguise the scars which, coupled with Losey's enthusiastic excesses, resulted in a product a long way removed from the novel. For example, instead of a narrow terrace house in a mean street, poorly furnished with no vestige of taste, rented by Tony as a temporary home, the setting was changed to an elegant house in Royal Avenue. Instead of being a war veteran returned to study for his law finals, Tony became a strangely effete architect involved with a grandiose scheme for three new cities in the Brazilian jungle. Barrett, the manservant, in a mesmerising performance from Dirk Bogarde, no longer needed to be a petty crook, 'the king of the local black market'. Instead he became a superb chef, a talented interior designer, valet, flower arranger and all-purpose domestic who could keep a large house spotless with the wave of a duster. Vera, the child waif, became the very un-waif-like, glamorous Sarah Miles.

The most drastic change was to the role of Tony's childhood sweetheart Sally. She became a major figure, absorbing the function of Richard Merton, but her social status seemed uncertain. Penelope Gilliatt later observed that the character wavered 'between a confident Pont Street loudmouth and an outwitted provincial'. Robin, if asked, could have clarified this and other problems of class and behaviour which arose from Losey's ignorance and were glaringly evident in the film. Sally, he would have explained, was a typically well-bred product of the upper-middle class, probably not unlike his own sisters. Losey claimed he could not find the type he wanted and cast Wendy Craig, an actress of warmth and sensitivity. When he asked her to assume an upper-class manner and accent 'it was utterly hopeless', he said, with hindsight, to Tom Milne in 1968. This ungallant comment did not absolve him from directorial responsibility for shaping her strident and bad-tempered interpretation; her attitude to Barrett was petulant and ill-mannered instead of being coolly correct. This made it difficult to see how Tony tolerated her. James Fox, at least, a newcomer blessedly free of actory tricks, played Tony with more plausibility than a glamorous box-office star might have done.

Losey often directed like a demented Orson Welles, sometimes with pyrotechnical effect. His orgy sequence towards the end of the film disastrously failed to emulate the German cinema which it appeared to ape and instead was painfully comic, while the final scenes were inadequate and exposed the pretentiousness of his approach.

*The Servant* was shown at the Venice Film Festival and the New York Film Festival but distributors were indifferent to it. In London, when a film failed at Warner Brothers' Leicester Square cinema, a frantic reconsideration of rejected films took place and it was decided to take a chance with *The Servant*. It was shown at a time when the public was engrossed in the Profumo affair, and the critics appeared to see it as a parable for the new age. It was acclaimed as the best film of 1963 and has since become a legend, although time has not been kind to it.

The novel of *The Servant* waits to be rediscovered and reassessed in a completely new dramatisation which incorporates the original situation that inspired it and manifests understanding of its complex sexual relationships. Such a reassessment should not lose the social milieu of the late 1940s that Robin captured with unwitting accuracy, like an old photograph which reveals more than was originally intended.

# Harold, Guy, Kurt and Ken

Robin initially had some difficulty with his parents about *The Servant*. When pre-publication copies of the novel arrived at Cadogan Square, they knew nothing of its contents, but his mother was intrigued by the elegant cover design and his father by the title. Somewhat reluctantly Robin gave them each a copy to read, anticipating correctly that they would not like it. He was not prepared for Freddie's demand that, whatever the cost, on no account must it be seen by the public with the Maugham name on it. Disconcerted by this, Robin telephoned Harold Nicolson for advice and Nicolson immediately wrote a long letter to Freddie explaining that, however shocking and abhorrent some of the sequences in the novel might be, its publication would make Robin's reputation as an author. Slightly mollified Freddie withdrew his objection in deference to Nicolson.

Freddie had no idea, of course, of Robin's intimate relationship with Nicolson. This had nothing of the emotional commitment that marked Vita Sackville-West's lesbian romances. Unlike his wife's homosexuality, Nicolson's was a light-hearted fantasy of jolly romps between well-built boys gleefully masturbating themselves and each other. The concept of a man in love with another man repelled him and he avoided any relationship which looked as if it might become serious. He was not only a good friend to Robin but a mentor; it has been suggested that he had some influence on the style of the early books, among them *Come to Dust* and *The Servant*.

Nicolson was responsible for introducing Robin to Guy Burgess who was only too delighted to welcome the future Viscount Maugham into his circle. The friendship between Nicolson and the Soviet agent which began in the thirties was much closer than generally realised. Like so many, from Churchill downwards, Nicolson was duped by the Burgess mixture of flattery and charm. He may not have understood the value of the titbits of fact and gossip that he passed on in chatty conversation, which went to build the mosaic of data that Burgess assembled to give his masters in Moscow. Nicolson might have been less sanguine if he had known that Burgess spoke of him behind his back as 'A rose-red sissy half as old as time'. Generally supposed to have referred to Hugh Walpole, from Burgess's lips this became a neat jibe at Nicolson's mild socialism and sexual propensities.

In his autobiography Robin described Burgess as a romantic with a brilliant, fertile brain but emotionally unstable and aggressively homosexual. No one knows how much of Robin's knowledge of Middle Eastern affairs may have been milked by Burgess, for he had no reason to mistrust a man so well established at the Foreign Office and if, as seems likely, he knew that Burgess worked for MI6, Robin could have spoken freely of his own intelligence work.

In 1948 Robin gave a lecture to the Royal Empire Society on the problems of North Africa. When the chairman invited questions Burgess, very drunk, lurched to his feet:

> The distinguished lecturer has in his speech used the phrase 'Fascism does not seem to matter so much in Spain.' But inasmuch as this meeting is being reported by the World Press, the lecturer might decide to qualify this statement in view of the fact that it might be quoted out of context.

Robin thanked him for drawing his attention to the slip. As he put it in his book: 'With typical kindness he had done me a good turn.'

At the party afterwards Burgess, with a boyfriend in tow, became progressively more drunk. He was not an attractive sight with his grubby clothes and dirty fingernails and, as he sprawled 'burly and truculent' on the floor in front of the fireplace, his talk was wild and pro-Russian. He kept repeating E. M. Forster's dictum that if he had to choose between betraying his country and his friends, he hoped he would choose to betray his country. Kate thought he must be a communist but Robin said this was nonsense; if he were, surely he would not act the part of a 'parlour' communist so obviously. 'Perhaps it's a double bluff,' she retorted.

Whether or not Robin slept with Burgess is unimportant but Burgess introduced him to a young man called Kurt (not his real name) with whom he fell in love and he allowed the two to use his flat at New Bond Street for their assignations. By doing this he tied Robin even closer to him. It is not too outlandish to suppose that for Burgess it was also a form of insurance. Burgess probably had a secret camera; if he had not, he was missing a trick taken for granted by his Soviet colleagues.

As a physical type, Kurt exemplified Robin's taste. He was of medium height with powerful shoulders, a narrow waist and long legs. He had blue eyes and his hair was a mass of blond curls. His nose was small and delicate and when he smiled he revealed even and very white teeth. His background was working class and he was flattered by Robin's attention but, like many of his lovers, he was not completely homosexual, an aspect which added to his appeal but which was to have an unexpected sequel.

Unable to settle down in England, Robin decided to follow the example of many of his countrymen and make a new life in the Colonies, in his case as a gentleman farmer in Tanganyika. He took Kurt with him and this proved a disaster. They were soon bored with a lonely lifestyle which had little to offer by way of distraction, and the men of the British colony were in no rush to accept the 'queer couple' into the narrow social life centred on their club. But then initial impressions were jolted when rumours spread about Kurt's behaviour. He had turned out to be a skilful womaniser with an insatiable sexual appetite. An irate husband vowed to kill Kurt and lashed him with a cattle whip. This scandal and the financial uncertainty of the farming venture forced Robin to give up. When they returned to England, he and Kurt parted.

While Robin was in Tanganyika *The Servant* was published in America and much was made in publicity of several critical comments which compared him to his uncle. The *New York Times*, for example, said that it was written with a skill and pace that Somerset Maugham might envy. Willie was furious when friends, eager to cause trouble, sent him cuttings of a full-page advertisement containing the offending reference to himself. He blamed Robin for approving the advertisement; Robin knew nothing about it but had some difficulty in persuading Willie of this.

Robin's second novel, mostly written in Tanganyika, was *Line on Ginger* (1949), a fictional spin-off of *Come to Dust*. Once again he used Merton as narrator. Merton discovers Ginger Edwards, an ex-trooper from his old regiment, burgling his flat. Ginger escapes and Merton sets out to find and, if possible, rescue him from a criminal life. Eventually he traces him through various ex-comrades and learns of his tragic childhood, his happiness in the army and his disillusionment with civilian life. Merton has suffered similar disillusionment and plans to find a new life abroad. He suggests that Ginger accompanies him: 'He looked at me for a long time. His eyes met mine. It seemed ages before he spoke. "Thanks. I'll think it over." ' In the final scene on board ship, Merton does not know whether Ginger will join him. He asks himself what has happened to men he knew in the tank corps:

> We are the same people. Why then do we feel we have changed? Then (in the war) we had a common aim . . . Now, we are alone and bewildered . . . And when we meet, we can only deal kindly with one another in our distress, hoping that kindness may do some good.

It would be easy to dismiss the story as trite, the execution as competent, if lachrymose, but in 1949 it had a poignancy which touched thousands of readers who identified with its sentiments and the search for a solution to the complexities of life. Perhaps unknowingly he had identified the pattern of his own future, an endless quest for Nirvana. Also, though the book is in no sense overtly homosexual, hovering just below the surface is Robin's longing for the ideal male companion who, time after time, was to be a working-class youth like Ginger. In 1953 a film version called *The Intruder*, with a screenplay by Robin and John Hunter, directed by Guy Hamilton, did reasonably well. But even with a cast of distinguished actors headed by Jack Hawkins, Dennis Price and George Cole, and with Michael Medwin as Ginger, it emerged as a mechanical retelling of the story without the poignancy of the book.

During his stay with Eric Duke in Alexandria, Robin's imagination was stimulated by stories of Siwa, once the site of the temple of Ammon. It was said that homosexual marriage ceremonies going back to ancient times were still carried out, despite government attempts to stop them. It was at Siwa that Alexander the Great was assured by the oracle that he was a god-king who would become lord of the earth. The involvement of one of the great gay icons of all time fascinated Robin, and he spent days at the English Library studying the history of Siwa and Alexander's association with it. He learned, for example, that Alexander had vowed to be buried in the temple of Ammon but his wishes had been ignored. (It is now believed that the body may have been transferred to Siwa and, at the time of writing, attempts are being made to locate the tomb.)

Robin was determined to investigate Siwa for himself and, with the help of Eric Duke, he obtained the necessary permits for himself and a photographer, Dimitri Papadimou. A friendly Egyptian colonel supplied an army truck and a driver who knew the desert route. They arrived after a journey of several days, were welcomed by the governor and shown to the official guest house. This was situated outside the town and run by a young Siwan called Ahmed.

The town, built on a rock plateau and surrounded by groves of date palms and olive trees, resembled a fortress, the result of its development to withstand attack from Bedouin tribes. To prevent trouble with the women and to provide the first line of defence, bachelors had always been excluded from the town at night and these zaggalas, as they were called, slept in shelters outside the walls. As soon as a boy reached puberty he was sent to join them and it was taken for granted that he would become the lover of one of the older men. But there were rules: if a boy did not like the zaggala who fancied him he could run away into the palm groves, but if he was caught the older man was allowed to make love to him and take him back to his shelter for the night. After this, the boy could still refuse to stay but if he decided he liked the man an elaborate marriage ceremony would take place.

It was assumed that, even if a man married a young girl, he would still have male lovers. Wives were changed frequently but the formal male-to-male marriages could last for years.

Robin discovered that the Siwan reputation for a casual attitude to sex in all its variations had not been exaggerated. He described returning to the guest house one afternoon to find Ahmed in the middle of fucking a teenage boy. Both, unabashed, smiled at him and Ahmed, pausing for a moment or two, asked Robin if he would like to have him too. The boy, to show that he approved of the idea, stuck his tongue out and waggled it from side to side in the age-old gesture of invitation. Robin, shocked by this hospitable offer, lied politely that of course he would, except that he had an assignation later. 'As long as you're happy,' smiled Ahmed and carried on with what he was doing.

Some nights later, when Robin and the photographer were eating their evening meal, Ahmed ushered in a young Senussi soldier called Salem who, it appeared, had become detached from an army patrol and had wandered around lost until he saw the lights of the guest house. As Ahmed was about to go home to his young wife, could he leave the soldier with them to sleep in one of the empty bedrooms? Robin nodded and the new guest joined them to eat. As a Senussi he followed the strict rules of his Moslem sect and declined the wine and tobacco which, as hosts, they were bound to offer him.

Later Robin showed him to a room, explained how the shower worked in the primitive bathroom and then settled down to read by the light of the oil lamp by his bed. Suddenly the door opened and Salem appeared naked, except for a towel round his waist. According to Robin a stilted conversation took place in which Salem explained that he had never slept in a room alone before and could he stay with him? Robin made space in his bed; Salem dropped the towel, got into bed and lay perfectly still by his side. In a frenzy of desire and uncertainty Robin lay equally still until he could not control himself; tentatively he touched Salem's shoulder. The boy turned to him, put his arms around him, kissed him and they made frantic love.

Robin was not able to use this story until *Search for Nirvana* thirty years later, by which time it had become lengthy and highly romanticised. He said that four days of love-making ended when

Salem went to find his army colleagues, but they were now so infatuated with each other that there had been wild talk of the boy deserting and going to London with Robin and even of Robin joining the boy's tribe.

Back in London Nellie had made the nursery floor of the house in Cadogan Square into a flat for Robin and here he wrote two books based on his experiences. The first, *North Africa Notebook*, was a straightforward travel book but the second, *Journey to Siwa*, which appeared in 1950, was of greater interest because so little was known of Siwa. Of the second book Freya Stark, under the heading 'Reticent Traveller', commented in the *Observer*: 'It is strange, when one thinks of it, how one hesitates over sodomy . . . when contemplating the history of Egypt. The fact is that we would like Robin Maugham to let himself go a little more.' As he said later, he was constrained by what Harold Nicolson called 'the nursery governess' who peered disapprovingly over the shoulder of every English writer of a certain class. This disapproval had also constrained Cecil Beaton in his poetic description of Siwa which he visited during the war, saying of it: 'Life is very pleasant here, almost a living enchantment.'

After completing *Journey to Siwa* Robin was at a loose end; superficially all seemed well and he managed to cope with blinding headaches and periods of amnesia. There was no lack of social life and he often entertained at his flat, but his friends, frequently young working-class males, did not please Freddie. One night Robin and Harold Nicolson returned to Cadogan Square after dinner at the Travellers' Club. The household was asleep and they crept up the stairs. When he left, Nicolson told Robin not to bother to see him out as he knew the way blindfolded but he stumbled and fell down the stairs, ending up with a crash against the door to Freddie's bedroom. Expecting his father to emerge at any second, Robin helped the stunned Nicolson down to the street, put him in a taxi and crept back to his own room.

The next morning Freddie delivered a short lecture on the type of company Robin kept. Surely he could find somebody other than the common riff-raff he seemed so fond of entertaining: 'Who, for example, was the drunken young hooligan who crashed against my bedroom door last night?' 'Harold Nicolson,' Robin replied.

After the failure of his affair with Kurt in Tanganyika, Robin longed for a permanent relationship but it was not easy to meet the right person in London. There were numerous places where bisexuals or homosexuals could be found but mostly they were interested only in anonymous one-night encounters, some at a price, and this was not what he was looking for. Sometimes urgent need drove him to make the rounds of the gay pubs like the White Bear in Piccadilly, the Fitzroy Tavern in north Soho, the Queen's in Leicester Square or the Salisbury in St Martin's Lane. They all attracted large crowds and sometimes he was lucky but then, as now, it was dangerous; he could never be certain whether the bit of rough would beat him up, rob him or attempt blackmail. He had to be very careful whom he took back to Cadogan Square and generally preferred to go back to the boy's home. Alternatively there were small hotels where no questions were asked. It has been suggested that, like many in his position, he leased a flat in the back streets where he could preserve his anonymity.

One night, after doing the rounds of the pubs, he visited a well-known, members-only gay drinking club in Archer Street called the Rockingham which prided itself on having 'class'. The interior was decorated in genteel style and the clientele it attracted matched it, a mixture of older business types, young clerks and shop assistants, all in suits and stiff white collars with silk ties, chattering quietly over their drinks. After ordering a gin and tonic Robin noticed that an attractive boy standing near him was not playing up to the surroundings, much to the embarrassment of his middle-aged companion who could have been a stockbroker, a bank manager or a cleric in mufti. Intrigued, Robin listened to their conversation which went something like this:

'This place is too piss-elegant and I don't like it,' said the boy.

His companion bridled. 'If you don't like it, go, but don't come to me next time you're in trouble.'

'Right,' said the boy, 'I'll fuck off, then.'

Robin slipped away and waited by the entrance. As the boy came out he said, 'You're perfectly right. It is bloody piss-elegant. Let's go and have a proper drink in a pub.'

Startled, the boy stared at him. 'What you want?'

'Nothing, except a pint of bitter.'

The boy grinned. Together they went into the nearest pub and, over their beer, Robin asked him about his life and heard a familiar story. Ken had quarrelled with his stepfather, left home, arrived in London, could not get a job and, desperate for money to pay for the rent of his room, had gone on the game.

They ended up in Ken's bedsit in a broken-down house in Fulham. The next morning Robin decided he had found the ideal companion, someone he could love. The attraction was mutual but the immediate problem was where they would live. It was solved when Robin found Ken was mad about boats and impulsively decided to buy one. They found what they wanted moored at Teddington, an old motor yacht called *Clio*, vintage 1910. The fittings were impressive and it had an Edwardian air of luxury. Robin paid £2,750 for it. Ostensibly Ken was employed to run the boat. Although he was a mechanic by trade, he was eager to learn seamanship.

Robin invited Harold Nicolson to dinner at an hotel by the river at Wargrave to be followed by a night on *Clio*. Robin insisted it be Tuesday 15 August so that he could meet friends from Cairo, a Mrs Dunlop and her daughter Hughine. They were to spend the afternoon on board and would join them for dinner before returning to London.

Tuesday was cold and stormy. During the afternoon the amateur sailors wedged *Clio* in mud on the wrong side of the river and drove the engines to free her until they gave out. Ken met Nicolson at Wargrave Station and wrapped him in oilskins to row him upriver in the pouring rain to the boat. As Nicolson put it in a letter to his wife two days later, Robin now conceived the 'idée funeste' of using their tiny dinghy to tow *Clio* out of the mud to a mooring by the hotel so the guests could step ashore to have dinner. After several hours of effort Robin admitted defeat and conceded it would have been easier to ferry everyone over the river instead of trying to move *Clio*. It was now ten o'clock, pitch dark and the hotel dining room closed up. After a snack of bread and cheese and remnants of fruit cake in the dim lights of three stubs of candle which Ken had found after the batteries failed, the Dunlop couple were anxious to go home.

Robin vowed to get them to the station and because it was so cold he dressed Hughine in his army greatcoat and gingerly lowered her into the dinghy where Ken was ready to take her. Mrs Dunlop handed down her handbag and climbed down herself. There was a loud splash and shouting as the dinghy capsized. As the child, weighed down with the heavy coat, was dragged underwater, Ken saved her. Back on board they changed out of their wet clothes and the Dunlops, wrapped in blankets and revived with coffee and rum, were given Nicolson's cabin.

Nicolson spent a grim night in Ken's bunk while the boy slept on the floor and Robin snored in the other bunk. Next morning Robin was up at six diving in the river to find Mrs Dunlop's handbag which had been lost in the confusion; he eventually recovered it, a muddy, sodden mess. Then he found the dinghy's oars and swam off to rescue the dinghy which had drifted downstream. Nicolson eventually reached London unscathed, the only one not to end up in the river. Hughine's verdict on the multiple disaster was: 'This is what comes of knowing Robin.'

# XIII

## Death of a Lady

On 12 October 1950 Nellie died peacefully surrounded by her family. Among many tributes to her in the press was one from A. A. Milne which appeared in *The Times*:

> She just bubbled over, even in her old age (but one could never think of her as old), with an absurd travesty of everything which had been happening to her, illness, war troubles, domestic difficulties, became, equally with the good, an irresistible saga of nonsense. Hysterical laughter from one end of the telephone meant that Nellie Maugham was at the other.

Nellie was buried at Hartfield Parish Church, in the new part of the churchyard looking across the Sussex countryside to Tye House.

In *Escape from the Shadows*, Robin argued that his parents were an ill-suited couple and that his father's ambition, allied to a neurotically violent jealousy and the need to make money to keep the family in comfort, dried up his humour and love and caused him to retreat into a lonely world of his own making. It is true that there was something inherently enigmatic in the psyche of the male Maughams, which friends and relatives have tried to define; was it fear, insecurity, guilt, or inadequacy? This Maugham enigma may explain a certain reclusiveness in Freddie's character but it did not make him the hermit-like creature that Robin described; in fact, the evidence of Freddie's busy social and professional life contradicts the assertion.

To say that Freddie and Nellie were ill-suited is also unfounded; indeed, they were foils to one another. In matters where he held strong views and she a contrary opinion, he would fix his monocle firmly and, looking at her solemnly, declare, 'Allow me to know better, Nellie.' This exaggerated pomposity was a component of his laconic humour which she and her daughters understood but others sometimes did not. Similarly, one of his favourite phrases was 'No income could stand it'. Robin quoted this to demonstrate a mean streak in Freddie but it was a saying originated by Nellie's wealthy father which he used with much tut-tutting over small items of expenditure like the cost of a short bus journey – in other words a family joke. This banter did not conceal the fact that Nellie was in charge and that Freddie was happy that this should be so.

It is evident that he had difficulty in expressing his feelings for her to others. But the many reasons for his devotion were encapsulated in Lord Asquith's tribute to her in *The Times*:

> Apart from a kindness to which Nature had set no limits, what her friends, I think, found so deeply satisfying was her spontaneity, her zest and her total lack of affectation or any other kind of smallness . . . In her presence, shyness was disarmed, diffidence melted, spirits rose, dullness began to emit sparks, or to think it was doing so, while the most exacting were held, charmed and exhilarated.

# All at Sea

Willie was visiting America when Nellie died and could not get back to England in time for her funeral. He must have recalled with gratitude that, without her affection, encouragement and support, he might have ended up as a family doctor instead of one of the most revered figures of popular literature.

It was to be Willie's last trip to the States, and his schedule was packed with events that paid tribute to his eminence. It included his presentation of a paper on Kant at Columbia, his gift to the Morgan Library of the manuscript of *Ah King* and the presentation of his manuscript of 'The Artistic Temperament of Stephen

Carey' to the Library of Congress (on condition that it would never be published).

On his way back to France in November he spent a few days in London at the Dorchester and saw something of the family including Robin who was full of news of his new lover Ken, and their plan to sail *Clio* to the Greek Islands. After months of work on the boat, the pair sailed in May across to France, up the Seine to Paris, then through the canals to Marseilles and on to the harbour at Villefranche.

When they visited Willie at the Villa Mauresque he was in a bad mood and took an instant dislike to Ken whom he thought common. At lunch he turned to him and remarked: 'You may think you are eating gruel but it is in fact zabaglione – and very expensive to make.' A few days later at dinner Willie said, in a sudden rage, that Robin was making a complete hash of his life and he saw his future as an ageing, impoverished viscount on the fringes of society. Robin retorted: 'And do you know how I see my future? Precisely the same.' The other guests laughed while Willie glowered.

Some days after this Willie told Robin that he would never be a writer and advised him to give it up before he made a fool of himself. If he did this and broke off his association with Ken, he would give him fifty thousand pounds provided he found a wife and went into politics. This offer had now been made on several occasions and Robin said that he would think it over.

The next day Harold Nicolson, anticipating some gentle sailing, arrived to stay on *Clio* but the old yacht had broken down again and the weekend was spent in harbour. Robin told Nicolson about Willie's offer and was advised to refuse the bribe. Nicolson added that he found Willie's hypocrisy unpleasant. But Robin had not told him the whole story, for, as he explained to Myles Hildyard, his uncle was very keen to see the title perpetuated and considered it was Robin's family obligation to marry and have a son; if he did so, Willie promised to make him and his hypothetical heir the main beneficiaries of his fortune.

Nicolson did not want to see Willie on this occasion and said his visit to France should be kept secret, but Willie found out and was enraged. He summoned Robin to the villa to complain about this and then lectured him on the 'scandal' that his affair with Ken was creating: 'In the bars he frequents he flaunts his relationship with you. Everybody in Villefranche knows that you are my nephew and you're getting me a bad name.' He ended with a veiled threat to tell Freddie. This seems questionable. Firstly, Alan Searle was well known for cruising the bars for sailors or rough trade and pimping for Willie. Secondly, in his many letters to Robin, Willie wrote as a loving uncle and never threatened. Thirdly, Freddie already knew of his son's sexual proclivities and preferred, as far as we know, to keep silent. But, as already noted, Robin knew how to conjure a story out of nothing. Keith Monk and Peter Burton have said that anecdotes invented over the dinner table could become actuality in Robin's mind. If this story is accurate, however, its lack of logic may be an early indication of Willie's failing mental powers.

After *Clio* had been refitted in Voisin's boatyard, Ken and Robin set sail, joined by Michael Davidson. In his autobiography, *The World, the Flesh and Myself*, Davidson remembered Willie coming to the quay but refusing to come on board, 'being averse to small craft', a witty but bitchy reference to Willie's grand status. As a dinner guest at the villa, Davidson recalled Willie being in unusually good humour and himself talking about Malaya to Lord John Hope, 'a nice, bony, youngish man'.

It was Davidson who proposed going to Capri to meet Norman Douglas, the author of *South Wind*. Douglas, eighty years old, dressed in baggy grey trousers, frayed braces, open-necked shirt and a shabby coat, had in attendance a twelve-year-old boy whose task was to guide the tottery old man. Douglas, smiling at the boy, murmured: 'I've always loved a very small boy attached to a very big cock.'

They spent several days with the old man, during which they all drank far too much, while Douglas reminisced about the past, but if he gossiped about the old Capri set, neither Robin nor Davidson recorded it. He spoke kindly of Harry Maugham but

Robin missed the opportunity to learn more about him. Of Wilde's friend, Reggie Turner, Douglas said: 'He wasn't one of the greatest conversationalists. He told me the same old stories; it got awfully boring. We used to run miles to avoid him.' He chatted openly about his sexual preferences and when he noticed some English tourists listening, agape, he snapped, 'Do them good!' 'Yes,' he replied to a question, 'I left England under a cloud, a cloud no bigger than a boy's hand.'

Robin was entranced by him and disagreed with Brian Howard who said that he had not really moved with the times 'as much as some of his frenzied admirers like one to believe'. Douglas was treated obsequiously wherever they went but, as he generated business, this may partly account for it. Robin, needless to say, paid the bills for all of them. Douglas's son (the result of 'too much Negroni' as his father put it) warned that the old man's health was too frail for a hectic life. A few months after their visit he died and Davidson wondered if their drinking sessions were responsible.

The next place of call was Ischia, one of Robin's favourite islands. He often stayed there in one of the villas built as an investment by Sir William Walton's wife. His was called Casa Drina and he leased it with Michael and Aileen Balcon. It was next door to Terence Rattigan's villa where he and Rattigan had once spent fourteen days on a drinking binge. Despite his success, Rattigan, like Robin, suffered from introspective depressions. He was doomed to ill-matched affairs with men where one of them was more involved emotionally than the other. Chips Channon, for instance, pursued him relentlessly but Rattigan never felt as strongly and had problems when he tried to convince Chips it was over. Conversely he fell deeply in love with a young actor, Kenneth Morgan, who felt so smothered that he left him for someone else. Rattigan believed he would return, and was distraught when Morgan killed himself. Robin was a shoulder to cry on and could be trusted to remain discreet. In 1976 Rattigan sent Robin a telegram congratulating him on his birthday: 'I thought you'd never make it to sixty! Willie thought you'd never make it as a writer!' In a bitchy remark to someone else he said that Robin couldn't write bum on a wall, and if he did, he would spell it 'BAUGHAM'.

While they were on Ischia Robin met Robert Clarke, the head of Associated British Pictures, who offered him a job to learn the technicalities of film-making and screen-writing. Robin, ever generous, entertained lavishly and held a party for Burt Lancaster, his wife and a large entourage, plus Robert Siodmak who was directing Lancaster in *The Crimson Pirate*.

From Ischia they sailed gently down the coast to Sicily. As Davidson put it: 'One goes where one will and leaves when one wants and one looks with pitying disdain upon the feeble, ordinary folk who can't go yachting. It's absurd and unreal, but delightful.' Reality took its revenge when, on the crossing to Malta at night, the yacht nearly sank in a storm because the amateur sailors, merrily drunk, forgot routine tasks. One engine went dead and the other worked erratically, the bilge pumps failed, the engine room flooded, the yacht plunged into darkness and without navigational lights it limped through pounding seas. Robin struggled up to relieve Ken in the wheelhouse; he appeared to be saying something but then Robin realised that his eyes were shut and he was praying. Down in the small saloon Davidson also prayed and drank himself into oblivion.

Shortly before dawn they saw the outline of a vast naval vessel. Robin guessed they were in Sliema Creek, out of bounds to all but the Royal Navy. Past caring they tied up to a stern buoy and fell into their bunks exhausted. Later, Captain Trevor Lean, DSO, was making his morning rounds of *Manxman* and, glancing over its stern rail, saw the little yacht fastened to the buoy. 'Good God,' he exclaimed, 'I've laid an egg!' By midday he had the bedraggled threesome drinking pink gins with him in his cabin while he listened to their barely coherent account of the night.

As Davidson observed, quoting Aubrey Beardsley: 'Boats are such blessed things, one loses all sense of responsibility.' But this latest mishap convinced Robin that, delightful though it might be, freedom from responsibility cost too much and he sold poor, battered *Clio* for little more than scrap value.

Back in London Robin installed Ken in the flat in Cadogan Square under the disapproving, monocled scrutiny of his father and he took up Robert Clarke's offer of a job. While he was away his novel *The Rough and the Smooth* had come out and sold well. It was no more than a potboiler and a lacklustre film version, directed by Robert Siodmak in 1959, only emphasised its faults. In America the title was changed to *Portrait of a Sinner*. But, as a critic put it with succinct accuracy, 'It is a preposterous melodrama about unreal people.'

Without the yacht as their mutual interest Robin and Ken had nothing in common except sex and that soon became a zestless routine. It was no surprise when Ken fell in love with a pretty young girl and left Robin to get married.

# Companion of Honour

Willie completed his career as a writer of fiction with a volume of short stories and two final novels. *Then and Now* (1946) was a return to an historical theme, the story of Machiavelli and his mission as an envoy from Florence to the court of Cesare Borgia. Its success prompted an incident in the dining room of the House of Lords. Freddie was entertaining Alexander Frere to tea when he overheard someone boasting that he was the top-selling English author in America. Irritated by the man's manner, Freddie leaned over and said: 'Young man, I don't know who you are or how many copies you've sold in the United States but I have a brother whose latest book has just sold a million copies.' The 'young man' was Evelyn Waugh who gave a different version in his diary entry of 8 August 1946, thus removing any sense of rebuke. The story is usually cited as a rare example of Freddie praising his brother, missing the point that it was primarily a put-down for Waugh's boasting.

*Then and Now* received mixed reviews. Edmund Wilson in *The New Yorker* not only damned it out of hand as little better than what a boy might write for a school magazine but also attacked Willie's status as an icon of modern literature. This typified the exasperation of those who resented Willie's years of success. *Catalina* (1948), also with an historical theme, was described by Orville Prescott in the *New York Times* as 'a sleekly clever book, a cynically and cold-bloodedly clever book'. *Creatures and Circumstance* (1947), the collection of short stories, merely illustrated Willie's habit of re-using old material from magazines.

In 1948 Willie appeared on the cinema screen to introduce four of his short stories in *Quartet*, filmed by Gainsborough Studios and produced by Sydney Box. The studio went to endless lengths to reproduce Willie's study. When he saw it he blinked but said nothing and then walked around examining every detail. Finally, when he reached the duplicate of his favourite chair, he touched the worn patches on the arms and, looking up, exclaimed: 'Christ!'

He was taken with the rejuvenating effect of make-up and said to Cyril Butcher: 'I think it is very fetching and I would wear it all the time if it were not for the possibility that people might get the wrong impression.'

Cinema-goers were fascinated to find that this old man, who seemed so bad-tempered, ugly and witchlike in press photographs, was apparently of a sweet disposition and endearingly modest. Willie, who had acted a role for the public ever since it took an interest in his work, found the experience and the fee much to his liking and when the film was a box-office success he was easily persuaded to do more. *Trio* followed in 1950 and *Encore* a year later. Television executives were not slow to see the possibilities his short stories provided for the new medium and CBS in the States produced nearly forty of them, all introduced by Willie and each signed off with a few words at the end. In England the BBC was equally successful with a similar series.

Stanley Millar, a television writer and novelist, was once deputed to fly to the Villa Mauresque to obtain Willie's final approval to scripts. It was suggested that he might care to explore the grounds while he was waiting. Millar wandered about until he found himself at the swimming pool where two beautiful youths were cavorting naked in the water. He was gazing at them with appreciative longing when a manservant arrived with a note on a silver salver: it read, 'You may look, but you may not touch. W. S. M.'

No other author before or since has used the new media with such effective cunning to advertise his own product and been paid so handsomely for it. The roll-on effect of Willie's promotion is still with us and the battering he has taken from the literary pundits has failed to diminish interest in his books. They forget, in the scramble to belittle him, that, though in their collective view he may be lacking in modish virtues such as verbal obscurity, he tells a good story in plain, unpretentious prose in a manner that remains unique.

In 1948, Liza married Lord John Hope in London. Willie, who had been fond of her first husband, Vincent Paravicini, was sad when that marriage failed and he may have been a little apprehensive of the new bridegroom. It had been John Hope's father, the Marquess of Linlithgow, who had infuriated Willie in 1938 by not including Haxton in an invitation to lunch at the Viceroy's palace when they were touring India. Such an invitation was a signal honour but Willie did not comprehend that, as Viceroy, Lord Linlithgow could not be expected formally to entertain someone who was forbidden entry to Britain. He refused to attend out of loyalty to his friend but it was a deliberate and peevish snub to the Monarch's representative. However, Liza's new husband became as much of a friend as Willie would permit.

During the fifties Willie's status as a Grand Old Man of English Letters was recognised with honorary degrees from the Université de Toulouse, Heidelberg and Oxford but he refused similar honours from several American universities because he said he could not stand the strain of the journey to the States. The fact was that he had no other reason to visit America and the degrees did not equal in prestige those he had accepted. Acutely aware of his value as a guest, he applied severe criteria to social events of a quasi-public nature. An invitation to sit next to the Queen of England at a dinner was highly desirable but an invitation to the wedding of Grace Kelly to Prince Rainier of Monaco only just qualified as acceptable. On that occasion, the press found it difficult to get near to the newly-weds and instead focused their attention on Willie who stole the limelight from other famous guests.

On one occasion Freddie received a letter addressed to 'Lord Somerset Maugham' and, thinking it might be for him, opened it and found it was a fan letter for Willie. So he sent it on with a note to which he received this reply (according to Robin):

My dear Freddie,
    I know what this is going to be – it will be another Bacon–Shakespeare affair because posterity will ascribe all my works to you thinking that you preferred to use my poor plebian name rather than sully the great name of a Lord Chancellor of England.
        Your loving brother – Willie

Freddie ruminated over this and then showed it to Robin. 'Do you detect a faintly unpleasant tone?' he asked. Robin, who admitted he enjoyed fanning any spark of animosity between the brothers ('when they ganged up on me to get married, life was quite unbearable'), considered for a moment and replied firmly: 'Yes.' Freddie composed the following:

My dear Willie,
    Indeed you may well be right. Certainly I have observed a certain adulation of your name in the more vulgar portions of the popular press. But one word of advice, do not attempt sonnets.
        Your loving brother – Freddie

Robin thought this reference to Shakespeare's 'homosexual'

verses was intended as an insulting jibe but it could simply be an example of Freddie's wit.

On the eve of his eightieth birthday Willie was given a dinner at the Garrick; only three writers before him, Dickens, Trollope and Thackeray, had been so honoured. In his speech responding to the toast he suddenly stopped speaking. Beverley Nichols, one of the organisers of the occasion, described this as an incident of acute embarrassment, a painful example of his stammer getting the better of him, but, in preparing work to be spoken in public, Willie carefully avoided words of potential danger and always memorised his speeches. Nichols claims to have rehearsed him and, at the last minute, suggested the substitution of the fateful word 'verandah' for 'terrace'. If this is true it could explain the incident, for Willie spoke without notes and, as St John Ervine, the playwright, said in a letter to Richard Church of 19 February 1954, it was like an actor drying on a line. But as Willie had nobody to prompt him it took him several seconds to recover himself; once he did, he sailed on to the end in smiling triumph.

As a contribution to the celebrations Willie's publishers, Heinemann, thought it would be a good idea to publish a book of tributes from British and American writers. Some thirty were approached but most, including Evelyn Waugh, Noël Coward, Vita Sackville-West, Cecil Day-Lewis and Peter Quennell, found reasons to decline. Quennell observed in 1993:

> What on earth could we all say except that he was a good writer even if we did not believe it, or what a splendid fellow he was even if we heartily disliked him? The book would have become rather like those fat charity programmes in which individual sponsors buy space to wish the cause success. It was a thoroughly silly idea that deserved to fail.

In June, Willie went to Buckingham Palace to be made a Companion of Honour. He told Cecil Roberts that he almost turned it down and would have preferred the more distinguished Order of Merit. He also told Kate and Robin that, many years before, he had declined a knighthood 'because, if I went into a party and they announced Mr Arnold Bennett, Mr H. G. Wells, Mr Hugh Walpole, Mr Rudyard Kipling and Sir William Somerset Maugham, I thought I'd look rather silly'. In fact, gay men were often excluded from the list, though inevitably some slipped through the vetting process. Willie's association with Gerald Haxton was well known and it is doubtful that he was ever considered for a knighthood. Hugh Walpole was knighted in 1937 but it was his close friends only who knew that Harold Cheevers, ostensibly his servant, was also his lover. It was not until 1967 that attitudes were relaxed and Robert Helpmann and Noël Coward, for example, were both honoured in this way.

Following his visit to the palace Willie dined with Robin and Barbara Back at Boulestin's in Covent Garden. He was late but excused himself by saying that he had met Syrie in the foyer of the Dorchester. In *Conversations with Willie*, Robin provides two pages of their conversation as recounted by his uncle. But these exchanges were actually based on a scene from Robin's unpro-duced play, *Willie*. It concludes with Willie saying, 'Goodbye'.

'Do you want our farewell to be like that?' she asks. 'Like what?' 'Like a farewell between two distant acquaintances,' she says quietly. He replies slowly but sharply: 'I wonder if we were ever anything more.'

Exit Syrie, holding back her tears.

When Barbara Back's husband Ivor died in 1951 without insurance provision, with him went the income which had enabled her to live in lavish style and she was forced to sell her house in Regent's Park, dispose of the Rolls-Royce, sack her servants and go out to work. The *Daily Mirror* employed her as a beauty columnist and she also taught etiquette at a finishing school for young ladies. Ostensibly Willie, remaining a loyal friend, helped with a regular allowance and paid for trips to the Mauresque but gradually he saw less of her. Others, like Rebecca West and Beverley Nichols, took against her completely. In 1982 Cyril Butcher, Nichols' companion since the thirties, explained that she made up scurrilous stories about her friends to entertain Willie who wickedly reported them back to those who featured in them. 'We refused to have anything to do with her eventually, particularly after she said terrible things about Syrie when she was dead. Of course, she liked the company of queer men. Today, we'd call her a faggots' moll.'

Willie also gave generous financial help to G. B. Stern when she fell out of favour with the reading public and was forced to leave her impressive Albany address for a country cottage. Here she lived an impecunious existence and suffered a long illness, finally dying in obscurity.

Willie's cheques bought him freedom from personal involvement with both women, who grew as cantankerous and tiresome the older they became, as he did himself. He much preferred his female friends to be financially independent and one such was Emily Borie Sherfesee, an American neighbour who, as Mrs Borie Ryerson, had been the close friend of Sibyl Colefax and of Mrs George Keppel. Willie had a great affection for Emily and often told the story of one of her visits to the Mauresque for dinner. As soon as she arrived, she had an urgent need to relieve herself and rushed to the nearest bathroom. She was sitting on the lavatory when she noticed with alarm that the bath was occupied by a man staring at her in astonishment. With considerable aplomb she finished her business, washed her hands, tidied her hair and left without a word being said. Later, during cocktails, the man appeared and Willie led him to her. 'I don't believe, my dear Emily, that you know Mr H. G. Wells?' Straightfaced, she held out her hand. 'On the contrary, I think we have met before.'

In her final years she lived alone at the Villa Bontac and Willie visited her several evenings a week to read one of his short stories to her. Beverley Nichols, who had first met her when he was on a government mission to America in 1918, asked Willie if she had a favourite story. 'Why, my dear Beverley, *Rain*, of course.' '*Rain*? That surprises me.' 'It should not. Like all really nice old ladies she sees herself in the role of Sadie Thompson.'

# Anti-climax

After Nellie's death, Freddie stayed on in Cadogan Square, but without her it was merely a house, not a home, and he became increasingly lonely. To occupy his time he wrote his autobiography to give posterity an idea of his place in history, or so his family thought. They rallied together to ease his loneliness and Kate, who still lived a few doors away, spent as much time with him as she could. As well as his life story he also wrote poetry and short stories which appeared under his pen name of Ormond Greville. In 1950, he published *UNO and War Crimes* in which he questioned the legal effects of three new categories of war crime as defined by the United Nations.

In old age, no longer weighed down by legal responsibilities, he mellowed and became, as Diana put it, 'an affable old gentleman'. Affability, though, is not the keynote of Robin's accounts of Freddie's visits to Willie. According to him they continuously antagonised each other and, after one fortnight's stay, Willie complained that the entire time had passed without Freddie making a single civil remark. Alan Searle is quoted as having had a terrible time keeping the peace between them. It is likely that both Robin and Searle failed to understand a relationship based on laconic humour; the two brothers, now old men, enjoyed the barbed familiarity of verbal jousting.

Robin reported with some relish that Willie invited three ancient princesses to lunch in Freddie's honour. At the end of the superbly presented meal the youngest princess, aged seventy, said: 'Tell me, Lord Maugham, how do you find the Riviera suits you?' After fixing his monocle as if to appraise his questioner, he let it fall and replied: 'Yes, I find the Riviera suits me well and I find this plain cooking agrees with me.' According to Robin, this non sequitur did not please Willie but, as others of the family have pointed out, it was typical of Freddie's sense of comedy, for he was something of a gourmet and was always highly appreciative of the cuisine at the Mauresque. It was also a covert rebuke of the patronising tone of the princess who may not have known that Freddie was French born and probably knew the country better than she did. For his part Willie was being deliberately provocative in inviting three old ladies of not the slightest interest to Freddie who, as he knew very well, delighted in the company of attractive young women.

Robin told another story, unique because it implies Willie could be disconcerted by Freddie.

One afternoon Willie had taken delivery of a commode which he had bought in Paris at enormous cost. He decided to ask some friends to come for drinks and view it but, convinced that my father would ruin the occasion, he used the ploy of making my father think he was very old and ill. Now father did not mind in the least being old and he was never ill but such was Willie's force of personality that he could make him *feel* old and ill. After lunch Willie commiserated with him. 'Freddie, my dear, you are looking so very pale and worn and if I may say so you are no longer a chicken. So I suggest you lie down in your room and we'll call you in time for dinner.'

Father, rather surprised and woebegone because he had looked forward to a jolly afternoon, went upstairs to his bed. Willie rubbed his hands happily and at cocktail time his friends arrived to admire the new acquisition which had been placed in the drawing room. Suddenly the double doors opened and my father appeared looking like Lear on the blasted heath. Willie lost his nerve and ran to him, clasped his hand and introduced him round the room. My father nodded but said nothing and in the chilling silence Willie gabbled: 'Freddie, I've asked a few friends in to celebrate the arrival of the commode which has just arrived from Paris and which I may tell you cost a King's ransom.' My father very slowly fixed his monocle in his eye and studied the magnificent object in silence. Then he let the glass fall and stared grim-faced at Willie. 'Rather florid, isn't it?'

In contradiction of reports that Freddie was every bit as much a dragon as Willie, Cole Lesley, in his biography of Noël Coward, wrote that Viscount Maugham was a smiling, witty, dear old gentleman. Coward himself admired the London Maughams and said so in his diary entry of 25 October 1952. Two years later he noted that he had lunched with Freddie and Willie, respectively eighty-eight and eighty, and he felt sorry for Freddie whose book had not been a success because it was dull and, in his view, wrong-headed.

Freddie's autobiography, *At the End of the Day*, was a baffling disappointment. Where were the enthralling stories he told friends and family of encounters with personalities from the law, arts and politics? Where indeed was the family? Nellie was referred to lovingly but briefly and Willie got three mentions in 587 pages. For some unfathomable reason most of the space was taken up with a detailed study of campaigns fought in the two world wars; erudite as this was, it had nothing to do with his life. The text revealed little of the man himself and there was no hint of his wit. It was an opportunity thrown away and the sad consequence is that Freddie is inaccurately remembered as one of the appeasers of Munich.

# XIV

## 'Society Takes Upon Itself'

> 'Society takes upon itself the right to inflict appalling punishments on the individual, but it also has the supreme vice of shallowness, and fails to realise what it has done.'
>
> Oscar Wilde, *De Profundis*

In 1953, Captain Trevor Lean invited Robin and Michael Davidson on board HMS *Adamant* for the Coronation Review of the Fleet. The evening before, they were both guests of Edward Montagu at Beaulieu. The next day was spent in what Davidson described as 'patriotic drinking' on *Adamant*, while Lord Montagu celebrated on the aircraft carrier allocated for the use of members of both Houses of Parliament. Later, they met him in a Portsmouth bar to round off the occasion.

Before Robin and Davidson left to spend a few weeks on Ischia, they were shocked to hear that Montagu had been charged with 'certain offences' concerning boy scouts. In the event, he was acquitted of these by the jury which, however, failed to agree on a lesser charge brought by the Director of Public Prosecutions at the last minute. A retrial on this charge was ordered amid a blaze of publicity. By the time Robin returned to England, events had moved rapidly and now his old friend Michael Pitt-Rivers was implicated in further developments involving RAF servicemen.

By a coincidence, another friend of Robin's, the writer Rupert Croft-Cooke, was arrested in July on a charge of gross indecency with two Royal Navy men. At the trial held at Lewes in Sussex it was the sailors' word against denials by Croft-Cooke. His counsel, the brilliant 'Khaki' Roberts, gave a passionate performance mocking the absence of evidence and the dubious behaviour of the police. But the jury followed the lead of the judge and brought in a guilty verdict. Roberts pleaded for a fine, then usual in London, but the sentence was nine months' prison. When Croft-Cooke was released, Hermione Baddeley held a celebration for him which she described as a 'coming-out party', adding grimly that the way things were going, it was the first of a series.

The driving force behind these cases was Sir David Maxwell Fyfe, the Home Secretary, best remembered for his refusal to reprieve nineteen-year-old Derek Bentley in the notorious Craig–Bentley case. At the time of Munich, he had supported Chamberlain but then recanted, explaining that he had suffered a temporary delusion. Now he deluded himself that homosexual behaviour could be stamped out by police action. According to the *Sydney Morning Telegraph* of 25 October 1953, Commander E. A. Cole of Scotland Yard had spent three months in America consulting FBI officials on a plan to weed out homosexuals from British government jobs following the defection of Burgess and Maclean. Under a new Commissioner at the Yard, Sir John Nott-Bower, the plan grew into a campaign against all 'vice', with homosexuality given priority. Local police forces were encouraged to increase the number of gay arrests and much time and money was spent in pursuit of this.

The campaign culminated in the arrest of Lord Montagu, Peter Wildeblood, Michael Pitt-Rivers, Edward McNally and John Reynolds. The last two, both RAF servicemen, admitted committing homosexual acts and were persuaded to turn Queen's Evidence in exchange for immunity. The parallels with the Croft-Cooke case were striking, for, without the two servicemen, the Crown had no case. The prosecution counsel, none other than Khaki Roberts, echoed the Oscar Wilde trials in an appeal to bigotry and middle-class snobbery, and made much of a proposition that had covertly sinister implications in a democracy, namely that it was improper for upper-class individuals such as

Montagu and Pitt-Rivers to mix with men of a working-class background such as Reynolds and McNally. For this purpose Wildeblood was elevated to a social grandeur he did not share with his fellow defendants. A bottle of cider, for instance, enjoyed with McNally, was transformed miraculously by Roberts into champagne. It was clear that a few useful lessons had been learned from the Croft-Cooke case. At the end of the proceedings, watched with astonishment by other, less sexually inhibited countries, the defendants were found guilty: Montagu received a sentence of twelve months and Wildeblood and Pitt-Rivers eighteen months each.

The satisfaction that Maxwell Fyfe gained from the campaign turned sour as public disquiet grew about police methods. Responsible voices claimed that the law failed to act as a deterrent and encouraged blackmail, suicide and police corruption. It was argued that, for adults, the question should be a moral, not a legal one. In the House of Commons, Sir Robert Boothby pressed for a Royal Commission which Maxwell Fyfe refused. Public pressure forced him to concede and so began the long process which led to changes in the law in 1967. Significantly, Maxwell Fyfe ignored these cases in his autobiography.

At the height of the furore Robin left the country when he was warned that his name was on a list of candidates for police investigation. Assuming such a list existed, his acquaintance with Guy Burgess might have counted against him. Without knowing it, Beverley Nichols may have helped to convince the powers-that-be that matters had gone too far when he began to contact highly respected public figures whom he knew to be gay or bisexual with the proposal that they join him in taking a full-page advertisement in *The Times* to declare their sexuality. He was persuaded that his enthusiasm for self-destruction was not shared by those whom he approached.

Willie's gay friends expected him to reinforce the general anger and they were surprised when he did not. Surely, they asked themselves, after he had experienced the persecution of homosexual men following the Wilde trials and was even forced into semi-exile to be with his own lover, he could not be indifferent? Did he not realise that something very important was happening in Britain where, for the first time since the Labouchere amendment of 1886, a revolt was beginning against the injustice of the law? But Willie rejected all approaches to become involved, however peripherally, even when non-homosexual men spoke out in favour of decriminalisation. Arthur Jeffress, the wealthy art collector and owner of the Hanover Gallery, who had helped pay defence costs for the recent trials, broached the subject when he was hosting a small dinner party but Willie, the chief guest, said nothing. Beverley Nichols, another guest, could see the danger signs in the set expression on Willie's face.

> Arthur was too intent on emphasising his point to notice and then he begged – you have to understand he was very theatrical – he begged Willie to write a letter to *The Times*. And the more vehement he became, the darker Willie's expression grew until he started trembling, went white with rage, stood up and left without a word.

# Syrie

Syrie died in July 1955 at her flat, 24 Park Lane, where for some time she had been nursed by Liza. Willie told Barbara Back in a letter that he could not pretend any deep grief and he wondered if, looking back at her life, it had ever occurred to Syrie what a mess she had made of it. This appeared to be a case of what Rebecca West once described as the capacity of people to believe what they know to be untrue.

Despite the failure of her marriage to Willie, Syrie had made the best of the situation. She continued to entertain and be entertained by the famous, and she carried on her design business until prevented by ill health. She continued also to proclaim her love for Willie and her wish for a reconciliation. Perhaps if she had faded from view and died forgotten in a Bournemouth hotel,

Willie might have hated her less. Inexplicably he loathed her even more after her death than when she had been alive. He once told Robin that out of many mistakes he had made, Syrie was the greatest.

It is probably impossible to produce a balanced portrait of Syrie, who has suffered from champions attributing saintly qualities to her which she probably never possessed, and detractors who have been astonishingly vicious. A contemporary, for example, remarked: 'How two such despicable people as Syrie and Willie could be the parents of such a delightful person as Liza is an impenetrable mystery.' Others have spoken of her sharp business practices and roundly condemned her as 'poisonous'.

The men in her life made a weird trio: her father, complex, domineering, intolerant, hypocritical, shrewd and quick to see opportunities to make a good living for himself as a champion of destitute children; Henry Wellcome, very similar to her father, too old as a bridegroom, his behaviour suggesting a sexually repressed man sublimating his lust by bursts of physical and mental brutality; and Willie Maugham, the ideal successor to the first two, embodying their faults but adding his own brand of misogynism. It is hardly surprising that Syrie developed a hardness of character, but she might have responded as does Catherine in Henry James' *Washington Square*: 'I have been taught by masters'.

# Odd Man In

Syrie's death heralded Willie's decline into senility. The year before he had formed a company to take over the Villa Mauresque and given Liza the shares. It had been a stratagem to avoid death duties but he now developed a fantasy that, as he legally no longer owned his home, he was liable to be thrown out of it, and verbally attacked Liza's husband to the point where it became impossible for him to visit. There were other examples of a childish illogicality influenced and encouraged by Alan Searle who saw Liza as a rival and feared for his financial future after Willie's death.

Willie's attitude to Robin, however, continued to be affectionate, though privately he had complained in a letter of October 1952 to his financial adviser, Bert Alanson, that Robin was a great disappointment, unable to stick to any occupation; he added contemptuously that Robin was now writing film-scripts and drinking too much. In another letter to Alanson in July 1955 shortly after Syrie's death, he conjectured that Robin would come to a shabby end and again commented that he was too fond of drink.

It was true that Robin's drinking was a source of worry, not because it was then a major problem but because of what it could lead to. Willie's slur on Robin's career was completely unjustified. In ten years he had achieved as much, if not more in purely commercial terms than Willie who, in a similar period, had enjoyed a limited success with *Liza of Lambeth*, followed by public lack of interest and commercial failure until *Lady Frederick*. Willie had been a professional writer for eighteen years before *Of Human Bondage*, which in any case owed its major success to the influential American critic Theodore Dreiser who rescued it from oblivion.

Robin could not, therefore, be criticised for lack of output, but it was highly questionable whether he had the talent and stamina to match the quality of his uncle's writing, however hard he tried. Financially Robin was doing well but he spent freely and was over-generous to friends. Two factors may explain his nonchalant attitude to money: he had expectations when Freddie died, and Willie continually assured him that he was to be a major beneficiary along with Liza. He saw himself as the future viscount living in style, able to pursue his political idealism in the House of Lords while becoming a respected author.

His novel *Behind the Mirror*, published in America and Britain in 1955, represented a major step forward in his development, though it seems likely that Michael Davidson can take some credit for this as he was actively involved in the development of several books. The plot of *Behind the Mirror*, based on Robin's experiences in Tanganyika, has clear characterisation and description of ambiance strongly reminiscent of his uncle's work without being a pastiche of it. The contrast between the vastness of the country and the claustrophobic lives of expatriates is vividly caught. Kurt, now Bill Brand, is the catalyst who forces the dramatic climax that causes the death of his friend, a fictional projection of Robin himself. Diverse sexual themes are dealt with in a bolder manner than Willie dared to employ, but without the explicit vulgarity of which Robin was later guilty. Its faults lie in over-plotting and too many twists and surprises which Willie, at his best, would have simplified or eradicated.

Robin was also to do well financially from cinema, but on a minor scale compared to Willie whose contempt for screen-writing was surprising in view of the fortune he had made from the medium. In addition to the sale of rights in his novels Robin wrote screenplays for at least twenty projects, all stillborn. The most ambitious was probably *Seven Pillars of Wisdom* with Dirk Bogarde proposed to play Lawrence and Brian Desmond Hurst to direct. This was one of several attempts to film what eventually became *Lawrence of Arabia* with Peter O'Toole in the leading role. Robin's other screenplays included *Cakes and Ale*, Beverley Nichols' *Evensong*, and a blend of three of his own short stories called *Speakers' Corner* written with Rodney Ackland.

In its transition to the screen his novella *The Black Tent* suffered like *The Servant* from over-elaboration. Set in the western desert during Rommel's offensive of May 1942, it told the story of David, a British tank commander left for dead by the Germans, who is rescued by a Senussi tribe and nursed back to health by Mabrouka, the daughter of the sheikh. When David leaves to find his regiment he gives the sheikh his signet ring, a promissory note for £20 and his journal of events since his rescue. David is never heard of again; the British, meanwhile, list him as missing, presumed dead. Six years later, the promissory note is presented for payment and a fellow officer sets out to discover David's fate. Eventually, he finds the tribe and learns from the journal of his marriage to Mabrouka and the birth of a son. The question is whether the boy should stay with the tribe or be taken to England where he is the legal heir to a considerable estate.

The writing is taut, without sentimentality, and displays Robin's understanding and affection for the Arab way of life; in many respects, it echoes *Come to Dust*. The screenplay, originally written by Robin himself, was considered inadequate and Bryan Forbes was engaged for rewrites. The film was a disappointment but the problem lay in some unwise casting and the haphazard direction of Brian Desmond Hurst who appeared unable to decide whether he was filming a small-scale story or a vast Hollywood-style epic.

Robin was emotionally close to Hurst who, like him, was an exponent of dream scenarios for living which never came true. A tall, handsome Irishman, he began his career in Hollywood working for his cousin John Ford. One of his first films in England was an adaptation of a twenty-five-year-old Willie Maugham drama, *The Tenth Man*, which he directed for Gaumont-British in 1936; it had done badly in the theatre and it did just as badly in the cinema. Hurst redeemed himself with several big box-office successes, though these did not often please the critics. In 1961 he returned to Ireland to direct the film of Synge's *Playboy of the Western World*. Ignored in Britain, it is highly thought of in the USA. It was shown to President John Kennedy at a special screening at the White House and was the last film he saw before leaving for Dallas.

Hurst, gregarious, funny and charming, was famous for his risky straight and gay parties at his home in Kinnerton Street. Here he was likely to have the latest pop group, a selection of hired guardsmen, a smattering of the famous – film stars, writers, politicians – and a support group of beautiful people of both sexes. Robin rarely left a party at Kinnerton Street without a bed-mate, usually selected by Hurst beforehand. Francis Crowdy, who worked with Hurst as scriptwriter for *Hungry Hill*, said of him:

'He was an exuberant character. I knew he was queer but he had none of the characteristics of the stereotype.' This contrasts with the description of him by Bryan Forbes who thought of him as an amiable and wicked old queen, or Peter Noble who said: 'He was outrageous and very camp.'

Surprisingly Robin did not go to Tripoli for the film shoot and Forbes wondered if he was miffed because his script had been rewritten – 'although Robin himself never seemed to bear me any malice'.

As well as his remunerative work for the screen Robin wrote a number of stage plays, but could not place any of them until Melville Gillam of the Connaught Theatre, Worthing, took *The Leopard* for production in May 1955. Though praised, it was not thought to be commercial theatre fare. The following year the Connaught tried again with *Mr Lear*, Shakespeare's story retold surprisingly as a comedy. In an ambitious piece of casting Henry Kendall was engaged to play the lead; a West End leading man for many years, he had appeared in the original productions of Willie's *The Circle* and *East of Suez*. (In the latter he was given a bad time by the director Basil Dean and Willie, watching rehearsals, was heard to remark: 'I see Basil is burning the Kendall at both ends.') In the cast of *Mr Lear* there were several actors who were to become 'names': Daniel Massey, Elizabeth Spriggs, Michael Bryant and Patricia Routledge. The director was Peter Wood and there were high expectations of a transfer to the West End but it did not happen.

Robin was convinced that he could not fail with *The Last Hero*, given a Sunday try-out at the Strand Theatre in 1957 with Nigel Stock in the lead. This was an exploration of General Gordon's reactions during the last months at Khartoum and it was highly praised by the press, but no West End management was prepared to back it. Later a version was seen on national television with Alan Badel, and Robin, never one to waste an idea, eventually used it as the basis for his novel *The Last Encounter* in 1972.

Robin then joined forces with Philip King to write *The Lonesome Road*, a play with a homosexual theme. King's name had been mainly associated with comedies such as *On Monday Next, Sailor Beware* and *See How They Run*. His attempts at serious topics were rare but in *Serious Charge* a slight whiff of homosexuality caused a sensation when it appeared in 1955. A version reached the screen in 1959 with the added attraction of Cliff Richard singing *Living Doll*.

*The Lonesome Road* dealt with the problems of a writer seeking solitude under a new identity in a remote village following a prison sentence for a homosexual offence. He cannot completely disguise his sexuality and the lonely seventeen-year-old son of the local vicar falls in love with him. The writer, too scared to respond, cruelly rejects the boy who, in a state of despair, commits suicide. The play was refused a licence in 1957 because of its content and it was produced at the Arts, a membership club theatre. It is fascinating to note that the Arts theatre was founded in the twenties by, among others, Willie's friend Walter Payne. The opening production was a revue largely written by Beverley Nichols who had been a lover of Willie's and was one of Payne's close friends for a while. It may be coincidence that after the war the theatre revived seven Maugham plays in as many years.

The stupidity of censorship in the 1950s meant that the West End's Comedy Theatre had to become a temporary club to present Tennessee Williams' *Cat on a Hot Tin Roof* and Arthur Miller's *A View from the Bridge*. Unfortunately, the quality of *The Lonesome Road* did not compare with the American offerings and it has not been seen since censorship was lifted. The press were kind to it but the critic of the *Daily Mail* suggested that the writers were 'a little too discreet'. This must have been the last occasion when this description was applied to Robin's handling of a gay theme.

Despite his continued commercial failure, Robin was commissioned by the producer Henry Sherek to write the English version of a French comedy by Claude Magnier, *Monsieur Masure*. Under its new title, *Odd Man In*, it featured Donald Sinden, Muriel Pavlow and Derek Farr. During early rehearsals, lunches at the Ivy, with Robin as the generous host, became so convivial that

Sherek put a stop to them. 'He had to,' Sinden remarked, 'because we were in no fit state for serious work afterwards.'

Willie went to see the play at the St Martin's Theatre while he was staying at the Dorchester with Searle in 1957 and told Robin that like everyone he had laughed a great deal and thought the play should run for ever. His optimism was not endorsed by the public and *Odd Man In* ran for six months; respectable enough, but not the success that Willie and others predicted. Three years later Robin adapted another Magnier comedy, *It's in the Bag*, which did well on tour and at the Duke of York's but closed prematurely when Terry-Thomas, the leading man, became ill with the debilitating disease that eventually killed him.

Before Robin had received the congratulations on *Odd Man In*, he had the impression that he was out of favour, but when Willie also invited him to stay at the Mauresque he knew he was persona grata again. By now the family was resigned to Willie's unexpected changes of mood encouraged, they believed, by Searle's machinations. In 1956, Ann Fleming, the wife of Ian Fleming, had written to Evelyn Waugh with some amusement about the atmosphere of intrigue at the Mauresque. Searle was inciting Willie against his daughter because of 'The Will' and what he considered to be his right to a share of the estate. According to Searle, Willie wrote a new will each week and his stutter grew worse at the mere thought of a visit from Liza. All seemed serene, however, in 1957 when Willie was guest of honour at his granddaughter Camilla's coming-out ball at the Savoy.

Noël Coward, who was fortunate never to have encountered Willie on a bad day, wrote in his diaries of his admiration for his lucidity, good-humour and charm in old age. In 1957, for instance, he described a day at the Mauresque and Willie's excellent physical condition at eighty-three, illustrated by his diving into the swimming pool from the board. Coward noticed that, if anything, he seemed younger than when they had last met two years earlier. But for those in regular contact it was uncertain how long these periods of tranquillity might last.

In the mid-fifties Robin decided to live part of the time in Brighton. The town still retained its raffish reputation acquired when the Prince Regent built his seaside palace, the Pavilion, and lived there with Mrs Fitzherbert. As a town created for pleasure it was not surprising that it became a focal point for gay men. During the Napoleonic wars, The Spotted Dog was known as a gay venue and carried on the tradition until the early 1980s. Even Victorian civic and religious leaders could not impose their ideas of virtue upon Brighton and it remained defiantly unconstrained. Subsequent attempts to enforce respectability also failed and, by the time Robin moved there, it was known as a haven for gay men and women, most of whom led their lives without attracting much attention. Among those gay residents associated with the arts were Terence Rattigan, Alan Melville, Douglas Byng, Sir David Webster, Collie Knox and Sir Francis Rose.

Robin found a flat in Brunswick Terrace in a house which had a history of gay tenants, among them Ivor Novello's long-time companion Robert Andrews, and Walter Crisham, the revue artist. His landlords were the Durnfords who owned a preparatory school in London and only used the house for weekends and holidays. As he put it, 'They became a kind of second family to me.' He was particularly fond of Winifred Durnford who, apart from a strong personality, bore no resemblance to the stereotypical seaside landlady of the comic postcards.

Among his Brighton friends was Gilbert Harding, a man of serious disposition, who had made a name for himself by accident as the easily angered member of television's 'What's My Line' team. Compton Mackenzie compared him with Dr Johnson, but although he was given to fits of deep depression, unlike Johnson he did not find tea a substitute for wine. To Harding, alcohol was essential and his capacity prodigious. On one occasion he and Robin went on a drinking tour by chauffeur-driven car. It began at six in the evening and ended twelve hours later in Harding's kitchen where they finished off the remnants of a crate of beer. Harding was forever searching for the ideal male lover but was doomed never to find him. Drink was a form of consolation but, as a convert to the Catholic Church, he could never free himself from the pain of sexual guilt.

It was through Harding that Robin met Keith Monk, a lusty ex-sailor with a bright and breezy personality and cute good looks. Robin took to him instantly and for three years they were virtually inseparable. Afterwards they remained close friends, seeing each other almost every day until Robin's final illness. Speaking of their relationship Keith Monk said:

> Robin was about forty and a glamorous figure caught up in the glittering world of films and theatre. He knew everyone and everyone knew him and socially he was in constant demand because he was such a vivid personality and so funny telling his stories. He had given up the flat at Cadogan Square so when we were in London we stayed with a friend of his who had a house off the King's Road near what was known as 'the guardsman's pub', a gay pub just down from Sloane Square.

Monk emphasised that they both enjoyed being with women and Robin was thrilled when a girl showed interest in him. 'Most men won't admit it but many swing both ways and Robin never made any secret of it.'

Monk took a room in the Durnford house and later that year went with Robin to Ischia to stay in his villa at Forio. He has vivid memories of a visit to Wystan Auden whose tiny apartment was appallingly squalid and stank of a curry cooking on the stove in the filthy kitchen area. When Auden served this for lunch Monk was nearly sick. 'I don't like curry much at the best of times but I tried to eat some of it. Fortunately there was plenty of wine to act as a disinfectant.' Robin, equally shocked, tactfully omitted any mention of squalor from his version in *Escape from the Shadows*. In this he telescoped points from several conversations with Auden. The poet accused England of being provincial and mean, which explained why he had become an American citizen: 'In America I won't open my mouth for less than three hundred dollars. In England I found people expected me to speak for five pounds.'

The couple went on to Tangier so that Robin could update

himself on the city for his next novel, *The Man with Two Shadows*, but it had barely altered. Dean's Bar still flourished with bogus barons, shady bankers, furtive foreign agents, phoney ex-army types, pretty boys and beautiful women. For a young man, the lure of the city was irresistible and Monk took full advantage of it. Robin soon decided that there were too many distractions and they returned to the dull sanity of England. However, he left with a notebook crammed with the sayings of Gerald Hamilton, who had been the model for the central figure in *Mr Norris Changes Trains*. Hamilton was delighted to talk about himself as Robin paid for drinks and kept his glass topped up. Auden had suggested that he might be worth another book but Robin could think of no way of eclipsing Christopher Isherwood.

# XV

## Freddie

The final example of Freddie's jurisprudence and skill as a writer appeared a year after his death in a paper contributed to *The Campden Wonder*, edited by Sir George Clark for the Oxford University Press. His article examined the 1661 case when three people were executed for the murder of Lady Campden's steward, even though no body was found; two years later the steward reappeared and told an extraordinary tale of his kidnapping and sale into slavery in Turkey. Freddie was fascinated by the conflict of evidence at the trial as he had been by the Tichborne case.

For some while Freddie had been devotedly looked after by Kate, helped by resident nurses, but he did not care for the discipline these strangers imposed. One, a middle-aged woman with heavily starched uniforms that crackled over her impressive bosom, particularly irritated him by her sergeant-major manner. Once, as she was going off duty, she asked if he needed anything. When she was out of earshot he said to Kate: 'I could have replied "Thee hither in a whirlwind – to Athens." ' (This use of an obscure line from *Timon of Athens* illustrates his life-long love of Shakespeare.)

It seemed, he now sensed, that death was not far off and he was anxious to see Robin. In his bedroom which had been moved to the ground floor, Robin sat with him for hours gazing out at the garden while the old man dozed fitfully. Suddenly he would wake and they would talk a little before he slipped into sleep again. Robin never divulged their conversations but it was clear to his sisters that a reconciliation had taken place. On the last occasion Freddie woke and, saying 'Hello, my boy', stretched out his arm, took Robin's hand and held it until he slept again.

Freddie died on 23 March 1958 and was buried three days later in the graveyard of Hartfield Parish Church. His fellow benchers gathered with the family for a memorial service in the chapel of Lincoln's Inn on 17 April.

To the end, he remained a fine-looking man with a trim, athletic figure. Indeed, when the brothers were together Willie looked the older. He stayed mentally in control, apart from the occasional lapse of memory to be expected in a man of over ninety, yet Willie tried to convince others that Freddie had lost his mind. In contradiction of this, Robin told the story of an inexpensive painting of the Dutch School that Freddie had bought which Willie dismissed as merely pleasant. To Willie's astonishment Freddie rang up the head of Christie's and asked him to come and value it. 'Your father really has the most enormous nerve,' Willie said admiringly.

When Willie was asked by R. F. V. Heuston to contribute a reminiscence of Freddie for his book *The Lives of the Lord Chancellors*, his reply gave a revealing insight into his state of mind, for he was ready to settle old scores, real or imaginary. He described Freddie as very strange, reticent and difficult. He omitted to acknowledge Freddie's loyalty and affection from which he had benefited over the years. He claimed that they met very seldom and, if it had not been for his sister-in-law, he would not have seen him from year's end to year's end. Yet apart from the obvious fact that they could not meet very often because they lived in different countries, Freddie was a regular visitor to the Mauresque and they saw each other frequently when Willie was in London.

Then, in a seemingly guileless paragraph, Willie mentioned that Dr Fane, in his novel *The Painted Veil*, was modelled on his brother. Anyone assuming, however, that here was an accurate portrait of Freddie would be badly misled; Fane is the type of man impossible for anyone to like, let alone love. Willie then referred Heuston to Robin, commenting that what Robin said could, on the whole, be relied upon, but knowing perfectly well that, in the aftermath of his father's death, Robin had reverted to his illogical dislike of his father. As an apparent afterthought, Willie ended with a jibe that was also used by Robin against his father: 'You probably know that he was very unpopular in the House of Lords because, as one member told me, he treated the peers as hostile witnesses.'

It was a diabolically clever letter calculated, under the guise of frankness, to put Freddie in the worst possible light; it ignored the sentiments of the family and the feelings of those who liked and admired Freddie. For Willie, who was so sensitive to public opinion, it marked a failure to anticipate that the publication of the letter could reflect badly on himself in the long run.

Of the latter-day male Maughams, Freddie was the best balanced and probably the happiest. In one of his few references to Nellie in his autobiography he attributed much of his happy life to her and to his children. If he had not become a lawyer he might have gone into the theatre, for he had much of the actor about him and, in addition to his good looks, he knew how to use his eyes and his hands to good effect. He passed on his love of the arts to his children. He never lost an intense interest in the theatre or the cinema and he read the latest popular books with an eager anticipation not always as fulfilled as he had hoped.

Professionally he was admired for his work in steering through major law reforms, and for his ability to disentangle complicated sets of facts, as well as for his energy, clarity and efficiency. As a man, he was appreciated for his charm and humour, but he could become cool and supercilious if annoyed. He also possessed the often underrated attribute of integrity which did not always make for easy relationships in the political arena. He was not a religious man but he approved of the notion of death as a prolonged sleep. He once said that, like most old men, he was willing to greet death with composure, if not with a smile.

# The Man with Two Shadows

Robin's 1958 novel, *The Man with Two Shadows*, was a ramshackle thriller which fell far below the standard set by *Behind the Mirror*. Like Robin, its central character, Peter Grant, has been wounded in the head during the 1942 campaign and suffers from periodic amnesia. During these bouts he changes mentally from a Dr Jekyll into a Mr Hyde and becomes 'Tommy'. To understand the origin of this alien personality, there is a flashback to childhood when Tommy was at first Peter's imaginary friend and then able to take control of his body. (The logic is somewhat obscure.) The common enemy of Peter/Tommy is his father for whom 'they' develop a passionate hatred. Tommy suggests the solution – 'Kill him.'

The opportunity comes one summer's day. Father lies asleep on the lawn which slopes up to a level area. Poised near the edge is a heavy garden roller, wedged for safety. Tommy sees that by manoeuvring it a little, taking out the wedges and giving it a push, it will crash down the slope and crush father's head. But Peter, horrified by the thought of this, moves the roller so that it is aimed at his legs, and then kicks out the wedges. He does not wait to see the result but flees in a panic. Later, when father is taken to hospital with a fractured leg, there is an investigation into the cause of the 'accident'. It remains a mystery; when Peter is questioned, Tommy takes over and provides a convincing alibi.

Tommy reappears in the autobiographical *Escape from the Shadows*. Afterwards Robin explained that until then he had kept his existence a secret and, by writing the novel, he had virtually exorcised him. Later Tommy was resurrected to become a useful device to use when explaining bad behaviour. Tommy was, of course, the 'naughty boy' in the song Robin's mother sang to him in the nursery. Michael Pitt-Rivers commented: 'I do not know whether Robin claimed to have a split personality and I do not know anything about "Tommy". Robin had a multi-personality. He lived the lives of fictional personalities whom he invented.'

Robin's *Escape from the Shadows* and Beverley Nichols' *Father Figure* were published in 1972. Both men disliked their respective fathers and gave similar examples to justify their attitudes; the tale of the garden roller was told in almost identical terms in both books. If Robin and Nichols sympathised with each other and swapped family yarns it might explain the coincidence. In the unlikely event, however, that they were both telling the truth, it suggests, as Confucius might have put it, that 'Stern father who sleeps in path of heavy garden roller tempts vengeance of chastised son.'

In August 1958 Robin went off to Vienna for a long stay, taking his friend Keith Gossop with him. By coincidence Colin Spencer's Australian lover John Tasker was living in a flat in the Sudtiroler Platz which he hoped to sell. Spencer thought Robin might buy the lease and a cable was sent to Tasker who took an instant dislike to the idea of an English peer without having met him. When he did, his worst expectations were realised, for Robin rejected the flat, then seemed to treat his voluntary efforts at finding them an alternative apartment as a right, not a favour, as if Tasker were a local flat-hunting agency. In a furious letter to Spencer on 14 August Tasker wrote:

> The Lord is a silly, fucking bore. I got them part of a villa, I've taken them round, will likely land them a boy servant, have procured for them and got fuck all in return except for a lot of 'bless you, dear boy' and a load of frankfurters anytime we're together near meal times . . . Although it was the second time I'd trammed it out there – it takes an hour – there was no offer of a lift into town or a taxi fare. And when I suggested that Keith drop me, the Lord assumed his 'Governess of Tooting Bec Reform School for Girls' look and let 'Good night' slide out from between tight arsehole lips. By God, they're mean . . . I hate going out with mean rich people. And they have shocking manners. I'm embarrassed by the way waiters treat us.

For some years Robin contemplated writing a novel with a strong homosexual theme that would go beyond the limits then acceptable in Britain. The more he thought about it, the more he saw it as a mission and he solemnly told Pitt-Rivers: 'I have decided to write a queer book,' to which Pitt-Rivers replied: 'Not another one! All your books are queer!'

Robin did not find this retort amusing and later sent his friend the manuscript to prove that it was to be a profoundly important work. Pitt-Rivers read it and was appalled; he had once joked to Robin that he might have the brain of a Lord Chancellor but he had the mind of a housemaid. This seemed to prove his point. From the first line, 'Tangier is a very strange place', it got worse and, in the second paragraph, a beautiful, sloe-eyed youth appeared followed by a succession of others. It was sentimental, semi-pornographic tosh lacking stylistic sophistication. Robin had asked for his comments but Pitt-Rivers did not know where to start: instead he retyped the opening chapters so that it began, 'Shanklin is a very strange place.' He then changed all the beautiful boys into girls and sent it off, hoping that the transformation would illustrate the banality of the original. Robin did not reply but began again, the first of a series of new beginnings. At an interim stage he asked his uncle's opinion of the latest version and Willie replied:

> It's easily the best work you've done. Having told you that, I must tell you that if you publish it, it will kill you stone dead. Do you think anyone could write such a book about the queer life that goes on in Morocco without having experienced it? Do you seriously imagine that, apart from a handful of queers, the public are going to be interested in the goings-on of a few pederasts in Tangier? The public will dislike the book. The critics will slay you and you'll lose such sales as you've got at present. Why do you think that Noël and I have never stuck our personal predilections down our public's throats? Because we know it would outrage them.

Terence Rattigan urged him to publish but Noël Coward agreed with Willie, adding that he was irritated by 'queer books' in which all the characters were miserable. 'As you know perfectly well, dear boy, you have only to look at me to see that there are queers who are very happy indeed, morning, noon and night!'

Robin decided to continue refining the book in the hope that he could overcome the problems envisaged by Willie without weakening the homosexual theme. As a working title he christened it *The Tainted Wether*, taken from a line in *The Merchant of Venice*: 'I am the tainted wether of the flock.'

In the meantime a living had to be made and he investigated the possibilities of popular journalism in which there had been a long tradition of titled people writing in the Sunday papers for high fees. Robin had no wish to lend his name to trivia and chose for his first subject the existence of slavery on the African continent which, he believed, would come as a shock to those who thought it had died out. He had heard that the trade in humans still centred on Timbuktu as it had done for centuries but when he approached the editors of quality newspapers with his proposal they turned him down. They were not prepared to gamble money on a subject which had no obvious attraction for their mainly middle-class readership. Robin eventually sold the idea to the *People*, a down-market popular paper whose editor could see the sensational possibilities it offered.

Robin invited Michael Davidson to go with him to Timbuktu and on the way they spent a week or so in Dakar. Robin was later reticent about his own activities there but for Davidson it was a cornucopia of boys. He boasted that he declined an invitation to dine with the French governor general in favour of a night with a shoeshine boy who had picked him up in the Place Protet. While Robin acted his new role as Lord Maugham at the governor's palace, Davidson pursued the dominating interest of his life elsewhere.

After the joys of Dakar it was a great disappointment for Davidson to find Timbuktu apparently devoid of homosexual activity of any kind. As for slavery there was no sign of that either, at least not in the form Robin had expected, but a domestic version of it existed among well-to-do families whose servants had been born into bondage, a tradition that went back to the time when an open slave market existed. Similarly, the nomadic Tuareg also had black African bond servants to wait on their womenfolk and look after their herds of camels. The French authorities who had made slavery illegal nearly seventy years before ignored a tradition it was impossible for them to change.

Davidson accepted their pragmatism but to Robin the existence of bondage was a moral outrage which must be exposed. Davidson made his own enquiries and discovered that the bond servants he questioned were appalled at the thought of being freed and left to fend for themselves. Robin was unconvinced by this and journeyed into the desert to stay with the hospitable Tuareg in order to examine the situation away from the city. He was appalled at the treatment of bond servants who were underfed, brutally beaten for the smallest misdemeanour and, if ill, left to die. The girls and the boys were sometimes sexually abused when little more than toddlers and he was particularly revolted by the discovery that boys were often castrated from the age of about ten by the cutting away of both the penis and the scrotum. Whatever French law might say slaves were bought and sold as they had been for hundreds of years. He even met a sheikh who had taken six children on his holy pilgrimage to Mecca and cheerfully admitted selling them off like human travellers' cheques. To prove his case, Robin bought a youth from his Tuareg master while Davidson took photographs of the transaction. Later, before they returned to England, the youth was given his freedom. The story, amplified with information obtained from the Anti-Slavery Society in London, appeared as a series in the *People* from 27 September to 25 October.

The stir the articles caused persuaded Robin to write a book on the subject to shock public opinion into action. In February 1960 he journeyed to Morocco to begin research. He took with him Keith Gossop as his assistant and driver. In Tangier he bought a car and they began their journey to Agadir, stopping on the way in Marrakesh which, apart from its splendours as an ancient capital city, was known for its relaxed acceptance of homosexual behaviour. T. S. Eliot and his wife were in Marrakesh. Over dinner they strongly advised the couple to stay at the Hotel Saada which had recently been built on the shore at Agadir. Eliot was so enthusiastic about it that Robin telephoned to cancel the reservations he had made at the Hotel Mauritania and switch to the Saada instead.

They arrived in Agadir on 29 February and Robin applied to the governor for permission to drive further south where he planned to investigate stories of an active slave trade. In the evening there was a slight earth tremor which everyone ignored, but when Robin's agent Eric Glass telephoned from London to discuss the sale of the film rights of *The Man with Two Shadows* to Hammer Films, the line was so bad that it was agreed that he would telephone later that night. By eleven o'clock the call had not come through so Robin undressed and climbed into bed to doze and read.

The story of what happened next was frequently retold by Robin to friends and acquaintances, and versions of it appeared in the *People* and *Escape from the Shadows*. Suddenly there was a mighty earth shudder and simultaneously a sound like rumbling thunder. Through the bedroom window it seemed to Robin as if the stars were flashing by while he experienced a sensation of floating and falling. Abruptly this stopped and he found himself in total darkness. His whole body seemed numb but gradually sensation returned, bringing pain with it, and he felt blood trickling downward from his chest. Through a haze of shock he realised that he was still in the bed trapped up to his neck in debris. Cautiously, he called out but there was no reply.

Keith Gossop had been drinking in a bar along the beach when the first shock of the earthquake came at 11.39 p.m. In the chaotic aftermath he somehow found his way back to the hotel. The entire building had telescoped into the sand and only a little of it was visible; grotesquely, the marble steps to the entrance were undamaged and the electric sign, previously on the roof five storeys above, straddled them intact.

Over the next few hours a rescue team formed of men from the nearby French naval air base, working in the light of vehicle headlamps, burrowed their way into the wreckage. They brought out nineteen people trapped underneath a concrete floor and then found others. Eventually they got to Robin. His head and shoulders were visible in a space formed by a massive concrete beam that seemed to rest precariously on the wooden headboard of the bed. The men, working like miners in a three-foot seam, shifted the debris from his body until they saw that one leg was trapped under the beam. With clasp knives they cut away the mattress beneath Robin, lowering his body by a few inches, but the situation appeared hopeless and the officer in charge said that they would have to sever his leg below the knee. Robin, terrified at this, begged them to try to pull him out. As he screamed in agony, they slowly wrenched him free and then passed him from man to man until he found himself lying on the sand. In a semi-coma he begged for an injection to ease his pain but was refused because supplies were short and needed for others in a worse condition. Gossop, who had been assisting the rescue team, told him that rumours of the numbers of dead were alarming, ranging from several thousands to twenty thousand. The whole of Agadir was devastated and hardly a building was left standing. Ironically the only hotel to survive was the Mauritania.

When the French military flew in additional supplies of morphine Robin was at last given an injection which put him out for hours. He woke up in a Casablanca hospital and, with the help of the British ambassador, Sir Charles Duke, got a place aboard a plane for England. Before leaving, he telephoned the editor of the *People*, Stuart Campbell, who arranged for stenographers and photographers to be waiting at Heathrow. He subsequently gave the £1,000 fee he was paid for his story to the Agadir Relief Fund as a thanksgiving for his rescue.

Robin spent the next month in the Lindo wing of St Mary's Hospital, Paddington where he went annually for tests to check that the shrapnel lodged near his brain had not moved. The fresh damage to his body exacerbated his poor physical condition and, despite constant warnings, he later relied even more on alcohol and prescribed drugs to relieve recurring bouts of pain. Psychologically he appeared to be unaffected by the experience and rarely spoke of it, though during the hours entombed in the wreckage of the hotel he suffered frightening claustrophobia, fear of death and periods of unconsciousness tormented by hallucinatory dreams.

In an interview in 1977 he was able to look back on the

experience with cool detachment and tell the readers of the American magazine *Gay Sunshine*:

> I didn't think with regret of all those silly things I'd done: I only regretted the dreary hours I'd spent studying the law and all the moments of boredom which I had suffered during the period of time when I tried to persuade myself and the world around me that I was an ordinary, blustering, predominantly heterosexual young man. Agadir taught me a sharp lesson – which was that one must not be afraid of enjoying oneself in life provided that you can afford to physically, mentally or spiritually. I'm all for having a good time whenever it's possible.
>
> I am absolutely scared stiff of any sort of pain. I am not afraid of dying – I do hope it will be a painless death. In Agadir I could just move in the blackness of my confinement and when I thought there was no hope I could just move my left arm on a jagged piece of stone. I wanted to cut my veins so that I would slowly bleed to death and not go out in anguish. So that [now] I take such precautions as are possible against such an eventuality.

On 14 July 1960 he was fit enough to make his maiden speech in the House of Lords in support of a question put by Lord Shackleton on the subject of slavery. In it he recalled his own experiences in Timbuktu. The speech was carefully composed and delivered with impressive coolness which did not disguise his passionate feelings. It suggested that he had a future role in the Lords as an advocate for those who suffered unjustly but had no public voice. The following year his book *The Slaves of Timbuktu* received an excellent press. The *Observer* reminded readers of Robin's speech in the Lords and commented: 'The sensation it created did more for the anti-slavery movement than many pamphlets.'

One of the most valuable items Robin received from his father's estate was the original manuscript of *Cakes and Ale* which Willie had given Freddie as a mark of affection; otherwise his inheritance came nowhere near what he had hoped it would be. With his share he began searching for a permanent London base and found what he wanted at 25 Seaton Street, a working-class road of narrow terraced houses at the unfashionable end of the King's

Road, Chelsea. It was very like the house he had lived in after the war and had used as the setting of *The Servant*.

The place was in a bad state of repair and he paid only a few hundred pounds for it, convinced that for very little more it would make a pleasant home. Once renovation started he was caught by a fever of invention and could not stop. The basement became a separate flat which he rented to a friend. On the hall floor he created a new dining room and a large, ultra-modern kitchen leading into an extension with a bedroom and bathroom for Keith Monk. The top floor became his own bedroom with a luxurious bathroom off it and the middle-floor rooms were knocked into one to make a drawing room. This was costly enough, but he insisted on a genuine Adam fireplace for the drawing room and four slender Adam pillars to decorate the arch in the middle of it. It was impossible to find genuine second-hand pillars, so moulds were made from an original, and pillars cast in metal, although plaster would have done just as well.

The reckless expense continued with the furnishings. Though he was able to find what he believed to be bargains in junk shops, it cost a small fortune to have them restored. As a final touch, a terrace was made on the roof of the extension and the garden itself expensively landscaped. At the end of all the work he had a beautiful house which astonished visitors when they stepped through the front door into an extravaganza of luxury completely out of keeping with the rest of the street. The total cost was somewhere in the region of £15,000 which, at the time, would have paid for somewhere far superior in a better location at the Sloane Square end of the King's Road. When friends remonstrated, he pointed out that this enclave of Chelsea was bound to improve and it was a good investment. 'It will go up,' he said. But, far from going up, the local authority had plans to pull it down for municipal housing. Five years later they slapped a compulsory purchase order on the property, offering a few thousand pounds in compensation. After much haggling this was increased but it represented a dramatic loss on his investment.

He still kept the flat in Brighton where, with the co-operation of the Durnfords, he instituted a series of celebrity Sunday lunches. The guests included local residents Sir Laurence and Lady Olivier, Dame Flora Robson, Terence Rattigan, Gilbert Harding, Hector Bolitho with his boyfriend Derek Peel, and, from London, members of the family and a string of well-known names: Graham Greene, Hermione Baddeley, Eric Portman, Beverley Nichols, Hermione Gingold, Joseph Losey, Cyril Connolly, Rupert Croft-Cooke, Donald Sinden and Noël Coward. Keith Monk acted as assistant host and ferried the London visitors from the station in Robin's Bentley, nicknamed 'Bessie'. Cocktails were served in Robin's living room and then everyone moved down to the large Durnford dining room where the table was presided over by Robin at one end and the striking-looking Mrs Durnford at the other. Beverley Nichols' friend Cyril Butcher, an ex-actor turned television director, assumed the house belonged to Robin and that Mrs Durnford was a glorified housekeeper, possibly a poor relation. 'It was never quite clear and one didn't ask. Robin was a good host, the food was all right, there was always plenty to drink and people made useful contacts.' Donald Sinden recalls that it was all rather impressive, complete with a manservant who waited at table. He later discovered that the 'manservant' was actually the master of the house, Mr Durnford!

Robin was instinctively hospitable, keen to be well-thought-of and compared favourably with his uncle, but in the Durnfords' slightly shabby home he could not begin to compete with the ambiance of the Villa Mauresque. Nonetheless, he had a childlike capacity for make-believe and could transform the surroundings of No. 2 Brunswick Terrace into Versailles and be anyone from the Sun King to Cary Grant – anyone as long as it was not Robin Maugham.

Robin's housekeeper, Mrs Roberts, cooked his lunches and, although she was already excellent, Robin paid for classes to extend her talents and to put her on a par with Willie's cook, Annette. Mrs Roberts was a lady of strong moral opinions, but she accepted without question the young men she found in

Robin's spare bedroom. The fact that they had come back for sex never occurred to her and she happily prepared breakfast for two. One morning, however, she discovered a young girl in the spare room and was outraged by the impropriety of a woman spending the night in a bachelor flat. Robin had some difficulty in placating her with hastily manufactured reasons. She would have been even more outraged if she had known that he had picked the girl up in a public house near the station but as he preferred sleeping alone after sex she had been shown to the spare room like her male counterparts.

Once, while Robin was in London, Keith Monk held an impromptu late-night party for the cast of a touring musical playing at the Hippodrome Theatre. Mrs Roberts, arriving unexpectedly early the next morning, was horrified at the state of the flat and the sight of bodies slumped in drunken sleep. Monk, with a boy in Robin's bed, was not sure if she saw him, but it was enough for her that the master's room had been used. Monk tried to explain that he intended to clean the flat up but he could not calm her or stop her telephoning to complain and to give her notice. Robin rushed down from London and persuaded her to reconsider but her price was the expulsion of Monk forthwith. Robin agreed to this and moved him into a flat nearby in Adelaide Crescent. As Robin put it to him: 'I can always replace you but I can't replace her.' It was an amicable arrangement but Robin built it up into a dramatic incident for *Escape from the Shadows*. According to this version, he found 'Jim' and a boy in his bed and ended the long-running affair. Jim disappeared from his life and later joined the merchant navy. It was a neat way to rid the book of a character of whom he had begun to tire. In real life Monk, who was one of several lovers used to create the composite Jim, remained as a member of Robin's entourage.

In a small town, it was inevitable that social circles should overlap and consequently Robin knew many of the gay set but did not necessarily want them as close friends. The Hon. George Kinnaird, Peter Churchill (the second Viscount) and Sir Francis Rose, for example, were a little too outrageous for his taste and though he went to their parties and they went to his, he kept them at a distance. Francis Rose in particular irritated him, as he assumed a form of kinship because Freddie had been his guardian, and he took it for granted that Robin would help him financially. Rose had lost most of his fortune in the thirties and, though he made a living as an artist, designer and author, he was always short of cash and sponged off friends, particularly his ex-lover Cecil Beaton. He did not endear himself to the Brighton set when, in 1961, he made an extraordinary attack on English gay men in his memoir, *Saying Life*, in which he compared them unfavourably with their Continental counterparts. They were, he said, effeminate and pretentious and had invaded every aspect of public life. In a sentence of considerable ambiguity he exempted several 'masculine types' including Peter Churchill and Louis Mountbatten!

At one of Churchill's parties Robin met Rose's young actor friend Alan Helm and invited him to afternoon tea. Helm was under no illusions about his sexual interest and went along prepared for the obvious to happen but, as they sat chatting over tea and cake, nothing could have been more innocent. Some days later however they encountered each other at the Curtain Club in Brighton and there began a relationship which lasted for nearly two years. After Robin returned from a trip abroad Helm found him entirely altered: he was drinking heavily and could be difficult to cope with and so the friendship petered out.

Ever since Robin had read press accounts in 1955 of a seventy-ton motor vessel, the *Joyita*, found abandoned in the South Pacific, he had toyed with the idea of a novel based on the story. The sixteen-man crew and nine passengers had vanished without trace and the ship had been stripped of its cargo and all removable fittings. Attempts had been made to sink it but, unknown to the perpetrators, the refrigerated hold was lined with 640 cubic feet of cork which kept the vessel afloat. The press had a field day with sensational theories of freak storms and piracy but an official inquiry could find no acceptable explanation and the *Joyita*'s fate became a maritime mystery along with the *Marie Celeste*.

In 1961 Robin went to Fiji to investigate the story and the acting governor, P. D. Macdonald, allowed him access to all the inquiry papers. The journey took him to some of the places visited by his uncle and Gerald Haxton in 1916. Levuka, once the capital of Fiji, was now a dilapidated ghost of a town. The waterfront was virtually abandoned compared to when Haxton had visited it and there had been over fifty bars packed with sailors of every nationality. The locals had vivid memories of Willie, and Robin was often asked if he was a relation, but his reply was not received with any sign of pleasure. Several of them warned that 'Whonsbon' wanted to see him and finally he received an imperious demand to visit the Venerable C. S. Whonsbon-Ashton, the Archdeacon of Fiji. As soon as Robin arrived the cleric was on the attack, brushing aside protests. The diatribe went along these lines:

> I read in the papers that Somerset Maugham was your uncle and we all know what he did when he came here, don't we? So I decided I'd better tell you straight, without prevarication, that we want no more heathen tricks from the Maughams. He'd visit Sumatra, Singapore and Samoa and listen to gossip about local people and write it all down, just changing the names. Look at that story about the missionary in *Rain*. I knew that man and there are relatives of the victims of the *Joyita* disaster who are alive today. I don't want the victims traduced in your book; there are some very odd stories going round about what you are up to. So do I have your word? No heathen tricks?

Robin promised solemnly that he would not upset anyone but in defence of Willie he pointed out that the missionary in 'Rain' was not based on a specific individual. The Archdeacon dismissed this: 'I've met the man. I know him. I've seen him. He's flesh and blood.'

Robin wrote two books from this visit, both published in 1962. The first was a factual account, *The Joyita Mystery*, the second a novel, *November Reef*. For this he took the *Joyita* story as a base and invented a plot about Clift, a millionaire who establishes a colony on a remote island for people with practical and artistic skills. The island is taken over by fascist-style thugs but Clift ignores their brutality and pays to be left in peace. There is enough action to enthral the reader who enjoys a thriller but it is also a warning against appeasement. Robin was gratified by praise from Anthony Burgess in the *Observer* while Willie called it 'fresh and stirring'.

Robin was in Fiji when he learned that Kate had died of a heart attack at only sixty-four, very young for a family traditionally noted for longevity, but she had suffered from the effects of diabetes for many years. She had been mother, sister and friend to him and he was devastated; no longer could he pour out his problems to her in long telephone conversations while she gave him understanding, common sense and optimism. Kate, an inveterate party giver, had inherited from her mother the cheerful humour characteristic of the Romers, and had little in her make-up of Maughamesque cynicism. Professionally, her career as a novelist had not been as successful as early books promised. Willie had warned her frequently that she had to work harder, but she was too easily diverted by family and friends from the solitary life of a writer.

# XVI

## The Scandal of *Looking Back*

When Robin had stayed at the Villa Mauresque in August 1959 he had jotted down scraps of conversation and comment in his diary. On 12 August he had recorded Willie casually mentioning that he was writing his autobiography:

> this and that, a kind of journal, obiter dicta about things I haven't had time to write about before. I've become so used to writing two or three hours each morning that I don't know how to make the hours go by. But this does the trick. When I've finished it, I shall start all over again because setting it down as I'm doing – just as it comes into my head – it's all muddled and I want to get it straight.

Robin said later that Willie had subsided into silence and he thought it tactless to remind him that an announcement had already appeared in the press: the book was to be called *The Ragbag* and would be published posthumously. When Willie was out of earshot, Alan Searle confided to Robin that the book was 'terrifyingly bitter' on the subject of Syrie and he was certain that Liza would try to suppress it. He added that the central truth of Willie's homosexuality was ignored but this was hardly a surprise in view of Willie's paranoid fear that the public might learn about it. At the time it seemed highly unlikely to Robin that Willie would attack Syrie in print, even posthumously, and he assumed that the story was gossip invented by Searle to cause dissention in the family.

The next morning Willie had wandered aimlessly between the house and the pool asking unrelated questions such as: 'How do you spell Shah as in Shah of Persia?', as if he was mentally adrift.

By lunch-time he seemed his usual self and talked about Freddie, repeating almost parrot-fashion the contents of the letter he had written to the author of *The Lives of the Lord Chancellors*.

Earlier the doctor had been called because Searle's back had been so painful that he could not sleep. Tough-looking, hairy and ebullient, the doctor had told Searle the pains were caused by 'the change of life'. Searle had been infuriated by this flippant reference to his sexuality and, when Willie had gone for his afternoon siesta, he broke down: 'I can't bear it any longer,' he wept, and kept repeating: 'You don't understand.' Calming down a little, he said that Liza was due to stay for two weeks and Willie would be torn to pieces emotionally because he thought he'd made a great mistake. (Searle did not explain what he meant by this.) Then he broke down again and declared hysterically that he wanted to leave the Mauresque: 'If I could, I'd leave today.' There were more tears and then, in a complete change of mood, he said he could not bear to leave Willie after all. 'What am I to do? I can't carry on any more.'

It is all the more astonishing that on 5 October Willie and Searle sailed for Japan on the French liner *Laos*, a trip that had been planned for a year; this after Willie had refused to go to America because the voyage might be too exhausting. The incentive was an exhibition honouring him as the greatest living English writer. Francis King, then based in Kyoto for the British Council, said of Willie in *Yesterday Came Suddenly*:

> So many people have written so many unpleasant things about Maugham. But in all truthfulness, I have little but good to report of him. He was in Kyoto for more than a week and, during that week, I saw him every day, often for hours on end. Such continuous proximity is an excellent test of character. He was extremely frail and tired easily but never once did he show any anger or irritability towards Alan Searle or anyone else.
>
> Maugham's reputation at that period was far higher in Japan than in England – a fact on which he commented to me, with the sardonic ruefulness of so much of his conversation. 'University professors queue up each morning in my hotel to get me to sign copies of my books. But when I stay in London, no one cares a damn that I'm there.'

Freddie Maugham

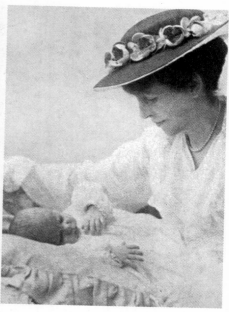

Nellie and Robin

Robin at Highfield

Robin at Eton

Helen 'Nellie' Romer Maugham

The Maugham sisters: Diana, Kate and Honor

A scene from *He Must Return*,
Robin's first professionally produced play

Robin as a subaltern
in the Sharpshooters, 1940

Programme of Robin's
first professional play, *He Must Return*

Rebecca West,
Cap d'Antibes, 1951

Derek Peel,
about 1956

Robin with Michael Davidson,
Ischia, 1953

Colin Spencer,
1952

Keith Monk

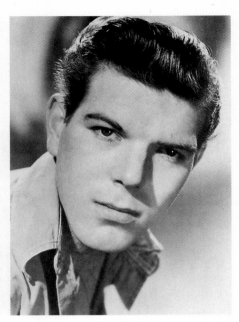

Alan Helm

Robin with Peter Burton, Casa Calapada,
during the writing of *Escape from the Shadows*

Casa Calapada

Peter Burton 'at work' on
*The Last Encounter*, Ibiza, 1971

William Lawrence
collaborated with Robin on several works

Robin with Honor at an exhibition of her work

'Robin Maugham, England 1977' by Ian McGee

Robin Maugham by Michael ffoulkes for *Punch*, 1975

Francis King admired Willie's consideration for others, but on one occasion he glimpsed another aspect of his character:

John Haylock and I had dinner with him and Alan Searle in the Miyako Hotel. In Maugham's absence, Alan whispered to us, 'I want you to show me the queer bars and clubs. Willie will trot up to bed as soon as dinner is over.'

Willie did indeed trot up to bed as soon as dinner was over. But, when he heard that Alan, John and I were going out for a drink (that was how Alan put it to him), he at once objected: 'No, Alan, I'm not f–f–feeling at all well tonight! I'd like to have you n–n–near at hand in case I need a d–d–doctor.'

Seeing us out, Alan exclaimed, 'Oh, how I long to be *free!*'

On the return journey Willie and Alan visited Bangkok, Singapore and Johore where they were guests at the coronation of the eighteenth Sultan. For Willie the five-month tour had been a personal triumph comparable to the final farewell of a great star, but it took several weeks of medical treatment and complete rest for him to recover. Searle, who had organised the trip and was constantly at Willie's beck and call, took longer to regain his energy.

Francis King and others who met Willie at this time were amazed by his stamina and general alertness, probably unaware that he had the actor's need for admiration and also the ability to rise to the occasion in order to get it. Those who knew him intimately noted the increasing signs of mental disintegration when he was off guard and free of pressure to perform for his admirers.

If Robin's diary suggests that the first draft of *The Ragbag* contained the unreliable and embittered ramblings of an old man, it also underlines that in 1959 Willie did not plan to have the book published while he was alive. This was further emphasised in a conversation over lunch at the Dorchester in May 1961 when he said: 'I'm afraid my autobiography reveals me in such an unpleasant light that it can't be published until after my death.'

Two months later Robin was astonished to hear that a completely rewritten version of *The Ragbag*, renamed *Looking Back*, was to be published the following year. According to Searle, quoted in *Time* magazine of 11 August, Willie had decided after all to publish in his lifetime because he had bloodied so many of his 'colleagues' and, if he left it until after his death, 'they might well pull him out of his grave'.

The news that *Looking Back* was to be published prompted Robin to go ahead with a project he had already discussed with his uncle; this was to be a chatty history of the family with the emphasis on charm rather than scholarship. He saw it following profitably in the wake of *Looking Back* as a sort of addendum to it. In January 1962 he was delighted when an American publisher who must have known about *Looking Back* offered him an advance of $50,000 provided he developed the proposed family history into a detailed biography of his uncle. This was something he had always hoped to do but Willie was fiercely opposed to anyone investigating his life and had gone to great lengths to frustrate any attempt, burning valuable documentation and even, as Robin later discovered, inserting a clause in his will expressly forbidding his literary executor, Spencer Curtis Brown, from assisting potential biographers. But Robin was convinced that he enjoyed a privileged relationship and, if Willie could be persuaded to break his embargo, he would have an asset worth far more than $50,000.

In the previous few years Willie had become almost completely reliant on Alan Searle whose influence the family saw as increasingly sinister. Robin already knew from his visits and from what Willie had told him with some glee in 1959 that Searle wrote and signed all his correspondence; whether this included letters purporting to be in Willie's own hand was not clear. But Robin bore this in mind when he composed a long letter dated 14 February 1962 designed to avoid antagonising either of them. Having outlined the American proposal, he explained his financial situation: the money left to him by his father had been spent on his 'little house' and he now needed to buy an annuity for his old age. Robin apparently thought that this indication of financial responsibility from one who was notoriously profligate with money would appeal. He ended by saying that the offer was too tempting to refuse but he would only accept if Willie gave his blessing and full co-operation for the project. He was not to know that in *Looking Back*, apart from leaving out any clue which might indicate his homosexuality, Willie had falsified history to present himself as a red-blooded womaniser. Robin, who had an intimate knowledge of Willie's life going back nearly thirty years, was one of the last people Willie was likely to entrust with a biography now or in the future.

In his reply of 16 February 1962, possibly composed by Searle, Willie explained that he was already checking the proofs of his memoirs (this was not true) and it would be stupid for anyone to go over similar ground again. Provided, however, that Robin refused the American offer and in addition left him out of the family book completely, he would gladly make him a gift of $50,000 to buy his annuity.

The letter put Robin into a dilemma; Willie and Searle had seen through his disingenuous approach and he was now worse off, for the family history was not worth publishing if it omitted its most important figure. Before replying, Robin took advice from his associate Derek Peel who set out the pros and cons in a detailed memo, emphasising that Willie's 'generous' gift represented some £30,000, whereas the American offer, after tax, would only amount to about £10,000. In an affectionate response dated 20 February 1962, Robin gratefully accepted his uncle's gift, promising to omit him from his family history and vowing never to write a biography of him in the future.

*Looking Back* was never published in book form, though extracts appeared in the press, so the raison d'être for the family history vanished. Subsequently Robin rewrote his book making Willie the central figure but delayed publication until his uncle died in 1965. He called it *Somerset and All the Maughams*, a title taken from Noël Coward's version of Cole Porter's 'Let's Do It'. In the end he believed he had got the best of both worlds – £30,000 from Willie and a good advance for his book – but he had also believed from what Willie had told him, verbally and in writing, that he was to be a major beneficiary. He was not to know that ten years previously Willie had instructed his financial adviser, Bert Alanson, that of the trust fund of $25,000 set up for Robin, which had grown to $75,000, only $50,000 would be paid; this, in effect, was the gift of 1962. In spite of Willie's promises, which persisted until his death, there was no mention of Robin in the will, drawn up in 1964.

Rumours circulated about the contents of *Looking Back* months before the first instalment appeared. Rebecca West, visiting New York in the early part of 1962, was appalled to be told that Willie denied 'in a characteristically reptilian statement' that he was the father of Liza. When West returned to London Barbara Back confirmed that he had written something of the sort, although she was not sure if it would appear in the excerpts, but she added that Willie had convinced her it was true that he was not the father. West, rarely at a loss for words, became so angry at this that she could not articulate a response. In her letter to Beverley Nichols of 4 May, West affirmed her conviction that Willie's story was nonsense. She said that never during her close friendship had she detected any falsity in Syrie's attribution of the child to Willie. If he now rejected his daughter, it must be the result of some senile fancy. For her part, if she believed herself to be the child of 'that obscene toad', she would be awfully glad if she were suddenly told she was not!

*Show – The Magazine of the Arts*, sophisticated and elegantly designed, serialised *Looking Back* over three months, from June 1962. When the *Sunday Express* began publishing re-edited excerpts from the book, the restrained presentation of *Show* gave way to glaring headlines such as 'The anguish my marriage to Syrie brought me' and 'One of my wife's closest friends told me of her affairs'. Admittedly, most of the readers may have treated the series as no more than Sunday-morning entertainment, but those who knew Willie even slightly could not remain entirely detached. The mildest reaction was that he had behaved dishonourably by telling the stories, even if there was some truth in them. The family could only keep a dignified silence and pray that the matter would be quickly forgotten.

Alexander Frere, Chairman of Heinemann, Willie's publisher for nearly sixty years, had been anxious that the book should be in the shops following the *Sunday Express* serialisation. In anticipation, an advertisement appeared on the dust jacket of *Purely for My Pleasure* in April. But when Frere received the full manuscript in the spring, he was so alarmed that he refused to publish. Following his rejection, no further attempt has so far been made to publish the book in its entirety.

It was clear that Willie had rewritten history to suppress anything that might suggest he was homosexual. While nobody expected him to tell the truth, all his talk about what he termed 'sexual congress' with a string of women caused eyebrows to be raised among those who had known him for many years. Beverley Nichols could not take it seriously: he believed it was all fiction and that Willie was claiming other people's experiences with women as his own. As he pointed out, he had very elderly friends who had known Willie since the 1900s, and there had never been a whiff of gossip about women, only about men.

Willie's dismissal of Haxton as no more than an efficient employee caused scorn among those in the know. This angered even Nichols who disliked Haxton. As he put it: 'Willie loved him, left England because of him and was distraught when he died. Surely someone as important to his life deserved more gracious acknowledgement. As for darling Syrie, I was so furious, I determined to put the record straight.' As it turned out, Nichols, for all his sincerity, was the wrong person to do this.

While Willie did not deny that he was Liza's father, he revealed the well-kept secret that she was born out of wedlock. In the pre-permissive society of 1962, the conventional attitude to illegitimacy was still one of stern disapproval and for any family, let alone the Maughams, it was painful and shocking for such information to be exposed to the public. It was made worse by Willie's bitter denigration of Syrie. His spleen reached its climax in a letter sent to her three years after their marriage, a copy of which he claimed he had 'recently found'. In it he blamed the failure of the relationship entirely on her, pointing out that she had married him knowing that he did not love her and that he agreed to the arrangement because she loved him and he wanted her to be happy; also because he was concerned for their daughter's welfare. It was unreasonable of her to reproach and torment him for not loving her when he had never deceived her into thinking he did. She had made his life such a misery that he could not face her without a drink to fortify himself and, because she had nagged, harassed and terrorised him, she had killed all the affection he had for her, driving him almost to suicide.

He attacked her for her empty-headedness and recalled how he had tried to arouse her interest in art and literature but failed. In an unwittingly comic touch he reminded her that he had even bought her needles and wool so that she could take up knitting but she had not even been interested in that. In one of his cruellest sentences he asked what she had to offer apart from sitting around in superb clothes looking picturesque. He ended by giving her an ultimatum: either she agreed to allow him complete freedom to come and go as he pleased without making scenes or they should agree to separate. For his part he would prefer the former, if only for Liza's sake, but he could not continue as they had been; he did not have the physical strength to live a life of unhappiness and would only die.

It is said that Willie carried out drastic rewriting in the months leading up to serialisation to give coherence to the muddled first draft of what was then *The Ragbag*. But was he physically capable of doing this? His sight and hearing were failing rapidly, he was cursed with circulation problems and he was forced to wear a leather and canvas harness on his writing hand to alleviate pain. Was he still able to give the task the prolonged periods of concentration it required? The first version in his own handwriting apparently exists but was the final version prepared by Searle?

The letter, for example, was so badly constructed and so full of melodramatic language that it is difficult to believe that Willie could have written it. Calder thought it 'almost certainly a fabrication, one last piece of fiction'. In his book *A Case of Human Bondage*, Beverley Nichols asserted that the letter was not written by Willie. With unerring snobbery, he dismissed it as the type of concoction a Victorian scullery maid might write under the influence of a cheap romantic novel. This pointed at the humbly-born Alan Searle but, as he was still alive, Nichols was unable to name him as the author of the letter for fear of legal action. Cyril Butcher was not so reticent, pointing out that if Willie had not written it, there was only one other person at the Mauresque who could have done.

A question that has confounded commentators is why Willie allowed serialisation. Various explanations have been offered but none is satisfactory. It has been suggested that he was flattered by the size of the offer made by Lord Beaverbrook. Others contend that Alan Searle, who had owned the book since Willie assigned it to him in 1960, masterminded the sale but he denied this in the wake of the hostile backlash. The charitable answer is that Willie was so mentally confused that he did not know what he was doing and may even have thought that the publication of the excerpts was to be delayed until after his death, as he once intended. It was, after all, only in May 1961 that he had admitted to Robin that its contents showed him in a bad light and it seems inconceivable that a man so protective of his reputation could change his mind so soon, unless his mind was out of control. Apparently, the full implication of what he had written did not dawn on him until he paid his usual visit to London and became aware of the coolness of friends. When he visited the Garrick, some members showed their disapproval either by ignoring him or by leaving the room. It was to be his final visit to England.

Unless Searle kept the newspapers from him, he could have been left in no doubt of the strength of feeling when Rebecca West started a fund to purchase a 1771 bust of Catherine the Great by Fedor Shubin to be presented to the Victoria and Albert Museum in memory of Syrie. This was unveiled on 9 October 1964 at a ceremony hosted by Cecil Beaton. Among those associated with this gesture of loyalty to her were John Pope-Hennessy, Lady Aberconway, Elizabeth von Hofmannsthal, Noël Coward, Sacheverell Sitwell, Victor Gollancz, Diana Cooper,

Oliver Messel and Beverley Nichols who commented: 'None of these people, myself included, would have gone out of their way to be publicly associated with the fictitious Syrie of *Looking Back*.'

# Second Childishness and Mere Oblivion

Willie's periods of mental lucidity were lessening, though Robin's diary notes show that these could last for as long as two days. Searle was the only person who could control him, though sometimes with difficulty, and he went to great lengths to disguise his true mental state. Like many old people Willie could speak lucidly about some events in the past but became confused about the present. His memories followed no perceptible theme but leapt from one incident to another as if the brain had decided to dispense with linking colloquy. In August 1962, for example, when Robin was listening to a familiar monologue about the past, Willie suddenly announced that he was leaving for St Moritz the following Monday. When Searle pointed out that Diana and Kim were coming to stay, Willie stared uncomprehendingly and asked who they were.

Both Willie and Freddie suffered nightmares in their final years but Willie's were rather more spectacular. On this visit Robin was awoken, as he often had been before, by the ghastly sounds of groaning and shrieking. He opened his bedroom door and heard Searle get up and go through the bathroom that connected his room with Willie's; gradually the sounds faded away and Robin went back to bed.

It was usual at the Mauresque for Willie not to appear until 12.30. Cocktails were served by Marius at 12.45 precisely and luncheon was announced at exactly one o'clock. But after the nightmares of the night before, Willie was very silent, leaving

Robin and Searle to chat. At 7.20 that evening they met again. As Willie lit a cigarette he pointed out that he no longer had special boxes of matches with his sign against the evil eye printed on them. 'Guests pinched them as souvenirs. I stopped it because I simply couldn't afford it.' He then repeated for the umpteenth time an explanation of the sign provided by the British Museum. According to this it was a symbol of a sword piercing through darkness into light; alternatively it was the cross of Lorraine. After a pause he said, as he did every night referring to pre-dinner martinis, 'How much longer have we got to wait?' Searle automatically replied, 'Two and three-quarter minutes,' and at exactly 7.45 the drinks were served.

The following day Searle was unwell and did not emerge from his room. In the early evening Robin found Willie strolling in the garden in a disgruntled mood. He bemoaned the fact that he could no longer play tennis or golf and could only just swim the length of the pool.

> This place is no use to me any more. Even when we're not here it costs £2,000 a month to run . . . It now belongs to Liza – though the contents belong to me. So I could sell all the contents and say, 'Take the Villa.' I'd like to live somewhere – perhaps in Venice – with a large living room and two bedrooms and nothing more. I'm fed up with this place.

He then complained that all his friends were dead and he couldn't even remember their names.

Depressing as this monologue was, Robin found Willie was a little more in command. The thought processes did not flicker as erratically and there was no automatic repetition of old anecdotes. When Robin suggested it was time for a drink, Willie remarked that he had had one at six o'clock. This in itself was an unusual change from routine. 'What about another?' Robin suggested. 'If you insist,' Willie replied laughing. 'I do and I'd like one too.' Off Willie went into the house and to Robin's amazement reappeared staggering under the weight of a large tray with whisky, ice and glasses. 'There was no one about so I did it myself. I even broke up the ice.' He was like a triumphant child.

The next day at lunch Willie was again on good form, apart from a few driftings into family history and a jibe or two at Syrie. Over coffee he spoke of his writing and doubted if it would stand the test of time. 'My success means nothing to me. All I can think of now are my mistakes. I can think of nothing else but my foolishness and I've made mistakes all along the line.' Then, in what must have been a twist of sardonic humour although Robin did not register it as such, Willie added, 'And the awful thing is, if I had my life to live a second time, I'd make the same errors all over again!'

Robin was due to return to England that afternoon and Willie insisted on walking to the chauffeur's cottage to make certain the car would be ready to go to the airport. Jean asked, 'Le Rolls ou le petit auto?' 'The little car of course. Monsieur is of no consequence.' 'Mais monsieur est Vicomte,' Jean protested. 'Monsieur is only my nephew,' Willie replied laconically.

Diana, who arrived soon after with her husband, says without prevarication that Willie was suffering from senile dementia. While she was there, her impression of Alan Searle as an Iago figure was confirmed when she heard him feeding Willie vicious lies about Liza, unaware that anyone was within earshot. When she confronted him, Searle admitted that he had lied but shrugged his shoulders as if to say 'So what?'

Robin returned to spend Christmas at the villa and was met at Nice airport by Searle, with Jean at the wheel of the Rolls-Royce. On the way Searle warned him that Willie had deteriorated since August but to Robin he seemed rational enough, even affable and benign. He was eager to see the photograph Robin had obtained of a statuette of Robert Maugham which had been found in the offices of the solicitors who were successors to Maugham et Dixon. The terracotta figure showed a plump man seated on a low, high-backed, upholstered chair, one leg tucked under the other, ankle behind calf. His hair had receded but he had luxuriant mutton-chop whiskers. The jacket of the suit he wore was buttoned once, high on the chest, over a high collar and stock with diamond pin. There was nothing to identify the figure, but on the base was the sculptor's signature, Jeras Boehm, and the date 1862. Willie studied the picture intently and remarked that ever since his father's death he had never been able to remember what he looked like. He was fascinated by the pose and Robin pointed out that he had often seen Willie sitting like that. Willie smiled. 'So I do.'

He was not so affable when Robin told him he had been to see the house Robert had built at Suresnes. He had been surprised to find the house apparently intact and easily recognisable from a description given to him by Aunt Beldy, who had said it looked like a Swiss chalet. She and Charles had thought about occupying it but Suresnes, once a rural village, had grown into an ugly suburb and there were cheap little shops and cafés built on the land before the house. After consulting his brothers, Charles had decided it should be sold. The mystery, to which she had no answer, was why it had been left empty and neglected for so long. Logic suggests that the growth of Suresnes gave rise to over-optimistic projections of land prices which did not happen.

Willie reacted furiously:

Why should you want to see the house your grandfather built in his folly? He must have known his financial condition. He must have known he had four sons . . . I suppose he said to himself . . . I don't care. Let them fend for themselves. Has it occurred to you that you have suffered from my father's folly? If he'd left your father a proper amount of money, your father wouldn't have been the despicable shit that he was.

The vehemence of this remark about Freddie was typical since he now saw his brother as a demonic figure. What had once been sibling rivalry played out as mildly malicious verbal cut-and-thrust had solidified in Willie's mind to become unmitigated hate. To attempt to discover an uncomplicated explanation for this is probably not possible. It could be that Willie hated his brother for not accepting his homosexuality or for the role he may have played in excluding Gerald Haxton from England. Alternatively, Freddie's tolerance, albeit limited by concern for the effects of scandal on his family, could have in itself become, in retrospect, a loathsome form of patronage.

After bathing and changing for dinner, Robin joined Willie and Searle in the living room. The room now looked much lighter since the bookshelves that had once occupied the whole of one wall had been removed and most of the books given to King's School. Willie often told a story which could be illustrative of Freddie's humour, or taunting malice, Willie's tone depending on whether one heard it before or after Freddie's death. On his first visit to the Mauresque Freddie had adjusted his monocle, gazed at the collection of some three thousand books and then turned to his brother. 'And where do you have the library?' On being asked his opinion of the furnishings he had looked about him and said, 'Too much gilt.' The possibility of a pun never occurred to Willie.

As usual, Willie's valet had dressed him for the evening in black silk trousers, a white shirt, a black double-breasted quilted jacket with a purple design and a loose white silk scarf. Searle wore a dinner jacket with a satin waistcoat with diamond buttons and matching cuff-links. Both wore black velvet embroidered shoes. Cocktails arrived promptly, one dry martini each for Willie and Robin and a tomato juice for Searle.

As recorded by Robin, dinner began with oyster soup with white fondant on top. (Robin may have meant a swirl of cream.) This was followed by prawns with rice and a curry sauce, crêpes au rhum, cheese, dates and nuts. This, a typical dinner at the Mauresque, was accompanied by pink champagne which was always served on the first night of a guest's arrival. In response to all Willie's utterances Searle provided an automatic repertoire of appropriate noises of approbation, surprise or sympathy. If he got it wrong, Willie did not appear to notice.

For no particular reason Willie spoke about 'Peter' – G. B. Stern. 'She was a vulgar Jewess. Broke now. I have to help her. But for thirty years she led a showy, vulgar life flaunting her success with two secretaries and all other kinds of nonsense. She was so common she'd sit on the lavatory talking to them.' Then without a pause, 'Barbara Back's thoroughly common as well and persecutes me.'

After dinner the intermittent flow continued, darting from one topic to another, until he began talking about Lady Bateman who was to be a guest at lunch the following day.

> She did something I've always envied. She decided to visit India so she hired a train – a steam engine and what goes behind it: there were carriages for herself and her companion and her secretary and ladies' maid and the other servants. There was a restaurant car. People can't afford to do that today however rich they are. One can have no idea of the luxury they lived in in those days.

Seating arrangements for the lunch next day were discussed at tedious length. Searle in a jolly voice said, 'We're having a grand lunch because it's Christmas Day.' 'Christmas Day? Oh, is it really?' Willie asked wearily.

The next morning Willie got into a frenzy about the seating plan agreed the night before and visited the dining room three times to arrange and rearrange the plan. 'You'll have to help me with the guests,' he told Searle. 'I'm bound to make a balls of it.' Robin wished the servants 'Joyeux Noël' but tension over the lunch was so high that there was no chance of a happy Christmas until it was over.

In the event everything went smoothly after a brief hiatus when Willie introduced Robin in a firm voice as his niece. Lady Bateman arrived announcing that she had got up early to get ready. She was swathed in sables and, when she had been relieved of these, unwound a scarf, took off a woollen sweater and was revealed dripping in diamonds; then she put on a mink stole and was ready for cocktails. Robin thought her remarkable for ninety-two. At lunch Willie withdrew into himself, finding it difficult to join in the chatter much of which he could not hear properly because of his increasing deafness and, if he could, would have found of little interest. During a pause Willie turned to Searle and said inconsequentially, 'What was that book I was reading by an American?' Searle stared blankly but, before he could speak, Willie snapped: 'For fuck's sake try to remember.'

When the chattering guests eventually dispersed, leaving the house suddenly silent, the three returned to the living room where Willie sat, his head buried in his hands, completely exhausted. At five o'clock he demanded to be taken to his room, then found his signet ring was missing and, in a rage, ordered a thorough search of the house. It was soon found and he settled down for a sleep before changing for pre-dinner cocktails. Searle, in tears, rushed Robin down to his favourite bar in Beaulieu in a desperate need to get away briefly from the fraught gloom of the house. He kept saying: 'This isn't a life, it's a nightmare.' Then they rushed back to the villa so that Searle would be on hand when Willie woke up. After a sombre dinner, and Willie put to bed for the night, they went out again to cruise the bars of Villefranche.

Over lunch the next day Willie rambled on disjointedly about journeys he had made with Gerald Haxton, substituting Searle for Haxton. 'Alan and I are planning to sail on the *Caronia* to the Far East.' Later: 'No one will ever know what a sensation I caused . . . the King of Johore gave a party for me. I sat next to Edwina Mountbatten . . . three weeks later she was dead.' After a long pause: 'I shall never understand why all these grand people made such a fuss of me.'

While the scandal of *Looking Back* was still brewing, Willie became convinced that he was penniless and he sold thirty-five of his paintings at Sotheby's in April 1962. Nine of them, however, had been assigned to Liza and she had documentation to support this. Following litigation, the proceeds from the sale of these pictures were frozen in a bank account pending a hearing of the action. In the meantime Willie took the extraordinary step of signing papers to adopt Searle and this was approved by the Nice court on 7 June. On 27 December the earlier rumour that he had intended to deny Liza was his daughter in *Looking Back* took tangible form when a statement from his lawyers said that he planned to sue to deny legal recognition of her. His declaration stated that she was legally the daughter of Henry Wellcome, who had never denied paternity, and he proposed to revoke all his gifts to her including shares in the Villa Mauresque company under

Article 950 of the French civil code. The suit contended that Liza had never taken care of him and that her claim to the paintings constituted ingratitude. In the *Daily Telegraph* of 29 December she was reported as saying that she was 'shocked, surprised and absolutely mystified' by her father's action and that 'when people get very old they become a little strange sometimes'.

An added bonus for the press was the disclosure for the first time of Searle's adoption and his new position as Willie's chief beneficiary. During his Christmas visit, Robin avoided discussion of this development which appeared to put his own expectations into jeopardy. It was now impossible to interpret Willie's actions in any logical fashion. For a man who had contrived to avoid public knowledge of his sex life, the laborious attempt to rewrite his own history in *Looking Back* had aroused the anger of people who knew the truth and the suspicions of those who otherwise might not have given the question any thought. Now, the adoption of the middle-aged Searle confirmed even to the most obtuse that something very odd was going on. The press had known the details of Willie's sex life for decades but for fear of legal action could say nothing; instead it was left to the cartoonists to make the point covertly with humour. One showed Willie in his dressing gown at the door of a bedroom saying, 'Nurse, he's just said "Dada".'

In February 1963 Liza appealed against the adoption and the case was heard in camera on 12 June in Nice. The court ruled that Liza was Willie's legitimate daughter and that the adoption of Searle must be annulled. In August Willie appealed, but at the subsequent hearing in January 1964 it was stated that an out-of-court settlement had been reached in Liza's favour and, as part of this, Willie had dropped his appeal over the adoption of Searle. He also paid legal costs. A terse joint statement was issued: 'Mr W. S. Maugham and his daughter, Lady John Hope, are happy to state that all differences between them have been settled.'

The entire saga, starting with the sale of the paintings, had been absurd and unnecessary and the family have nominated Searle as the villain of the piece. He had a strong motive: until the final years, his only expectation was a comparatively low pension from the interest on a trust fund, conditional on his 'remaining in service' until Willie's death. It was not much of a reward for years of devotion as lover, secretary and general factotum.

It is clear that throughout this period, once Willie's mental powers began to fail, Searle was in control of the Mauresque with access to information about Willie's business and financial affairs. He was able to originate letters and sign them as 'W. S. Maugham', or whatever was appropriate, and he used his position to plot against the family whom he thought to be more generously treated than they deserved. Even the sale of the pictures may have been deliberate provocation on his part to test Liza's reaction. He must have known that nine of them were designated to her but he said nothing when they were removed from the house; indeed it would have been part of his function to organise this with Sotheby's and supervise the removal. In his role as spokesman for Willie he reported that he was 'distressed and shocked' by Liza's writ; privately he told friends that he thought she was bluffing. The loser, he said, would be the Royal Literary Fund but this was not true. During the legal proceedings he had gone to great lengths to keep the press from Willie, ostensibly to protect the old man from the strain of interviews, but also to hide his senility and to prevent him saying anything that would damage the case. Some might speculate that Willie had very little idea of what was being done in his name and in his periods of lucidity would have been horrified at the adverse publicity and scorn he was attracting.

Anyone who has experienced cases of the manipulation of elderly people, senile or not, will find the story of Searle depressingly familiar. He always contended that he had nothing to do with Willie's business affairs and conveyed the impression that the old man was in complete control, when this was untrue. He went out of his way to be ingratiating to everyone and he was always charming to the family while working to dispossess them of as much as he could. If this scheme was to succeed, it was essential that he kept Willie hostile to his daughter and he had no scruples about the way he did this. His greatest fear must have been the possibility of a reconciliation. To defend himself against filial affection, he had to make himself indispensable to Willie in every respect, however distasteful; because he was crafty rather than intelligent he feared even the influence of professional nurses. Willie came to rely on him more and more and this may have induced a form of laziness, for, ironically, he could be better mentally and physically when Searle was not there to fetch and carry and act as a foil to his temper.

The circumstantial evidence against Searle appears to be strong but if he was guilty the blame lies initially with Willie who could have made generous financial arrangements for him much sooner instead of classifying him as a superior servant. In support of Searle there were many who saw him as selflessly devoted, motivated only by love. That the last years were difficult is something of an understatement but somehow Searle managed to create some semblance of dignity for the old man. It was more than simply 'difficult' when Willie had sudden, frightening changes of mood in which he imagined demons taunting him and swore and raved at them. If friends were present Searle used humour to ease any tension and embarrassment. Once Willie went into a fury for no apparent reason and demanded to go to bed; Searle helped him out of the room and, when he returned, quoted from Harry Graham's *Ruthless Rhymes*:

> Now when the nights grow long and chilly,
> No one wants to poke poor Willy.

On another occasion, when the old man had become incontinent, and messed a carpet, Searle, hurrying to deal with the problem, remarked cheerfully: 'Whoops, there goes another priceless Aubusson!' He did not exaggerate when he described life at the Mauresque as 'absolute hell' but a hell partly of his own choosing and creation.

He was the enthusiastic force behind celebrations for Willie's ninetieth birthday; behaving like an archetypal stage mother, he encouraged selected interviews, prodding and prompting his charge to perform. Lionel Hale attempted to interview Willie for the BBC and found that he was lucid for up to ten minutes at a time and frequently forgot what was happening. At one point he whispered to Hale that 'they', whoever 'they' might be, 'were plotting to keep me here in Venice'. All the while Searle smoothed over difficulties and translated what Willie said. He told Hale that he actually had to hold the old man down to get him to go to bed at night; it conjured up an unpleasant picture. Hale said to Calder: 'I wish to God that I'd never gone.'

A long interview appeared in the *Sunday Express* of 26 January 1964 which completely belied the reality of Willie's condition; indeed, anyone reading it in the hitherto uncollected 'writings' published in 1984 would find it difficult to believe any of the stories of his senility. Ewan MacNaughton has, however, explained the circumstances. During two interviews at the Mauresque in the presence of Searle, he found the old man feeble and slow to remember, 'just this side of dotage', and he had to guide his thoughts to likely topics, even using quotations from the preface and postscript of *A Writer's Notebook*. The final transcript was a patchwork of guided thoughts and quotations of his work skilfully put together by MacNaughton.

Robin was the only guest staying at the Mauresque for the celebrations on 25 January. The day before, as he went into the living room for pre-lunch cocktails, Willie asked what he was doing there and, when he explained, said: 'Well, I hope you don't expect any food, there isn't enough and I don't see why Alan and I should go short merely because you've arrived. I can't imagine why you've arrived anyhow.'

By the evening he was in a calmer mood and seemed pleased by the hundreds of letters, cables and greetings cards that kept arriving at the house. Robin noted in his diary that Willie was glad that Prince Pierre of Monaco had sent him a telegram. On the other hand he was proud because the Queen of England had not sent him a greeting. 'She's much too sensible for such nonsense,' Willie had said.

The next morning Robin went to his bedroom to wish him a happy birthday and found him sitting up in bed with a bright-red shawl round his shoulders. The room was filled with flowers. He is alleged to have said of the display: 'Looks as if I'm in a fucking graveyard.' This was quoted in the press as 'One would think I was in a graveyard' which does not have the same ring to it. He was in a reasonably good mood, though not expressing much interest in the morning mail. Robin's present of the Old Testament pleased him because it was in large print which compensated for his failing sight. 'I can read it,' he exclaimed and opened it at the Book of Samuel and read out the passages about Saul, David and Jonathan. 'There's no doubt about it, they were all in love.'

His physician Dr Rosanoff arrived to see him and Willie, now dressed for his birthday lunch, became angry because he did not recognise him and thought he was a press photographer. When he realised who it was he accused Rosanoff of trying to poison him.

In defiance of the doctor's advice, Searle had planned an elaborate day with a formal luncheon followed by dinner that evening with Lord Beaverbrook. He claimed that he was merely carrying out Willie's instructions. By the time they were due to set off in the Rolls, Willie was white with rage over something but no one knew what. When they arrived at the Château de Madrid, where Searle had arranged lunch for fourteen people, Willie refused to leave the car and demanded to be taken home. It was quickly surrounded by television cameras and photographers and Robin, by now standing on the pavement, asked whether they were bothering him. 'No, I don't see any of them but I don't want to meet all these people.' He then beckoned Robin to come closer. 'Where are we?' Robin explained about the lunch party in his honour. 'Well, no one ever told me,' Willie complained. Searle asked Robin to go ahead to the guests and promised they would follow. Ten minutes later Willie arrived looking grim and refusing to acknowledge any greetings, while Searle, bright as usual with social bonhomie, covered the hiatus.

According to Robin, the guests were an odd mix: ageing men with bodies carefully nurtured but minds left unattended, crumbling old ladies beautifully gowned, faces heavy with maquillage, frail hands laden with jewels, heads protected by hats and hair pieces, an aura of conflicting scents hovering around them. Several had royal titles, reminders of half-forgotten regimes, others plain names redolent of wealth from the New World.

Unable to see or hear properly, Willie sulked until the food, fresh asparagus, followed by baby lamb and then strawberries, a menu chosen to please him, soothed away his frustrated anger, and by the end of lunch he was quite relaxed. Then abruptly press photographers burst in and he was pulled to his feet for a shot of him blowing out the single candle on the special cake. When the press had finally been persuaded to leave after more photographs, an uneasy silence settled on the company. A female guest remarked loudly: 'I'm told there's a pensioner in Nice who's still alive and kicking at one hundred and four.' Willie glared. 'Fuck one hundred and four.'

When they arrived back at the Mauresque, Robin took Willie's arm to assist him but he turned away in a rage. 'Why do you do that? Can't you see how it annoys me?' The reaction recalled Willie's fastidious dislike of being touched by strangers and, at that moment, Robin probably was a stranger in Willie's disturbed mind. It was clear that he was exhausted and might become increasingly cantankerous so Searle cancelled the dinner party with Lord Beaverbrook. The rest of the time passed miserably.

On the following day the papers again referred to Willie's amazing longevity and the *Sunday Times* quoted him as saying, 'There is no reason to be happy at ninety,' which was exactly the type of comment the public expected. The longevity might have been accounted for by the treatment he had begun receiving in the late 1930s at the Niehans clinic in Vevey. Paul Niehans claimed to have discovered cellular therapy which involved injecting patients in the buttocks with a serum containing cells scraped from the foetuses of unborn goats or lambs. Instead of sharing the doubts of medical men, Willie accepted the treatment enthusiastically. He was in good company, for, over the years, the Duke of Windsor,

Pope Pius XII, Thomas Mann, Gloria Swanson, Charles Lind-
bergh and Bernard Baruch were among his fellow patients. In
1962 Searle asked Niehans if the injections could hold back
Willie's mental deterioration but the doctor could not promise
anything.

Searle, who also received the treatment, claimed that both he
and Willie were sexually rejuvenated by it and this may have been
true, for, even at his great age, Willie was capable of sexual
activity that a man twenty years younger might regard with some
awe. His physical prowess partly accounted for the restless energy
which had to find an outlet but was quickly exhausted when it
did. In his travelling days he had never stayed for long in one
place and moved on before he became bored; now he felt trapped
and wanted to get away from the confines of the Mauresque.
Searle gave in to him and they went to Venice in April, staying as
they often had at the Gritti Palace Hotel. Far from providing the
change they both hoped for, it was a miserable failure; Willie was
bewildered and lost and Searle, restricted by his duties as a nurse,
was unable to cruise the bars and enjoy himself.

Back at the Mauresque with its repetitive routine, the days
dragged wearily by. Willie sat silently brooding or, in sudden
bursts of frenetic energy, stomped up and down like a caged
creature. Searle, never far away during the day, now slept on a
bed in Willie's bedroom, permanently on duty. When Robin
arrived in June, Searle took the opportunity to go out one
evening, leaving him in charge. Robin often told the story of what
happened next, and a version was included in *Conversations with
Willie*.

At first everything went well. Cocktails were served on the
terrace as usual and, after he had finished his drink, Willie asked
(as usual) what time it was. Robin told him it was 7.23. 'Good,'
Willie responded, 'we've only seven minutes to wait.' Promptly,
at seven-thirty Marius announced dinner. Afterwards, as they sat
in the living room, Willie began to get worried. He asked Robin
the time and was told it was about nine o'clock. Then he asked
where Alan was and Robin explained. After a brief silence, Willie

repeated his questions. This happened four times in ten minutes. Finally Willie fell silent and about twenty minutes later demanded once again to know the time. When Robin told him he became angry and wanted to know where Alan was. 'Do you know what town he is in?' Robin said he was not sure – probably Nice.

Willie lit a cigarette with trembling hands and asked: 'When will Mr Searle be back?' Once again Robin explained but Willie retorted: 'You must know.' Robin protested that he did not. By now Willie was in a towering rage. 'Where do you live?' 'In Brighton.' 'Don't be wilfully stupid, I mean where are you staying tonight?' 'Here in your villa. I'm your guest.' 'No, you're not. There's no room for you. Who are you? What room do you think you are going to sleep in?'

Abruptly Willie stood up and tottered out. Robin could hear him screaming at the staff in the kitchen, then he came back. 'Where is Alan?' he screamed. 'I'm asking you, when is he coming back? When will Mr Searle be here? What are you doing in this house? What is your name?' Then he went out again and came back with Marie, Annette's assistant in the kitchen.

> 'Dans quelle chambre est-ce-que monsieur va se coucher?'
> 'Mais en haut, monsieur,' Marie answered.
> 'Dans quelle chambre?' Willie demanded.
> 'Dans la chambre à lui.'
> 'Montrez la moi.'

They processed upstairs. Marie, terrified, opened the door of Robin's bedroom. Willie glared into the empty room. Then he flicked the light switch. 'These lights will be turned out in five minutes. I'm not going to pay for any more electricity for you than that.' 'Good night, Willie,' Robin said. 'Thank you very much for an excellent dinner.' Willie tottered towards him shaking with rage. Robin thought he would strike him. 'That's the very least you should say to me,' he shouted. 'I expect more than that.' And he shuffled angrily to the door.

Marie, in tears, gave Robin a look of commiseration before she left. Willie slammed the bedroom door shut and, screaming and shouting, went away. Alan returned at about ten-thirty and went up to see Robin. 'The staff are in tears. I haven't had an evening out for a whole year and now I shall feel I can never go out again.' Then he went off to cope with Willie.

Commenting on this experience Robin said: 'I'm sure that if Willie had a knife or gun he would have killed me. He·is, I'm now convinced, a maniac. It is his quality of malignancy that pierces me with fear.'

The next morning Willie had completely forgotten his fit of lunacy but he seemed to be left with the vague impression that he had been unpleasant to Robin and felt that he should make amends for it. When Robin came out of his room on the way to swim in the pool, Willie was on the patio and greeted Robin affectionately: 'You're looking very smart.' Robin was wearing one of the ordinary white towelling dressing-gowns that belonged to the Mauresque and hung behind the door of each guest bedroom. Later Willie arrived at the pool where Robin was sunbathing. 'You know, I've slept all morning,' he said. 'I don't know what I've been working myself up about . . . But I've been trying to sleep my life away . . . You must realise that it was all right for Jesus Christ, every bit of it. He could arrange things just as he wanted them. But my problem is that I simply can't. That's the whole difference between the two of us. And I am tired – so dreadfully tired. And I don't really know anything and I find it very humiliating. But I don't really care a fer-fuck. Is it morning or afternoon?'

'Morning.'

'I hoped it was afternoon . . . But presently Alan will make us a cocktail, and if it's Sunday morning, then perhaps we could have a second cocktail.'

After lunch followed by his siesta Willie appeared on the terrace. 'I'd like a drink,' he announced, 'and then I'd like my lunch.' 'But you've already had lunch,' Searle said. 'No, I haven't. And I'm thirsty and hungry and miserable. And I'm not Jesus Christ – because he could do things that I can't. And the whole business of life was infinitely more simple for him than it is for me. And I haven't had any lunch.' 'Would you like a biscuit?' Robin asked. 'I don't want a biscuit,' he said furiously. 'I just want my lunch.'

Searle went to the kitchen and came back ten minutes later with a sandwich by which time Willie seemed to have forgotten about lunch but accepted the sandwich with surprised pleasure.

On the last day of Robin's visit the three of them moved on to the terrace after lunch to be served coffee. While they waited Willie said that when he died everything would be taken from him. 'I shan't have anything left,' he said, and burst into tears. 'I am so old and tired. Why can't they let me die? . . . I want to die so much.' When coffee was served he calmed down, smoked a cigarette and, in a change of mood, began planning a trip to Tahiti.

Robin visited the Mauresque twice in the last year of Willie's life and the pattern of behaviour was similar. Yet Willie was capable of remarkable mental and physical recovery. In March 1965 he left hospital after a bout of pneumonia which would have killed most people and was able to entertain Robin and Derek Peel to dinner when they stayed at a local hotel in May. Peel, at first very nervous after all that he had heard about the senile tantrums, saw him for what he was, a very small, shuffling old man, very deaf, with a memory almost gone. Willie was attentive to Peel over dinner, making sure that he was being looked after. Later in the sitting room as Willie sat in silence, Searle implored Peel to talk to him as he hated to be left out. In an attempt to break his strange silence, he asked him: 'What is the happiest recollection of your life?' To this mundane enquiry Willie eventually said, stammering slightly, 'I ca-can't think of anything,' as if his mind was a total blank. As his guests left, Willie shook hands and said, 'It was good of you to come. Enjoy yourself – if one can in these days.'

Visitors continued to arrive in these final months. Noël Coward, temporarily putting aside his anger over *Looking Back*, hoped he had cheered Willie a little – 'poor beast'. George Rylands found him incoherent, convinced that someone was behind him about to stab him and that Searle was leaving. Romaine Brooks, the lesbian wife of Willie's first lover Ellingham

Brooks, got the impression that Searle was being bequeathed to her as a companion. Godfrey Winn's usual self-absorption was shattered by Willie's mental and physical condition. Idiotically he handed him a programme of a recent production of *Othello*, forgetting his sight had almost gone. Willie eventually made out the title and remarked sadly: 'D'you know, I can't remember when I wrote that.' Winn passed on quickly to describe the National Theatre's success with Noël Coward's *Hay Fever* and Willie cut in: 'Noël who?' Winn repeated the name loudly. There was a very long pause while Willie ruminated: 'I seem to recollect the name but I cannot recall the face.' 'It was terrible,' Winn said. 'For most of the time he sat silently staring into space as if there was no one there. It was frightening to look into those eyes and see no flicker of recognition. This was the man I loved when I was twenty and now, nothing. Such is the whirligig of time!'

On 10 December Willie tripped and fell while in the garden and later fell again, this time hitting his head. The servants carried him to his bed, but during the night he fell out of bed and Searle found him lying on the floor. Before becoming unconscious he said, apparently quite lucidly, 'I've been looking for you for two years and we have much to talk about. I want to thank you and say goodbye.' These were his last words as Searle repeated them to Calder. Robin took down a more elaborate version after speaking to Searle on 11 December. 'This time I know I'm going to die and I'm happy that I've come to for a moment because now I can say goodbye. I want you to promise me one thing. I want you to let me die in my bed.'

He was taken by ambulance to the Anglo-American hospital in Nice where he slipped into a coma. On 15 December he died. However, because of a complication in French law, he was taken back to the Mauresque and Searle announced his death on 16 December.

Willie had left instructions that Searle – and Searle alone – should take the body to Marseilles which housed the nearest crematorium in the area. Liza asked Robin on the telephone whether he thought that she ought to go to France but without hesitation he replied no; he felt there was no reason for her to do so. There were no instructions in the will about the disposal of the ashes and it was decided that they should be interred within the precincts of Canterbury Cathedral, as Willie had discussed a decade before when visiting his old school. (There is a curious circumstance about the choice of resting place which has not been noted before. It was subsequently found that, on his mother's side, Willie was descended from Reginald de Brereton, one of the four knights who murdered Thomas à Becket, Archbishop of Canterbury, in 1170.) After the cremation it was intended that Searle was to take the casket to King's School personally; instead, he sent it on a scheduled flight from Nice.

A private ceremony was held on 22 December attended by Liza, her husband and members of the family. The casket was plain mahogany with two red seals on it and a plate with the inscription 'Somerset Maugham 1874–1965'. In the centre of the lawn, beneath the walls of the library, the turf had been neatly removed and laid on one side. A small grave had been dug, a yard square. Around it were five simple wreaths. From the headmaster and the boys of King's School there was a replica in white carnations and violets of the school coat of arms which was laid alongside the little grave by the senior boy. Around the casket were wreaths from Liza and her family. The fifth spray of flowers came from: 'Skipper Brittle and the crew of the tanker *Somerset Maugham*.' Ranged to the left of the grave was a semi-circle of boys in their school uniforms. To the right stood the small group of mourners. Close to the grave stood the Dean, who conducted the committal service. The headmaster said a short prayer and the casket was lowered into the ground.

Later, a plaque of stone was put into the wall of the library close to the grave. The letters K. S. C. stand for King's School, Canterbury. The engraved plate reads:

WILLIAM SOMERSET MAUGHAM

K. S. C. 1885–1889

BORN 1874 – DIED 1965

# Willie: The Dissection

Willie had battled so desperately to convince the world at large that he was heterosexual that he may have believed he had succeeded. In his final deranged years, if he thought about it at all, he probably assumed that the press, who had ignored his homosexuality while he was alive, would have the good taste to continue doing so when he was dead. It would have horrified him to read the *New York Times* of 17 December where, without giving it a moment's thought, his homosexuality was mentioned in passing as if it was of no importance whatsoever. So within hours of his death the edifice of hypocrisy, lies and half-truths exemplified by *Looking Back* began to collapse.

In Britain, discretion was maintained for the time being, many of the obituaries reading like hastily updated orations that had been mouldering on the files for many years. Cyril Connolly in the *Sunday Times* of 19 December called him the last of the professional men of letters 'whose name is a household word in every country'. He failed to mention that most of the literary intelligentsia had long since written Willie off because of his popularity.

The *New York Times* tribute quoted W. H. Auden's response to the valedictory resonance of the last paragraph of *A Writer's Notebook* which he had reviewed in 1949.

> We shall miss you. Of course we shall find new writers to read, but art like friendship is personal, that is unique – and no writer is replaceable by or even comparable with another. Thank you for having given us so much pleasure for so long, for having never been tedious.

Willie took practical steps to make sure that his name would be kept alive, albeit in a limited manner, even if the public forgot him. The Somerset Maugham Award, originally set up in 1947 and administered by the Society of Authors, is given annually to British writers under the age of thirty-five who show promise with a published work. The winners are required to use the money to travel abroad 'to enrich their writing by experience in foreign countries'. Over ninety authors have so far benefited, including Paul Bailey, Doris Lessing, Francis King, Humphrey Carpenter, Peter Ackroyd, A. N. Wilson, Lawrence Norfolk, Helen Simpson, Duncan McLean and Alan Warner.

He bequeathed his theatrical oil paintings which he began collecting before World War I to the Royal National Theatre. At the time of writing, however, it lacks suitable and secure conditions to display the pictures permanently so the public is unable to see a unique record of the acting profession, as Willie intended.

His lavish generosity to King's School, Canterbury began in the thirties with a set of mezzotints for the masters' common room and, by the time he died, he had paid for a science building and a library to house his donation of some 1,600 volumes, many of them inscribed by their authors. To this valuable collection he also added the manuscripts of his first and last published novels, *Liza of Lambeth* and *Catalina*. Because he always emphasised his unhappiness at the school, commentators have had difficulty in explaining this apparent volte-face. They have not examined the possibility that he was no more happy or unhappy than any other pupil of Canterbury, but happy schoolboys make for dull reading, hence the suffering hero Philip Carey in *Of Human Bondage*. But, assuming that Willie was genuinely unhappy, the return in triumph of the once despised and bullied pupil to dispense largess and receive the fawning acknowledgement of a grateful establishment has the elements of both comedy and revenge.

Willie also did good by stealth and was frequently generous to fellow writers who had fallen on hard times; in the case of aspiring youngsters, he often provided encouragement by acts of kindness which were free of obligation. We now know that among those who benefited were Alec Waugh, Karl Pfeiffer, Klaus Jonas, Ralf Gustafson, Glenway Wescott, Hector Bolitho and Norman Douglas. Others have already been mentioned but there were still more who remain unknown. According to Beverley Nichols, he had a secret list of people he helped financially.

In a revised will dated 9 July 1964, the main beneficiary of the estate was Alan Searle who received £50,000 in cash and the contents of the Mauresque. He also received all income from royalties and other sources while he lived; this would then pass to the Royal Literary Fund. Liza was left shares not already owned by her in the Mauresque company, Annette Chiaramello and Willie's valet, Jean Larregle, received £2,000 each and the other servants £500. While he waited for the estate to be settled Searle claimed to be penniless, but he was shrewd enough to avoid approaching a bank and escaped interest charges by borrowing from friends.

The real value of the estate fell substantially short of what was anticipated. Kenneth Marr-Johnson, an executor, suspected that Searle had defrauded Willie, but he had no way of proving it, while Lord Glendevon considered Searle completely untrustworthy and capable of fraud. It was also suggested that Willie, who had developed a habit of hoarding large sums of cash, usually in US dollars, had operated a Swiss bank account to deposit money and avoid tax or death duties. It was a credible explanation but there was no evidence that such an account existed or, if it did, what became of the funds.

The house went on the market in 1969 handled by Knight, Frank and Rutley who advertised it as 'an opportunity to acquire one of the most beautiful and famous properties on the Riviera ... for forty years the home of Mr Somerset Maugham'. It may have been forgotten that the house allegedly had a curse on it when Willie bought it but now it seemed as if the misery of his final years had soaked into the fabric and added to the weird atmosphere of the place. This impression was not helped by the absence of furniture or by the lack of light fittings, switches and even door handles, supposedly stripped out in a fury by Searle. The price asked was around $1,000,000 and in theory it should have attracted the new breed of pop stars or business tycoons but it did not, and eventually went to a developer who broke the estate into building lots.

Searle sold the best of the contents of the house on 20 November 1967 at Sotheby's where they realised nearly £32,000. In a day the collection of a lifetime – furniture, carpets, various works of art, antiquities, icons and paintings – was dispersed around the world. Distressing as such events are, with possessions looking curiously diminished in strange surroundings, there is a special dimension of poignancy when books are put up for sale. The dedications written by authors often convey admiration, affection, even love to the recipient of the book. In Willie's collection there were gifts from Michael Arlen, James Joyce, Jean Cocteau, Dame Edith Sitwell, Hugh Walpole, Raymond Chandler and many others. There was also a series of books by Norman Douglas, four of them inscribed to Gerald Haxton; this raises intriguing possibilities.

Sotheby's included in the sale 'The property of Mrs Barbara Back', a package of letters and postcards of which nearly one hundred and fifty were from Willie with five from Haxton. There were books dedicated to her by Willie but also several dedicated to Ivor Back including *Ashenden*, *The Constant Wife* and *The Magician* which, with its alleged plagiarism of Aleister Crowley's works, either amused or annoyed Back, a faithful disciple of 'The Beast'.

Several weeks after Willie's death Searle had a nervous breakdown which heralded a series of medical problems including Parkinson's disease. He quickly discovered to his dismay that most of those people he had assumed to be his friends as much as Willie's either deliberately ignored him or carelessly forgot about him. A few, such as George Cukor, Beverley Nichols and Robin, maintained contact but Searle became desperately lonely and sought company in the camaraderie of bars, where he spent lavishly to try to impress. He travelled extensively, often revisiting places he had first seen with Willie, in a sadly pathetic attempt to relive the past.

He sought consolation for his soul in a revived interest in

religion and pandered to his body by overeating. Francis King gives a frightening account of his gluttony in *Yesterday Came Suddenly*. On two occasions he was Searle's guest at Claridges.

> His once handsome face bloated and his body swollen, he insisted on eating course after course. 'Do have an hors d'oeuvre before your soup . . . Do have sole before your duck . . . You must have a savoury . . . Do have a brandy.' Each time I refused an offer, it was as though I had slapped him across the face.

When Spencer Curtis Brown, Willie's literary executor, agreed to endorse Ted Morgan's biography and persuaded the family to co-operate, Searle, horrified by what he saw as a betrayal, refused to be interviewed officially. This, he realised later, was a mistake and he willingly co-operated with Robert Calder who had already proved his academic credentials with *W. Somerset Maugham and the Quest for Freedom* (1972). Calder interviewed him over a period of five days and thought him a sad and pathetic figure. Speaking of this in 1993, he wondered if his portrait of Searle in *Willie* had erred on the harsh side but, if anything, it was too charitable. Searle died in 1985, aged eighty.

Searle could never hope to replace Haxton in Willie's affections. It must have come as a shock when he arrived in America in 1945 to find that he was expected to be on duty twenty-four hours a day, in strong contrast to his life in London where he had lived rent free and received a salary for doing very little. By all accounts he was a gentle creature, not very bright, ingratiating to Willie's family and friends, a touch common, his social class betrayed by a cockney accent. On the surface he appeared harmless, but underneath he simmered with resentment at his own inadequacy and at being treated like a glorified servant. ('I thought he *was* a servant,' said Lord Glendevon.)

His state of mind was revealed when he began to complain about Willie's treatment of him to anyone who could be trapped into listening. Willie, for his part, apparently believed it was necessary to threaten Searle with a poverty-stricken future to keep him in line. (Glenway Wescott, who knew of this, opined in his diary for January 1955 that without money Searle would find it very hard to shift for himself.) Willie may even have derived some pleasure from bullying him but could not have foreseen that, driven too far, Searle would take revenge and plot against the family to ensure his own survival.

Whatever may be said against him, Searle undoubtedly loved Willie but it is a pity that, out of loyalty, he honoured the instruction that no biography should be written. If he had recorded his memories of their friendship it might have given a purpose to the remaining fifteen years of his life which he let go to waste.

Just a month after Willie's death, the *Sunday Telegraph* began serialising Robin's *Somerset and All the Maughams*. It was the Book Society choice for April, became a bestseller in the UK and the States and was translated into several languages. The critics united in praise; typical was Peter Quennell in the *Financial Times*: 'His portrait of Uncle Willie – sad, sardonic, self-tormented – stands out from the surrounding text like a grim fragment of medieval sculpture.' To Robin the most satisfying was from Cyril Connolly, the doyen of literary critics, who said in the *Sunday Times*: 'Lord Maugham is a brilliant observer and reporter.'

Robin had employed Derek Peel at a fee of £1,000 to research the family background; Peel later complained bitterly that he had written over half of the text and that he should have received recognition as co-author plus a percentage of the royalties. Peel, born in 1924, had been the lover of Hector Bolitho and his collaborator and ghostwriter. His situation was similar to that of Alan Searle, for Bolitho had made him his heir conditional on his being 'in service' at the time of his death and whenever Peel made a bid for independence Bolitho threatened to cut him out of his will. His grievance over *Somerset and All the Maughams* may have been genuine, as the stylistic differences in the text indicate, but it was hardly Robin's fault that Peel did not insist on clear contractual arrangements from the start.

*Somerset and All the Maughams* is two books – a history of the

family and a biography of Willie – but coupled together with a
lubricant of nostalgia that makes the transition from one to the
other fairly painless. In holding the reader's attention the
biography is an easy winner, but the history sections are
charming, if over-romantic, containing several intriguing diver-
sions into the lives of relatives. There was for example the
Reverend William Maugham, the only one of the Westmoreland
Maughams to show any ambition to improve his station in life. By
his own efforts he got to Cambridge and was then ordained,
spending most of his life as headmaster of Moulton Grammar
School in Lincolnshire. One of his sons, Theophilus, ran away to
sea around 1790 when he was still in his teens and saw active
service during the French Revolutionary wars. He died unmarried
aged twenty-seven, probably of battle injuries. He left his savings
to his father, some £300, a large amount at the time. The money
was in the keeping of Theophilus (then a popular name) Tutt, an
uncle by marriage who had a millinery manufacturing business in
Covent Garden. W. Farringdon Maugham, another of the
Reverend Maugham's sons, was apprenticed to Uncle Tutt to
learn the trade. By 1798 he was in business for himself and he
appeared in London directories as a 'Hat and Cap Manufacturer
of 19 King Street, next to St Paul's Church Yard'.

The biographical sections on Willie were important for
disclosing the story of his long-lasting love affair with Gerald
Haxton. This was managed in a verbal hesitation waltz which, by
today's standards, was not even remotely shocking, but to its
mainly middle-class readers, particularly those trapped in attitudes dictated by tribal mythology, the revelation came as
startling and disgusting. But because of its wide appeal the book
may have achieved much more in putting the case for understanding and tolerance than more scholarly works.

Following on the heels of Robin's book came Beverley Nichols'
*A Case of Human Bondage* which was serialised in the *Sunday
Express* as 'the most explosive document of the year'. This claim
was correct, for it was destined to become notorious overnight. He
had submitted it for comment to Liza and, generously though

unwisely as it may now appear, she had pointed out factual errors and certain incorrect inferences. At no point did she approve or endorse the book though Nichols convinced himself, erroneously, that she had. In his dealings with media interviewers he behaved with crass stupidity and, when asked if he had consulted any members of the Maugham family about it, he smugly replied with the ambivalent 'No comment' when a truthful reply would have saved him a great deal of trouble. He grew to believe that Liza was under some moral obligation to rescue him from the mess he had got himself into.

It could be said in favour of Nichols' book that it attempted to right the injustice done to Syrie by *Looking Back*, but it was fundamentally dishonest in its attacks on Haxton and Willie. Nichols' holier-than-thou attitude nauseated the very people who approved of his basic premise. To make the situation worse the style he adopted was frequently laughably melodramatic and florid. What were serious readers to make of the following typical example: 'Here comes another memory and we will pin it down before it escapes, lest these pages drift away on the wings of butterflies'?

What hurt Nichols more than his imaginary grievance about Liza was the reception of the press, which saw his attack on Willie and Haxton as hypocritical and pilloried him for it. If anyone had been in any doubt about Willie's sexuality, they would have had none after reading the book, but nowhere in it was there the slightest hint that Nichols himself was gay or had once been Willie's lover. Legally, of course, he could not put himself in jeopardy but if he had not been in such a rush to make money, he could have resolved this by judicious word play.

Nichols sent Robin a copy of *A Case of Human Bondage* accompanied by a letter which ended, 'I dread to think what Alan [Searle] will say about all this. But considering I have practically nailed a halo on his behind I don't think he should have much cause to complain.' Robin replied on 2 May in tactfully congratulatory terms, adding: 'You cannot expect me, under the circumstances, to make any comment on the central theme because, of course, in my position as head of the Maugham family, that, you will admit, would be very difficult for me.' This miracle of understatement did nothing to comfort Nichols who had hoped for support from this quarter. He was consoled by Rebecca West whose view of Willie was governed by her blind devotion to Syrie. In one of her letters to Nichols she told the story of a journalist who had interviewed her about the Maughams and then, referring to Willie's place in society, asked: 'Tell me, why were you all so nice to the little bastard?'

Noël Coward thought *A Case of Human Bondage* a ghastly book, vulgar, tasteless and inaccurate. When he met Nichols at the theatre he avoided expressing his own opinion by saying (as Nichols noted in his diary): 'Willie must be spinning in his grave like a teetotem top.' But Coward had also condemned *Looking Back* as entirely contemptible, and on Syrie's behalf took revenge in his drama *A Song at Twilight*.

The central character of the play, Hugo Latymer, an old and dying grandee of British letters, bore an uncanny resemblance to Willie. In July 1965 Coward read the script to Robin who, he told friends with gleeful satisfaction, had nearly fainted because of the resemblance. Robin did not for a second believe Coward's protestations that the character was based on Max Beerbohm and sensibly advised him to wait until Willie was dead before producing it, as the old man was likely to sue. (A nonsensical story has appeared in print on several occasions to the effect that Robin himself threatened to take legal action.) In the event the play did not go into rehearsal with Coward in the lead until the January following Willie's death and it opened at the Queen's Theatre on 14 April 1966. There would have been those in the audience who recognised that Coward was doing to Maugham what Maugham had done to Hugh Walpole in *Cakes and Ale*. To make the point even clearer Coward, as Latymer, based his make-up on the Sutherland portrait and adopted Willie's walk and mannerisms.

Latymer, like Willie, has written an autobiography which ignores the central truth of his life; he has used women to mask his homosexuality without thought of the pain he might cause. His marriage to his secretary Hilde was to satisfy convention and his two-year affair with the shrewd Carlotta was prompted by expediency. She reappears in his life to seek permission to use his early letters to her in the memoir she is writing. When he refuses, she tells him she owns the passionate letters written to his male ex-lover which she proposes handing over to his prospective biographer. Latymer is horrified by the effect this revelation will have on his reputation. The situation is resolved in suitably theatrical fashion and she returns the incriminating correspondence to him. Alone on stage, Latymer, played throughout as cold, unsympathetic and completely selfish, settles down to read the letters and, for the first time, the audience sees the genuine emotion and despairing love he still has for the only person for whom he ever cared.

Two evenings after Coward's opening, the Friends of the Libraries of the University of California hosted a dinner in honour of Willie's memory. Afterwards, Garson Kanin read excerpts from his forthcoming book *Remembering Mr Maugham* interspersed with comments from Clare Boothe Luce, George Cukor and Kanin's wife, Ruth Gordon. If it had not been for the critical tone of Dr Aerol Arnold, Professor of English, who opened the proceedings, the evening might have been better called 'Adoring Mr Maugham'. 'Great literary works grow in the memory, so that phrases, scenes, characters become part of one's real environment. Maugham holds my interest while I read him . . . but the work collapses in retrospect.' While guests and audience absorbed this broadside, a recording of Willie's voice was played as a sort of ghostly overture to Kanin reading the first few pages of his book.

The general discussion was too sycophantic and rambling to get to serious grips with the subject until towards the end when Dr Arnold, cutting through the mindless adoration, suggested that the canon of work had a certain callousness and superficiality about it. Studying the transcript of the proceedings, it is clear that no one, including George Cukor, was prepared to touch on, even by the slightest implication, the fact of Maugham's homosexuality. But there must have been those present who realised that to ignore this was to distort any discussion which pretended to be analytical.

*Remembering Mr Maugham*, with a tactful introduction by Noël Coward, provided a honeyed antidote to Nichols' bitter attack. Kanin had made copious notes of every encounter with Willie over twenty years and from these he reconstructed conversations and gossipy stories which, for the most part, were sentimentally affectionate. Intriguingly, he repeated an elaborate story told to him in 1954 by a bitchy London queen (not named) about Willie's affair with a male (also unnamed) to whom he had written incriminating letters and the stratagem he used to get them back from his friend's widow after his death. The 'friend' could only have been Walter Payne who had died five years before.

Heavily biased in Willie's favour as he was, Kanin could not completely ignore *Looking Back* and though he deplored it, he also tried to justify it, but without much conviction. Strangely, he quoted someone unnamed who had described the writing of it as a 'wildly faggoty thing to have done', a remark which would have infuriated Willie by its direct reference to his sexual orientation. There are times reading *Remembering Mr Maugham* when it is possible to detect that Kanin might have written a franker book but was deterred from doing so by his admiration for Willie and by his own standards of gentlemanly good taste.

By the middle of 1966 Willie's life had been explored by three books and a play, the first of many. Surprisingly there has never been a scholarly examination of his work taking into account his homosexuality and his determination to conceal it from the public. If justification was needed, Willie supplied it himself in his essay on Herman Melville in *Ten Novels and Their Authors* (1954) when he argued that the sexual proclivities of writers are of no concern to the reader unless they influence his work. He gave as examples Marcel Proust and André Gide. Now that we know that Willie's best novels, short stories and even his later plays were influenced by his lover Gerald Haxton, such an analysis might illuminate the work and give it fresh meaning.

# XVII

## The Wrong People

Any lingering qualms Robin may have had about breaking his promise to Willie disappeared when he learned that he had been dropped completely from the 1964 will. A close friend said: 'I had never seen him so visibly shocked.' All Robin's fantasies vanished in seconds. There would be no trouble-free life with the leisure to hone his writing talent and prove to the world that he was heir to his uncle's literary reputation.

Later, he was not sure what to make of Alan Searle's surprising promise to name him as his chief beneficiary but it was a useful throw-away line when talking to his bank manager. He was forced to continue his strategy of working on two levels, for quick profit and for esteem, in the forlorn hope that the two goals might coincide.

Under the heading of quick profit came a series of sensational articles for the *People* about Gerald Hamilton, the model for Isherwood's character Mr Norris. Twenty years later Isherwood emphasised in his prologue to Hamilton's memoir, *Mr Norris and I*, that the fictional figure was quite unlike the original. He might have added that any author creating a character as fantastic as the real thing would be condemned for gross exaggeration. Hamilton was short and fat with a large bald head, a crooked, bulbous nose and heavy pendulous lips which parted in a ready smile to show crooked teeth flashing gold. A dedicated confidence trickster, he was not always successful but never gave up. In World War II he was interned briefly for attempting to mastermind a peace settlement with Hitler. Legend has him arrested in Edinburgh en route for Ireland disguised as a nun.

When Robin went to the Ritz Hotel, Madrid, to interview him he was told of the old man's grandiose plan to restore the Spanish monarchy. He claimed that royals were showering him with gifts but, despite their generosity, he was suffering from a temporary cash-flow problem and could not leave his suite at the Ritz until his bill was settled. Robin missed the opportunity to suggest that he escape disguised as a nun.

In a television programme Daniel Farson asked him: 'Is it true that you are the wickedest man in Europe?'

'That's very kind of you,' Hamilton chuckled. 'Wittiest, well—'

'No, not wittiest, wickedest.'

The reaction was one of outraged innocence. 'I'm just a harmless old man . . .'

Wicked or witty, he celebrated his seventy-fifth birthday in a Soho restaurant with a host of friends at the expense of Robin and Francis Bacon. He lived the last years of his life in a room above a Chinese restaurant in Chelsea called The Good Earth. 'Better above it than below it,' he repeatedly quipped.

When he died in June 1970 the few mourners at Putney crematorium included Peter Burton, Brian Desmond Hurst, Cecil Woolf, John Symonds and Robin who stared in disbelief at the coffin. 'My dear, we've got the wrong funeral. That's for a child; they can't possibly have got Gerald into it.' But death had deflated the huge body, the replica of which is on view in Parliament Square masquerading as Sir Winston Churchill, the great man having sat for the head and Mr Norris, alias Gerald, for the rest.

Still under the heading of quick profit Robin published *The Green Shade* in 1966, a potboiler about a middle-aged man's obsession for an eighteen-year-old girl. Supposedly set in contemporary London, it perversely ignored the radical changes of the sixties and there was no hint of the culture of youth with its provocative fashions and sexy music. He was on surer ground when the setting switched to Morocco and the girl fell for his favourite character, the ubiquitous beautiful Arab.

When his agent, Eric Glass, sold the film rights of *Somerset and All the Maughams* to Avco Embassy Films, Joe Levene, the head of the company, commissioned Robin to write a screenplay highlighting Willie's life. There was much talk about ideal casting and Robin threw star names into the discussion without thought of cost: Alec Guinness, Peter O'Toole or Peter Finch as Willie and, if Richard Burton played Haxton, would Elizabeth Taylor play Syrie? But what about Rock Hudson or Paul Newman as Haxton and Jean Simmons or Julie Andrews as Syrie? The flights of fancy went merrily on but nothing came of the film.

Robin was doing very well financially from *Somerset and All the Maughams* but it was pointed out to him that after tax he had little left to invest for the future. He was urged to move to a tax haven and though he found the idea distasteful in principle, he established residency in Switzerland and opened several accounts with Banque de l'Harpe of Geneva. He did not want to give up his tiny flat in London and small house in Brighton so he let them at nominal rents to friends.

Meanwhile, the much revised version of *The Tainted Wether* was consistently rejected by publishers in America and Britain. Harold Nicolson and Michael Davidson had strongly endorsed Willie's verdict that it should not be published because of the damage it would do to Robin's reputation. Homosexual themes were now acceptable in novels such as Gore Vidal's *The City and the Pillar*, Mary Renault's *The Charioteer*, Angus Wilson's *Hemlock and After* and Rodney Garland's *The Heart in Exile*, but Robin's book had a premise new to mainstream fiction, namely that sex with boys should be accepted as a fact of life. He differentiated, however, between boys who had reached puberty and those who had not. In a scene in the novel, an exhibition in a brothel involving a frail, child-like Berber boy and a large, well-built man reflected his revulsion and disgust with those who perpetuated this trade in sex and the slavery allied to it.

Arnold Turner, the central character, is a repressed homosexual, a kindly man who teaches boys in an approved school in England. (Robin based the horrifying description of this institution on extensive research, as his notes show. He hoped his revelations might lead to reform, but such was the complacency of the average critic and reader that it was thought he had exaggerated his case; subsequent scandals continue to show that he had not.) In an attempt to explore his sexuality, Arnold takes a holiday in Tangier. Here he is befriended by Ewing Baird, a wealthy Anglo-American who is a lover of young boys and deduces that Arnold is fundamentally similar but has never dared to confront his preference. He encourages a relationship with Riffi, a beautiful Arab boy of about sixteen, who has a deceptive air of guileless innocence but who has been working as a male prostitute since he was twelve. Arnold falls in love, blinded to the fact that, for Riffi, it is merely a pleasanter-than-usual financial transaction. When Arnold becomes so obsessed that he cannot reason clearly, Baird springs a trap. In return for a secure future in Morocco with Riffi, he needs Arnold to assist with the abduction of a young boy from his school in England. It transpires that over the years Baird has become insanely obsessed with the idea of taking a young boy and creating a Pygmalion and Galatea relationship. If Arnold refuses, Riffi will be taken from him and evidence of his sexual preferences provided to the authorities in England.

Robin's development of the plot and the resolution of Arnold's dilemma are persuasively engineered, though, in retrospect, questions are begged but not answered. In an unexpected twist, Dan, the boy selected from among Arnold's pupils, is an apparently willing accomplice but believes his real benefactor is Arnold with whom he is secretly in love. He does not reveal this until they meet in Tangier but Arnold has no emotional feelings for the boy beyond pity. He is brought to his senses when he learns that Riffi, true to character, has gone away with a new, wealthy lover. Realising he must make restitution for his own irresponsibility, Arnold contacts the British Consulate, knowing that he faces a possible prison sentence and that Dan will have to return to the horrors of an approved school. Before they are separated, Dan makes him promise that in a few years they can live together. To spare him further unhappiness Arnold agrees, even though he knows he can never reciprocate the boy's affection. Baird, the instigator of the plot, has covered his tracks and escapes scot-free to plan another attempt to satisfy his insane ambition.

In 1967 the novel was published by the Paperback Library Inc., New York, under the pseudonym David Griffin. Instead of being called *The Tainted Wether* it was entitled *The Wrong People*. There was little reaction to the book and when a German publisher, Wilhelm Heyne of Munich, showed interest, Robin allowed his real name to be used and it appeared in 1969 as *Anders als die Andern*. At last, in 1970, Heinemann published it in a slightly revised edition which Robin dedicated to his sister Honor. The jacket was almost deliberately dull and, to give it literary respectability, Cyril Connolly supplied a preface setting the story in the context of Tangier as it was before independence in 1956 when the authorities closed the boy brothels and more outrageous gay bars. He began by recalling Willie's comment after he had read the manuscript: 'They'll murder you.' He had originally assumed that 'they' referred to the critics, but 'they' could well refer to irate homosexuals who did not like Robin's description of them.

After the long gestation and the softening of any shock value that it might once have had, not much was expected of it. To the astonishment of all involved it became a bestseller and received excellent reviews, notably from the conservative press: 'A beautifully and sensitively written novel. The author handles his theme with enormous discretion and, at the same time, delivers a gripping thriller' (*Sunday Express*), and 'A very well told story, this, every move nicely calculated' (*Daily Telegraph*). The following year it reappeared in America published by McGraw-Hill who dropped the Connolly preface and, to be on the safe side, promoted it as a thriller.

*The Second Window*, an over-heated dramatic novel that Robin had published two years earlier, was sexually more explicit but caused no problems, probably because it was not exclusively homosexual. It was suggested by Robin's experience when he went to Ceylon for the *People* to find and interview Harold Musson, a Londoner who had become a Buddhist monk and then gone missing in the jungle. Robin eventually tracked him down to a remote location where he was living as a hermit, dependent for food on the charity of poor local villagers who had scarcely enough to eat themselves. He spent two days discussing Buddhism with Musson but did not challenge him when he claimed he had sacrificed everything for his faith, although Robin knew that he had retained property and funds in England in case his faith deserted him. Two weeks later he heard that Musson had committed suicide and the inquest disclosed that he had tried to kill himself on three previous occasions. Somehow Robin felt he had been partly responsible for the final and fatal attempt.

In the fictionalised version Martin Yorke, a journalist, mentally unstable himself, taunts the Musson character and drives him to take his own life. This experience induces a form of madness in Yorke who hides in a remote country house to write down random incidents in his life as a form of catharsis.

One of these incidents was taken from Robin's own childhood. When he was about nine years old he was erotically stirred by the sight of a farm lad, blond, blue-eyed and tough, riding a massive cart horse, his thighs stretched wide to straddle the animal. 'I thought he was the most beautiful person I had ever seen.' In the novel the incident is taken to a conclusion. Young Martin Yorke, aged nine, is aroused by the sight of Jim, a blond, beautiful stable lad of nineteen, and follows him around like a devoted puppy. From his bedroom he overlooks the stables above which Jim has a room and at night he sees the middle-aged butler creep across the yard to visit him. When this happens regularly, he investigates and sees Jim straddled across the naked body of the butler who lies face down on the bed. He does not understand what is happening but is disturbed by the man's groans. (In the original draft Robin gave graphic details which Heinemann thought it wise to cut.) Jim believes that Martin's interest in him is sexual and he makes love to the child but, at the first pain of penetration, the boy screams and wriggles free. In the hysterical aftermath Jim and the butler are sacked and Martin suffers a form of nervous breakdown. A coda provides the truth: Yorke's sister reveals the incident to be the product of her brother's imagination; she was the one Jim was interested in but the boy became so jealous that, in revenge, he told his father that he had been sexually attacked.

In the longest of the stories Yorke is sent to Mombasa to investigate the secret slave trade. He meets a staid and refined-looking elderly white woman, Mrs Clarke, who, it transpires, is a drug addict and, amid the trappings of faded gentility, is ready to sell her orphaned granddaughter for sex to pay for her habit. The girl, a frail, demure-looking child shows few signs of physical development and, with her blonde, pageboy bob, looks about eleven, although she is actually thirteen. Yorke agrees the price and finds she has an insatiable sexual appetite fostered by forbidden sex with a beautiful black boy who has been a prostitute since he was ten. Among his customers is Yorke's black driver Abe who is saving up his money so that he can pay for an hour of the little white girl's time. After Yorke returns to England, he becomes so obsessed by thoughts of the girl that he goes back to rescue her, but she has been sent to a special institution for delinquents. Abe, in the role of Nemesis, rapes and then strangles him.

The episodes in the journal are interspersed with stream-of-consciousness dialogue which serves several purposes: to supply footnotes, to link sections together and to convey the mental disintegration of Yorke. The perfunctory fashion in which this is done suggests that Robin had become tired of the project and could not be bothered to complete it. Afterwards he was very proud that he had written it without help from Derek Peel or anyone else and he believed it to be the apogée of his career. It was his most ambitious novel, over-plotted and confusing, but it sold well. Indeed, John Betjeman, a fellow guest with Robin at

Beverley Nichols' home, said over dinner that he was a genius. Nichols, in a burst of prophecy, declared that within five years, he would have eclipsed Willie. As Robin remarked to a friend: 'This is excellent for my quavering morale!'

# 'Always Remember, I am a Peer of the Realm!'

In 1966 Robin moved to a villa on Ibiza; this was long before the island was 'discovered'. The villages were much as they had been for centuries, the roads mere tracks and the airstrip an open space that became unusable when it rained. To the locals the foreigners who had built houses for themselves were harmless eccentrics who caused general amusement while adding usefully to the island's coffers.

One of the attractions of Casa Cala Pada, which Robin bought from Betty O'Shea, was its remote location and extensive garden, not unlike the setting of the Villa Mauresque when Willie originally saw it. The villa was a simple one-storey building with a large marble-floored living room opening out on to a terrace. A path wound through the grounds and down the headland to a private beach. Although secluded, there was a right of way along the top of the cliffs which became a source of nuisance as the island grew popular. Robin or his servants frequently had to ask tourists to leave the beach and, like Betsey Trotwood, would cry not 'donkeys' but 'trippers' at the first sight of them.

He soon decided his house was not grand enough for entertaining and at a huge cost he employed an architect to enlarge it. The result was an imitation Mauresque, an imposing villa on two floors with grounds landscaped to match. His friends Elizabeth Sellars, the actress, and her husband, who knew the house before and after its transformation, described the result, with its new furnishings, as 'English elegant'. It was Seaton Street all over again on a bigger scale and once more he convinced himself it was a first-class investment.

While the rebuilding was going on, Robin went to Australia where his stay in Sydney coincided with visits by Robert Helpmann and Cecil Beaton. They met up at a reception where another guest was the novelist Patrick White. He had an enviable flair for colourful vituperation and referred to 'Lord Maugham' in a letter dated 3 February 1968 as having a face like a 'wizened cow's twat'. From White this almost qualified as a compliment.

Robin's trip was ostensibly to research backgrounds for a novel suggested by his father's account of the Tichborne case. He had already devised a new twist to the story which he used in a stage version with the theatrically dull title of *The Claimant*. After a provincial try-out it opened at London's Comedy Theatre in April 1964 but even with the distinguished Eric Portman and Cathleen Nesbitt leading the cast it stood little chance. Word of mouth dismissed it as a stodgily written melodramatic bore and it came off after a few weeks. What hastened its demise and that of similarly old-fashioned pieces was the effect of forceful work such as Edward Albee's *Who's Afraid of Virginia Woolf?* and *Entertaining Mr Sloane*. Robin saw *Sloane* soon after *The Claimant* opened. He hated everything about it, probably because Joe Orton, from a working-class background, openly gay and indisputably a brilliant talent, was everything he could never be. Surprisingly, Robin's friend Terence Rattigan, who might have been expected to be equally reactionary, was deeply impressed and admired Orton for having the courage to go a stride or two further towards honesty than he was able to do. He marked his approval by financing the transfer of *Entertaining Mr Sloane* from the Arts Theatre Club to Wyndhams Theatre.

Robin's intellectual laziness was typified by his approach to turning *The Claimant* into a novel with the equally dull title of *The Link*. Instead of learning the lessons of the play's failure or reconsidering the mass of material left by his father, he used his own script as the core of the novel. This is painfully evident in the transference of dialogue and the incorporation of stage directions. Frequently passages of description read as if they had been written by someone else, possibly Derek Peel. Sex scenes, many unnecessary to the plot, have the semi-pornographic style that Robin developed for his novels – unerotic but unpleasant.

In 1969 Robin was taken ill on Ibiza where tests showed that he had diabetes. He returned to England immediately and was admitted to St Mary's Hospital, Paddington, where he was to stay from 5 April to the end of May. He was only too aware that Kate's premature death in 1962 had been induced by the same condition and he resigned himself to expect the worst, though it seemed unfair he would now have to cope with this as well as the ever-present consequences of his war wounds. As he remarked to a friend: 'I thought fate had given up kicking me in the balls.' Visitors found him remarkably good-humoured and uncomplaining, though he was weak, often in pain and also had to cope with the effects of an operation to remove his gall bladder, another surprise from fate.

While Robin was still in hospital, Eric Glass told him that his play *Enemy* had been accepted for production in the West End. After so many disappointments this was tremendous news and he put out of his mind the fact that when Kate had been in hospital with diabetes, her play had also gone into production.

The plot of *Enemy* was based on an incident in the western desert in 1942 when, from his scout car, Robin had spotted a man in the shadow of a derelict tank. Ordering his driver Jim to move cautiously towards it, he drew his pistol and a young German captain stepped forward, hands raised in surrender. Robin and his driver leapt from their vehicle and, while Jim disarmed the prisoner, Robin searched the tank, recoiling at the carnage of bodies he found inside. The officer's despatch case containing Rommel's operational orders, wireless codes and a bundle of high-value Egyptian currency was still intact. During the few minutes that had elapsed, Robin's unit of tanks had swept forward and he tuned into brigade frequency to assess the situation, while cursing that the scout car did not carry a transmitter. In the mayhem of battle, positions were gained and lost so rapidly that he was not surprised to learn that the enemy was now somewhere between him and his unit. All he could do was to wait in the hope that British vehicles would find him before the Germans did. In the meantime he began an interrogation of the officer who stared back, his eyes cold with hatred. Robin, speaking in German, got the non-committal response he expected although from the papers he knew his prisoner's name, number and division. In a theatrical gesture he handed the captain the Egyptian currency remarking that, under the Geneva Convention, he was bound to do so but that the captain would have no opportunity to spend it in Cairo. The German reacted angrily, saying that Cairo and Tobruk would be captured within a few weeks. Robin changed tactics and, offering him a cigarette, began questioning him about non-military matters. Gradually the man relaxed and for over half an hour they talked about their home lives until Jim reported vehicles in the distance. Robin held out his hand to the German: 'In a few minutes you may still be my prisoner or I may be yours. Just to show that we can see something beyond all this, let us shake hands.' The captain abruptly refused: 'I cannot. You are my enemy.' The vehicles emerging out of a cloud of dust were a British support unit and Robin handed his prisoner over to them. Later he was given a message that the German wished to speak to him. He found the young officer in the back of a truck, blindfolded so that he could see nothing as he was taken into the British lines. The officer held out his hand: 'I wanted to say goodbye,' and Robin, touched by this change of heart, clasped it: 'Good luck to you.'

He frequently told this story, with several variations, but for the play he altered it drastically to give it dramatic tension and changed the two men into ordinary soldiers from working-class backgrounds. Gradually they become friends and there is a sub-text which suggests, for those who wish to interpret it, that Paul, the German boy, is emotionally attracted to his English counterpart, Ken. Towards the end of the piece they plan to escape together to South Africa but a British officer arrives and, in a bloody climax, kills Paul.

Noël Coward, reading the final draft, described it as extremely moving, well-written and exciting but thought the ending too grim and upsetting for an audience. He suggested that Ken, instead of appearing defeated by the death of Paul, should be defiant and symbolise hope. Robin took his advice and rewrote the final page but this version was never performed because Ronald Eyre, the director, preferred the original.

Ensconced in his hospital bed Robin fantasised over casting and made visitors join in. As before, actors were listed in careless profusion as if budgets did not exist; could the young German be played by Hardy Kruger, Karl Boehm or possibly Horst Buchholz? Which of the new breed of British stars could play the other lead – Tom Courtenay, Michael York or David Hemmings? In the event, the play opened in Guildford with Dennis Waterman as Paul, Tony Selby as Ken and the small role of the British officer played by Neil Stacey. A long tour followed while the management waited for a West End theatre to fall vacant. Unfortunately this proved to be the Saville, a beautiful art-deco building seating over a thousand which was ideally suited to musicals or star-cast plays but far too large for a two-hander like *Enemy*. On the opening night, 17 December 1969, the theatre was packed with a celebratory black-tie audience headed by Noël Coward and Merle Oberon. If the reviews and the enthusiasm of the first-night audience were a guide, it appeared that a long run could be expected. But the public wanted something far less demanding for the Christmas season and *Enemy* closed after seven weeks. It was the last play to be staged at the Saville and after reconstruction the building reopened a year later as a multiplex cinema. *Enemy* was selected for inclusion in *Plays of the Year: Volume 39 1969–1970* by its editor, J. C. Trewin, the theatre historian, and it was also published in an acting edition by Samuel French. It has been seen in a television version and is revived from time to time in America and Britain.

While he was in hospital during the rehearsals for *Enemy* Robin had remarked to his friend Colin Spencer that he was lost without someone 'to run errands'. Colin mentioned this to Peter Burton, a twenty-three-year-old theatre critic and freelance journalist, who knew little about Robin apart from *The Servant* but was intrigued enough to go to St Mary's. Burton describes his visit in *Parallel Lives*:

He was then fifty-three but the wear and tear of his life, illness and drink had already begun to take their toll on his physical appearance. The dark hair was touched with grey – which completely disappeared in later years. Dye, I suppose. His face was tanned, but as with so many who expose themselves to the sun's rays at every opportunity, it looked slightly leathery. Lines were already deeply etched, particularly around the slightly patrician nose. His eyes were dark and could become – as I was to discover – black and beady when he was in a rage. Robin had a typical, almost exaggerated, upper-class accent. Sentences were punctuated with cries of 'hooo-ray' and 'splendid', and words like 'so' were extended in such a way that they came out oddly. ('So', for example, always sounded like 'Sue'.)

He was busily checking proofs of the American edition of *The Link* but put these aside to welcome his visitor and to offer him a drink. Warily, Burton eyed the bottle of Rose's lime juice at the bedside but Robin said, 'Just open the wardrobe and mix yourself whatever you want.' He was startled to find an impressive range of bottles of spirits, mixers and glasses set out at the base of the cupboard and poured himself a hefty gin and tonic.

This was his introduction to Robin's style of living. Robin, as Peter Burton was to discover, used hospitals and nursing homes as others used hotels; however awful he might feel physically, there was always a welcome for chums who soon learned that bottles of spirits were more acceptable than expensive hot-house grapes. On one visit Burton and a friend were getting quietly high on gin when Lady Assheton-Smith and Hermione Baddeley burst in and within seconds the clinical atmosphere was replaced by the hilarity of a successful cocktail party.

Burton had never encountered anyone quite like Robin.

Part of him was rigidly conservative – a dislike of most music after Tchaikovsky, an aggressive antipathy towards the drug scene, a belief in protocol and a correctness in appearance, which seemed to exclude such things as long hair, beards, the lack of ties and the wearing of T-shirts and jeans. The other side of him was Bohemian – a congenital inability to conform, a love of entertaining on a grand scale anyone from world-famous celebrities to street-corner hustlers, an honesty about his own sexuality and drink problems which could sometimes shock, and a sheer flamboyance of personality which often battled almost visibly with the conservatism. Nowhere was this clash more apparent than over money matters. Robin was generous to a fault, wildly extravagant, and yet had occasional moments of economy when he would order his staff to cut down on the food bill while, in almost the same breath, calling the wine merchant to order another case of vodka.

Burton, after carrying out the duties of a glorified hospital visitor, got a phone call inviting him to Brighton for lunch. Robin had rented the public rooms of George Kinnaird's house at 3 Burlington Street for entertaining. Kinnaird was living more or less permanently in Tangier with his lover-cum-servant, a wild Moroccan known affectionately as 'The Gorilla', and was only too pleased with the income. Oddly the bedrooms were excluded from this arrangement and Robin spent the nights in the spare room at his small house in Bute Street where Keith Monk lived. The celebrated Sunday lunches had been reinstated and the usual string of personalities travelled down to see him.

At one of the lunches he mentioned to Noël Coward that he was looking for a 'secretary'. His definition of this was flexible; he already had Nancy Hosegood in Ibiza and Jeanne Francis in Brighton but what he wanted was a personal assistant able to act as a sort of collaborator. 'He doesn't have to be a lover,' he told Coward, 'but at least he must be understanding.' 'And, heaven only knows, my dear boy, he'll have to be that,' said Coward drily.

The role of assistant may have been in Robin's mind when he invited Peter Burton to lunch. In addition to his other work, Burton had taken over the editorship of *Jeremy*, a strangely androgynous magazine which reflected the new permissiveness without committing itself. Subconsciously it appeared to be attempting to emulate the famous *Yellow Book* of the 1890s but without the benefit of Beardsley. Burton decided it might achieve the success that eluded it if it was rejigged as an openly gay publication. In an apparent afterthought to his invitation, Robin suggested that Burton bring down the beautiful boy who decorated the centre spread of the new issue. This was his sister's boyfriend, and Burton thought he would be unimpressed by the prospect of meeting a gay, middle-aged literary peer who would have designs on his body but he asked him anyway and was given a firm 'No'. Robin, unabashed, suggested that Burton find another equally beautiful boy to bring with him but Burton could not think of anyone who might be prepared to give up his Sunday for a free lunch and the prospect of being pounced upon. 'Don't worry, my dear,' Robin said, 'come by yourself.'

Bemused by being cast as a procurer, albeit failed, Burton arrived to find that his fellow guests were all celebrities, headed by Laurence Olivier and Joan Plowright. 'At first, I was overawed. But as time went by – and the champagne poured down my throat – I became more and more confident. God knows what the others made of me as I babbled drunkenly on.' Many hours later, as the final guests left, Robin suggested that Burton 'come back to my little slum house for a nightcap and you can stay the night. It's a bit of a bore getting back to London this late.'

The two walked unsteadily to Bute Street. Burton had assumed that 'little slum house' was a modest, lordly euphemism for a large Regency villa with a choice of guest bedrooms and he was surprised to see it was a small house of the two-up, two-down variety. Burton commented:

You may find this hard to believe but it's true. At twenty-four I was still rather naive about some things. As I'd known Robin for over a year and he'd never shown anything but a professional interest in me, I reasoned that I was safe from sexual advances.

We sat in the office, which doubled as a sitting room, drinking enormous gin and tonics. Slowly through my drunken haze – I had one hand clapped over my left eye in the vain hope that this would diminish the double vision and enable me to see only one Robin – the true picture began to form itself in my mind.

I realised that: a) there was only one bedroom, b) there was only one bed, and c) I was expected to share this with His Lordship. The idea didn't much appeal to me but it was rather too late to make excuses. Like a Victorian virgin about to face a fate worse than death, I resigned myself and determined to think – if not of England – then at least of humpy numbers from my past.

Burton was taken completely by surprise by the situation in which he found himself as he had never quite been able to cope when one kind of relationship changed unexpectedly into another. Once they were squeezed together in Robin's single bed everything became more improbable:

'I love you,' Robin declared, once what his uncle always described as 'congress' was out of the way. 'You're the one for me. Let's have a drink to celebrate.'

Still in a state of mild shock, I tottered back into the office-cum-sitting room and replenished our glasses.

'We will be able to travel the world together,' Robin continued once I had returned to the bedroom and he had a generous mouthful of gin. 'You will be able to assist me with my writing. You will be Gerald Haxton to my Willie Maugham. We must make plans. Can you fly out to Ibiza with me later in the week?'

Burton later discovered that extravagent commitment was part of Robin's post-coital routine if he took a particular fancy to a bed-mate. Sometimes he promised a life of monied ease and this was so successful that he often had several boyfriends in tow at the same time, each believing he was the only love of Robin's life.

The next morning Burton assumed that the drunken talk of the previous night would be forgotten but, to his alarm, Robin was still full of plans and told his secretary Jeanne Francis to book seats for them on the Tuesday plane for Ibiza. Eventually Burton got on the London train with Robin in tow, apparently now so besotted that he couldn't bear to be parted from his new discovery. In the buffet car Robin ordered drinks and spent the journey declaring his affection and repeating plans for the future. Finally Burton escaped at Victoria and arrived, hours late, semi-drunk, at the *Jeremy* office. 'I chickened out and did not turn up at the airport. I realised I had missed an important and tempting opportunity, but not one that I could accept on a false premise. I was not attracted physically and I had my own career to think of.'

Burton did not expect to hear from Robin again and was astounded when he contacted him the following year. The Brighton episode was apparently completely forgotten and he now had a business proposition to put to him. 'Carter de Haven has asked me to write a film script of *Cakes and Ale* and I also plan to start work on my autobiography. There is a lot to be done. Will you fly to Morocco with me?' Burton had never been abroad in his life and the idea of being paid a salary to see Tangier was an adventure he could not refuse.

Terms were agreed and they left London on 7 September 1970 travelling on the economy night flight to Malaga. From the moment they left, he and Robin drank; in Spain there was a long delay waiting for the connecting flight which they spent drinking and dozing on wooden benches. Burton, assuming that Lord Maugham would travel as a VIP, was mildly surprised by this but later discovered that Robin was loath to spend money on luxury when spartan travel, despite all its disadvantages, eventually got him to his destination. To Burton's disappointment Robin had decided to stay not in Tangier or Marrakesh but in Chechaouen, an ancient town in the Rif mountains. He had booked rooms at the Parador (now Hotel Chaouen), then the only luxury hotel. Burton admitted in a letter to Mike Gill of 9 September that he was instantly seduced by the atmosphere of the town:

> It is staggeringly beautiful up here, perched on a hill which looks down into an olive- and pine-tree-filled valley. Robin has a room overlooking the valley, I one on the other side of the corridor overlooking the Medina. The local boys are exactly as one would expect, they follow as steadily as the flies . . . at one point I felt as if I were transported into *Suddenly Last Summer* playing Catherine Holly to Robin's Sebastian.

To a gay young man used only to the repressive atmosphere of England, the uncomplicated attitude of the Moroccans to sex was an astonishing revelation, but Islam had been in advance of Western sexual conventions for centuries and treated homosexuality as a mere matter of personal taste.

Over six weeks the work progressed with amazing speed: first drafts of a film adaptation of *Cakes and Ale* and a stage version of *The Wrong People* were followed by an outline plan for Robin's autobiography and ideas for a novel based on *The Last Hero*, his play about General Gordon. 'He was brimful of ideas,' Burton recalled,

> and he encouraged my creative input but by midday he was mentally exhausted. We usually worked by the swimming pool and then went into lunch where Robin always got paralytically drunk. I went up to my room to type and rewrite the morning's dictation while Robin sat on the terrace drinking. After I'd finished I'd have a rest before changing for dinner and inevitably Robin would appear demanding sex. He was fresh from a late-afternoon siesta and in a lively mood after a couple of drinks to top up his alcohol level. Sometimes he was drunkenly affectionate and occasionally almost violent; there was this bullying element as if he were an officer and I a common soldier who had to obey orders. If I got angry it excited him and if I said nothing he took it for assent. I was afraid of his unpredictability, but at the same time fond of him. Unless you've been in this type of situation yourself it's probably difficult to understand and it's difficult to describe. Usually I gave in to keep the peace, hating him and hating myself. Afterwards he'd become terribly hearty and tell me I'd enjoyed it as much as he had; in fact it was dreary but mercifully brief.
>
> It was a ridiculous situation. Here I was abroad for the first time in my life, ready for anything in a country with endless opportunities, trapped in an hotel with a randy old peer who expected me to be on duty twenty-four hours a day. It seems laughable now but at the time it nearly drove me mad. I think if it hadn't been for the arrival of Brian Desmond Hurst I would have run off with the first available sheik.

Hurst's exuberant personality and sense of humour eased the pressure on Burton and diverted Robin who was content to act as audience while the Irish film-maker reminisced about the movie business. When they worked in the mornings, he wandered off to explore the town, attracting attention wherever he went because he was a male on his own and because he had a magnificent head of white, leonine hair which was much admired. Burton remembers finding him in the gardens smoking hash, surrounded by crouching boys as if he were an august prophet.

Tensions were bound to creep back and a climax was reached during a lunch-time discussion about Joe Orton. In September 1966, Burton had interviewed the playwright for the *Stage* and was charmed by his wit and friendly acceptance of what must have seemed callow questioning from his relatively inexperienced interrogator. Hurst found his account of this amusing and entertaining but Robin, getting more drunk, glared at Burton, his eyes dark and ferocious, and then a hank of hair fell across his forehead. This, Burton was to discover, was the prelude to a fit of icy rage. Slurring badly, Robin suddenly broke in: 'Terry Rattigan put on his play *Entertaining Mr Sloane* in the West End and Orton had the audacity to turn up on the first night improperly dressed in a polo-necked sweater! It was disgusting behaviour. Common little man.' Robin glared triumphantly as if this was the final word to be said on the subject of Orton.

At the time Burton did not know that behind this was dislike and even jealousy of Orton and other young writers whose work would accelerate the decline of popular playwrights like Robin and, indeed, Rattigan. Instead, infuriated by this attack on a man whose murder in 1967 was, by common assent, a tragic loss to the British theatre, Burton retaliated with a vicious jab: 'We were thrown out of the Savoy when we went to see your uncle's play, *The Circle*. When Evelyn Laye made her first entrance, she looked like a boiled lobster and we laughed ourselves sick. God, it's an awful play.' Not only had the generation battle been joined but Burton had also deliberately hit the most sensitive target because by now he knew that Robin regarded Willie as his own personal property, sacrosanct and beyond criticism by anyone other than himself. 'How dare you speak of my uncle's play like that. His play is a masterpiece.'

'And so is *Entertaining Mr Sloane*. It's a far better play than any play by your boring uncle.'

Red with rage, Robin brushed back the hair from his eyes and,

325

pointing his index finger at Burton, declared very slowly in a loud voice, his speech slurring: 'Always remember, I am a peer of the realm and a number-one bestseller. Don't you dare speak to me like that.'

In retrospect, Burton found this retort irresistibly comic but, at the time, near to furious tears, he stood up and, with a parting 'Fuck you', stormed off and spent the afternoon considering what to do next. He had little money, no return ticket to England and he was trapped in a remote town; should he hitch a lift to Tangier and go to the British Consul? If he did, what could he say? He could hardly complain that Lord Maugham was sexually molesting him and, if he did, who would be believed, a peer of the realm or a young East Ender? More than likely it would be treated as a lovers' tiff and he would be told not to be so hysterical. Subdued but no less angry, he returned to the hotel in the late afternoon to find Robin in a jovial mood drinking with Hurst. 'There you are, my dear. Come and have a drink,' he said, as if nothing had happened.

Later that night Robin arrived in Burton's room and solemnly declared: 'I can understand that you are homesick and missing Ian [Burton's lover] but this kind of behaviour really isn't on. During the war, the troopers under my command missed their homes and their loved ones, but they didn't carry on like that. Can we please have no more scenes?'

Commenting on this, Burton said: 'From his point of view, I had behaved badly by arguing with him, while he had remained a perfect gentleman. I was too astonished to say anything and just nodded. Then, with the relief of someone who had carried out a necessary but distasteful task, he smiled and said: "Now come to bed with me." '

The work completed, all three left Chechaouen and moved down to Tangier to stay at the Hotel El Djenina. Burton remarked: 'I realised that far from seeing anything of Morocco, or for that matter Chechaouen, I had been trapped for the whole of the time in the Parador which was only slightly more exciting than being locked up in a temperance hotel on the Isle of Wight.'

If he hoped to make up for lost opportunities he was to be disappointed.

> It was so respectable. We had lunch with David Herbert, the Queen Mother of Tangier, in his 'pink palace', drinks with Alec Waugh and paid a very unpleasant, rather alarming call on George Kinnaird and his Moroccan lover who was stoned out of his mind and kept trying to be the centre of attention by doing dangerous acrobatics on the balcony. The place was barely furnished and Robin explained that the lover had smashed everything up in a drunken fury. We got out just as he seemed on the brink of another violent fit.

Robin departed after a few days to meet his current boyfriend in Paris and left Hurst and Burton to themselves. The old brothel area in the alleys behind the Petit Socco had been closed soon after independence in 1956 and the sale of alcohol forbidden in the cafés. Dean's Bar off the Grand Succo still functioned but Joseph Dean himself had died of a drug overdose in 1963. To Burton it could not have been less like the Tangier of *The Wrong People*.

Robin's drunken outburst over Joe Orton may seem trivial in itself but it marked a change in his behaviour which people who had known him for far longer than Burton noted with dismay. Keith Monk said that, until he was diagnosed a diabetic, Robin had always been 'a jolly drunk' but afterwards he had sudden rages, often for no apparent reason. At first they died away as rapidly as they had arrived but, increasingly, they lasted longer. Afterwards he rarely remembered them but, if he did, or was told what had happened, he blamed everything on his alter ego, Tommy. Burton once asked him how he could drink so much when he was dependent on insulin injections in addition to other pills and potions; he replied that his doctor had advised him that, if he gave up drinking, smoking and stuck rigidly to the necessary diet, he would live to be eighty. 'In that case,' Robin had answered, 'I'll carry on as I am!'

# XVIII

## Liking Boys, Liking Girls

When Robin appeared on television in 'Late Night Line Up' to promote *The Wrong People*, he casually remarked: 'I like boys as much as girls.' Sheridan Morley, the interviewer, let it pass. After the show Robin joined a few friends for dinner and as he arrived in the restaurant they applauded him. Next day there were no press reports and no tabloid headlines of the 'Queer Peer' variety. Over the years Robin embellished the story at each retelling so that even his arrival for dinner resembled the entrance of a Broadway star to Sardi's after a brilliant opening night. As for his throw-away remark, it became 'a declaration of gay rights'. Americans in particular were awestruck by the courage of this 'British Lord' who had broken taboos and 'come out' in 1970. In fact he had done nothing of the kind; if he had stated that he preferred boys to girls, he might have made the impact he imagined. Two years later he described himself as mainly but not wholly homosexual in his autobiography and he became increasingly identified with the gay press in Europe and the USA with his short stories and interviews.

Back in Ibiza, plans to move to Switzerland fell to pieces when nobody showed the slightest interest in buying his house, so he resigned himself to making the best of the situation. This was not helped when his latest love affair broke up. Once again it was the story of infatuation with a young man who rapidly became bored, despite expensive baubles to tempt him to stay. There was little to choose between Robin in the throes of an affair or recovering from one; he suffered equally in either circumstance and so did his friends. It was useless for them to point out that his predictable response to a pretty face had about as much emotion in it as the antics of Pavlov's dogs. While he believed he was in love nothing could be done but wait for the fever to pass and hope for a period of stability until he met someone else. Michael Davidson, often finding himself selected as a shoulder to cry on, was startled and worried on this occasion and wrote to Robin:

> Your visit on Sunday has left me with a very heavy heart . . . so sad. I don't know whither this affair is leading you: you're becoming a different man altogether. In the old days one could be fairly certain where one stood with you; now you're never the same two days running; one can't count on your mood and intention or word from hour to hour. It's dreadful to watch a friend one loves who is basically so nice turn before one's eyes into a weakling whose promises and projects change hourly with what one might call the sexual situation.

Davidson also wrote to the errant lover:

> Robin is desperately missing you and is frantically lonely; he says if only you will go back to him permanently, he will consult a London doctor about how to go on . . . and stay on . . . the wagon. I believe that all the difficulties you and he have every so often are due to the Bottle: it's a sort of vicious circle; you hate the Bottle and show it in ways that send him back to the Bottle! . . . You and I both know that no matter how difficult he may be (nor how often), he is enormously lovable: a sweet, generous, charming person and, at his best, a wonderful companion.

Davidson grew tired of trying to be a comforter and a go-between but it took several years and several boyfriends before he finally gave up.

Robin could not face writing alone and he decided to approach Peter Burton again; he mentioned this to Michael Davidson who warned him that Burton had told him about the miserable period in Morocco and would refuse. Back in England for Christmas Robin telephoned Burton and invited him to his flat for drinks to discuss a business proposal. As it happened Burton had not found a job to replace his editorship of the now defunct *Jeremy* and freelance work was difficult to get. 'I was virtually broke,' he admitted, 'down to my last few quid and depressed by the prospect of having no cash for Christmas. But, of course, I didn't want him to know.' Remembering Robin's old-fashioned views on casual wear, he dressed carefully in his best clothes and spent the last of his money on a cab so that he could arrive with a dash of style.

Robin was solemnly professional: if Burton joined him in Ibiza to work on the General Gordon novel that they had discussed in Morocco, he would pay him a weekly salary and all expenses. He added that Michael Davidson had spoken to him and this time, he promised, there would be no question of sex. Relieved, Burton agreed. After toasting the renewed partnership Robin said in a complete change of mood: 'Now that's all settled, let's go to bed and have a glorious romp.' Burton stared at him in amazement. 'I thought we had just agreed about that side of things?' With a little shrug as if to say 'You can't blame a boy for trying', Robin smilingly conceded: 'So we did, so we did, my dear.' As Burton stood up to go Robin pulled out his cheque book: 'I'd like to give you something for Christmas.' Burton described it as a spontaneous gesture, typical of his generosity. 'I often wonder if he guessed that I was badly off. Anyway, his kindness saved the situation and meant a happy Christmas before I flew out to Ibiza on New Year's Eve.'

The origins of the Gordon novel went back to Robin's boyhood. When he was at prep school the history of England was taught chronologically so that he had a working knowledge of how Great Britain and the Empire had evolved. If the facts were often dull and the political arguments frequently incomprehensible, the tales of glory were not. The leaders who made England great were mystic beings with the aura of saints who could inspire men to follow in their steps by the mere mention of their deeds. What schoolboy did not yearn to sail with Drake and fight with Wellington or Haig? Woven into the tapestry of patriotism was the doctrine of Christianity so that every drop of blood shed and every enemy left dead on the battlefield was a step towards building 'Jerusalem in England's green and pleasant land', while at the same time keeping the rest of the world in thrall or in its place.

The great propaganda machine of Church and State was past its brilliant best when Robin was a child but still potent enough, and what it could not claim as a victory of arms it transformed into a victory of the spirit, a moral lesson to emulate. When he was taken to Madame Tussaud's in Baker Street the greatest hero of them all, Gordon of Khartoum, was there, enshrined in wax, life-sized, on the point of death, an awe-inspiring sight. It was conveniently forgotten that Gordon had disobeyed the order to leave Khartoum and that it was probably his intransigence which caused Gladstone to delay sending an expedition to save him.

Robin, deeply moved by his glorious death, wanted to know more and there, among his father's books, were *The Journals of Charles George Gordon*, published to assuage the insatiable interest of the British public (although Robin found them almost unreadable). Being an imaginative boy, he wondered what had happened to the final volume; the last known entry was on 14 December 1884 but the General was not killed by the army of Mohammed Ahmed until 26 January 1885 . . .

The concept of lost journals fascinated Robin. If only Shakespeare had left an account of his working methods, or Mary, Queen of Scots a secret diary. Why was there nothing written down to explain the fate of those aboard the *Marie Celeste*? Robin used lost journals in *The 1946 Ms, The Black Tent* and *The Second Window*, and in *Somerset and All the Maughams* family mysteries are solved by the papers found in an old box. Even *The Servant* is a personal account of events 'for your eyes only'.

The unsolved mystery of Gordon's last days kept coming out of Robin's mental filing cabinet and being tucked back until, after a gestation period of thirty years, the solution came to him. Not surprisingly, it relied on coincidence, but for once not at all unlikely. Gordon looked after the welfare of orphan boys at the Fort House in Gravesend and was admired for his Christian charity in feeding and clothing these strays whom he found leading rough lives in the streets. When he had built up the boys' strength, given them confidence in themselves and lasting faith in the saving grace of the Lord Jesus, he would find them work. He encouraged some to join the army.

Suppose, then, that one of these boys, one of his 'Angels' as he sometimes called them, is an army messenger who gets through the rebel lines to Khartoum disguised as a dervish. He is Willie Warren, an attractive lad of seventeen, worldly wise, who arouses in Gordon desires he has always subdued by prayer and self-discipline. Suppose that in the hopelessness of the military situation Gordon suffers a sort of breakdown and confides his frustrations to paper? But triumphantly he resists the temptation Warren willingly offers and praises God for it. Amid these innermost thoughts he manages to record the military events of the siege during the final days. Just before Warren escapes, Gordon gives him the journal, a slim, narrow volume, asking him to destroy it. Instead, he keeps it and it is eventually found among the family relics, with a letter of explanation from Warren.

Robin first conceived this story as a play, *The Last Hero*, in 1957 and with the legerdemain of the theatre covering the gaps in the logic it was acceptable. In the final scene Gordon appears in his white full-dress uniform, medals glittering in the spotlights, dress sword hanging at his side. Seconds before the curtain falls he moves forward, right arm raised, an expression of pleasurable anticipation on his face as if to greet death.

When he came to turn the play into a novel, Robin refused to rethink the project. It was relatively easy, Burton recalls, to transpose scenes from the play and provide linking narrative between stage dialogue. Far greater emphasis was placed on homosexuality in new speeches composed in the style used by Gordon in the journals, a curious mixture of hearty schoolboyish patriotism and religion. Fortunately Burton was able to persuade Robin not to add a scene of lurid sex between Gordon and young Warren. 'I argued that for Gordon to lose his fight against temptation and fail his God would destroy the character; it was essential that he go to his death a spiritual victor.'

To compensate for losing his sex scene Robin insisted on

adding the adventures of a Trooper Warren in Cairo, introducing another lost journal to accommodate them. In three sequences Warren visits a child brothel (presumably based on Robin's experience in Tangier), attempts to seduce a fellow army trooper who summarily rejects him, but gets full satisfaction from a fourteen-year-old Arab boy with whom he has a brief affair. Tacked on as a sort of afterword, it had nothing to do with the Gordon story.

Burton returned to England to research military and social material to complete the book, now entitled *The Last Encounter*, and wrote another ten thousand words or so to bring it up to the length expected by the publishers. It was Robin's name which would sell it and the question of co-authorship did not arise, although Burton's contribution was acknowledged in a note. (Later the credit for other books was to become a little more specific, using the phrase 'the preparation and writing of . . .')

When the manuscript was delivered, Dwye Evans, the head of Heinemann, refused to consider it until the journal of Willie Warren was deleted. When this was done and the necessary patching up completed, Evans pointed out that the book was now too short but Robin was bored with it and refused to do more work. In a fit of pique he severed links with Heinemann who had been associated with the name of Maugham for many years. Eric Glass offered the novel to W. H. Allen who published it in its shortened form in 1972.

The critics were impressed. Burton was particularly pleased with the review in the *Birmingham Post* which recognised one aspect of his input. 'When Lytton Strachey included "The End of General Gordon" in his *Eminent Victorians* some readers were surprised at his knowledge of military matters . . . Lord Maugham has done his homework even more thoroughly than Strachey.'

It reads well, yet is another example of a lost opportunity; if Robin had listened to Dwye Evans, a far more important work might have resulted. According to Burton it was not just laziness or lack of interest. 'Following my research there was a mass of material which could have been used to illuminate even more the complexity of Gordon's character but Robin was always pressed for money and needed to sell the book as quickly as possible, so that delay was out of the question.' The Warren sequence appeared separately in 1972 under the imprint of De Hartington as an elegantly bound edition of 150 copies entitled *Testament Cairo 1898* and later in *The Black Tent and Other Short Stories*.

While Burton was working at the Casa Cala Pada, Sal Mineo and his business partner Eric Williams arrived to discuss filming *The Wrong People* for which they had acquired the rights. Mineo is best remembered as the teenager who hero-worshipped James Dean in *Rebel Without a Cause* and died because of his devotion. In real life he was to die as tragically in 1976 when he was murdered outside his Hollywood home. By 1971 he had switched from acting to film production and *The Wrong People* was to be a major project. Robin had been commissioned to write the screenplay, but Mineo was disappointed with the result, even after making allowances for it being a first draft. He suggested various changes including a new ending which indicated some hope for the unfortunate Dan.

Business completed, Mineo suggested a tour of the gay night spots but Ibiza then was still quiet, old-fashioned and bereft of gay bars. Mineo was disappointed but Robin fixed him up with one of his own contacts, a youth with Germanic good-looks who was on vacation from college and was willing to provide sexual favours irrespective of gender. Nicknamed 'G. G.' ('God's Gift'), his charm and versatility made him popular for two summers running and he could often be found prettily displayed in the nude on Robin's terrace.

Social life on the island revolved around the homes of expatriates. The wealthiest of these were Laurel and Gerry Albertini who became Robin's close friends and whose lavish standard of entertaining he tried to copy. The acknowledged meeting place was a bar in Santa Eulalia, run by a Sandy Pratt, called The Black Horse but referred to as Sandy's Bar. At times it resembled a theatrical green-room where the likes of Coral Browne, Terry-Thomas, Lionel Bart, Ursula Andress, Denholm

Elliott, Diana Rigg and Elizabeth Sellars mingled with the 'civilians'. Otherwise, there was an endless exchange of visits for drinks or luncheon and dinner parties. Elizabeth Sellars and her husband Frank Henley described Robin as a generous host and a lively guest. Henry, a surgeon, also remembered his preoccupation with his health: 'He would describe his aches and pains and expect a diagnosis. He was clearly something of a hypochondriac.' Others remember that he liked nothing better than to plan projects for the theatre and cinema which seemed dazzlingly wondrous through a haze of alcohol but crumbled to dross when sobriety took over. Essentially the resident colony was small and, as dearly as they might like each other (and even then more from necessity than choice), tensions and petty jealousies were bound to occur. Privately, Robin admitted that it was frequently a bore and Casa Cala Pada nothing like the Villa Mauresque which he had hoped to emulate.

One of the more colourful party-giving residents was Elmyr de Hory, a diminutive figure with dyed hair and made-up face who had achieved dubious fame as an expert art forger. He was a vicious gossip and a fanatical snob, constantly reeling off information from the Almanach de Gotha. When Robin was helping Gloria Vanderbilt to find a holiday villa on the island, he took her to visit de Hory who, with a complete lack of sensitivity, went over the complicated custody case which had given Gloria such misery as a child. She restrained herself until afterwards: 'I couldn't live on the same island as that man,' she raged. The thought of her wishing to live on Ibiza had seemed unlikely from the start but, according to Keith Monk, she hoped to become Lady Maugham. Robin, however, declined to become Mr Vanderbilt.

There was some excitement in Sandy's Bar when it was learnt that Orson Welles was due to arrive to film footage for *F for Fake* at de Hory's villa. A large party was thrown for this but Robin refused to go as he thought it bad form to use guests as unpaid extras. It did occur to him, however, that Welles would be ideal casting as Ewing Baird in *The Wrong People* and he asked Peter

335

Burton to sound Welles out unofficially. Sadly, though usually only too keen to earn money to finance his own projects, Welles drew the line at portraying someone as evil as Baird. Whether he might have been tempted later is a matter of speculation because plans for the film began to founder when Sal Mineo approached the Moroccan authorities for permission to film locations in Tangier and elsewhere. When he was asked for details he outlined the plot, unaware that Morocco was determined to stamp out the reputation which the story perpetuated and he was refused. Alternative locations were considered but, as frequently occurs in the film industry, other problems arose and plans were put aside.

In 1971 Robin sold a screenplay called *The Barrier* to Triarch Productions. This was effectively a period version of *The Green Shade* set in an Indian hill station in the 1890s. Instead of the young girl falling for a beautiful Arab she falls for an equally beautiful but exceedingly exotic Indian prince with a thorough working knowledge of the Kama Sutra. It was announced as a lavish multi-million Anglo-American epic which would be filmed in Ceylon and directed by Fred Zinnemann, known for *Oklahoma!*, *From Here to Eternity* and *A Man for All Seasons*. As usual, Robin imagined star casting. Audrey Hepburn was a favourite for the girl but perhaps she was too old and too thin. Why not Susannah York or Natalie Wood or maybe a world-wide search for a newcomer? The young Indian prince was more difficult and Robin went off to Ceylon in a semi-official capacity to see what local male talent was on offer. His search caused raised eyebrows when young men besieged his hotel in Colombo begging to be seen. In interviews with the local press he explained what he was looking for: 'a tall, dark and handsome young man, preferably a Tamil. He must look beautiful, young and virile . . . he will have to make naked, uninhibited love' (this in the *Ceylon Daily News* of 13 June). In the *Weekend* of 15 June this was put slightly differently under the headline 'Literary Lord Will Put Ceylon on the Permissive Wave'. The piece ended:

> In the film he hopes the accent will be on torrid love scenes. Probably

the film would have scenes of violent, unrestricted, permissive love as Ceylon has never known before. He hopes to enrol the services of a young and virile man who will enthral the audience with plain animalistic desire and project the qualities of natural man.

After this nothing more was heard of the projected film but Robin and Burton rewrote the script as a novel for W. H. Allen. For the collector, it is a publication with rarity value because of the five sonnets written for it by John Betjeman.

On his own in Ibiza, a prisoner in the house he could not sell, Robin became melancholic. He told Burton how one night in a fit of drunken depression, looking through the growing collection of his own books, many successful enough to be translated into several foreign languages, he realised that they were not good enough to attract the lasting admiration given to his uncle. This made him more depressed than ever and, in an attempt to escape this mood, he listed those people who loved and admired him, but they were all in England and he was trapped in Ibiza.

A few days later after dinner with Laurel and Gerry Albertini, he drove home in the early hours aware that, though he was drunk, his mind was clear and strangely calm, as if subconsciously a problem had been examined and a decision made on how to resolve it. The house was silent, the servants asleep; he poured a large whisky and went into the bathroom to give himself his insulin injection. When he returned to the living room the glass was empty but he could not remember drinking. He poured another to the brim to wash down his sleeping pills and then another. Suddenly he knew what had to be done.

The servants found him on the floor of his bedroom when they broke open the locked door at midday. He was still alive and the ambulance rushed him to the clinic in the old town where the medical team saved him; he eventually recovered consciousness seven hours later. The Albertinis looked after him until he was well enough to fly to England to go into the Lindo Wing of St Mary's yet again. In a thorough examination, an encephalogram was taken of his head to make sure the shrapnel had not moved, and it was noted that there was a deterioration in the normal function of his heart. He was prescribed special drugs but craftily kept to himself details of other drugs he was obtaining from doctors who innocently believed themselves to be his only physician.

Faced with the prospect of a life governed by even tougher restrictions he chose to ignore them, though he now began to fight a belated rearguard action by visiting clinics to 'dry out'. But even this was on his own terms and, in defiance of his doctors, he cajoled friends to smuggle in a supply of vodka to top up what he described as 'the alcohol blood level'. Outwardly, he appeared to have suffered little from the suicide attempt and rarely spoke about it, but whether or not he was glad to be alive he did not say, though he admitted to friends that he was living on borrowed time.

As soon as he was able, he returned to Ibiza to begin work with Peter Burton on his autobiography, *Escape from the Shadows*. Their relationship had become one of mutual affection punctuated by blazing rows sparked by drink. Robin's intention was to tell a good story without much concern for truth and though he dictated several new sequences, the result was a compilation of incidents from previous books, fictional or otherwise. Sometimes he changed these to fit in, or merely marked passages to be quoted verbatim. He described it as a patchwork of old pieces and left Burton to do much of the stitching.

It was published in 1972 shortly after Beverley Nichols' autobiographical *Father Figure*. Not only were there similarities of structure but some scenes were interchangeable; the unusual attempt at patricide by garden roller has already been mentioned. Both portrayed their respective fathers as overbearing tyrants who mocked their talented sons' musical ambitions and tried to thwart their writing careers by forcing them to practise law. Robin could not compete with Nichols' venom but he was able to trump this with descriptions of the malign influence Willie had on his life, hence the title. The major difference between the books was the attitude of the writers to their own homosexuality. Nichols implied it, but Robin made it the central feature.

A colourful new version of the suicide attempt on Ibiza features his alter ego Tommy who had already appeared intermittently throughout the narrative in the role of whipping boy. Now his apparition manifests itself in the bedroom as a beautiful naked young male, seductive and evil. He tempts Robin with oblivion and smilingly shares sleeping pills before lying back on the bed. Robin, also naked, gazes in admiration at this beautiful creature: 'The person I knew I loved most of all – I found myself lying beside him and our limbs melted together.' The combination of desire, masturbation and death in this particular flight of fancy gave a glimpse into Robin's psyche which he may not have intended to be so informative. Burton refused to believe a word of it. 'I knew when Robin was fantasising. As for the so-called suicide attempt, he was either drunk or took an overdose of insulin by mistake. But it made a colourful tale, I suppose!'

The ending became a problem until late one evening when, very drunk, Robin suddenly said: 'I've got it!' and reeled off what became the conclusion, finishing with the sentence: 'Now at last without any fear and without any shadows spread out in the space before me – now, at last, I can stretch out my arms and reach the delivering sun.' Well satisfied with this burst of theatrical rhetoric, he paused and poured another glass of wine.

Reactions to *Escape from the Shadows* were mixed and Robin was angered when he was described as a 'drunken homosexual'. He told the *Observer* the story of General Eisenhower remonstrating with one of his officers. 'It's OK to call him a limey and it could be permissible in certain circumstances to call him a bastard. But "limey bastard", never!' That, said Robin, was how he felt about 'drunken homosexual'. Needless to say, it was Robin's honest admission of his homosexuality that fascinated the media. The tabloid *Sunday Mirror*, predictably combining prurience with disapproval, warned its readers that many would feel nothing but revulsion for his revelations. Its prophecy that it would be a bestseller was correct, but the publishers, Hodder &

Stoughton, eventually lost over £6,000 because they had paid Robin such a substantial advance.

In an introduction to *The Black Tent and Other Short Stories* Peter Burton neatly summarised Robin's output up to 1973:

> Robin Maugham has had a highly successful career as a novelist, a travel writer, a dramatist, a journalist, a family biographer and most recently as an autobiographer. He has written over a dozen novels, seven travel books and more than twenty plays for stage and television. In fact there can be few writers as prolific as Maugham with so few short stories to their credit.

One way or another the short story was out of fashion, partly killed, it could be argued, by television which now dominated homes like some garrulous relative. It was ironic that Willie, who had depended for a large part of his income and fame on magazines, had fed TV with short stories that had first appeared in magazines. It was a pity that the market had almost gone because Robin was at his best when disciplined by the short-story format. The fifteen examples in the collection illustrate the diversity of his moods and range of styles from 1943. The quality is not consistent and may reflect the influence of his mentor or collaborator at the time, whether it was Harold Nicolson, Derek Peel, Michael Davidson or Peter Burton.

Although Robin was grateful to Burton for the idea, and to Karen De Groot who tracked down copies of the older stories, the volume had no significance for him and he learned nothing from it. This was confirmed by *Lovers in Exile* (1977), four new short stories, 'new' being relative, for two were a regurgitation of plays and the others, supposedly contemporary, had more to do with the fifties than the seventies.

*Winter in Ischia* originated as a three-act tale of doomed love between Liza, an English lady of early middle-age, and Carlo, a mechanic who has broad shoulders, a narrow waist, 'a nose too broad for classical perfection' and a mouth too wide, for reasons unspecified. It reads like a play intended for matinée audiences, to be performed to the accompaniment of hearing aids buzzing and tea trays rattling. It was first performed in 1964 at the Worthing

Connaught Theatre and there was a television transmission later. The short-story version typified Robin's lazy adaptations and came complete with stage directions.

*The Two Wise Virgins of Hove* was about two elderly ladies, portrayed on television by Margaret Rutherford and Martita Hunt, who believe Jesus will come to dinner provided they set up house in Jerusalem. They do so and he does. This was a version of Mary Borden's short story about the ambitious society hostess, a thinly-disguised Sibyl Colefax, setting a place for Jesus at her table.

# Nirvana

Back in 1944 when Willie was in America and went into the equivalent of a 'Victorian decline', as Robin described it, he tried to find some comfort from reading the gospels and became fascinated by the discrepancies in the four accounts of Christ's life. He examined the stories as a police detective might do and postulated that Joseph of Arimathaea, a wealthy politician, had made plans to fake the death and resurrection to confirm Christ's claim to be the true Messiah. He would 'appear' to a number of reliable witnesses and then vanish apparently to heaven. By judicious propaganda throughout Israel he would become the symbolic figure to lead the uprising against the Roman occupation of the Jewish homelands.

Willie probably intended to write an essay or even a novel on this subject, but he did not get beyond preparing notes which were later destroyed in the notorious fires at the Mauresque. Remembering his discussions, Robin toyed with the idea of developing the story as a play for the theatre and discussed it with friends. John Betjeman pointed out that the Church would be outraged at the portrayal of Christ as a political pawn. Reluctantly Robin rethought the story; the Christ figure would be replaced by one of the many other young men who claimed to be the Messiah during the Roman occupation:

> I see this man as a kind of flower child. I see him as a hippy of those days, endowed with beauty, charm and what we would now call extra-sensory perception, clairvoyance and prophecy. He was what they longed for at that time. The hysteria was such that prophets who once might have said 'The Messiah will come in ten years time' were saying 'He will arrive at any minute.'

The revised version soon moved away from the gospel story. Joseph of Arimathaea became bisexual with a long-suffering wife and a boyfriend of ten years who was somewhat neurotic and jealous of Christ, now renamed Caleb. The central drama remained with the crucifixion as its climax and politics as the guiding motive. Robin did not yet put anything on paper but talked about it endlessly to anyone prepared to listen. Eventually the American theatre director Herbert Machiz was sufficiently encouraging to spur Robin into writing. They had met when Robin went to the Spolteo Festival to see his friend Hermione Baddeley in Tennessee Williams' *The Milk Train Doesn't Stop Here Any More* which Machiz directed.

Robin may have been overawed by the story he was trying to tell or even influenced by the verbal dexterity of Tennessee Williams; whatever the reasons, the play entitled *AD 20* turned out to be incredibly boring with all the action off stage and interminable speeches in pretentious prose on stage to explain what had happened and why, and what might happen and if . . . On the Machiz front there was silence and subsequently every management in London turned the script down. As was his habit, Robin eventually dug it out of the files, and turned it into a novel with the help of William Lawrence. The result was as turgid as the play but it now contained the proposition that the Christ figure, Caleb, was homosexual. In an entirely gratuitous sex scene following the stripping and flogging of Caleb, one of the centurion guards goes into his cell to anoint his back with oil and sodomises him. Later this centurion stands at the foot of the cross in tears.

The reviews were surprisingly generous but few appeared to

realise that Caleb was a lightly-disguised Christ; if they had, perhaps they might have been less sanguine. The novel, given one of those meaningless titles that Robin liked, in this case, *The Sign*, picked up several quotable reviews. The *Guardian*, for example, said: 'Robin Maugham performs with considerable technical skill.' It is probably an inexplicable coincidence that the poem 'The love that dares to speak its name' by James Kirkup, printed in *Gay News*, provided a sequel to the sex scene in *The Sign* and resulted in a conviction for blasphemous libel. Robin, aware of his own narrow escape, sent a cheque for £50 to the *Gay News* Fighting Fund.

As he became increasingly more disenchanted with Ibiza, Robin stayed away as much as possible. When he was not travelling, he had his bolt hole in Brighton and a tiny flat on London's Charing Cross Road which he had taken over from one of his gay friends, T. C. (Cuthbert) Worsley the theatre critic.

On one of his trips to London, Robin took Burton out to lunch to outline plans for a new autobiographical book. It would use material omitted from *Escape from the Shadows*, with new material to be gathered during a trip to India and elsewhere. 'Imagine,' he said, 'we could arrive, say, in Bali. I may be tired and wish to sleep, but you could go off and discover the louche bars in the town. In the morning, you would be sitting on the terrace of the hotel having breakfast with a beautiful prune-black boy of about seventeen, obviously deliriously happy after a night of love and wanting to bring the boy on the journey with us. All that could be included in the book.'

It seemed as if Robin was again casting himself as Willie, with Burton as Gerald Haxton, who in the new permissive age could tell all. Burton was uneasy: 'Private and public candour are two vastly different things.' By now, he was working as publicist to Billy Gaff, then manager of Rod Stewart, and was able to decline the offer. Robin invited William Lawrence instead and the two set off on what he described as a search for nirvana.

On his first trip to Ceylon in 1965 Robin had visited the little island of Tabrobane where in 1926 Count de Mauny had built a magnificent house and created a garden to complement it. Robin, overwhelmed by the beauty of the place, imagined himself living an idyllic existence in which he would write novels the world would hail as works of genius. Its attraction was enhanced by knowing that Paul Bowles, equally seduced, had lived there for a time with his wife Jane. Now, as the cargo ship MS *Tiber* sailed nearer to Ceylon, he thought of himself ending his days on Tabrobane. When they arrived, however, he could not believe the destruction he saw. The house was empty after a brief period as a tourist hotel and a new highway bisected the golden beach and shallows between the island and the mainland. As they watched, an old lorry thundered by belching clouds of diesel smoke. Only the beautiful gardens overgrown with orchids suggested nirvana. The house had been taken over by rats which scuttled through the abandoned bedrooms among the rotting bedding.

In Bombay, Robin suffered a minor heart-attack and fell, gashing his head badly. The doctor advised him to leave the heat of India and, remembering happy times in Beirut, Robin decided that they should fly there. When the plane touched down at the airport they were the only passengers to disembark and though they heard gunfire and explosions the truth did not dawn on either of them until they found their luggage dumped on the tarmac outside the deserted airport building. Then a battered taxi screeched to a halt and the Lebanese driver shouted at them to get in as a deafening burst of artillery fire opened up. Robin shouted back that they wanted to go to the Hotel St Georges and agreed to pay one hundred Lebanese pounds. Driving like a maniac he took them to another hotel instead because 'They will blow up the St Georges.' During this nightmare journey, they had been menaced by a mob, almost fired at by a tank and still did not know exactly what was happening until it was explained that the battle was between the Palestinian refugees, the Fedayeen, and the Lebanese Army and Air Force.

In his room Robin tried to rest, aware that he was unwell but attributing it, not unreasonably, to the recent upsetting sequence of events. Then he began slipping into a diabetic coma. Somehow, as second by second he became physically weaker, he managed to reach a plate of fruit. The natural sugar relieved the condition temporarily and Lawrence arrived just in time to give him his insulin injection.

According to the Beirut *Daily Star* the city was in a state of siege and everyone was trapped, but by paying an inflated price Robin was able to book passage on an Egyptian boat to Alexandria. He had spent some of his happiest times in 'Alex' and he expected everything to be the same but he was appalled to find it in a terrible state of neglect. The Cecil Hotel, once a centre of cosmopolitan life, was ramshackle, the interiors stripped of saleable furnishings, and the entrance to the luxury apartment block where he had stayed with Eric Duke to write *The Servant* was squalid and stinking of urine. The old friends he had hoped to surprise by his unexpected arrival had left the country. Sadly, he and Lawrence travelled to Tangier where, to Robin's relief, life continued much as before but without the old, outrageous café society. Paul Bowles, whom he had not seen for fifteen years, said that Morocco might soon shut the door against Americans and Europeans.

Back in England, Robin asked Peter Burton to work with him on a book about his disillusioning experiences and he was so charming and persuasive that Burton arranged leave of absence from the Billy Gaff organisation. Deciding it would be best to get away from the pleasures and distractions of London or Brighton, Robin rented a house near Dublin, recruiting Keith Monk to take charge of the domestic side. At first, everything went as planned, until Robin began receiving a series of abusive and threatening telephone calls. What they were all about neither Monk nor Burton knew but the effect on Robin was alarming and he began drinking heavily and going into terrible rages which teetered on the brink of violence. It looked to Burton as if it would be impossible to finish the book in the time he had allotted to it.

On 17 August 1974 Burton wrote to Mike Gill at C. M. Records and Tapes Limited, Wardour Street, begging Mike to send him a letter, preferably over Billy Gaff's signature, reminding Burton that he was needed back in London by mid-November. He wanted to show this to Robin to urge him on. 'The trouble is,' Burton wrote,

> Robin is fast reaching, drifting towards, the state he always described Somerset Maugham being in. He rambles. He doesn't make sense – frequently neither Keith nor I know what he's talking about. He becomes irritable and sits and fulminates about everyone who has ever upset him. Worse, he loses sense of exactly who we are and who the people he's talking about are. He keeps saying 'Let's leave here.' Apart from anything else, it is extremely worrying. For Robin is now an old man. He has the stoop, the pallor, the lines, the trembles, the wandering mind. He can still be very funny, entertaining, write, etc. But the periods between the wandering come round like the periods of the occlusion of a lighthouse.

It came as a relief when Robin decided that they should go to Ibiza to finish the book; there Burton made faster progress and completed corrections and revisions. But after a period of relative sobriety, Robin began drinking heavily again and Burton wrote to his office asking Mike Gill to organise a cable to the effect that he was needed in London immediately. Subsequently, while Burton was in New York on business for Billy Gaff, he completed work on the book, which was published by W. H. Allen in 1975 and called, predictably, *Search for Nirvana*.

# XIX

## Conversations with Willie

Robin finally sold Casa Cala Pada in 1977 for a figure that barely covered his costs. At the same time he sold his little house in Bute Street, Brighton for £9,000 from which he paid £2,000 to Keith Monk as compensation for giving up his tenancy. He relinquished the benefits of tax exile in Switzerland in favour of domicile in England and bought an unpretentious three-storey Victorian terrace house in Clifton Road, Brighton. After alterations, the interior closely resembled that of the Seaton Street house but without some of the more expensive refinements.

By now Brighton, dubbed 'The Gay Capital of Europe', had become more openly homosexual than at any time in its history. Exclusively gay hotels, pubs, clubs, discos and restaurants flourished. Most of this was of little interest to Robin who was too old for the young 'scene' and too well known and conscious of his status to appear at the more popular venues. Once, while staying at his London flat, he was coaxed across the road to Bang, the late-night gay disco; he had never seen anything like it and was stunned by the animal exuberance and overt sexuality of the young dancers. In Brighton he occasionally ventured into the staid Curtain Club but stories of him roaring around the town in an opera cloak like a crazed Oscar Wilde, with a troupe of pretty boys at his heels, are indignantly denied by his friends.

Between frequent trips abroad he was looked after by a faithful staff but no amount of genuine loyalty, blatant sycophancy or self-deception could protect him from the belief that he had consistently missed boats, burned bridges, backed wrong horses,

347

counted chickens prematurely and done all those evil things he ought not to have done. In this respect Michael Pitt-Rivers commented: 'I think perhaps his imagination prompted him to think more evil of himself than he in fact possessed.'

Robin always needed the assurance of having familiar faces around him and, if someone moved on, it caused emotional turmoil out of all proportion to the importance of that individual. Some young lovers stayed as long as his bank account could satisfy their demands or they could restrain their boredom. At sixty-one years old, he could only pretend that life was wonderful and try to obliterate the physical and mental wounds of the war and those he had inflicted upon himself by pouring another drink.

One of his favourite visitors was Kate's son David who was only three years younger and more like a brother than a nephew. David was a hero of the war and also its psychological victim; both his married life and his business ventures had suffered because of it. Like Robin he attempted to forget the past by drinking too much and together they frequently drank themselves into oblivion. It was during a drunken bout, although not with Robin, that David died as a consequence of falling down some stairs, an accident that might not have happened if he had been sober. Robin was deeply affected by losing someone with whom he had so much in common and was one of the very few friends who was socially his equal.

Robin continued to entertain as lavishly as ever and reinstated the famous Sunday lunches, but it was not the same. In the halcyon days when famous names decorated the table few, if any, had been close friends. They were merely playing a social game which, however diverting and delightful at the time, had no substance whatsoever. Now he had to make do with lesser lights who laughed at his increasingly familiar anecdotes, provided there was enough wine to wash them down.

Readers around the world admired his books and wrote to say so, but none of them matched James Blair Lovell, a wealthy young American who was obsessed by all aspects of his life and work. Lovell was only fourteen when his father pointed out a pristine copy of the first edition of *The Servant* on the shelves of a second-hand bookshop and suggested he buy it.

It was the best few dollars' worth of my life. It impressed me with its economy of word use, its spare, clean, almost spartan style. When I was seventeen I discovered *The Wrong People*. It was revelatory, helping me to sort out questions of my own sexuality. I became the typical fan and wrote to Robin, not expecting a reply but hopeful that I might. When he answered, I was overjoyed and we exchanged letters from then on. I persuaded my younger brother John, when he was in Europe with his tutor, to contact Robin who, it turned out, was in St Mary's Hospital, Paddington. John went to visit and said he was charming – a typical English gentleman.

Lovell finally met him in 1977 when he was staying in London on business. Robin came to lunch, and after that Lovell saw him eight or nine times, mostly at his home in Clifton Road, Brighton. Lovell could not get over the high degree of talent in the family on both sides going back several generations.

One Saturday we were talking after lunch at Clifton Road and he was being as charming and unaffected as ever when, without any warning, he underwent a total change of mood. His face twisted into a mask of evil, his eyes – always his prominent feature – glittered with hate and a hank of hair fell across his forehead. Slowly, very slowly, he rose to his feet and in a harsh voice unlike his own he said: 'I think it's time you left.'

This may sound melodramatic but it is exactly as it happened. I'd said nothing to offend him but I was too shocked and frightened to argue. His friend Andy Anderson drove me to the station and I took the next train to London. People have asked me if he was drunk but no, we had definitely not been drinking and all the times that we were together he drank only moderately as far as I was aware. The next day his friend William Lawrence who lived in London called me up and we met. I guess it was Robin apologising indirectly because William eventually said something about the incident, ending with 'Now you've met Tommy, Robin's alter ego'.

Lovell accepted this as a possible explanation at the time but became increasingly sceptical, though without finding an alternative that made any sense. The experience did not affect his

349

admiration of Robin. He saw his work as an important contribution to gay literature by a man who was 'out' long before others had plucked up the courage to declare themselves. His admiration was not indiscriminate and he deplored the trivial nature of some of Robin's later books and the lamentable failure to fulfil his early promise.

After Robin's death, Lovell continued to add to the Maugham collection that he had begun in his teens. During his visit to England in 1992, his new purchases included a head of Robin sculpted by William Lawrence and two portraits of Robin purchased from John Durnford, whose mother Winifred Durnford had been left them in Robin's will. Before his premature death in 1993, Lovell had made arrangements for his collection to go to Cornell University, New York.

Peter Burton persistently bemoaned the fact that no use had been made of much of the material he had assembled for *Escape from the Shadows*. At last Robin, realising that writing a full-length biography of Willie was now beyond his capabilities, agreed that his diaries and journals should form the basis of a volume of memoirs of his uncle. He may have been influenced by knowing that Robert Calder was already at work on a biography but he apparently did not know that Ted Morgan had received Spencer Curtis Brown's blessing for his version of Willie's life. Despite previous difficulties Burton, who had moved from London to Brighton, decided to work on the project because if the situation became unbearable he could escape to his own home. 'By this stage I knew Robin very well indeed but however stormy our relationship had been, and to be fair he probably found me as insufferable as I found him, fundamentally, despite everything, we were friends.'

The book was to be a sort of 'Robin's-eye-view' of Willie and Burton tried to persuade him to retain the diary format, leaving entries as they were without grammatical or stylistic tidying-up unless essential.

I have always been fascinated by volumes of letters, journals and so on, but Robin could not grasp the point. So instead of the book having the sharpness, relevance and value of archive material, it often had the tone associated with the popular Sunday press. There was nothing wrong with this but the result did not have the gravitas and immediacy I would have liked.

What Burton means is typified by Robin's romanticised explanation of the book's origin:

Willie died in 1965. Shortly afterwards, I went to live in Spain. The notebooks — together with many other documents — went into store.

When I returned to England after nearly ten years abroad, I was foraging through the various papers which had been stored and I came across — dusty and a little mouldy — my Willie diaries. As I read my almost indecipherable handwriting, suddenly the realisation came to me: I had found a treasure trove. In the pages which I was turning over in my hands were the observations, almost instantly recorded, of and about a great man. Two tasks remained to me: the first was to have typed out the quickly written notes from all my diaries — the second was to fill in the abbreviations in the text and to link the notes together.

This was nonsense, as the entire archive had been transported to Ibiza and then brought back to England, but it pleased Robin to create a colourful story because he thought it made the product more commercial.

Having failed to persuade him to adopt one approach, Burton succeeded with another when he suggested it might be modelled on S. N. Behrman's *Conversation with Max*. He agrees the result bore little resemblance to this except in the title *Conversations with Willie*, the additional 's' being at Robin's insistence.

Robin's method of writing his journal was not dissimilar to that of Garson Kanin. Both jotted down details of Willie's remarks as they remembered them. Kanin, in the role of adoring fan, was looking for wit, sagacity and sentimentality while Robin, with no illusions about his uncle, searched for comments which revealed the man behind the façade. His resulting portrait illustrated with horrifying clarity Willie's descent into madness and gave the overall impression that a slow, decomposing gloom had set in after Haxton's death.

351

The problem with conversation recorded hours, days, even weeks afterwards is that the writer may genuinely block out aspects that do not fit in with his preconceived ideas and so alter the original meaning. An example of this could be Willie's much-quoted comment that he tried to persuade himself that he was only a quarter queer and three-quarters normal, when it was the other way around. Commentators have always taken it as a serious piece of self-analysis but it was unlike Willie to say something so glaringly silly; he was the last person to believe that sexual preference can be subjected to mathematical definition. If he said it, or something similar, it was likely to have been one of the camp throw-away remarks that, in gay company, would get an amused reaction. It is not unlike John Osborne's response to Noël Coward's question, 'How queer are you?' – 'Oh, about twenty per cent.' Coward promptly volunteered that he was 'ninety-five'. Nobody has attempted to extrapolate some truth from this exchange, treating it as nothing more than flummery.

Instead of always going back to his journals, Robin insisted on saving time, by relying heavily on his screenplay, *Willie*, a romanticised account of events. From this he used dialogue between his father and Uncle Harry which may or may not have had a basis in truth, while 'scenes' with Haxton and Barbara Back were interpolated almost unaltered. The latter embodied absurd factual errors: for example, Back speaks of Syrie as an established interior decorator years before the idea had even occurred to her. Robin also used sections from previous books to save time and adapted letters into conversations. Burton had to accept that fiction and fact welded together in Robin's mind and metamorphosed into pure truth but he was startled when Robin casually asked him to pad out gaps with invented stories and dialogue. The sections in which Willie reminisces about Aleister Crowley, G. B. Stern and Hugh Walpole are an example of this.

In a slightly ironic dedication Robin acknowledged Burton's contribution: 'without whose help – as has often been said, but this time with truth – this book could not have been written'. Burton, commenting fifteen years afterwards, said:

If Robin had not been in such a frantic hurry to get the second half of the advance, *Conversations with Willie* could have been much stronger but no time was allowed for research and he refused to use pages of interesting material which provided valuable background or include dialogue which he thought the public might find a bit dull.

The book was launched with a blaze of publicity in February 1978 and critical reaction, from Auberon Waugh in the *New York Times* to Anthony Powell in the *Daily Telegraph*, was highly favourable, almost as good as that for *Somerset and All the Maughams*. A review of more than usual interest came from John Lehmann in the *Sunday Telegraph*. He was the godson of Violet Hammersley, Willie's childhood playmate in Paris and, as a youth, had met him frequently in her company. After the war his encounters were more random but, as a gay man, his remark that Willie 'disclosed a side of his nature that gets scant showing in this book' appears more meaningful than he was prepared to say.

Philip Toynbee in the *Observer* expressed his initial doubts as he began to read what appeared to be a clearly fabricated book, an impression strengthened by the 'fearful vacuity' of the earlier pages.

But long before the point of no return these conversations had begun to grip me with the sinister force of an Ancient Mariner's finger in my button-hole . . . The febrility and tarnished sparkle of the early pages are seen, as we get further into the book, to be the appropriate prelude to a horror story of the blackest kind; to something which has risen by the end almost to the level of tragedy.

After a run of books which sold well but were quickly forgotten, Robin had good reason to be pleased about the favourable reaction to *Conversations with Willie*, but instead it brought bouts of deep depression. It was as if its success reminded him of how much his writing career owed to Willie. He never denied that it helped to be the nephew of the most successful author of the day as well as the son of a viscount and he cheerfully exploited both Willie and Freddie to get maximum attention. When they died he changed his tune, frequently complaining that they had overshadowed his life, implying that this had prevented his talent from reaching its full flowering. From a publicity point of view it had the practical effect of reminding the public of his connections.

In the past, introspective depression may have led to a suicide attempt: now, as he tried to alleviate his mental condition by pills and heavy drinking, he knew perfectly well that his action was a form of self-administered death, admittedly slow, but as conclusive as a dose of cyanide. When he was sober he castigated himself for the effects his alcoholism had on his behaviour, such as the humiliation of passing out in the House of Lords and at Alec Waugh's eightieth birthday dinner, and he hated the unreasoning anger it triggered, often over matters of little consequence. Sometimes he tried to give up alcohol and Peter Burton speaks of his attempts to control himself by waiting until midday before his first drink, but rarely succeeding. Michael Lowrie recalls him pouring a tumbler of vodka, walking a few feet while drinking from the glass and then returning to replace the half he had gulped down. Lunch parties increasingly became an endurance test for hungry guests when the meal was postponed yet again in favour of another pre-lunch drink; those familiar with this routine ate a substantial snack before arriving. By the time the ruined meal was eventually served in the late afternoon Robin, switching to wine, only toyed with the food. Afterwards he often went to bed drunk and exhausted, only to reappear several hours later in pyjamas and dressing-gown ready to drink again. Even on days when he drank a medically-prescribed alternative of valium syrup diluted with tonic water, he cheated by taking secret nips of alcohol while pretending to visitors that he was 'off the booze'.

Then, just as his depressive moods began to lessen, the Banque de l'Harpe collapsed and he lost his only provision for emergencies and retirement. It was supremely ironic that the only apparently prudent financial decision he had ever made ended in disaster. When he had pleaded poverty in the past it was assumed to be a rich man's affectation and now, though he trimmed expenditure here and there, no one close to him took the situation too seriously because superficially he continued to appear affluent.

354

He refused to be sensible and accept that he could not afford to run several homes, employ staff, use private doctors, pay large amounts to lovers, travel abroad and pretend he was a millionaire. Yet over the years he had earned vast sums of money from his writing and, even with only a modicum of financial sense, he should have been comfortably off.

The Banque de l'Harpe crisis emphasised Robin's lack of ready cash, in itself nothing new, and his need to sell valuables to pay bills became more critical. His archive of letters from well-known people ranging from Glubb Pasha to Noël Coward and of course Willie, began to appear in sale rooms or went direct to various American universities. Billy Gaff bought four watercolours by William de Belleroche, and Michael Gill a painting by Sir Frank Brangwyn of Donald Sinden as a boy. Incredible as it may seem, close friends and employees still did not guess the truth. One of his ex-lovers had no idea of the seriousness of the situation until Robin died and then he was shocked to discover that the man he still regarded as a benefactor, who was always ready to help him financially, earned less in a year than he did.

Until *Conversations with Willie* the sale of Robin's recent books, although still satisfactory, had been slipping steadily. The potency of revived success should have had him overflowing with ideas and energy but, if anything, it had the reverse effect. It was reminiscent of a period in the late 1940s, after the success of *The Servant*, when he despaired of ever finding a subject for his next book. He talked about this to Michael Pitt-Rivers and then, changing the subject, went on to describe in his usual hilarious fashion a recent stay at an hotel in Devon. His fellow guests, he explained, were a dull lot and, in a mood of mischief-making and to keep himself from falling unconscious into his soup with boredom, he assigned completely unlikely characters to each of them. The flashy spiv and his girlfriend he treated as if they were the American ambassador and his lady; the dull bank manager became the revered billionaire benefactor of umpteen charities; the plain, fortyish spinster a sparkling star of Broadway musicals; and a grey-faced cleric the wickedest man in the world. Gradually they began behaving as cast and it was only when his own performance went too far that the bank manager realised what was happening. He was furious at 'being made fun of', but it had taken several days for the penny to drop.

'You've found the subject for your book,' Pitt-Rivers told him and, as they talked the idea through until the early hours, Robin became more and more enthusiastic until, without any warning, he broke down in floods of tears. His mood had changed into one of self-pity. Between sobs he kept saying, 'I can't do it', like a small boy defeated by an algebraic equation and fearful of punishment. It was clear that behind the emotion was some early experience which had left a corrosive lack of self-esteem and nothing that Pitt-Rivers said could help: 'The idea for the book had considerable potential but Robin abandoned it; it could have pre-dated Nigel Dennis's *Cards of Identity* by several years.' Pitt-Rivers discussed this episode with Harold Nicolson who agreed Robin had stumbled on a good idea for a book but said: 'I am always worried about that bit of shell in his brain. We shouldn't press him too much.'

Now Robin badly needed the sort of bestselling book that would attract high bids for the film rights, but to his despair he was devoid of ideas. Then after a few weeks, as if it had been lurking in his subconscious, the scheme for a new novel came to him complete in almost every detail. It would be based loosely on the life of Laurence Harvey who had died in 1973 from cancer. A Lithuanian by origin, he had arrived in England from South Africa as an ambitious young actor. Completely unscrupulous, he deployed his good-looks and bisexual athleticism whenever he saw the chance of advantage. His ruthless exploitation of Hermione Baddeley and Margaret Leighton was well known in theatrical and film circles; this and his association with influential gay men in cinema and theatre, the latter typified by the impresario Binkie Beaumont, earned him the stardom he craved. In 1958 he was nominated for an Oscar in *Room at the Top* and then went to Hollywood where he starred with Elizabeth Taylor in *Butterfield 8*, Frank Sinatra and Angela Lansbury in *The Manchurian*

*Candidate* and John Wayne in *The Alamo*. He returned to England for several projects, including a disastrous remake of *Of Human Bondage*, in which he was miscast as the sensitive Philip.

Robin had met Harvey frequently and knew the most intimate details of his private life from Hermione Baddeley, who relished the idea of revenge. He saw the story as a contemporary version of *Dorian Gray* with a touch of the Faust legend. Rodney Croft, otherwise Harvey, is the victim of a car crash. When he regains partial consciousness he is being wheeled down a hospital corridor to the operating theatre; as he slips into a coma he remembers dramatic episodes from his life. Weeks later, when he is recovering from a series of operations his mentor Quayne, the Beaumont character, tells him his beauty has been destroyed in the crash and his career is finished.

Robin engaged Peter Burton to collaborate and dictated the story outline, leaving him to research detail and write the chapters. Everything went well until Robin sent a long letter from Italy, where he had gone on holiday with William Lawrence and Gordon Anderson, complaining that Burton was working too slowly and costing too much. This came as a shock because Burton was carrying out precisely what they had agreed, as papers in his files confirm. These papers also show that his estimated earnings would amount to half the advance but he would have no further income from paperback, stage, film, radio or television sales or receipts.

When Robin returned from Italy Burton could not face a battle and decided to hand over the completed chapters and his research notes and leave Robin to work on the novel alone. The discussion had taken place over one of the solid 'school' lunches cooked by Robin's housekeeper, Mrs Sargent, and washed down with several bottles of claret. Burton had gone home relieved that he was free again. 'I am afraid I was not particularly sympathetic to the theme of the book but I think my work had gone fairly well. Robin's complaint about my speed was not justified but he was desperate to earn money from the advance.'

After Burton left, Robin continued drinking and worked

357

himself into a terrible rage over some imagined wrong. Early in the evening he telephoned, demanding certain material, but he was beyond reason and kept repeating himself and being abusive. Burton slammed down the receiver and when he picked it up half an hour later he found that he was still connected and Robin was still chuntering on. He slammed the phone down again and, in a fury, typed out a note to Robin. It began, 'Further to our telephone conversation – it is only because you are drunk all the time that you never remember a conversation or a business agreement,' and, after detailing events, ended, 'Therefore, with regret, I suggest you do not write to me or telephone. Your attitude, obviously partly due to ill health and alcohol, is becoming increasingly strange and unless you are careful it is apparent that you will be as mad and unpleasant as your descriptions make your uncle sound.'

He sent it round by cab and Robin, in a gesture of drunken theatricalism, scrawled a note which began, 'To whom it may concern, the attached letter is the cause of my death,' and then fell asleep in his armchair. This row with its ludicrous mixture of misunderstanding, self-indulgent drama and farce was the last the two men were to have. A few days later they were reconciled over another of Mrs Sargent's lunches.

Robin's decision to drop Burton was a mistake because, as he quickly found, he could not apply his mind to the work. He even used some of Burton's raw notes without any attempt to integrate them. He should have found another collaborator but it was as if he had pushed a self-destruct button. As a result *The Corridor* was never finished on the major scale that had been planned. The truncated version was rejected by W. H. Allen and other publishers until Patrick Newley persuaded William Kimber to take it. By the time it appeared there were drastic alterations and the narrative made little sense.

Surprisingly, it picked up a few favourable reviews, though the *Irish Times* noted: 'The exceptional and the commonplace are juxtaposed, so that the book seems to be written by two people.' The most perceptive comment was made by Stephen Glover in the *Daily Telegraph*: 'What Robin Maugham thinks about homosexuals I do not know, but they do not get a good write-up here.' He had highlighted Robin's covert dislike of many types of homosexual and his inability to invent gay men for whom the reader could have much sympathy.

# XX

## Sisters

Patrick Newley believed Robin was a little frightened of his sisters Honor and Diana, and did his best to hide his lifestyle from them. He recalled the fuss that Robin made when Diana was due to visit Brighton with some of her family:

> He told Andy [Gordon Anderson] to hide all the bottles, so I helped to clear the drinks table and the housekeeper put a big bowl of flowers in the middle of it. Then we locked everything away in the room where he kept the spare crates of booze. Robin stopped drinking the day before but he was still a bit shaky by the time Diana arrived.
>
> On another occasion I was taking him to catch the train to Brighton after we had recorded an interview for Japanese television when he suddenly decided to call on each of his sisters unannounced. He'd been drinking steadily all day, but he stopped off to buy a bottle of vodka, half of which he downed before we arrived at Mrs Earl's house. She seemed very jolly but slightly perplexed by Robin's mood. We didn't stay long. On the way to Mrs Marr-Johnson he warned me to mind my language as Diana was very strict about that sort of thing. When we got to Onslow Square he changed his mind about visiting her, saying we might not be welcome. By this time he was really drunk and obviously did not want her to see him in that state.

Robin told Newley that Diana was the better writer: 'I can't hold a candle to her when it comes to style.'

He described Honor as someone who lived in a world of her own and did so very successfully. Over the years she had painted the portraits of a large number of well-known writers, actors, musicians and dancers. Among her sitters were Paul Robeson, Peter Ustinov, Evelyn Laye, Noël Coward, Edith Evans, Danny Kaye, John Gielgud, Grace Kelly and Queen Elizabeth, now the

Queen Mother. But she derived her greatest satisfaction from painting young children and, however hostile, shy or bored they might be to begin with, she had the knack of coaxing them to co-operate. She sold much of her work to aid charities such as Dr Barnardo, Save the Children and the Actors' Orphanage. Among her exhibitions was 'Children of the Stars' in 1990, the proceeds of which went to the NSPCC.

Honor believed in life after death and she was puzzled by those who did not: 'It's going to be such an awfully big adventure. I can't wait!' (Her words echoed the line in *Peter Pan* which she recalled her father taking Kate and herself to see at the Coronet Theatre when they were children.) She died aged ninety-four in February 1996.

Diana was successful with short stories, novels and children's books. She has published seven novels and is working on her eighth. Her approach was summed up by the *Times Literary Supplement*'s review of *Face of a Stranger* (1963): 'The delicacy and precision of the author's analysis of her characters and their essential human qualities makes this novel disturbing and compelling.' Much the same was said of *Goodnight Pelican*, a Book Society recommendation which later appeared on television dramatised as *Boy Meets Girl*. The *New York Times* said of *Three for a Wedding* in 1975: '[It] combines wit and simplicity with unusual depth of psychological understanding ... her fresh, uncynical view of life is all her own.' This is particularly true of *Faces My Fortune* (1970). It tells of the impact of a woman portrait painter on an apparently happy family and their impact on her when she stays with them to complete a commission. As a result of the experience she becomes dissatisfied with the quality of her work and with her dull, well-ordered life, and suffers a form of mental breakdown. The resolution is completely unexpected but consistent with the temperament of an artist.

Like Robin, Diana hoped to make a name as a playwright and speaks with wry amusement of the disastrous first night of a drama at a London fringe theatre. The plot concerned a group of people trapped by snow in a mountain hut in the Alps. Their one hope of rescue is that the glow of a candle in the window will be seen across the valley. On the opening day London was hit by a freak heatwave and, as audience and players sweltered in the small theatre, the candle slowly drooped over into a pool of wax and went out.

She was luckier with another play, *Never Say Die*, which had a show-case production at the Strand Theatre with Gwen Watford in the lead and subsequently did well in repertory theatres and later with amateur companies. The public had no idea that Diana was Somerset Maugham's niece, a connection which, like her sister Kate, she had no desire to exploit. But, as Robin successfully proved, it might have made a difference if she had.

# Come to Dust

In 1980 Ted Morgan's biography of Willie appeared. Unwisely, perhaps, Robin had refused to be interviewed, unlike other members of the family, which may explain a certain coolness towards him from Morgan, who nonetheless made good use of *Somerset and All the Maughams* and *Escape from the Shadows*, indeed could not avoid doing so as Robin was the only Maugham to have written about Willie and the family. Even when Morgan wrote of Robin's war record, quoting praise from his commanding officer, he juxtaposed it with Willie's remark in a letter to Bert Alanson of 24 March 1942: 'Who would have thought that that flighty boy had it in him to do what he has done?' Morgan appeared to intend the reader to take the words literally as snide criticism when they were actually ironic words of praise. His lack of understanding of Willie's homosexual argot and camp speech rhythms can be attributed to heterosexual ignorance. But, in fairness to him, his logic was not helped by Robin's misleading use of quotations out of context to score points against Willie and

Freddie. Nor was he helped by Willie's habit of complaining about Robin behind his back.

Family, friends and admirers of Willie were predictably outraged by the book, but this was merely a sharp reminder that no biographer can ever hope to meet the expectations of those who wish to forget, or prefer to remain in ignorance of anything that they find impinging disagreeably on their own emotions. It was Willie, however, who had set the bandwagon rolling with his disgraceful *Looking Back*. It was a case of the biter bit.

One of the most virulent reactions came from Beverley Nichols who, as an ex-lover, claimed proprietorial rights over Willie's life. He was angry and bewildered that Willie's literary executor, Spencer Curtis Brown, had ignored the terms of the will in which it was stated that no biography was to be written or assistance provided to anyone who attempted one. But the main cause of his fury was Morgan's departure from Edwardian rules of social conduct by revealing in print, for the first time, the extent of Willie's promiscuity. 'The role of sex is absurdly exaggerated. He was not a sex maniac as the book implies but only as sexually active as the average man.' He vented his spleen in a very long article in *Books and Bookmen* in which he dismissed Morgan's work with contempt: 'Socially the book is written from the viewpoint of the servants' hall . . . There is no serious attempt to assess Maugham's position as an artist.' By the final paragraph he had calmed down sufficiently to say of Willie's life: 'It wasn't all bitchiness and hatred and money and going to bed with him or her. There were interludes of high comedy and incidents of simple kindness.'

If everything had gone according to plan, the publication of Morgan's book would have coincided with the production of *Willie*, a stage version of a screenplay based on *Somerset and All the Maughams*. Robert Selbie, administrator of the Chichester Festival Theatre, helped Robin with the adaptation. (Selbie remarked that Robin was 'an enchanting man', and easy to work with, though 'another round of drinks' before lunch delayed progress.) It was hoped that the play would form part of the

Chichester Season, but as the production called for a large cast and elaborate staging, it was too costly to be undertaken during the world recession of the early 1980s.

Eric Glass had confidence in the box-office potential of the play and a conference was held to discuss its future. Peter Burton proposed scrapping the screenplay structure, with its many short scenes and settings, and instead devising a much simpler piece with Willie, surrounded by the detritus of his life, recalling the main events. This approach was welcomed but matters were left in abeyance while Robin went to India on holiday.

While he was away Robin's health was not good and he drank heavily. As one friend put it: 'I don't understand why he goes abroad so much; being drunk in Calcutta is much the same as being drunk in Brighton.' On his return, following a now established routine, he went into a private nursing home to rest and, if possible, dry out. A brain specialist warned him in the most serious terms that tests showed that progressive mental deterioration had set in and would become more rapid unless he gave up alcohol immediately. Even the fear of insanity did not deter him and he was soon drinking as much as ever, between brief periods of semi-abstinence.

To help pay for his costly lifestyle he continued to sell off assets and even talked of giving up the house and moving into a flat. From time to time he earned moderate amounts from journalism which he split with Peter Burton who ghosted for him.

His name sold the articles and I received half the fee. Typical examples included a piece for the *TV Times*: £500, and a review of a life of Wavell for the *Evening News*: £100. I was particularly pleased with an article I wrote for the American magazine *MD* called 'The Art of Biography'. Robin liked the image it conveyed of his breadth of reading when, in reality, he had stopped reading anything of consequence years ago. He had a few books in his house but, apart from a set of Proust, they were mostly novels sent to him by fellow authors in response to those he sent them.

In March, work began on turning the play *Enemy* into a novel. Called *The Deserters* in England and *Enemy* in the USA, it expanded the theme of the play and included sequences from *Come to Dust* and *Nomad*. Burton made the adaptation and wrote new chapters telling the background story of each soldier, Ken in London and Paul in Berlin. The young German emerged as the only likeable gay character in the entire canon of fiction published under Robin's name. The bond between the men was understated so that the violent death which ended their relationship came as a greater shock than it might have done if there had been the usual graphic descriptions of mechanical sex. Robin wanted them but Burton refused:

> I persuaded him that prurience was out of place. If he'd felt strongly about it he could have written the scenes himself but I don't think he could be bothered. He'd even stopped writing his daily journal which he had begun in 1944. I am haunted by the final entry in November 1978 in which he admonished himself for drinking and vowed to stop.

On 17 May Robin was sixty-four and celebrated with what was to be his last birthday lunch. In addition to the Brighton friends – Gordon Anderson who had become one of the most dependable in these final years, Keith Monk, Peter Burton and Jeanne Francis – there were guests who came down specially from London: his sister Diana, her husband Kenneth, William Lawrence and Lady Assheton-Smith.

Mrs Sargent always prepared lunch on the assumption that there would be two or three guests and there often were. When someone special was due, the soup was more heavily laced with sherry, the joint a better cut, the fresh fruit salad floating in cointreau, the brie just right and the wines carefully selected. Among the 'special' guests were Beverley Nichols and Cyril Butcher who remembered that the fruit salad was 'positively paralytic'. Nichols was no longer so sure about Robin's role as successor to Willie:

> I only saw him on rare occasions in the last decade of his life and delightful as he always was the sparkle had grown duller each time. I could not avoid noticing that he only dabbled with his food but drank almost continuously. To me, only too familiar with heavy drinkers

and their habits, this was ominous. He also had a puffy look about the face and carried too much fat. I am afraid he had not fulfilled the earlier promise and I doubted whether in his sixties he would live long enough to surprise us.

Francis King said that Robin's conversation became increasingly trivial: 'Unlike Willie, he was never an intellectual, there were never piercing insights but in the last years he seemed only interested in gossip about the politics of Brighton's gay life, an exceedingly dull subject.'

To some it seemed as if Robin found his performance as the jolly Lord Maugham increasingly difficult to maintain. But those who saw it through a haze of conviviality might dispute that behind the mask was deep unhappiness, preferring to remember him as all-joking, all-laughing, always generous with his hospitality and free with his money. Francis King said it was embarrassing in restaurants when Robin insisted on paying the bill for everyone and made a scene about it. There was always something of 'the small boy showing off' in his character which he rarely suppressed; this could be endearing when it was not being infuriating.

Many of Robin's emotional problems stemmed from failure to come to terms with his sexuality. This may explain why some of his relationships had difficulties which led to frightening rows and violence. As an ex-lover put it: 'I don't think he would have been so interested in some of us if we had passively complied. He liked his friends and lovers to be aggressively independent.' An old friend said:

> You could not ignore his social background and, though he enjoyed shocking people, at heart he was thoroughly conventional and middle class. Unfortunately, he was trapped in an adolescent attitude to sex. Like many other bisexual men, he should have married and coped with any extra-marital diversions just as heterosexual men do.

Robin's sister Honor observed:

> He needed the stability of marriage: if he had had this, he might have been a better writer and would certainly have lived to a grand old age

provided his wife could keep him off the bottle! He would have made a delightful and understanding father and, though he never admitted it, lack of a wife and children was, I believe, his greatest sorrow. He was very keen on Gillian Dearmer for a time, but the real love of his life was Mary Churchill, Winston's daughter. I think he'd have married her but the war caused so much upheaval.

A Cambridge contemporary, on the other hand, remarked: 'Robin's trouble was that he was born with a silver spoon in his mouth and a silver knife in his back!'

In August 1980 Robin visited Charles Fletcher-Cooke in Gloucester for a few days and then went on to stay with Myles Hildyard in Nottinghamshire. Apparently all was well. He also stayed at Winifred Durnford's home in Cornwall with William Lawrence to work on a short novel called *The Refuge*. Back in Brighton he went into a Rottingdean nursing home for the third time that year for a ten-day rest. He returned to Clifton Road, neither better nor worse, to draft the script of a play for BBC Radio working with Burton again. After Christmas spent with his Brighton friends he began another short novel which was intended to accompany *The Refuge* in one volume.

*DAN 31*, as he called it, was inspired by his infatuation for the young actor Jimmy Hanley who subsequently married the actress Dinah Sheridan. As an adolescent Hanley was gangly, with blond hair, a cheeky grin and an infectious laugh, not sufficiently good-looking to attract a teenage following but the effect he had on Robin was extraordinary. Apparently they never met but he remained Robin's sexual ideal and in his dreams Hanley stayed the young boy whom he had first seen at the London Coliseum in 1931 in *White Horse Inn*. But there had to be more than this for the infatuation to last for fifty years and there was, for young Hanley worked with Chapman's circus in 1932 as a bareback rider. The sight of him in tights and spangles astride a horse had sent Robin into a mental spin from which he never recovered and a blond boy on a black horse or a black boy on a white horse always caused instant sexual delight, hence his repeated use of this image in his books.

In February 1981 Robin went into a private clinic for a minor operation and for what everyone assumed was one of his 'drying-out sessions'. On 16 February Burton received a telephone call from him: 'He sounded dreadful. Twice during our conversation he had to break off to be sick. "If I'm not better by the end of the week," he said, choking, "I hope I'm dead." ' He had similar conversations with other friends but they assumed that he was dramatising the situation. It came as a complete shock when on 22 February he was rushed into intensive care at the Royal Sussex County Hospital and put onto life-support equipment. On 13 March this was switched off and he was pronounced dead; the causes were listed as diabetes, uraemia, pulmonary embolism and broncho–pneumonia. It was two months before his sixty-fifth birthday.

Discussing death in 1977 for *Gay Sunshine*, Robin said:

> I don't believe in physical resurrection. I am not sure about spiritual resurrection. I expect it exists. I am in the position of an agnostic who would like to believe definitely in something but if I had to declare my religion I would say Buddhist. Let them bury me at Hartfield with my parents and just hope for the best. Maybe death is like walking through a door. Maybe one is reborn but maybe, though I doubt it in my case, one reaches some form of nirvana and the spirit is joined in the Infinite Godhead.

Peter Burton wrote in *Parallel Lives*:

> It may sound heartless to say this but I firmly believe that Robin's death came at the right time for him. Such creative abilities as he possessed had gone – destroyed by drink. The amount of money he made from writing was dwindling year by year and, anyway, he had nothing left to say. He could no longer afford the lifestyle to which he was used but he couldn't manage without it. In a sense, Robin was lucky to die when he did. An infirm, alcoholic and penniless old age would have been the ultimate nightmare.

Michael Pitt-Rivers remarked: 'If he [Robin] could have written as well as he talked, he might have been greater than Willie.' Francis King said something similar in the *Sunday Telegraph*, noting that, unlike most novelists, Robin was always willing to talk about a book while work was in progress – 'When the volume was read, it never, for all its merits, quite measured up to his superlative telling of it.' Of Robin's sometimes-voiced, strange, self-deluding notion that Willie had been jealous of his writing success, King thought it highly improbable: 'If indeed Somerset Maugham was jealous, it is more likely to have been of an ability, cruelly lacking in himself, to be at ease with people of every class and type, to be totally frank about the vagaries of his nature, and to create fun, joy and excitement wherever he found himself.'

Collaborating with others or on his own, Robin's industry could not be faulted: eighteen novels, three collections of short stories, twenty plays, twelve filmscripts and ten volumes of biography and memoirs. Regrettably, much of it was ephemeral and none of it reached the high standard set by his uncle. *The Servant* and *The Wrong People* may last and *The Second Window* might retain its curiosity value. But his first book, *Come to Dust*, deserves to survive for its passion, immediacy and simplicity, qualities rarely recaptured in later work.

Robin – Robert Cecil Romer, Second Viscount Maugham of Hartfield – the last of his line of male Maughams, was buried with his parents. A memorial service was held at St Paul's, Covent Garden on 2 April 1981.

# The Ghost of Ashenden

The value of Robin's estate amounted to around £67,000, most of this being the estimated selling price of the house at Clifton Road. While they waited for probate to be granted, the executors, Diana Marr-Johnson and B. J. Wheeler, and Peter Burton as co-literary executor, decided to publish Robin's private diaries.

Peter Burton was formally contracted to give coherence to the material and to prepare a folio of extracts; this was circulated in

1981 to whet the appetites of would-be publishers. In a foreword he said:

> The following diary entries form no more than a very small sample of the whole work – which when transcribed and edited should present a picture which represents a fascinating example of the correlation between creativity and alcohol and creativity and emotional struggles. It is as if F. Scott Fitzgerald had left behind a detailed self-examination of his life and work processes.

He proposed a title taken from a verse by John Betjeman with an appropriately bitter ring to it: 'What on earth was all the fun for?'

This caused a flurry of excitement and several publishing houses sent representatives to Brighton to examine the original material. Robin Baird-Smith, then of Collins, spent several hours reading the diaries: 'I could not see their publication as a viable commercial proposition. There had been losses on that kind of work and publishers were nervous because of the world recession.' His view was shared by other potential buyers and after a year with no prospect of a sale, Burton asked to be released from his contract and Diana Marr-Johnson took charge of the material.

Towards the end of 1991 all but six volumes were stolen from her Kensington flat. As the diaries were contained in several packages and kept in a cupboard it seems that the thief knew where to find them. It is significant that other items a burglar might be expected to steal were completely ignored.

Burton, the only person to have studied the material in depth, remains baffled as to the motive. He points out that for many years the diaries stood in a row on the shelves in Robin's study and were over a year in his care without special precautions against theft. 'If someone wanted them so badly, why not take them when it was easy to do so? Why wait until nearly ten years after Robin's death?' The police found no ready answers and the case remains unsolved.

Perhaps the diaries were stolen 'to order' in the belief that they contained scandal about famous people. If so, the thieves were disappointed, for Robin omitted anything that might rebound to the disadvantage of himself, his family or friends, or could be construed as libellous. If the diaries had contained such material, Robin would not have allowed them to be so accessible in his own home, or Burton in his.

It is not so easy to dismiss another theory to the effect that the thieves believed the diaries to contain coded references to Robin's work for British intelligence. But even in the bizarre world of espionage this seems unlikely, for there would be no reason for him to keep a record unless he hoped to write his own version of the Ashenden stories. But it is doubtful that Robin had Willie's ability to transmute fact into fiction in such a way as to evade a charge of betraying national secrets, and there is no indication that he ever attempted to.

There has never been any doubt that Robin worked for British Intelligence, but there has always been a mystery about the degree of his importance as an operative. Part of the answer was provided by the dramatic discovery early in 1996 of documents in Robin's handwriting which appear to be draft notes of the report he prepared following his visit to the Middle East in 1946. It is possible to deduce from the documents that this mission was prompted by the British and American belief that Stalin intended to take over the Middle East. Robin's plan of 1943, which had already been approved by leading figures including Churchill, postulated a German invasion; now it was to be adapted to suit the new situation in which Russia was the enemy. (This explains the annoying lack of information in Robin's autobiographical *Nomad*.)

In the context of the scale of Soviet ambitions, Robin's plan may seem of minor importance, but as an element in a complex strategy it would have had a vital role to play. Briefly it assumed Russian infiltration prior to a military presence. In response, a network of anti-communist groups was to be set up urgently in each North African country to monitor hostile forces and to maintain strong relationships with powerful Arabs. At the centre of the network was to be an agent, probably based in Cairo or Tangier, ostensibly working legitimately in the type of profession which would permit freedom to travel.

Included in the papers was a list of names of Arabs, apparently interviewed by Robin, who were to be considered for specific tasks as secret agents. He provided an assessment of the strengths and weaknesses of each man and expressed his view of their suitability. In 1946, and for several decades afterwards, this list of potential secret agents would have been highly confidential and, to put it mildly, politically sensitive. Presumably the rest of the papers were destroyed by Robin when he had finished with them. How these remnants survived is a mystery, unless he retained them as a form of insurance against future developments which might not be in his interest.

His assertion to several friends that he was on a death list may not, after all, have been a drunken delusion. It has been assumed that, if his story was to be believed, he was targeted because of his pro-Arab sentiments: it is now more likely to have been his anti-communist activities.

Today the American OSS involvement in the Middle East is a matter of record. It is possible that Robin's visit to the USA in the winter of 1944 may have had a covert purpose linked to this. Is it relevant that Brendan Bracken arranged the visit and that Willie worked with the OSS? It might be that Willie, in his role of secret agent, was instrumental in recruiting Robin into the twilight realm of Ashenden while he was still at Cambridge. And finally, was the revised plan implemented and did Robin continue to work for British Intelligence after 1946? There are many other unanswered questions.

# W. S. M.: A Summing Up

Unlikely as it may now seem, there was a possibility after Maugham's death that he would fade from public awareness. As Cyril Connolly observed in the *Sunday Times* of 19 December 1965, it was difficult to foresee the verdict of posterity.

Today, over thirty years after Willie's death and over fifty since he wrote his final bestselling novel, *The Razor's Edge*, it is possible to provide an answer. His films still flicker across our screens, his plays are performed, his best novels and short stories are still read. Whatever the effect of *Looking Back* on his reputation as a man, it appears to have had none on his popularity as a writer. The substantial sums earned annually by his work have helped to rejuvenate his beneficiary the Royal Literary Fund, enabling it to be far more generous than previously to writers in financial difficulties, such as the late Sir Angus Wilson.

To put these earnings into context: if, by some miracle, Willie was alive today, he could continue to live at the Villa Mauresque, spend several weeks every year at the Dorchester Hotel and travel abroad to his favourite haunts.

Posterity's decision on his place in the literary hierarchy has yet to be made but in his premature critique of his own career, *The Summing Up* (1938), Willie appeared to accept with modesty and good grace Lytton Strachey's verdict: 'Class Two, Division One.' Behind the façade of good manners, however, Willie deeply resented this and longed for Strachey to be refuted. Instead, English critics occasionally provided a word of felicitous yet condescending praise and then agreed with Strachey.

When, in the last stages of his life, Willie was dubbed 'a grand old man of letters', this had more to do with longevity than with a reappraisal of his standing in English literature. There were exceptions: Cyril Connolly, for example, called him the last of the great professional writers, but even this had a tinge of snobbishness, as if Willie was more artisan than artist.

Outside England attitudes were different. Critics such as Paul Dottin in France and Richard Cordell in America showed Willie deference and admiration, while not being blind to his faults.

Willie's commercial success is beyond dispute but the psychological reasons for it are not easy to establish. There has to be something more than his ability to tell a good story, a skill he shares with many of his peers who are now almost, if not totally, forgotten. Many attempts have been made to define the Maugham

373

appeal but, like star quality, it may be indefinable. In the meantime, while pundits debate the subject and question Willie's literary status, the public, chiefly in Japan and America, demonstrate that the world of W. Somerset Maugham is as seductive as ever.

# Select Bibliography

## General

Acton, Harold *Nancy Mitford*, Hamish Hamilton, 1975

Agate, James *First Nights*, Ivor Nicholson & Watson, 1934

Alexander, Peter F. *William Plomer*, Oxford University Press, 1989

Baddeley, Hermione *The Unsinkable Hermione Baddeley*, Collins, 1984

Bankhead, Tallulah *Tallulah*, Gollancz, 1952

Barnes, Malcolm *Augustus Hare*, Allen & Unwin, 1984

Baxter, Beverley *First Nights and Footlights*, Hutchinson, 1955

Beardmore, George *Civilians at War*, John Murray, 1984

Becker, Heinz and Gudrun *Giacomo Meyerbeer: A Life in Letters*, Amadeus Press, 1983

Beecham, Thomas *A Mingled Chime*, Hutchinson & Co., 1944

Bell, Quentin *Bloomsbury*, Weidenfeld & Nicolson, 1968

Bishop, George W. *My Betters*, Heinemann, 1957

Bloch, Michael (ed.) *Wallis and Edward: Letters 1931–1937*, Summit Books, 1986

Blow, Sydney *Through Stage Doors*, Chambers, 1958

Bogarde, Dirk *Snakes and Ladders*, Chatto & Windus, 1978

Bolitho, Hector *Marie Tempest*, Cobden-Sanderson, 1936

Box, Muriel *Odd Woman Out*, Leslie Frewin, 1974

Brandon-Thomas, Jevan *Charley's Aunt's Father*, Douglas Saunders with MacGibbon & Kee, 1955

Brook, Donald *The Romance of the English Theatre*, Rockliff, 1945

Burke, Billie *With a Feather on My Nose*, Peter Davies, 1950

Carpenter, Humphrey *W. H. Auden*, Allen & Unwin, 1981

'Cato' *Guilty Men*, Gollancz, 1940

Cecil, Hugh and Mirabel *Clever Hearts*, Gollancz, 1990

375

Childs, David *Germany in the 20th Century*, B. T. Batsford, 1971

Clark, Kenneth *The Other Half*, John Murray, 1977

Clarke, D. Waldo *Modern English Writers*, Longmans, 1947

Clarke, Gerald *Capote*, Simon & Schuster, 1988

Collier, Constance *Harlequinade*, The Bodley Head, 1929

Collier, John and Lang, Ian *Just the Other Day*, Hamish Hamilton, 1932

Connell, John *Auchinleck*, Cassell, 1959

Connolly, Cyril *Enemies of Promise*, Routledge & Kegan Paul, 1938

Connon, Bryan *Beverley Nichols*, Constable, 1991

Cooper, Artemis *Cairo in the War: 1939–1945*, Hamish Hamilton, 1989

Coward, Noël *Autobiography*, Methuen, 1986

Croft, Taylor *The Cloven Hoof*, Denis Archer, 1932

Croft-Cooke, Rupert *The Verdict of You All*, Secker & Warburg, 1955

Darlow, Michael and Hodson, Gillian *Terence Rattigan*, Quartet Books, 1979

Daubeny, Peter *My World of Theatre*, Jonathan Cape, 1971

Dean, Basil *Seven Ages*, Hutchinson, 1970

De Wolfe, Elsie *After All*, Heinemann, 1935

Donald, Frances *Freddie Lonsdale*, Heinemann, 1957

Drake, Fabia *Blind Fortune*, William Kimber, 1978

Drawbell, James *The Sun Within Us*, Collins, 1963

Dudley, Ernest *The Gilded Lily*, Odhams, 1958

Eade, Charles (ed.) *The Unrelenting Struggle*, Cassell, 1942

Ellis, Mary *Those Dancing Years*, John Murray, 1982

Ellmann, Richard *Oscar Wilde*, Hamish Hamilton, 1987

Falk, Bernard *He Laughed in Fleet Street*, Hutchinson, 1933

Farson, Daniel *Sacred Monsters*, Bloomsbury, 1988

Forbes, Bryan *A Divided Life*, Heinemann, 1992

Forbes-Robertson, Diana *Maxine*, Hamish Hamilton, 1964

Freeland, Michael *Jerome Kern*, Robson Books, 1978

Fryer, Jonathan *Isherwood*, New English Library, 1977

Gerhardie, William *God's Fifth Column*, Hodder & Stoughton, 1981

Gielgud, John *Early Stages*, Heinemann, 1939

Gilbert, Martin *Churchill: A Life*, Heinemann, 1991

Glendenning, Victoria *Rebecca West*, Weidenfeld & Nicolson, 1987

Glyn, Anthony *Elinor Glyn*, Hutchinson, 1955

Graves, Robert and Hodge, Alan *The Long Weekend*, Hutchinson, 1940

Grenfell, Stephen (ed.) *Gilbert Harding*, André Deutsch, 1961

Guinness, Alec *Blessings in Disguise*, Hamish Hamilton, 1985

Hamilton, Lord Frederic *The Days Before Yesterday*, Hodder & Stoughton, 1920

Hamilton, Gerald *Mr Norris and I*, Allan Wingate, 1956

Hart-Davis, Rupert *Hugh Walpole*, Macmillan, 1952

Hassall, Christopher *Edward Marsh*, Longmans, 1959

Hastings, Patrick *Famous and Infamous Cases*, Heinemann, 1950

Hawtree, Christopher and Greene, Graham (eds) *Yours, etc*, Reinhardt Books, 1981

Hayman, Ronald *Gielgud*, Heinemann, 1971

Hewison, Robert *In Anger*, Weidenfeld & Nicolson, 1981
    *Under Siege*, Weidenfeld & Nicolson, 1977

Hichens, Robert *Yesterday*, Cassell, 1947

Hicks, Seymour *Night Lights*, Cassell, 1938

Hoare, Philip *Serious Pleasures*, Hamish Hamilton, 1990

Hobson, Harold *Theatre*, Longmans Green, 1948

Hodge, James H. (ed.) *Famous Trials*, vol. 5, Penguin, 1955

Howarth, Patrick *When the Riviera Was Ours*, Routledge & Kegan Paul, 1977

Huggett, Richard *Binkie Beaumont*, Hodder & Stoughton, 1989

Hyde, H. Montgomery *The Quiet Canadian*, Hamish Hamilton, 1962

Jackson, Holbrook *The Eighteen Nineties*, Jonathan Cape, 1913

James, Robert Rhodes *Henry Wellcome*, Hodder & Stoughton, 1994

James, Robert Rhodes (ed.) *'Chips': The Diaries of Sir Henry Channon*, Weidenfeld & Nicolson, 1967

Judd, Alan *Ford Madox Ford*, Collins, 1990

June *The Glass Ladder*, Heinemann, 1960

Junor, John *Listening for a Midnight Train*, Chapmans, 1990

Kazan, Elia *America, America*, Collins, 1963

Kendall, Henry *I Remember Romano's*, Macdonald, 1960

Kennedy, Ludovic *On My Way to the Club*, William Collins, 1989

King, Francis *Yesterday Came Suddenly*, Constable, 1993

Kirkpatrick Jnr, Lyman B. *The Real CIA*, Macmillan, 1968

Knox, Collie *It Might Have Been You*, Chapman & Hall, 1938
Korda, Michael *Charmed Lives*, Random House, 1979

Lahr, John *Prick Up Your Ears*, Allen Lane, 1978
Lambert, Angela *1939: The Last Season of Peace*, Weidenfeld & Nicolson, 1989
Lancaster, Marie-Jacqueline (ed.) *Brian Howard: Portrait of a Failure*, Anthony Blond, 1968
Lang, Iain *Just the Other Day*, Hamish Hamilton, 1932
Lees-Milne, James *Harold Nicolson*, 2 vols, Chatto & Windus, 1980 and 1981
Lehmann, John *Christopher Isherwood*, Weidenfeld & Nicolson, 1987
Lesley, Cole *The Life of Noël Coward*, Jonathan Cape, 1976

Mackenzie, Compton *My Life and Times*, Chatto & Windus, various dates
MacQueen-Pope, W. *Twenty Shillings in the Pound*, Hutchinson, 1948
Marcosson, Isaac *Charles Frohman*, John Lane, 1916
Marshall, Arthur *Life's Rich Pageant*, Hamish Hamilton, 1984
Massey, Raymond *A Hundred Different Lives*, Robson Books, 1979
Matthews, A. E. *Matty*, Hutchinson, 1952
McGilligan, Patrick *George Cukor*, Faber & Faber, 1991
McLeod, Kirsty *A Passion for Friendship*, Michael Joseph, 1991
Melville, Alan *Merely Melville*, Hodder & Stoughton, 1970
Middlemass, Keith *Diplomacy of Illusion*, Weidenfeld & Nicolson, 1972
Milton, Billy *Milton's Paradise Mislaid*, Jupiter Books, 1976
Ministry of Information *The Eighth Army*, HMSO, 1944
Modin, Yuri *My Five Cambridge Friends*, Headline, 1994
Monk, L. A. *Britain 1945–1970*, G. Bell & Sons, 1976
Montgomery, Viscount *Memoirs*, Collins, 1958
Morley, Sheridan *A Talent to Amuse*, Heinemann, 1969
Morrison, Arthur *Tales of Mean Streets*, Boydell Press, 1983
Mosley, Charlotte (ed.) *The Letters of Nancy Mitford*, Hodder & Stoughton, 1993

Neville, Peter *Neville Chamberlain*, Hodder & Stoughton, 1992
Nichols, Beverley *The Sweet and Twenties*, Weidenfeld & Nicolson, 1958
Nicolson, Nigel *Portrait of a Marriage*, Weidenfeld & Nicolson, 1973

Noble, Peter *Ivor Novello*, Falcon Press, 1951

O'Connor, Gary *Ralph Richardson*, Hodder & Stoughton, 1982

Palmer, Geoffrey and Lloyd, Noel *E. F. Benson*, Lennard, 1988
Palmer, James and Riley, Michael *The Films of Joseph Losey*,
    Cambridge University Press, 1993
Patmore, Derek *Private History*, Jonathan Cape, 1960
Pearson, Hesketh *Beerbohm Tree*, Methuen, 1956
Pearson, John *Façades*, Macmillan, 1978
    *The Life of Ian Fleming*, Jonathan Cape, 1966
Penrose, Barry and Freeman, Simon *Conspiracy of Silence*, Grafton,
    1986
Pinter, Harold *The Servant and Other Screen Plays*, Faber & Faber,
    1991
Pound, Reginald *Arnold Bennett*, Heinemann, 1952
Powell, Anthony *Infants of the Spring*, Heinemann, 1976
Price, Nancy *Into an Hour-Glass*, Museum Press, 1953

Richards, Grant *Author Hunting*, Unicorn Press, 1934
Roberts, Cecil *The Bright Twenties*, Hodder & Stoughton, 1970
Roberts, Major-General *From the Desert to the Baltic*, William
    Kimber & Co. Ltd, 1987
Rose, Sir Francis *Saying Life*, Cassell, 1961

Schmidgall, Gary *The Stranger Wilde*, Dutton, 1994
Shadegg, Stephen *Clare Boothe Luce*, Leslie Frewin, 1973
Short, Ernest *Theatrical Cavalcade*, Eyre & Spottiswoode, 1942
Sinden, Donald *A Touch of the Memoirs*, Hodder & Stoughton, 1982
Skelton, Barbara *Tears Before Bedtime*, Hamish Hamilton, 1987
Smith, Timothy d'Arch *Love in Earnest*, Routledge & Kegan Paul,
    1970
Spears, Sir Edward *Fulfilment of a Mission*, Leo Cooper, 1977
Speedie, Julie *Wonderful Sphinx*, Virago Press, 1993
Stevenson, William *A Man Called Intrepid*, Macmillan, 1976
Stokes, Sewell *Without Veils*, Peter Davies, 1953
Swears, Herbert *When All's Said and Done*, Geoffrey Bles, 1937
Swinnerton, Frank *Background with Chorus*, Hutchinson, 1950
Symonds, John and Grant, Kenneth (eds) *The Confessions of Aleister
    Crowley*, Routledge & Kegan Paul, 1979

Thwaite, Ann *A. A. Milne*, Faber & Faber, 1990

Trewin, J. C. *We'll Hear a Play*, Carroll & Nicholson, 1949

Vanbrugh, Irene *To Tell My Story*, Hutchinson, 1948
Vidal, Gore *A View from the Diners Club*, Random House, 1991

Watt, Donald Cameron *How War Came*, Heinemann, 1989
Waugh, Alec *A Year to Remember (1931)*, W. H. Allen, 1975
Wescott, Glenway *Journals: 1937–1955*, Farrar Straus Giroux, 1990
    *Images of Truth*, Hamish Hamilton, 1963
White, Patrick *Letters*, Jonathan Cape, 1994
Wildeblood, Peter *Against the Law*, Penguin, 1955
Williams, Francis *Nothing So Strange*, Cassell, 1970
Williams, Tennessee *Memoirs*, W. H. Allen, 1976
Wilson, A. E. *Playgoer's Pilgrimage*, Stanley Paul

Young, Kenneth (ed.) *The Diaries of Sir Robert Bruce Lockhart*,
    Macmillan, 1980

Ziegler, Philip *Diana Cooper*, Hamish Hamilton, 1981

## Concerning the Maughams

Aldington, Richard *W. Somerset Maugham* (including *Sixty-Five* by
    W. Somerset Maugham), Doubleday, 1939

Brophy, John *Somerset Maugham*, Longmans, 1952

Calder, Robert *Willie*, Heinemann, 1989
    *W. Somerset Maugham and the Quest for Freedom*, Doubleday,
    1973
Cordell, Richard A. *Somerset Maugham*, Indiana University Press,
    1961
Curtis, Anthony *Somerset Maugham*, Weidenfeld & Nicolson, 1977
    *The Pattern of Maugham*, Hamish Hamilton, 1974
Curtis, Anthony and Whitehead, John (eds) *W. Somerset Maugham*,
    Routledge & Kegan Paul, 1987

Fisher, Richard B. *Syrie Maugham*, Duckworth, 1978
Friends of the Libraries, University of Southern California
    'Remembering Mr Maugham'

Jonas, Klaus W. *The Maugham Enigma*, Citadel Press, 1954

*The Gentleman from Cap Ferrat*, Centre of Maugham Studies, New Haven, Connecticut, 1956
*More Maughamiana*, Bibliographical Society of America, 1950

Kanin, Garson *Remembering Mr Maugham*, Hamish Hamilton, 1966

Loss, Archie K. *W. Somerset Maugham*, Ungar, 1987

Mander, Raymond and Mitchenson, Joe *Theatrical Companion to Maugham*, Rockliff, 1955
Maugham, W. Somerset 'Of Human Bondage' (an address), 1946
McNight, Gerald *The Scandal of Syrie Maugham*, W. H. Allen, 1980
Menard, Wilmon *The Two Worlds of Somerset Maugham*, Sherbourne Press, 1965
Morgan, Ted *Somerset Maugham*, Jonathan Cape, 1980

Nichols, Beverley *A Case of Human Bondage*, Secker & Warburg, 1966

Pfeiffer, Karl G. *W. Somerset Maugham*, W. W. Norton, 1959

Raphael, Frederick *Somerset Maugham*, Cardinal, 1989
*Somerset Maugham and His World*, Thames & Hudson, 1976

Sanders, Charles (ed.) *W. Somerset Maugham*, Northern Illinois University Press, 1970
Sargent, John T. and Doubleday, Nelson *W. Somerset Maugham* (an appreciation), Doubleday, 1965
Sotheby & Co. 'The Villa Mauresque' (catalogue of contents), 1967
Stott, Raymond Toole *A Bibliography of the Works of W. Somerset Maugham*, Kaye & Ward, 1973

Ward, Richard Heron *William Somerset Maugham*, Geoffrey Bles, 1937
Whitehead, John *Maugham: A Reappraisal*, Vision/Barnes & Noble, 1987
Whitehead, John (ed.) *A Traveller in Romance* (uncollected writings 1901–1964), Anthony Blond, 1984

# Index

395